A HISTORY OF
THE CROATIAN PEOPLE

●

VOLUME II

FRANCIS PREVEDEN

1890—1959

A HISTORY

OF THE

CROATIAN PEOPLE

from their arrival on the shores of the Adriatic

to the present day,

with some account of the

Gothic, Roman, Greek, Illyrian, and Prehistoric

periods of the Ancient Illyricum and Pannonia

•

Volume II

FRANCIS R. PREVEDEN

PHILOSOPHICAL LIBRARY

NEW YORK

This volume is affectionately dedicated to my wife MARY and our two daughters: TATYANA MARGARET and IRENE DOLORES, in grateful acknowledgment of their devoted assistance in bearing with me the crushing burden of study and research.

Plate 1.
BOSNIA

Dedicated to the worship of Allah through the suras of Al
Kuran, the magnificent mosque of Husref Bey in Sarayevo
shows a remarkable architectural likeness to Diocletian's
Mausoleum both through the polygonic shaping of its nave,
and the arcade of wide arcs supported by appropriate columns of less elaborate Egyptian capitals. (Library of Congress
Collection)

(Engraving by courtesy of Prof. Paul K. Kufrin.)

FOREWORD

The burden of adverse historical circumstances conspired heavily against the very survival of the Croatian people since the beginning of the fifteenth century. The Ottoman Empire, during the era of its dynamic offensive against Europe in the fifteenth and sixteenth centuries, sent almost every one of its armies into and through Croatian lands. It conquered Croatian provinces, destroyed castles, crushed resistance, accompanied the waging of some of its major battles with a prolonged and incessant series of guerilla skirmishes in the hinterlands, and finally transported appalling numbers of the Croatian people into slavery.

With the fall of Bosnia and Herzegovina, a considerable segment of the native population in these lands accepted the religion of the conquerors and joined forces, both spiritually and militarily, with the Turks in their drive against the European states, and more significantly, against the rest of Croatia, until the latter was reduced to a mere sixth of her former historical size. As a result, it was characterized in one of the contemporary documents of the time—*reliquiae reliquiarum olim inclyti regni*—the "remnants of the remnants of the former glorious Kingdom."

The decline of the Ottoman Empire, and the subsequent battles of its gradual retreat from the West during the seventeenth and eighteenth centuries, made the times hardly any easier for the Croatian people. Every inch of Croatian soil was bitterly contested, changing and re-changing masters many times. Such continuous conflict further weakened the unity and identity of the Croatian people, for a clear division had been created between those who helped to defend against the onslaught into Europe and those who had joined and aided the Turks.

For many Croatians of both the Christian and Moslem faiths today, the documents of these long and bloody struggles evoke bitter and unpleasant memories. They prefer to plan a better future of mutual constructive understanding and national unity, rather than to dwell upon their violent history. Yet, if we wish to portray the Croatian history of these centuries truthfully, as well as the specific events which have shaped the present Croatian situation, we cannot ignore these struggles. History is a science, a study of facts and not a compilation of fairy tales. All "conditioned" histories are eventually bound to be discredited, not only to the detriment of their authors, but also of the causes which such authors seek to promote by their conditioning.

The narrative of Francis Preveden should be evaluated in the light of these considerations. This volume of his, a prolix but always accurate and exciting narrative, recounts the wars between the Turks and the Croatian Moslems of Bosnia on one side, and the rest of Croatia on the other.

An historical documentation of civil or revolutionary war, if honestly told and properly explained, should neither provoke resentment nor weaken unity within any civilized nation. On the contrary, the bitter lessons of the past should teach subsequent generations to avoid some of the historical errors and to imitate the virtues as well as the edifying examples of such a past. Our great nation does not conceal or embellish the cruel facts of the battles of her Civil War. Contemporary Americans discuss freely the causes and effects, the development and aftermath of the bloody conflict between the Union and the Confederacy. We are equally proud of such figures as Lincoln and Lee, Grant and Jackson, and their monuments stand side by side on the battlefield of Gettysburg. America's attitude regarding her interior struggles of the last century did not harm her unity in the building of her greatness.

With due variances, the same may be said about Great Britain, France, Germany and Italy. Each of these countries has undergone severe domestic strife, where one segment fought against another. However, they do not attempt to conceal the facts of such struggles. They relate truthfully all the battles, both shameful and honorable, and have learned to honor the defeated as they honor the victorious, all part of their great heritage.

I am certain that this same spirit of civilized maturity prevails today amongst the Croatian people, be they Christian or Moslem, and that they will equally honor the great contenders of their past.

As a final remark, it should be said that although this volume consists primarily of objective documentation and impartial commentary, there does emerge, almost inadvertantly, a certain amount of subjective judgment on the part of the author which may not meet with universal approval. Certainly on this point Francis Preveden may be criticized; yet it was impossible to get him to work out changes because before he was able to submit the manuscript to any of his colleagues for constructive suggestion, Preveden was dead. Now, out of respect for his memory, his friends and advisors have decided that the text (with some negligible changes) should be published just as he wrote it.

REV. DR. CHARLES KAMBER
Lynch, Nebraska

TABLE OF CONTENTS

ix

ILLUSTRATIONS

Non Platoni, sed veritati.

TWELFTH-NIGHT

Act One

Scene Two

The Sea-coast.

VIOLA. And what should I do in Illyria?
    My brother he is in Elysium.
    Perchance he is not drown'd. What think you sailors?

CAPTAIN. It is perchance that you yourself were sav'd.

VIOLA. O my poor brother! and so perchance may he be.

CAPTAIN. True, madam: and, to comfort you with chance,
    Assure yourself, after our ship did split,
    When you and those poor number sav'd with you
    Hung on our driving boat, I saw your brother,
    Most provident in peril, bind himself,—
    Courage and hope both teaching him the practice,—
    To a strong mast that liv'd upon the sea;
    Where, like Arion on the dolphin's back,
    I saw him hold acquaintance with the waves
    So long as I could see.
                   William Shakespeare

PREFACE TO THE SECOND VOLUME

The second volume of this history of the Croatian people tells the story of the Croatian lands under the impact of the Turkish invasions. This is followed by the life-and-death struggle of the Croats against the overwhelming forces of the Ottoman empire.

As elsewhere throughout the Balkans and Central Europe, the Turks wrought tremendous damage to the Croatian people, not only through their exactions of booty and tribute but mainly through the massacre and extermination of the population. While in the 10th century the Croatian population was at par with that of England, at present it does not constitute more than 5% of the English-speaking people originating from Great Britain.

However, unlike Greece, Albania, Bulgaria, Serbia, Wallachia and Moldavia, which had been overrun by the Turks and were for centuries held in Turkish bondage, the kingdoms of Croatia and Hungary retained control over their borderland areas, and in a desperate resistance for nearly two centuries, earned the flattering epithet: "antemurale Christianitatis" (Bulwark of Christendom). In a similar style and for the same merit the Albanian hero, Skanderbeg Castriota, with his forces, was honored with the title: "scutum Christianitatis" (shield of Christendom)

throughout the world. After his death the Albanians were left without an inspiring leader and under the menace of pillage and massacre the majority of the Albanians left their Christian faith and passed over to Islam, in order to avoid the threatening doom. The same transpired in Bosnia and Herzegovina, neither of which could place in the field a general of Skanderbeg's genius, and the greater half of the population became Mohammedan.*

With such distressful and agonizing changes throughout the Balkan peninsula and central Europe, it seemed to the author imperative to place in full perspective the motive forces of the OTTOMAN empire (section II of the third volume), rooting themselves in the history of Islam both as a religious and political organization. In the political field it is known as caliphate, which conquered and controlled vast areas of three continents.

Elucidation of these developments will help us to understand, and appraise in their international ramifications, the heroic struggle, not unlike that of Skanderbeg Castriota — of the Senian Uskoki, uncompromising fighters of the Turks and of the Venetians who were the age-old business associates and occasional allies (section III of the third volume) of the Turks.

---

* Preveden often uses the terms Mohammedanism meaning Islam and Mohammedan meaning Moslem.

Plate 3.

A. Another view of the Husref Bey Mosque, with its arcade.

B. Interior of the Mosque in the town of Fotchaw, reputed
to be the most beautiful in Bosnia.
(Engraving by courtesy of Rev. Ljubo Cbuvalo.)

Section I

CROATIA AND SLAVONIA FROM 1396 TO 1664

Plate 4.

A. A section of the city of a hundred Mosques, another name for Sarayevo.

B. The Catholic cathedral in the same city, testifying to peaceful co-existence of the Catholic and Moslem population.

(Engraving by courtesy of Mr. Valent Susa.)

THE REIGN OF SIGISMUND

Rebellion in Croatia*

THE long absence of Sigismund from the country after his defeat at Nicopolis created great confusion for it was generally believed that the king had fallen in the battle. In this belief a faction of Croatian and Hungarian magnates decided to invite king Ladislaus of Naples, to occupy the vacant Croatian-Hungarian throne. This faction was headed by banus and palatin Styepan Latskovich of Chakovats (Mura-district).

In the meantime, Sigismund arrived in Dalmatia and Croatia and when he discovered what had happened, he summoned Styepan Latskovich and his friends to Parliament in Krizhevats, ostensibly for a friendly parley. Moreover, he gave them a written guarantee, a "salvus conductus", that no evil would befall them at the parley. In spite of that both Latskovich and his friends were massacred in the midst of a quarrel by the partisans of Sigismund and their lifeless bodies hurled through the windows of the parliament house. This atrocity took place on February 19, 1397.

The news of the "bloody Krizhevats Parliament" produced a violent reaction. General rebellion broke out in Croatia, which was joined also by Bosnia, under the leadership of duke Hervoye Vukchich Hervatinich, master of the Lower Regions (Dolnji Kraji). The whole kingdom and the neighboring countries were seized by unrest. In retaliation Sigismund undertook, the next year (1398), a campaign against the rebels in Croatia and Bosnia, but it ended in failure. Moreover, duke Hervoye attached the entire region from Banjaluka to Una and Sava rivers to his possessions. This was the turning point in Sigismund's career. With his extravagance and light-mindedness he aroused the major part of the Hungarian nobility which joined hands with the Croatian rebels against the king. Thus it happened that in April, 1401 Sigismund was

seized in Vishegrad, dethroned and imprisoned in Shiklosh, a city in south-western Hungary. However, through mediation of the Croatian banus Nicholas of Gara (Goryanski), a part of the Hungarian magnates made a truce with him, while others, together with Croatians, supported Ladislaus of Naples and named him for coronation. Ladislaus of Naples, relying chiefly on duke Hervoye, arrived in the summer of 1403 in Zadar and on the 5th of August was crowned there by the Ostrogon archbishop king of Croatia and Hungary. Remembering the tragic fate of his father, Charles II,* Ladislaus was unwilling to go to Hungary in spite of the pleading of the magnates who attended his coronation. Instead, after a short stay in Zadar, Ladislaus returned to Naples, having appointed the duke of Split, Hervoye, his vicar in Croatia and Dalmatia. All of Croatia south of Velebit and all the Dalmatian cities remained loyal to Ladislaus, even after his departure from the country.

End of the Croatian Insurrection

By 1403 Duke Hervoye was at the peak of his power and glory. Because of this the Bosnian king Styepan Ostoya turned away from the overlord, but Hervoye soon dethroned him and proclaimed the legitimate son of Styepan Tvartko, the youthful Styepan Tvartko II Tvartkovich, king of Bosnia, (1404-1408). This change aroused king Sigismund who undertook three ineffective campaigns against Bosnia, 1405, 1406 and 1407. At the beginning of this struggle queen Maria died and Sigismund married in Krapina (1405) Barbara, daughter of count Herman of Tselye (Zell) who owned the city of Varazhdin and the major part of Zagorye (Croatian Tramontane). Seeing that he alone could not overcome the resistance of Bosnia and Croatia, Sigismund sought aid from Pope Gregory XII. In his turn, the Pontiff made a religious issue out of the conflict and summoned the Western World to a "crusade" against the "Patarenes" and other "heretics" in Bosnia, Dalmatia and Croatia. In 1408, after gathering a large army

---

* For history of Croatia prior to the reign of Sigismund see Vol. I of this series.

* Assassinated in the royal palace of Budavar in February, 1386. See Vol. I, p. 120.

1

Sigismund broke deep into Bosnia, defeated the Bosnian forces and took prisoner, king Styepan Tvartko II, with about 126 Bosnian barons, whom he had beheaded. Upon the news of this disaster duke Hervoye bowed before the king. Thus, after a quarter of a century the Croatian insurrection was put down and Sigismund was recognized king by all Croats.

In the midst of a hopeless situation Ladislaus of Naples realized that he could not maintain himself on the Hungarian—Croatian throne, and decided to make the best of a bad situation. After protracted negotiations and bargaining, in July, 1409 he sold the cities of Zadar, Novigrad, Vrana and the island of Pag, together with his sovereign rights over the rest of Dalmatia to Venice for 100,000 ducats.* This deal greatly benefited Venice which, during all this struggle, kept on the sidelines. Furthermore, since 1409 Venice established herself in Dalmatia permanently until her suppression in 1797, when possession of this territory was taken over by the Revolutionary France.

Loss of Dalmatia

The transfer of Dalmatia through a commercial deal to Venice came as a lightning stroke to all concerned, and especially to king Sigismund and the city of Zadar. The indignation of the Zadar citizenry developed into an open rebellion against the treacherous king and the Neapolitan guards were forced out of the city. Then rather than engage in a bloody war with Venice, the citizens of Zadar decided to join the Republic of St. Mark of their own free will and the Venetian flag was hoisted on the plaza. The Doge confirmed the municipal autonomy and appointed the city patricians Venetian citizens. But, at the same time he settled a number of Venetian families in the city (September, 1409).

This event was to play an important role in the city's history. By the end of the 14th century Zadar became a Croatian city and with the importation of Italian populace from Venice, it assumed, as time went on, Italian characteristics which became a source of friction and conflict with Italy in the post-Venetian period and even to this day. The example of Zadar was emulated by all the northern islands, including Rab and

* About $250,000.

Osor. The only exception was the Frankapan island of Kerk, and the city of Nin. Many other cities invited the Venetians of their own accord, placing themselves under the protection of the Serenissime Republic. However, the cities of Trogir and Shibenik refused to follow suit and the Doge summoned them to surrender, claiming right of ownership through purchase in due form from the "legal king", Ladislaus of Naples. Yet they refused to submit, upon which the Venetian fleet laid siege to Shibenik.

The sale of Dalmatia by the Neapolitan weakling caused worse damage to the Croatian people than a series of lost battles. "Pacta conventa" with Hungary under Koloman was a mild affair compared to this calamity. With the loss of Dalmatia, the Croatian State was deprived of the very foundation upon which all its importance and national essence rested. True enough, that state did not disappear after this fatal event, but henceforth it was to carry on merely a shadow existence. Being drawn into the orbit of alien influence, it lost its former striking power and ceased to develop within the framework of traditions derived from the times of the national dynasty. And it was precisely from these traditions that the Croatian people drew their power of cohesion and national consciousness.

On the other hand, a closer tie with the cultured and prosperous West was established. Yet, in the domain of the Croatian political and national life, Dalmatia relinquished its leadership, and from 1409 on—the center of gravity shifted more and more toward the north.

The First War with Venice

While the Dalmatian cities, one after another, were surrendering to Venice, Sigismund called to account the Venetian Council and demanded release of all his former towns and provinces. The negotiations, however, bore no fruit, since neither party was willing to yield. Thus, the first Venetian war broke out. The campaign was conducted for two years, (1411-1413) both in northern Italy and Dalmatia. In Lombardy the commander of the king's armies was count Pipo of Ozor, while in Dalmatia hostilities were carried on at first under a Czech general, Peter of Myshlin, and later under banus Peter Alben. The struggle was bitter, yet indecisive. Sigismund's generals could not wring out a clear-cut victory from their opponents. After unsuccessful campaigning in northern Italy and following the loss of Skradin, Ostrovitsa and Shibenik, which surrendered to Venice in October, 1412, a five year truce was concluded in Trieste. By the terms of this agreement each warring party retained exactly that part it possessed at the moment of negotiations (April, 1413).

Sigismund and Hervoye

After the conquest of Bosnia in 1408, and the capture of king Styepan Tvartko II, the Bosnian throne remained vacant for a short period of time. Sigismund wished not only to annex Bosnia to his own dominion, but also to crown himself, together with his consort, Queen Barbara, king and queen of Bosnia. But his plans were thwarted when the Bosnian barons raised for the second time, Styepan Ostoya (1408-1418), to the throne, and the new king found recognition throughout Bosnia, except in the domain of duke Hervoye.

In the face of this adverse situation, Sigismund denounced the enthronement of Ostoya and in 1410 he set out on a new campaign against Bosnia. The war lasted for nearly a year. Hervoye sided this time with Sigismund. Nevertheless, the conflict ended with a compromise, by virtue of which Sigismund recognized Ostoya as king of Bosnia, while the latter bowed before Sigismund as his sovereign. However, not even this arrangement lasted long, for a new rebellion broke out under the leadership of duke Sandal Hranich. This resulted in a new intervention, during which Sigismund finally crushed the Bosnian resistance.

All this time duke Hervoye took Sigismund's part and remained either neutral, or actively supported the king. His own might remained unchallenged. He ruled as a sovereign over the city of Split, Omish and the Maritime Province extending from Tsetina river to Neretva. Furthermore, he established his power over the three large islands: Korchula, Brach and Hvar (Lessina). In addition, Hervoye enjoyed the friendship of Sigismund who acted as his god-father when the duke embraced the Catholic faith. But this exalted position earned him wide-spread envy and enmity among the magnates of Bosnia, Croatia and Hungary. By continuous slander and denunciations, his opponents tried to under-

mine his position at the royal court. Yielding to this pressure, Queen Barbara in the absence of Sigismund, denounced him as a traitor. Later Sigismund himself joined the queen and declared all of Hervoye's possessions forfeited to the Crown.

Far from losing his head in this adversity, Hervoye sought allies for a show-down with Sigismund himself. Failing to find them among Christians, he sought and found them among the Turks. The Sultan was only too glad to have his troops move toward Sigismund's frontiers. Hervoye retired with his forces in the newly-built stronghold of Yaytse. From there he watched the movements of the enemy eager to attack Sigismund's army at the right moment. In August, 1415 a bloody battle was fought in Usora, near the place called Maklyenovtsi, in the neighborhood of the town of Doboj. The allied forces of Hervoye and the Sultan scored a great victory over the Hungarian-Slavonian army of banus Paul Chupor of Moslava. Banus Chupor himself was taken prisoner, with many other magnates, and was put to death.

The victorious allies broke into Croatia and Styria up to the city of Zell (Tselye). This was the first Turkish invasion of Croatia (1415). Unchecked by any power, Hervoye became the sole master of western Bosnia, while the remaining part of the country gradually came under the Turkish sovereignty, so that the Hungarian influence was eliminated from Bosnia altogether. Thus, in his last test of force, Sigismund lost with one blow, what he acquired through so many years of struggle and with the loss of so much blood, in the undaunted country. From that time on Sigismund never crossed the Sava river. Neither did duke Hervoye survive long the crowning success of his brilliant career for he died in April, 1416. In his last days he drew comfort from the realization that throughout his life he maintained himself in power, imperious, adamant and unconquered.

With the passing of the Duke all his possessions became scattered. His Bosnian estates were inherited by his son Balsha Hertsegovich, a man without the genius of his father. The stronghold of Omish, with the Maritime Province, went to his brother-in-law, prince Ivanish Nelipich, while the three large islands were taken over by king Sigismund.

Victorious Campaign of Venice

Sigismund's reign was beset by grave problems both within the borders of his extensive empire, and in foreign lands. For years he had to stay out of Hungary. In 1411, while campaigning in Bosnia, he was elected King of Germany. The Great Schism in the Church occupied his mind, while the Hussite problems added to his worries. Thus, he paid little attention to the fact that his five-year truce with Venice was about to expire, and neglected to take any defensive measures in case of attack.

On the other hand, the Venetian Senate decided to take advantage of the king's difficulties and began hostilities in 1418, immediately after the expiration of the truce. War was carried on in Furlandia (Venezia Giulia) and Dalmatia. The Venetians were successful on both theaters of war and scored a series of important victories. In 1420 Trogir and Split surrendered after a long and heroic defense. In addition Kotor (Cattaro) and the three large islands: Korchula, Brach and Hvar followed suit. The war petered out without truce or peace and almost the entire Adriatic coast came under Venetian authority. Only Senj and Kerk in the north, and Omish, with the Maritime Province as well as the diminutive Republic of Polyitse in the south, remained within the borders of the Croatian kingdom. Here the powerful prince Ivanish (John) Nelipich held sway, extending his authority over the entire Croatia south of Velebit, with the exception of the royal cities of Knin, Ostrovitsa and Bribir.

Sigismund's Campaign in Serbia

With the death of King Styepan Ostoya and after the overthrow of his son, Styepan Ostoyich, in 1421, the former King Styepan Tvartko II Tvartkovich (1421-1443), ascended again the Bosnian throne.

Eager to reduce the power of Ivanish Nelipich, Venice made an alliance with Tvartko, offering him all of the prince's possessions, with the exception of the stronghold of Klis. The plan was doomed to failure because of a new Turkish invasion of Bosnia, staged at the time when Tvartko was making ready for the attack. The unexpected turn of events forced Tvartko II to seek aid from Sigismund, a natural ally of Nelipich.

The Turkish incursions into Serbia also compelled the Serbian despot, Styepan Lazarevich to seek protection from Sigismund. In his turn the Despot bound himself to cede Belgrade which he had administered since 1403, to the king. After his death, not only Belgrade, but also the stronghold of Golubats on the right bank of the Danube would be given to Sigismund. Styepan Lazarevich died in 1427 and was succeeded by his nephew, George Brankovich (1424-1456), son of the heroic Vuk Brankovich of Kossovo fame. He promptly fulfilled his uncle's pledge. Thus, Belgrade passed again directly under the authority of the Hungarian-Croatian king, remaining in his possession until 1521.

But upon the news of the Despot's death, Murad II (1421-1451) broke into Serbia, captured Krushevats, capital of the country. Through the work of traitors Murad II made himself the master of the powerful stronghold of Golubats. Sigismund promptly declared war on the Sultan, and laid siege to Golubats. But Murad hurried to the aid of the beleaguered city and beat the king's army so decisively that Sigismund had to retire, with heavy losses, to Hungary (1428).

Abandonment of Hungary and Croatia

After his defeat at Golubats the restless king left his State, turning over its administration to his wife Barbara, the "black queen", and her father, banus Herman of Zell. During this period Sigismund achieved his life-long ambition to become Roman Emperor. This crowning glory of his reign was reached in 1433 when Pope Eugene IV crowned him in Rome with the imperial crown. Subsequently, he made another truce with the Venetians, prolonging it once more before his death. Thus, through his neglect and indolence, the problem of Dalmatia and the Julian Alps was solved in favor of Venice for several centuries. Moreover, Dalmatia was never united with Croatia again until October, 1918.

At that time the banus of Croatia was Nicholas Frankapan (1426-1432), the first of his clan to make this name famous in Croatian history. Even before he became banus, he owned as the only member of his clan, the island of Kerk, and the districts of Vinodol, Modrush, Senj, Gatska and Lika in Croatia, with the towns of Tsetin, Slun and Ozal in Slavonia. When he became banus, King Sigismund left him in return for a loan of 28,000 ducats, also the town of Bihach on Una river, further Knin, Lapatsgrad, Verlika, Ostrovitsa (near Bribir), Skradin, the county of Luk between Zermanya and Kerka rivers, and the district of Polyitse. Thus, Nicholas Frankapan owned nearly all of Croatia.

In Slavonia the banal authority belonged to prince Herman of Zell (1423-1435), father-in-law of King Sigismund. Herman was the master of a large part of Slavonia. Because of family quarrels the two powerful clans clashed. Each of them had partisans among the powerful barons. Thus, two factions were formed, ready to start a bloody feud. Those who sided with the princes of Zell strove to extend their sway also over Croatia, and to annihilate the Frankapani. However, the outbreak of civil war was prevented by Sigismund's return from abroad. Peace was further consolidated by the passing of banus Nicholas on June 26, 1432. He left behind nine sons, each of them becoming the founder of a branch of the Frankapan family, which supplied leaders and generals of great renown. Its illustrious role in Croatian history is annually commemorated to this day when the tragic end of Kersto (Christophore) Frankapan on the scaffold of Wiener Neustadt (April 30, 1670), and the extinction of the Frankapan family, is mourned throughout the nation.

Croatian and Hungarian Defenses

The numerous campaigns of Sigismund, few of which were successful, exposed the short-comings and weaknesses of the military organization, both in Croatia and Hungary. Being threatened on all sides: by Venetians, Turks and Hussites alike, Sigismund decided to introduce reforms in his defensive system. Thus, he decreed that every baron and magnate, together with his subjects, serfs and employees, had to join the king's banners in case of war. On the other hand, lower nobility had to fully equip fighters, according to their means.

Croatia was divided into three military zones. The first zone embraced the northern Croatian sea-coast and Dalmatia, including the territories of the banus of Croatia, city of Dubrovnik, districts of Kerbava, Tsetina and Senj. The rest of lower nobility also belonged to this group. The second was the Slavonian district extending toward Una river. It included the forces of the Croatian banus, the important principality of Blagay, priorate of Vrana, diocese of Zagreb and the possessions of Susyedgrad barons. Equally important was the Usora district, grouping the military resources of the magnates and noblemen of lower Slavonia and southern Hungary. By this plan a defense system was created which not only outlived its century, but also provided a firm foundation of military security in the age-old struggle with the Ottoman Empire until the later part of the 19th century.

Passing of Sigismund

The half-century long reign of Sigismund in Croatia ended in an atmosphere of grave internal disorders. When wealthy prince Ivanish Nelipich, who was the last male member of his illustrious clan, died in 1434, the problem of inheritance became acute. According to her father's will, Catherine, his only daughter, was to inherit all of his extensive possessions from the Velebit ranges to Tsetina. Her patrimony was to be shared by her husband, Ivanish Frankapan, son of Nicholas Frankapan, since his father's death, banus of Croatia (1432-1436). In spite of the legality of this bequest, and his consent to such an arrangement during the life of Ivanish Nelipich, King Sigismund denounced the testament and demanded that Ivan Frankapan turn over to him the legacy of Prince Ivanish. When the latter refused to obey, Sigismund proclaimed him a rebel and deprived him of all honors and possessions. Then he ordered the banus of Slavonia Matko Talovats (1435-1444), to subdue him by force. Thus, in 1436, civil war broke out in Croatia. It, however, was of short duration. The sudden death of Ivan Frankapan halted hostilities and provided a decisive victory to the king. In a revengeful mood Sigismund now retaliated by giving the legacy of prince Ivanish Nelipich to banus Matko Talovats and his brothers, Peter, Frank and John.

On the 9th of September, 1437, Sigismund died in Znaym, Moravia, after a reign of half a century. This circumstance alone would make him one of the outstanding rulers of history. However, his talent was not equal to the problems besetting him in the turbulent era of his reign. Indeed, it was unfortunate for both Hungary and Croatia. He was born for peaceful occupations, and not for generalship and the din of many battles. He could neither successfully defend Dalmatia from the Venetian onslaughts nor was he able to properly protect the frontiers of his State from the Turkish invasions. His long, but inauspicious reign weighed heavily both on the careers of his successors, and on the destinies of Hungary and Croatia for generations to come.

KINGS FROM MISCELLANEOUS DYNASTIES

Emperor Albert of Hapsburg

Sigismund's only child was Elizabeth and she was married in 1422 to Albert of Hapsburg. In compliance with Sigismund's wishes both the Hungarian and Croatian estates elected him King of Croatia and Hungary (1438-1439). Since Albert became both Bohemian and German king, he was the first Hapsburg to sway his scepter, even for a short time, over all those lands which in less than a century were to become the Hapsburg domain until 1918.

But besides valuable assets, Albert inherited depressing liabilities from his father-in-law. One of them was war with the Turks caused by complications in Serbia. Because of continuous attacks by Sultan Murad against Serbia, Despot George Brankovich was in a desperate situation. In a mood of despair despot George gave his daughter Maria to grace the Sultan's harem as one of his many wives (August, 1436), but even that could not alter Murad's conquests in Serbia.

Thus, late in 1438 Murad made another attack against Brankovich's country, intent on capturing Smederevo (Semendria), his new capital. The unfortunate Serbian Despot fled to Hungary, pleading with King Albert for aid. But at that time Albert had to face a hostile Parliament, which was bent on stripping the king of his sovereign powers. Accordingly, the king could not take any action in matters of foreign policy without the consent of the Estates. In view of the urgency of the situation Albert consented to humiliating terms, but was permitted by the Parliament to declare war on Turkey. Albert promptly set to field, without even mustering sufficient forces. So he never advanced further than the towns of Slankament and Titel, at the confluence of Danube and Theiss (Tissa) rivers. The Hungarian magnates withdrew their support and left him lingering helplessly in camp.

In the meantime, Smederevo fell to the Turks (August, 1439), while the Hungarian Army was stricken with disease from which King Albert himself died (October 27, 1439) while on his way to Vienna.

The promising career of Albert, even though short lived left behind some momentous achievements. In the first place he renewed the Severin banate in southeastern Hungary, centering around the city of Orshova, near the famous Danube island of Ada Kalay. He appointed governor of that district the brilliant Roumanian officer Yancu de Sibiu, better known in Hungary by the name of Hunyadi Janos and in southern Slavic folk-lore as Sibinyanin Yanko. As a leader of Christian armies in his thunderous campaigns against the Turks, he carved his name deep in the hearts of Roumanians, Hungarians, Bulgars, Serbs and Croats alike, as a symbol of heroism for centuries. The folk-lore of these countries sings his praise to this day.

Albert's sudden death created new confusion and strife over throne succession, both in Croatia and Hungary. The internal struggle further weakened the two countries, and sapped their energies needed so badly for the gigantic struggle with the Ottoman Turks.

Wlodzislaw I and Ladislaus IV (V) (1449-1457) Succession Problems

The ill-fated King Albert left behind two daughters and his widow Elizabeth, an expectant mother. Considering herself chief heir of Sigismund and rightful successor to the throne, she took the reins of Government and introduced an arbitrary rule, both in Hungary and Croatia. Firmly believing that she would give birth to a son and act as a regent until his maturity, she was eager to lay her hands on the crown of St. Stephen. With the aid of her chambermaid, she actually obtained the crown, yet she could not muster up sufficient support among the barons. Only a few relatives, including princes Frederick and Ulric of Zell, some Frankapani and prince Nicholas of Ilok rallied to the support of the queen. On the other hand the majority of magnates and nobility, both in Hungary and Croatia, and even her own relative, the banus of Machva (north-western Serbia), Ladislaus Goryanski, turned away from her.

As true patriots these magnates wanted to see

on the throne a forceful ruler who could steer with firm hands the ship of State amid the grave dangers of their time. They wanted a man, able to defend both Hungary and Croatia from foreign enemies, and especially from Sultan Murad II. One party wanted to elect the son of the Serbian Despot George Brankovich, but the large majority of both Hungarian and Croatian Estates decided early in January, 1440, to elect the 16 year old Polish king Wlodzislaw of the House of Yaghiello. This was an especially clever move, since Sultan Murad II sought Polish alliance against Hungary. This choice, however, was not without its complications. While a select embassy of Hungarian and Croatian magnates, and among them banus Matko Talovats himself, was on its way to Krakow, Queen Elizabeth gave birth to a son named Ladislaus Posthumous on the 22nd of February, 1440. The mother had the infant crowned by archbishop Dionysius Szechy of Ostrogon, with the crown of St. Stephen. This event took place on the 15th of May of the same year.

In the meantime, Wlodzislaw left Poland and at the head of a small force arrived at Budavar. At this turn all the magnates, with the exception of the princes of Zell, deserted Queen Elizabeth and her infant son, joining with the partisans of Wlodzislaw. The Polish king was again unanimously elected Hungarian—Croatian king. At the same time the Estates proclaimed the crowning of the infant prince null and void. On the 17th of July Wlodzislaw was crowned by the same archbishop Dionysius Szechy of Ostrogon in Szekes Fehervar, however, not with the crown of St. Stephen, for it was in the hands of Queen Elizabeth, but with another crown taken from the crypt of St. Stephen. As king of Hungary and Croatia he was known under the name of Wlodzislaw I (1440-1444).

The First Siege of Belgrade

The factional strife that broke out in connection with throne succession was cleverly turned by Murad II to account for his plans of conquest. His next move was to capture the strongly fortified Belgrade. The city was heroically defended by the prior of Vrana, Ivan Talovats, brother of Matko, banus of Slavonia. The Sultan surrounded the city from the land and from the banks of Sava and Danube, and started to bombard it from large siege engines and guns. From May to October, 1440, the Sultan sent wave after wave of his troops to storm Belgrade and to scale the walls of the Danubian stronghold. But all his efforts were in vain for Ivan Talovats defended the city with such skill and determination that Murad II finally withdrew to Adrianople after sustaining a loss of 17,000 men.

Civil War and Territorial Shrinking of Croatia

The retreat of the Sultan from Belgrade enabled King Wlodzislaw I to decide the question of inheritance of the Croatian-Hungarian throne. This was possible only by settling the accounts with Queen Elizabeth and her party. The Queen's faction was headed by a Czech general Yan Yiskra who owned extensive estates in the northwestern part of Hungary. The more important members of this faction were Frederic and Ulric of Zell, princely masters of a considerable part of Slavonia, and some Frankapani, also holders of estates in Slavonia. The rest of Croatia and Hungary, on the other hand, sided with Wlodzislaw I.

Realizing that she was too weak to fight it out with the king, Elizabeth sought and obtained aid from her relative, and guardian of her infant son, Ladislaus. This was the German king Frederick III of Hapsburg. For any Hapsburg prince this was a propitious occasion to promote the Hapsburg policy which strove to unite Hungary and Croatia under the Hapsburg scepter. Moreover, Elizabeth left her infant son in August, 1440, in Frederick's custody. The child was to be raised at the German court, while Elizabeth was given a loan of 5,000 ducats for the upkeep of an army.

After these preparations a bloody civil war broke out in Hungary and Croatia between the two factions. In the course of this struggle Zagreb suffered great damage, from the excesses of Ulric's soldiery. Finally the party of King Wlodzislaw I won out chiefly through the efforts of the papal Legate, cardinal Julianus Cesarini who moved the warring factions to compromise. The peace was concluded on the 16th of December, 1442, in the Hungarian city of Gyoer (pronounce: Jur). Both parties agreed that Wlodzislaw I would rule until his death and then be succeeded by Ladislaus Posthumous. The prospect of a new era of domestic peace seemed fully assured after Queen Elizabeth died shortly after the promulgation of the treaty.

The civil war between the factions of the two rulers was of baneful consequences for the integrity of the Croatian territory. Taking advantage of the general confusion in Croatia, duke Styepan Vukchich (Kossacha), nephew and successor of duke Sandal Hranich, seized the Maritime Province (i.e. the area between Tsetina and Neretva rivers), together with the stronghold of Omish, and the district of Polyitse. However, his control of his new possessions was short-lived because Venice forced him out of Omish and Polyitse, leaving in his hands only the Maritime Province. Except for the Venetian seizure of Dalmatia at the opening of the century, this was the most serious blow Croatia had to suffer. By the combined attack of the Grand Duke and Venice, Croatia was finally separated from her sea-coast in the south, while her counties in the interior of the country were torn away, little by little, by the king of Bosnia and his dukes. Preoccupied with wars with the Turks, King Wlodzislaw could not prevent this dismemberment of the Croatian territory. His tragic death prevented him from recovering what had been lost.

The Great Turkish War (1443-1444)

After the internal peace was restored, and unmindful of the complications arising at the southwestern tip of his realm, Wlodzislaw mobilized all the forces of his three kingdoms to crush the Ottoman Empire. His was not only an army of crack forces, but he also had a brilliant general whose military genius was to lead the combined Christian forces to victory. That was the famous Roumanian fighter Yancu de Sibiu, or Hunyadi Janos (in Hungarian) banus of the Severin province.

Still in 1441 banus Yancu (John Hunyadi) was campaigning in Transylvania with such success that plans were formed to declare a general European war against the Turks with the intention of ejecting them from Europe. Voices to that effect, couched in passionate appeals and eloquent words, were heard in the first place from the papal Legate, cardinal Julianus Cesarini. Then from the King of Bosnia, Styepan Tvartko I, and from the exiled despot George Brankovich.

Moved by the warlike spirit of the day, the Hungarian Estates decided in January, 1443 to declare war on Turkey. The campaign was carried out on a grand scale. The king himself, assisted by banus John Hunyadi led the Christian host. Without much effort Wlodzislaw and Hunyadi penetrated into the interior of the Balkans. Near the city of Sofia, at the foot of the Balkan mountains, they pitched camp on Christmas Eve, 1443. In the course of this advance they defeated the Turks in several decisive battles.

This date was also the turning point of the campaign. Suddenly great cold set in and, in addition, embarrassed by lack of food supplies, Wlodzislaw decided to withdraw. Encouraged by the king's embarrassment, the Turks attacked him during his retreat at the Kunovitsa pass near Nish, but suffered such a crushing defeat that their forces disintegrated, and were abandoned by their Albanian allies under George Skanderbeg Castriota.

Convinced that the war was lost for Turkey, Murad II sued for peace which was concluded on the 13th day of July, 1444 in Segedin, for a period of ten years. By its provisions Serbia was delivered from the Turkish rule and despot George Brankovich could return to his country.

But no sooner was the peace signed, than cardinal Julianus Cesarini again undertook to persuade the magnates to embark on a new crusade. In his exhortations he repeated the allegation that oaths given to the "infidels", had no value. An ill omen to the new campaign was the stubborn opposition to it by George Brankovich, who denied assistance to the king, or even passage of his armies through Serbia. In spite of this the Hungarian Diet declared a new war on Murad II.

Fired again with the zeal to expel the Turks from Europe, Wlodzislaw mustered up an army 16,000 strong. Under the command of King Wlodzislaw and John Hunyadi the forces set to field advancing along the right bank of the Danube and then turned to Varna on the Black Sea. But here the further advance of the invading army was checked on the 10th of November, 1444, by Sultan Murad, who drew out at the head of a force 40,000 strong. By his surprise attack the Christian army was caught unprepared and annihilated. King Wlodzislaw himself, perished in battle. Together with the king, many magnates and Church dignitaries,—including Cardinal Julianus Cesarini, lost their lives.

However, banus John Hunyadi and banus Frank Talovats broke through the enemy ranks with the remnants of their army. This was the last offensive war the Christian rulers and their army leaders waged in the Balkans and Central Europe, against the rising might of the Ottoman Empire.

Ladislaus IV (V) and Governor John Hunyadi

News of the king's death spread like wild-fire, both in Croatia and Hungary. Since the throne became vacant, the Estates, in concurrence with the representatives of the royal free cities, elected in April, 1445 Ladislaus IV (V), the posthumous, (1445-1457) Hungarian-Croatian king. But even such a simple and legitimate move was not without serious complications. The guardian of the 5 year old child interposed here his selfish policy. The German king Frederic III, the boy's keeper, refused to return either the boy or the crown of St. Stephen to the magnates.

Confronted with the unexpected turn, the Estates elected, two months later (June 5, 1446), the most popular hero of his time, John Hunyadi, Governor of the country (1446-1452).

The Estates invested Hunyadi with the exercise of sovereign power over Hungary and Croatia. Without wasting time the Governor summoned Frederic to send Ladislaus to him, together with the crown of St. Stephen. The Hapsburg king refused to comply and Governor Hunyadi declared war on him. However, the campaign ended quickly and indecisively for King Frederic, as before, kept both the boy and the crown. On the other hand, Hunyadi was loath to forcing the issue for it was to his advantage to postpone the decision for as long a time as possible.

Instead of fighting in the north, John Hunyadi again directed the attention of his country to the situation in the south where the Turks took advantage of their victory at Varna for further expansion and conquest in the Balkans. He convinced the Estates of the necessity for a new campaign against the Turks. The war was declared and Hunyadi decided to strike this time at the opposite end of the Ottoman Empire, namely in the south-west, along the Albanian border. This was the opposite of the tactics followed at Varna, when the plan was to capture Adrianople, the Turkish capital, by invasion of south-eastern Bulgaria. On the other hand, proximity of Croatia as a convenient base, and the struggle of Albania with the Turks under the leadership of Skanderbeg, were the incentives for the new plan.

However, the weak point of this campaign was the hostile attitude of despot George Brankovich of Serbia who again refused to join the crusade. Aroused over this attitude and in requital for the Despot's treachery, which was responsible for the disaster at Varna, Governor Hunyadi laid waste the Serbian country-side during his advance south. The crusaders met the Turkish hosts on the fatal Blackbird Field (Kossovo Polye), where nearly sixty years ago the Serbian empire was reduced to ruins. Under Governor Hunyadi the battle raged as fiercely as under prince Lazarus. In 1448 the fighting continued for three days (October 18, 19, 20), as in 1389 (June 16 through 18), with the same effect. The Hungarian and Croatian armies were crushed, with great loss of life. The Croatian banus Frank Talovats and Slavonian banus John Szekely (Sekula) were among those who fell on the battlefield.

Neither did Governor Hunyadi fare well. While retreating with the remnants of his army through Serbia, he was attacked by despot George Brankovich and taken prisoner. The Despot threw him in the dungeon in the fort of Smederevo, but after two months of captivity he set Hunyadi free upon promise of a substantial ransom, and by keeping the Governor's son Ladislaus as a hostage. Upon his release from prison, Hunyadi made a truce for three years with the new sultan, Mehmed II el Fatih (1451-1481).

After his tragic failures in the south Governor Hunyadi again turned north in order to improve his position. He made a secret treaty with King Frederic III, by which he would keep his position of Governor-Regent until the boy-king Ladislaus became eighteen years of age. This arrangement would prolong Hunyadi's regency up to 1458. However, in 1452 the Austrian Estates rebelled against Frederic and forced him to pass the 12 year old king into their custody. This turn of events upset all the plans of Frederic and Hunyadi. The residence of the boy-king Ladislaus was established in Vienna, and he was made a sovereign of Austria, Bohemia, Hungary and

Croatia. However, being a minor, king's power was exercised in his name by Ulric Einzinger in Austria, by George Podyebradski in Bohemia, and by John Hunyadi in Hungary and Croatia. On the other hand, the authority of Frederic III was restricted to Styria, Carniola and Carinthia. Prince Ulric of Zell, a distant uncle of the young king was appointed his educator. In the new set-up John Hunyadi resigned his Office as Governor, but the young king appointed him in 1453 as Commander-in-Chief of the armed forces and director of the Royal Treasury in Hungary and Croatia. In addition, Hunyadi was given the title of prince of Bistritse (Hungarian: Beszterce). Here we should add that the emblem of Hunyadi carried the image of a raven (Latin: corbus, corvus), hence the surname; *Corvinus*.

Conditions in Croatia

Throughout this period of momentous struggle, inside and outside her borders, Croatia contributed her part in blood and resources. Attacked on her outlying districts by scheming and greedy barons, Croatia could not defend her borders successfully. Her efforts were concentrated on the crusades against the Turks and on supporting such leaders who could lead the Christian armies to victory. Hence she neglected her own vital interests and dissensions at home. The troubles began in 1445 when after the death of banus Matko Talovats, the Slavonian banate was seized by the princes Frederic and Ulric of Zell.

As they were seizing the estates of Talovats and those of the Zagreb diocese, fighting flared up in many districts of Slavonia. Tragically, the heroic defender of Belgrade (1440), Ivan Talovats, prior of Varna, lost his life in this struggle.

The unbridled violence of the Zell princes aroused the magnates of the kingdom, and they brought complaints on judgment day (August 20th of each year) before the Royal Court in Szekes Fehervar. With a verdict of guilty the Royal Tribunal ordered Governor John Hunyadi (1446) to force the Zell clan into submission by resorting to arms.

In execution of the court order the Governor organized an armed expedition against the overbearing princes. He soon took their town Djurdevats and set on fire Varazhdin, another Zell-owned town. From Varazhdin he broke into Styria, ravaging their estates. Finally, passing through the Mura district (Medjimurye), he laid siege to Koprivnitza, another town in possession of the Zell family. Confronted with military disasters, the Zell princes surrendered, promising to return all the towns and estates to their rightful owners. In return they were permitted to retain their own legal possessions and the office of the Slavonian banus. However, in the exercise of banal authority, both they and the Croatian banus Peter Talovats, were limited by submission to Ivan Szekely, a relation of Hunyadi's who was appointed prior of Vrana, banus of Croatia, Dalmatia, Slavonia and also Vice-Governor of Croatia and Slavonia.

In spite of the apparent settlement of the administrative affairs, Vice-Governor Ivan Szekely had still to go through serious fighting with the princes of Zell who even then, possessed great power. Moreover, banus Peter Talovats, who controlled the area south of Velebit, had his hands full fighting the Venetians. In addition he was embroiled with the King of Bosnia, Styepan Tomash (1443-1461), successor of Styepan Tvartko II. Likewise he had to fight Styepan Vukchich Kossacha, who in 1448, proclaimed himself Duke (Herzog) of St. Sava (St. Sabbas) —(hence the name Herzegovina).

Unmindful of the stormy events, the princes Frankapani ruled over northern Croatia as true sovereigns, paying no attention to either the minor king, to the Governor or to any of the bani. In 1449 they divided their huge estate into eight parts, thus establishing eight branches of the Frankapan famliy. Some of these branches died out, while four of them survived. Those perpetuating themselves into the 17th century were the branches of Terzhats, Ozalj, Slunj and Tsetina.

Things went from bad to worse when Peter Talovats died and the Croatian—Dalmatian banal Office was given to the Governor's elder son, Ladislaus Hunyadi (1453). The young man never even saw his banate for he left it to the mercy of domestic strife and disorders. In Slavonia, again, after the death of Ivan Szekely on the Blackbird Field (1448), the princes of Zell, Frederic and Ulric remained in power as bani, until their death. Frederic died in 1454 and Ulric died two years later.

Second Siege of Belgrade (1456)

In the meantime, Mehmed II el Fatih captured Constantinople on the 29th of May, 1453. This colossal achievement earned him undying glory in the Mohammedan world and the title, still in use, of Fatih, "the conqueror". Thus, the last bastion of the Lower Roman Empire, after 1,000 years of struggle crumbled into dust. While to Islam, the capture of Constantinople was a feat of glory, to western Europe it was a catastrophe. Consternation was wide-spread and misgivings were especially depressing in Bosnia, Croatia and Hungary. On a wave of indignation John Hunyadi declared war on the Turks in 1454, but with little success. He then decided to organize and lead a crusade, with the aid of western Europe. Pope Nicholas V sent the fiery and eloquent friar John Capistrano to raise as many crusaders as possible throughout Austria, Bohemia and Hungary. His activities were a phenomenal success, for when Sultan Mehmed el Fatih laid siege to Belgrade in 1456 with an army of 150,000 men, Capistrano's crusaders swooped down on the Turks, under the leadership of Hunyadi, with such force that Mehmed's army suffered a crushing defeat. The Turks were defeated at first on the Sava and Danube Rivers, and a few days later, on land (July 1456). This was also the most glorious victory for "Sibinyanin Janko", but also his last one.

Victim to a plague, the great hero died on the 11th of August in Zemun, opposite Belgrade. Two months later John's companion-in-arms, John Capistrano died, probably from the same cause, about sixty miles up the Danube in the stronghold of Ilok. He was buried at Ilok where a cathedral was built in his honor. Thus, the two greatest Christian fighters of the 15th century joined their graves at almost the same time on the blood-drenched soil of Croatia, on the right bank of the Danube.

Blood Feud Between the Hunyadi and Zell Clans

At the peak of the struggle with the Turks, Governor Hunyadi became embroiled in a bitter quarrel over the custody of the youthful king Ladislaus IV (V), the Posthumous. After the death of the Croatian banus, Peter Talovats, Ulric, resorting to violence, got hold of the Croatian-Dalmatian banate, seized some personal estates of the late Talovats, and soon made himself master of all Croatia, with the exception of the stronghold of Klis and the Frankapani estates. In his expansionist adventures he was aided by Duke Styepan Vukchich Kossacha. Inebriated by his success, Ulric lost sight of the fact that Ladislaus Hunyadi was appointed banus of Croatia, even before he set out on his path of violence. In consequence, a momentous conflict broke out between them.

The struggle ended on the 9th of November, 1456, in Belgrade, where young Hunyadi had Ulric seized and beheaded. Banus Hunyadi came to Belgrade in company with King Ladislaus IV (V) on a sight-seeing visit after the great victory of that year. The tragic end of prince Ulric of Zell brought along the extinction of that family, for he was the last male member of the House of Zell (Celski). The spectacular rise and military exploits of this clan were much to the detriment of the Croatian lands where they caused much grief, ruin and wanton bloodshed.

Yet the sudden execution of King Ladislaus' relative and educator was not left without equally cruel requital. The boy-king craved revenge and schemed the doom of Ladislaus Hunyadi. In the meantime, he bound himself by oath before Elizabeth Hunyadi, widow of the Governor, that he would not harbor any plans of revenge on her foster-son. Breaking his oath, the king had Ladislaus Hunyadi seized and beheaded on the 16th of March, 1457, in Budavar, where he treacherously called him, together with his younger brother Mathias, for a conference. In addition, he took Mathias prisoner and sent him to his residence in Prague.

Before reaching his eighteenth year, King Ladislaus IV (V) suddenly died in Prague, on the 23rd of November, 1457. With his death the personal union between Austria, Bohemia, Hungary and Croatia was promptly dissolved, and since the king left no successor, Hungary and Croatia had to elect a new ruler. Early in 1458, after a prolonged debate, the Estates, chiefly under the pressure of the lower nobility who were devoutly attached to the name of Hunyadi, decided to select Mathias, the younger son of Governor Hunyadi, king of Hungary and Croatia. Thus began the reign of one of the most brilliant monarchs of medieval Europe and probably the greatest of all the rulers who occupied the throne of Hungary and Croatia.

MATHIAS I. CORVINUS (1458-1490)

(In Hungarian: Matyas Kiraly;
in Croatian: Kralj Matija)

Consolidation of Power

Upon the news of King Ladislaus' death, Mathias Corvinus, still the king's prisoner in the royal castle of Hradchany (Prague), was promptly set free. Moreover, the Bohemian king George Podyebradski (1458-1471) had him betrothed with his daughter Catherine.

Being only 15 years of age when elected Croatian-Hungarian king, Mathias was placed under the tutelage of his uncle Michael Szilagyi who was to act as Governor of the two kingdoms for a period of five years. But Michael's nephew asserted himself right from the start. Through display of unusual will power and self-reliance the teen-age king rid himself of his uncle's guardianship and seized the reins of Government in his own name.

Mathias' first task was to raise the prestige of royal authority in Croatia where it was nearly obliterated during the civil wars. The crude force applied for a long time by the Zell princes undermined the law and authority. In turn, the princely offenders were also severely punished by the ultimate extinction of their clan. In addition, the raids of Stephen Thomas, king of Bosnia, Grand Duke Stephen Vukchich of Herzegovina, and the Venetian Republic, upon the Croatian territory, with seizure of Croatian towns and districts, created a precarious situation in the ravaged country.

King Mathias took the situation in earnest and decided to clear the territory of its invaders, and restore to Croatia her former authority and power. With this purpose in mind he appointed Paul Speranchich, an able general, Croatian-Dalmatian banus (1459-1463). However, the assignment of the task was not supported by sufficient military force, so that despite the skill and superior leadership of banus Speranchich the preponderant forces of outsiders could not be overcome. The only worthwhile accomplishment of Speranchich, after much fighting, was the capture and retention of the all-important stronghold of Klis.

Even with the best of intentions, Mathias could not accomplish much toward setting Croatia back on her feet, for trouble brewed right in his own court and capital. Under the leadership of Nicholas Ujlaki (Ilochki) and his own uncle Michael Szilagyi, a plot was formed to overthrow him and deprive him of his throne. The conspirators offered the crown to Frederic III, King of Germany. Yet Frederic was not a man of energy and determination who could take advantage of the offer and go through with the coup. In the meantime, Mathias effected a compromise with the rebels. Moreover, he made up with King Frederic himself who gladly accepted a ransom of 80,000 ducats for the return of the crown of St. Stephen. In addition, he dropped his plan to establish an effective rule in Hungary and Croatia. He became satisfied with the title of the king of Croatia and Hungary. Furthermore, he was given the promise that in case of Mathias' death without a male descendant, he or his sons would inherit the throne of Croatia and Hungary.

After the conclusion of this treaty (July 23, 1463) and the return of St. Stephen's crown, Mathias was crowned with pomp on March 29, 1464, king of Croatia and Hungary. For a period of six years the reign of Mathias was successful and prosperous. During this time he restored internal harmony and prosperity both in Croatia and Hungary which these two kingdoms had not enjoyed since the times of Louis the Great.

Turkish Advance in the South

Right at the beginning of Mathias' reign, disasters overtook the countries south of his dominion. After the fall of Smederevo in 1459 Serbia was conquered by Sultan Mehmed II and turned into a Turkish province (pashalyk). In 1463 the same fate befell Bosnia, whose first crowned king, Stephen Tomashevich, was beheaded (June, 1463) in the Sultan's tent below the walls of Yaytse, Stephen's former capital. The fall of Bosnia aroused Mathias and his kingdom, since everyone became conscious of the impending danger threatening Croatia and Hungary alike. In a counteroffensive staged in the fall of the same year, the Croatian and Hungarian troops pushed deep into Bosnia and reconquered the northern part of the country. Out of the reconquered territory Mathias formed two banates: one with the capital of Yaytse, and the other with the center in the town of Srebrenik. These two districts were to serve as ramparts for the defense of Slavonia and Hungary in the east, and of Croatia in the west. However, the Turkish tide of conquest was running too high to be stopped for a long time.

Hussite Complications and War with Austria

From a more effective deployment of his power against the Turks, Mathias was prevented by his intervention in the affairs of Bohemia. In that country the Hussite reformation was in full vogue and King George Podyebradski extended it his protection. In retaliation, Pope Pius II excommunicated George and deprived him of his crown. At this turn Mathias I, as an ally of the Holy See, broke into Moravia and Bohemia where he was elected king by the Catholic nobility. Nevertheless, he could not establish himself in the country, since the majority of the Bohemian (Czech) magnates elected and crowned Vladislav the Yaghiellonian, a Polish prince, king of Moravia and Bohemia. Furthermore, his own throne was threatened at home. Irritated over his foreign wars and strict enforcement of the new law, the higher nobility rebelled both in Croatia and Hungary. After the overthrow of Mathias the rebels planned to invite Kazimir, a royal prince of Poland, to the Croatian-Hungarian throne. But the swift and forceful measures of Mathias nipped the rebellion in the bud, and order was restored throughout his kingdom.

Having quashed all opposition at home, Mathias I again turned his attention north. Finally, he realized that he could not subdue Bohemia, and negotiated a peace treaty with King Vladislav in Olmuetz (1479). By the terms of this treaty Mathias recognized Vladislav king of Bohemia, but he was given the title of Bohemian king. Further, the administration of Moravia, Silesia and Luzhitse (Lausitz) was assigned to him, and after his death the Czechs could redeem this area for the sum of 400,000 ducats.

Mathias' campaigns were not restricted to Bohemia alone. Even before his conciliation with King Vladislav, Mathias declared war on the German king Frederic III. His quarrel with Frederic was of long standing and the hostilities between the two monarchs were bitter and protracted. The war lasted for nearly twelve years (1477-1488) and the Hungarian troops took Vienna in 1485. Mathias attached great importance to his new Austrian possessions, and moved his court to Vienna. But while Mathias scored success in the north, he neglected the situation in the south where events were taking an ominous course.

Situation in Croatia

Ever since the fall of Bosnia (1463), the Turks embarked on a course of inroads, devastations and plunder in the neighboring lands. Especially attractive for the forays of the invaders were areas adjacent to the provinces of Lika, Kerbava and northern Dalmatia. In their dash northward, the Turkish outposts frequently reached Senj on the Adriatic coast and the Alps of southern Carniola (Slovenia). On their way back the Turks used to drive thousands of Christian slaves in front of them whom they attached as serfs (rayah) to the Bosnian estates of the Mohammedan warlords, or sold them on the eastern slave markets. Women were sold to procurers, while men were driven for hard labor as far as the cataracts of the Nile. By 1469 the picture of devastations was so terrifying that individual Croatian magnates and especially the princes Frankapani, began to apply to Venice and German King Frederic III for aid, since their own king Mathias Corvinus was immersed in his Bohemian adventures, and could not give them protection or military aid.

Apprised of this turn, King Mathias feared that under the pretext of aiding the Frankapani, the Venetians would seize the city of Senj, and in a counter-move he sent an army into Croatia. The stronghold of Senj was promptly captured, and the town was made a free royal city at the expense of Frankapani. Furthermore, he made it a focal point of a large military district equipped to meet both the Turkish and Venetian attacks. In organizing these defenses King Mathias seized also the other Frankapani possessions along the sea-coast and inland. So he took away from them the whole coast from Tersat, near Fiume, down to Senj, or the area known as the Croatian coastland (Hrvatsko Primorje), together with the rich district of Vinodol.

The dispositions of Mathias struck a heavy blow at the fortunes of the Frankapani family, and bitter enmity developed between this clan and the king. Relying on Venetian support Prince Ivan (John) of Kerk (Veglia) attacked the cities of Novi and Bribir on the nearby mainland. This move aroused Blaise Podmanitski, commander of the royal forces, who invaded the island of Kerk. But before the struggle was ended prince Ivan Frankapan surrendered the island in 1480 to Venice. As a result of this, new strife arose in the course of which the Frankapani family was cut off from the sea, and Croatia lost her last island in the Adriatic. On the other hand, Croatia obtained in 1477 the right to select in her parliament (sabor) the commander-in-chief of her armed forces (capitaneus regni), independently from the office or authority of the banus.

Administrative Unity Between Croatia and Bosnia

Even in the midst of his northern campaigns, King Mathias devoted a part of his time and forces to fight the Turks in Bosnia and Herzegovina. After recapturing the northern part of Bosnia, Mathias sent a part of his forces to Herzegovina, in order to aid Grand Duke Stephen Vukchich Kossacha in the defense of his country. The chief line of defense was the Neretva defile, with its estuary. Its stronghold Pochitel was well fortified and ably defended. After the death of the Grand Duke (1466), the country's forces were frittered away in quarrels over inheritance. The Neretva defense line collapsed, and in spite of its stubborn defense, Pochitel was captured by the Turks in 1471. With the exception of the coastland (maritime province) the whole district between Tsetina and Neretva was now conquered.

In spite of this set-back, King Mathias decided to continue his campaigns against the Turks and in 1472 he restored the Bosnian kingdom, elevating Nicholas of Ujlak (Ilok) to the throne and had him crowned king of Bosnia. In addition, he appointed Nicholas also banus of Croatia and Slavonia, and prior of Vrana. Thus, the administrative unity of Bosnia with the other Croatian lands, restored in part the situation as it existed under the national Croatian kings. The task of the new Bosnian king was to liberate all of Bosnia from the Turks. But his premature death (1477) prevented him from carrying out the momentous assignment.

After Nicholas' death, King Mathias decided to undertake a campaign in Bosnia under his personal command. He fully succeeded in his undertaking, for in 1480 he took Sarayevo and Upper Bosnia (Vrhbosna). However, his success was ephemeral, for two years later (1482) the Turks recovered the lost territory, and, in addition, conquered all of Herzegovina. King Mathias was helpless in the face of Turkish expansion, for he engaged in a bitter and prolonged war with the German king Frederic III. He never resumed his struggle with the Turks again, for he suddenly died in 1480 at the age of 47. Mathias passed away in Vienna, the city which he had made the capital of his empire.

Mathias' Reign

With the premature death of Mathias Corvinus, a benevolent despot and outstanding ruler of his time, both Croatia and Hungary suffered a heavy loss. Mathias was quite independent in his actions which he prosecuted with great will-power and unyielding energy. Adamant in his opposition to high nobility, he was a true friend of the small gentry, farmer and burgher alike. His lowly subjects found in him their protector and friend, and up to this time the popular devotion to his memory is reflected in the survival of proverbs "Passed on King Mathias, passed out the Justice" (Meghalt Matyas kiraly, oda az igazsag) in Hungarian, and "as long as King Mathias is asleep, there is no justice" (Pokle Kralj Matijas spi, nikakve pravice ni) in Croatian.

Mathias made his name famous by his successes, victories and conquests in the north. For Croatia, however, his exploits are synonymous with disasters, since they disabled him to make a successful stand against the Turks in the moments of their greatest striking power. Temperamental and gifted, he was a convincing orator and learned man, and an admirer of arts and sciences. Men of letters and arts were invited to his court from far and wide, for he was an enthusiastic champion of renaissance. During his reign the art of printing was introduced both in Hungary and Croatia.

Mathias raised his kingdom to a position of glamor and power unmatched at that time in Europe. He could easily put in the field an army of 150,000 men and dispose of a fleet of 330 naval vessels, partly in the Adriatic and partly on the Danube.

After the death of Mathias strife over throne succession further paralyzed the country. Even though he was married three times, Mathias had no children. But he had one son born out of wed-lock whom he dearly loved. He named him John Corvinus (born in 1473 in Breslau, Silesia), gave him large estates and raised him at his court as a royal prince. He had the Estates' promise under oath that they would make his son king of both Croatia and Hungary. But as soon as Mathias died, both the magnates and royal free cities turned away from the undesirable youth.

THE LAST YAGHIELLONIAN KINGS (1490-1526)

Election of Vladislav II (Ulaszlo) 1490-1516

The death of Mathias Corvinus was wel-come news to the Hungarian magnates and they promptly rejected the claims of John Corvinus to his father's throne. They pointed out that his illegitimate origin disqualified him to wear the Hungarian crown. But what they actually aimed at, was loosening up of the royal authority which Mathias established in his kingdom.

On the other hand, Lawrence of Ujlak (Ilok), son of the former king of Bosnia, and his Sla-vonian friends, stood by prince John. But the vacant Hungarian-Croatian throne was coveted by three other contenders: Maximilian, son of Frederic III, king of Germany; Vladislav Ya-ghiellovich, king of Bohemia; and John Albert, royal prince of Poland. Each of them claimed the right to the throne succession either through their Angevin blood-ties, or by reference to some political treaty or agreement. So Maximilian, a Hapsburg prince, invoked the treaty concluded between King Mathias and Frederic III in 1463.

The tangle was unravelled through the power-ful influence of prince Stephen of Zapolye, a Carpathian magnate, who had elected the Bo-hemian king Vladislav II, and obtained from John Corvinus the hereditary title of the duke of Sla-vonia. Later on, he was appointed also Croatian-Dalmatian banus, and was promised also the crown of Bosnia.

When Vladislav crossed the Hungarian border he was asked to take the electoral crown-oath (capitulationes electorales), by which he became dependent upon the magnates. Thus the high nobility made a new bid for power, which had been drastically reduced under King Mathias.

Vladislav was taken to Budavar with great pomp. On the 18th of September, 1490 he was crowned by Oswald Thuz, bishop of Zagreb, king of Hungary and Croatia in the ancient royal capital of Szekes Fehervar.

Struggle for the Throne

Upon his accession to the throne Vladislav had to contend with two rivals: his younger brother John Albert and King Maximilian of Germany. In an armed contest with his brother John, Vlad-islav forced a quick decision, for he defeated him in the battle of Koshitsa (Kassa) and made him abandon his claims.

By way of contrast, his second adversary, King Maximilian, was favored with good luck in the war. Without difficulty he recaptured Vienna and drove out the Hungarians from Austria. More-over, he broke into Hungary, raiding the very vicinity of Budavar and taking Szekes Fehervar where he proclaimed himself king of Croatia and Hungary.

This move earned him the support of many Croatian magnates, including Lawrence of Ujlak (Ilok), two branches of the Frankapan family, descendants of the Talovats clan, and the city of Zagreb. On the other hand, Maximilian was op-posed by John Corvinus, and the Ozal group of Frankapani, together with some other barons of the kingdom. In the meantime, Maximilian was forced to withdraw from Hungary, because of lack of funds, while the Hungarian troops occu-pied the towns evacuated by the Austrians.

Confronted with the failure of his plans, Maxi-milian made peace with King Vladislav, which was confirmed in the treaty of Pozhun (Press-burg, Bratislava). According to this treaty (No-vember 1, 1491) the Hapsburgs were guaranteed for the second time in a few years, the right of succession, should the male descendants of the royal house die out. Hungary also renounced her claim to Austria, while Maximilian's supporters in Croatia were given full amnesty.

In order to have this treaty ratified by the Estates, Vladislav called a Diet in Budavar in February, 1492. He also wanted to obtain the sanction of the kingdom for a prospective en-thronement of the Hapsburgs. Assembled in the Parliament were numerous members of the lower and higher nobility, church dignitaries and rep-resentatives of royal cities both from Croatia and Hungary. The Estates were irritated over the Pozhun treaty and its ratification was denied.

After a whole month of wrangling in the Diet the two kingdoms made separate decisions to accept the Hapsburgs. The Hungarian Estates issued a patent in the name of Hungary, while the Croatian magnates and nobility guaranteed the right of Maximilian and his descendants to inherit the Croatian crown, in the name of Croatia and Slavonia, when the male line of King Vladislav II became extinct. This decree in the name of Croatia was issued on the 7th of March, 1492, and signed by sixty-three Croatian barons and knights headed by the Croatian-Slavonian-Dalmatian banus Ladislaus.

Constitutional Reforms

With these arrangements the internal order in the two kingdoms was restored, but the country began to show alarming signs of weakness. Exhausted by the military campaigns of Mathias Corvinus both Croatia and Hungary were afflicted with financial troubles and military disorganization. New laws were enacted to meet the situation. The royal authority suffered a grave setback. By the decision of the Budavar Diet the system of taxation, together with army regulations enacted by King Mathias, were abolished, and the old laws dating back to the reign of Albert and Sigismund were reinstated.

The king lost the right to start an offensive war on his own initiative. The old privileges of the barons and warlords were restored, both in Hungary and Croatia. In Slavonia the nobility fared best, since its rights were guaranteed by eleven sections of the new constitution, and its taxes were reduced to half the size of those paid in Hungary. The Palatin of the kingdom was appointed by the king upon the advice of the prelates and barons, yet with the consent of the lower nobility.

On the whole these provisions, made out of a bad situation, became much worse for soon the country was plunged into grave financial difficulties. Due to many tax-exemptions, the treasury remained empty in the times of need and stress.

Prince Stephen of Zapolye was appointed Palatin of Hungary by Vladislav, in recognition of Stephen's effort to have him elected king.

Croatian Disasters

From its inception Vladislav's reign boded ill for Croatia. Through loosening up of the king's authority the barons raised their heads, eager to regain their former power and possessions. The king's weakness was promptly seized upon by the Frankapani princes whose estates were confiscated by King Mathias, in order to regain the coastland and recapture the city of Senj. In the ensuing turmoil John Corvinus, banus of Croatia, resigned his Office, and Emeric Derenchin was appointed in his place. The new banus engaged in a bitter struggle with prince Bernardin Frankapan for the possession of Senj.

Before either party won a decision in the armed contest, the Bosnian Sanjak, Hadum Jakub Pasha at the head of a large army, broke into Croatia, Carniola and Carinthia. This made both parties make up and join forces against the Turks. The united Croatian armies lay in wait for the return of the Turks to Bosnia, and attacked them on the Kerbava field near the town of Udbine. On the 9th of September, 1493, a fierce battle was fought between the two camps, and through inferior generalship of the banus, the Croatian forces suffered a crushing defeat. Banus Derenchin himself was taken prisoner, and shortly after died in Turkey. The disaster suffered by Croatia on the Kerbava field can be compared with the battle of Kossovo in which the might of the Serbian empire crumbled. By country folk the Kerbava field was very aptly called "Bloody Field (Kervavo polye)" because of the heavy losses sustained by the Croatian warriors.

After the Kerbava battle, Croatian history resembles much that of Serbia, for province after province was overwhelmed by Turkish might, until the once powerful Croatian kingdom was reduced to a few counties in the Alpine region, with Zagreb as the southernmost outpost of the country's defenses. Unlike Belgrade and Budapest, Zagreb was never captured by the Turks, but the country's reduced size was frequently complained about in official documents, as "reliquiae reliquiarum olim magni et gloriosi regni Croatiae." ("Relics of the relics of the once great and glorious kingdom of Croatia.")

Indeed, with the disaster on Kerbava field, a two-centuries long life-and-death struggle is ushered in in which the Croatian people fought with the powerful Ottoman Empire. In the course of this unequal struggle the Croats won the admiration of Western Europe and entire Christendom.

Popes sent them their blessing and showered them with such flattering epithets as "ante-murale Christianitatis" and "Scutum Ecclesiae."* Hungarians, too, shared in these honors, for they, too, fought under similar conditions, and were bleeding white. The intimate union between Croatia and Hungary, cemented by four centuries of happier existence, was not dissolved in the crucial moments of their ordeal, but was still further cemented by common struggle against the Hapsburgs whose generals at times were no less oppressive than the Turkish pashas themselves.

Throughout this era of bloody struggle far-reaching social changes took place on the Croatian territory. The population of Bosnia, Dalmatia and Lika, fleeing before the Turkish hordes, settled temporarily or permanently in Slavonia, southern Hungary and the Burgenland district along the Austrian and Hungarian border. Also, the administrative center shifted north, making Zagreb the capital of the Croatian territory. Furthermore, the area north of Gvozd Mountains (Alpes Ferrae) and south of the Drava, which was called throughout the Middle ages "Slavonia," became known as "Croatia," and as such it figures in the constitutional law of the country to this day.

After the Kerbava disaster the Croatian magnates looked around for aid. Since King Vladislav was not able to help them at all, they applied to King Maximilian and Pope Alexander VI for aid. In response to their pleadings Maximilian sent them troops from Carniola, while the Pope provided them with money, food supplies and arms. But all this was a drop in the bucket considering the fierce onslaughts of the Turkish troops. The situation became worse with every coming year, since the Bosnian Mohammedans started their own inroads into Croatia and Slavonia, with ever increasing momentum. Having no alternative, the Croatian barons and noblemen consented to pay them annual tribute and to give free passage to their troops on their forays further north. This humiliation gave the barons a semblance of personal security and continued use of their property. This situation did not change for the better even when King Vladislav in March, 1495 made a truce for three years with Sultan Bayazid II (1481-1512).

* "Bulwark of Christendom" and "shield of the Church."

Internal Strife and Constitutional Changes

The weak and ineffective rule of Vladislav II caused great disappointment both in Croatia and Hungary. Croatia was exposed to continuous Turkish attacks, while the king made no move to defend the country. Hungary herself was in economic prostration, and unprepared to ward off the fierce Turkish attacks.

The general anxiety produced a cleavage in the ranks of high nobility, and two parties were formed. The court-party headed by the Archbishop of Ostrogon, Thomas Erdody, was in opposition to the party of Duke Lawrence Ujlaky (Ilochki) which aspired to overthrow King Vladislav. As master of Sirmium and a part of Slavonia, the richest provinces of the kingdom, Duke Lawrence was a formidable opponent to the king himself. Out of this political friction a war broke out in which King Vladislav hurled all his forces against the Duke. After a protracted struggle the opposition was subdued. But at the next Diet in Budavar the lower nobility scored a brilliant victory by enacting a law which entitled every nobleman to a seat in Parliament, thus securing for the small landowners a majority in the Diet and political control of the country.

Enactment of this important law was the work of Palatin Stephen of Zapolye, father of John, a rival king after the disaster at Mohach. Stephen's plan was to enlist, after Vladislav's death, the support of the lower nobility in his effort to raise his son John to the throne. This plan was very promising since Palatin Stephen enjoyed the support of the famous jurist Stephen Verboczy, the influential leader of the lower nobility. In the meantime, Palatin Stephen died (1499) and his son John inherited every office held by his father, except that of the palatin.

Pursuing the ambitious plans of his father, John submitted on the 12th of October, 1505, before the Estates assembled on Rakos mezo (Crabfield), near Budavar, a bill by virtue of which no one, under penalty of high treason, might propose in the Diet to invite an alien to the Croatian-Hungarian throne. Approved by the king this decision became a law. This Act was obviously directed against the Hapsburgs who already considered themselves legal heirs to the Croatian-Hungarian throne. Apprised of the enactment of this Law, King Maximilian prepared himself for a war against Hungary in order to enforce his succession rights. But the birth of Louis, son of Vladislav, prevented the bloodshed. The dispute was settled by a new treaty concluded on July 19, 1505, in Vienna, by which again—and now for the third time—the right of Hapsburg succession was confirmed by the Croatian-Hungarian king.

Separatist Tendencies in Croatia

Left in the lurch by King Vladislav II, Croatia had to face the formidable realities of the day, relying on her own resources and on the initiative of such leaders who would defend the country. Besides Bernardin Frankapan, such was John Corvinus, son of the late King Mathias. Dismayed over the internal struggle in Hungary, prince John returned to Croatia to exercise the authority of his high office. Here he married Beatrice, daughter of prince Bernardin and established himself alternatingly in the stronghold of Bihach on Una, and in the picturesque town of Krapina, in the Croatian Tramontane (Zagorye). Worthy of the heroic traditions of his grandfather, Yancu de Sibiu, John organized a stubborn defense of Croatia against the Turks, and especially of the Bosnian banate, with its capital at Yaytse. He scored two impressive victories: one under Knin, and the other near the stronghold of Yaytse. John's successful campaigns moved the sultan to make a seven years' truce with King Vladislav (1504).

Unfortunately, prince John died in the same year. His death was felt throughout the kingdom as a heavy blow to Croatia, and his remains were laid at rest, among general mourning, in the Church of the Paulician Monastery of Lepoglava, near Zagreb. The epitaph on his tomb still can be seen. As a consequence of this tragedy, another dynastic tie was made when his widow, Beatrice Frankapan, married prince George of Brandenburg, a member of the Hohenzollern family.

Even in the face of Turkish peril, the sovereigns of Christian powers continued their suicidal wrangling. So King Vladislav II was inclined to join the League of Cambrai in a war against Venice. As a reward for his alliance with King Maximilian, Vladislav had to obtain Dalmatia. But at the court of Budavar there was a strong party, headed by Archbishop Bakocz and palatin Thomas Erdody, which was friendly to Ven-

ice, and which kept frustrating Vladislav's move against the republic. The campaign was ended in 1512, with status quo, and Dalmatia remained under Venetian authority.

In the same year Vladislav II appointed the bishop of Veszprem, Peter Berislavich, banus of Croatia. Berislavich, a native of Trogir in Dalmatia, added to his spiritual calling the skill of a general, and undertook many defensive actions against the Turkish raiders. His brilliant victory won on the 15th of August, 1513, near the town of Dubitsa on the banks of Una, made his name famous throughout the kingdom.

Aroused by Croatian successes, Hungary, too, made preparations for a war against Turkey. A sizable army was gathered to move against the Turks. Since this was not a noblemen's army, which carried the burden of fighting in the past, but an army drafted from the peasantry, which had bitter grievances against both the lower and higher nobility, it was not enthusiastic about the war. Under the leadership of Julius Dozsa, the peasant-army mutinied and ravaged the estates of the knights and barons, instead of fighting the Turks. Before making much headway, the rebellion was crushed by the forces of the Transylvanian duke, John of Zapolye. Dozsa and the rest of the ring-leaders were beheaded.

The duke's victory over Dozsa and his rebels which he won in 1514 near Temeshvar (Tamiscara), still further raised his prestige, both before the gentry and the magnates. John's ascendancy had a bad effect upon the aged and weak king Vladislav who sought support abroad. So he still further tightened his ties with King Maximilian and the two sovereigns met in 1515 both in Vienna and Pressburg (Bratislava).

In a new agreement between the two kings, the right of the Hapsburg succession to the throne of Hungary and Croatia was confirmed for the fourth time (July 22, 1515). As a guarantee for the execution of the covenant, a double marriage was arranged: Vladislav's son Louis was betrothed to Maria of Hapsburg, grand-daughter of Maximilian, while Anna, Vladislav's daughter, was engaged to Ferdinand, brother of Maria.

In spite of these guarantees the above arrangements had merely the value of private contracts, while the Diet's decision of 1505, by which the aliens had been excluded from the Hungarian-Croatian throne, was enacted, by the king's sanction, as a basic law of the two kingdoms. This unfortunate situation became the source of grave troubles in an era of fatal events.

Louis II (1516-1526)

On the 13th of March, 1516, King Vladislav II passed away, and was succeeded by his son, Louis II, a boy ten years of age. Still an infant, Louis was crowned king of Bohemia, Hungary and Croatia. This time there was no complication about throne succession. The king being a minor, a board of regency took the reins of Government, while the boy was under the care of tutors and guardians. The entourage of the youthful sovereign consisted of selfish and greedy courtiers who exploited the situation to their personal advantage. This reduced the authority of the court, and corruption set in in all the branches of administration. The revenue of the crown was squandered by high officials, and the treasury was filled with debased currency. The luxury of the magnates was contrasted by the misery of the peasants and town residents. To cap the climax, there was a bitter struggle between the court party headed by the Palatin Stephen Bathory, and the people's party under the leadership of the popular John of Zapolye. In a hopeless situation, no one seemed to know the remedy.

Croatia's Predicament

Civil strife and internal weakness in Hungary was a welcome opportunity for the Turks to continue their attacks against Transylvania, Hungary and Croatia. Because of the growing power of Moslem Bosnians the incursions into Croatia and neighboring Alpine lands assumed menacing proportions. Fighting an uphill battle the Croats defended their territory at a high price in blood and possessions. The heroic bishop and banus Berislavich contained the powerful Turkish attacks to the limit of his troops and financial resources. Even with full cooperation of the Croatian Diet and sacrificial efforts on the part of Croatian nobility, banus Berislavich could resist the Turkish onslaughts only with great difficulty. But especially precarious was his position when the Turks conquered the whole Bosnian banate up to the banks of Una. Only the Yaytse stronghold, with the surrounding area, remained undaunted, as a Christian island in the Moslem sea.

Since the fort was surrounded on all sides, it was necessary to provide the garrison with food and ammunition by breaking through the Turkish cordon.

In such a break-through operation, banus Berislavich defeated the Turks in the vicinity of Yaytse early in 1518, and supplied the garrison with ammunition and necessities of life. In 1520 the Turks again raided Croatia and invaded Istria. Banus Berislavich planned a large-scale action and withdrew with his troops to Bihach on the banks of Una. On the 20th of May he offered a decisive battle in the mountain-ranges of Plyeshivitsa, and was totally defeated. Banus himself was killed in action, but his body was rescued and taken to Veszprem, the seat of his diocese, where it was given a solemn burial. His death was mourned at the Hungarian court, the Imperial court of Charles V, and in Rome.

In the meantime, the Turkish attacks continued with increased fury, and the situation both in Croatia and Hungary went from bad to worse.

The Height of Turkish Power— Suleiman II (1520-1566)

In 1520, when Peter Berislavich met heroic death, a brilliant young man ascended the Ottoman throne under the name of Suleiman II. Under his scepter the Turkish empire reached the climax of its power and glory, and the grateful Islam honored him with the title: Magnificent. Suleiman spent the major part of his life on the throne (1520-1566). His career was one of irresistible expansion and conquest. The year following his accession to the throne he captured Belgrade (August 29, 1521), the key-stronghold of Hungary and Slavonia, which had resisted so many Turkish attacks in the past.

After the fall of Belgrade the situation became critical both for Hungary and Croatia, for no serious obstacle was in the way of the Turkish tide. It was obvious, therefore, that momentous events and decisive conflicts were to follow. Croatia, for the moment, was exposed to more immediate dangers than Hungary, and the country was bleeding in a hopeless war. Wonders of heroism were performed under the new banus Ivan Karlovich, a member of the Gussich clan. Overcoming Croatian defenses, the Turks took the formidable stronghold of Knin (1522) in the highlands, and in the same year the fort of Skradin (Scardona) on the sea-coast. In 1523 the coastal fort of Ostrovitsa fell. Only the stronghold of Klis near Split withstood the Turkish attacks in 1524, under the heroic defense of captain Peter Kruzhich.

The Diet of Krizhevtsi

Abandoned to their tragic fate, the Croats began to lean on the power of the German king, Ferdinand of Hapsburg, who aided them both with money and troops. This aid came quite naturally, since in this way he effectively protected his own possessions in Carniola, Carinthia and Styria. In fact, Ferdinand gave them more aid than King Louis II did, and Croatia in her dark moments naturally veered away from Hungary and inclined more toward the Hapsburgs. This tendency took root under Maximilian, and was ready to bear fruit under Ferdinand.

Outliving other Croatian strongholds, the Bosnian Yaytse was still holding out, but in conditions of great distress. Surrounded on all sides by the Turks it had neither ammunition nor fighters to hold out much longer. Upon the frantic appeals of its garrison, prince Kersto (Christopher) Frankapan, son of Bernardin, decided to bring aid to the defenders of Yaytse. He organized a rescue expedition and carried it out with such courage and skill that after several days of continuous fighting he reached the beleaguered stronghold, causing sensitive losses to the enemy. Upon his return he was hailed as a hero of Christianity throughout Europe.

In spite of episodes of bravery and self-sacrifice recorded throughout the Croatian territory, the country was heading to its doom, and some stern emergency measures had to be taken. Under this impression the Croatian Estates met early in 1526 in Krizhevtsi to deliberate on the situation. Some magnates headed by Kersto Frankapan demanded that Croatia separate from King Louis II and Hungary, and to elect another sovereign who would be able to protect and defend it. Their hopes were pinned upon Ferdinand of Hapsburg, also designated as the future king of Croatia. Prince Kersto declared his willingness to head a crusade against the Turks for reconquest of Bosnia, as a result of which Ferdinand would be proclaimed also king of Bosnia, since that country belonged to Croatia. However, another group of magnates favored union with Venice, and the

Diet adjourned without solving the fundamental problems of the day.

To the tragic consequences of the ebbing power of Hungary following the death of King Mathias, belongs also the fact that the ties between Croatia and Hungary loosened up with increasing momentum. The Croatian Estates' loyalty did not stand the fire test of such critical times. The political power of the House of Hapsburgs, on the one hand and the wealth of the Venetian Republic on the other had a force of attraction for them, and again in their despair they were looking for security under Turkish authority, since Hungary no longer was able to give them such. Even such phenomena came to sight which indicated a hostile attitude against the Hungarian race.

While for centuries the Croatian grandees entertained relations with Venice, the beginnings of their political contacts with Austria fall in the second half of the reign of Louis II. Archduke Ferdinand in the summer of 1523, undoubtedly upon the request of the Croatian nobility, directed a summons to King Louis to turn over Croatia to him. But this plan was rejected by the Hungarian nobility.

Then Ferdinand chose another path in order to establish his hold and power over the Croatian lands. He took in his employ certain Croatian magnates and persuaded them to turn over their strongholds to him. Count Nicholas Zrinski, father of the hero of Sziget, entered in such relation with him and likewise Count John of Korbavia as well as Count John Kobashich. In the summer of 1524 the Archduke made preparations to start a campaign for the recapture of the Croatian bordertowns occupied by the Turks; but this campaign was prevented by the war that broke out between the Emperor and the King of France.

Francis Batthyany and John Tahi, Hungarian magnates who were invested at that time with the banal authority, were not of a caliber to restore the sympathy of Croatia toward Hungary. Especially Tahi, with his violent character and arbitrary proceedings, made himself hated. The assembly of Hatvan, upon the complaints of the Croatian Estates, urged the removal of Tahi. They expressed a desire to appoint as his successor the popular Croatian magnate, Count Christopher Frankapan, the savior of the stronghold of Yaytse. But the primate Szalkai who for a long time had a personal grudge against Frankapan prevented the execution of this appointment. At the royal council held on August 30, 1525, a violent debate took place between them, in the course of which, Frankapan, carried by anger, slapped the face of the first Grand Priest of the land.

The king punished him by imprisonment in a tower, but upon intervention of the queen and papal nuncio, he was released, provided he apologized to the Grand Priest. The enemies settled their grievances, but Frankapan, fully aware of Szalkai's vindictiveness, left the royal court, and his appointment as banus of Croatia was dropped. Then the king, in order to satisfy the Croatian Estates and for the purpose of offering protection to the country against Turkish threats, prepared for a personal visit to Zagreb. This apparently excellent and salutary plan ran into stiff opposition by the papal nuncio, since he was well aware of the fact that the royal troops themselves were short of their pay and that he would not be in a position to pay the salary of court personnel. So he would be forced to set out to journey without proper attendance. He was also afraid that the Turks, informed of the king's trip, would break into Slavonia, upon which the king would shamefully return. Therefore he suggested that the king should stay in Buda and the magnates' troops, which were to protect the king on his journey, should be sent to Zagreb and thence to the protection and defense of the bordertowns. The trip was thus cancelled but the magnates refused to send their troops to the bordertowns under various pretexts.

Early in October the bani of Yaytse and the soldiers' representative arrived at Buda and threatened to retire from the stronghold unless they received immediate aid, to an otherwise hopeless resistance. The royal council was greatly confused over these tidings and assigned a portion of the royal income from Transylvania for the needs of Yaytse's defense. However, it could not be collected promptly. Then the papal nuncio and the Archbishop of Ostrogon produced several thousand florins as advance money for a provision of food supplies for Yaytse.

At the same time the Croatian magnates, in whose circle now also Christopher Frankapan became an advocate of complete separation from Hungary, sent still more threatening messages; should they be left in the lurch, they would make

an agreement with the Sultan, from whom they had received enticing offers on the condition that his troops be allowed to pass freely through their country. Early in December all the Croatian Estates declared that they would accept the Turkish offer if they did not get aid immediately. The king could do nothing but induce them to be patient and perseverant until the next national diet which would assist them in every problem. The Croatian magnates then invited the envoys of the Sultan to appear at their Diet on the 25th of January (1526) in the town of Krizhevtsi so that they might strike a bargain with them.

Consequently the king instructed the Banus, Francis Batthyany to hasten to Krizhevtsi and to do everything in his power to promote the interests of the royal crown. But Batthyany replied with undisguised cynicism that he should appear in as brilliant array as the Turkish envoys at the Diet Assemblies, and that he would not budge until he was paid 2,500 florins. The National Treasury did not dispose over such a sum, and thus the king was not represented at the Diet of Krizhevtsi. Fortunately, neither did the Turkish envoys appear. Thus the assembled Estates declared that since the king did not worry about their defense, they had the right to look for such a king whose chief worry would be the defense of Croatia.

Then they turned to Archduke Ferdinand requesting him to give protection to their country. The Archduke accepted their offer with pleasure, and even made plans to assume the title of king of Bosnia. He also sent a message to the Pope to the effect that he was taking Croatia under his protection.

However, Ladislas Szalkai, the primate of the Hungarian Church was determined to keep his high office of Chancellor of the country in spite of the decision of the Hatvan Diet. And by the power of his Office, Szalkai was able to prevent the king from appointing his successor. Upon this the papal nuncio recommended Abbot Brodarich (a Croatian name meaning "Shipman") for this important post. Brodarich shied away from squabbles of political parties, but attested in the course of his diplomatic assignments an excellent culture, and statesmanship. Furthermore, his clean character commanded general respect. However, precisely for these excellent qualities, both the primate and the Queen, who was siding with Szalkai, resorted to all means of intrigue, in order to prevent the appointment of Brodarich, even though the Pope himself, in a series of commending letters urged the appointment of Brodarich. Yet Szalkai was in a position to override all this, and prevent the appointment.

The attitude of the primate Szalkai was sharply criticized by the papal nuncio, who found him unworthy either to keep his position as a chancellor or, to be appointed Cardinal of the Church. After eight months of evasive tactics, Szalkai finally resigned early in March, and a week later Brodarich was appointed Chancellor and also named Bishop of Sriyem (Sirmium).

However, the nuncio did not sleep on his laurels in view of his successful policy. He was now worried about the conditions in Hungary and the plight of the Hungarian army so his effort was directed towards getting a capable supreme commander of the Hungarian and Croatian forces. Several men were named for the position. The most capable military leader was Christopher Frankapan, the saviour of the fortification of Yaytse. But Frankapan was somewhat evasive and did not promptly accept the offer. So as their final choice they placed the name of Archbishop Paul Tomori of the Archdiocese of Kalocha in southern Hungary. At first he declined this honor, but upon continuous insistence of both the king and Pope, he finally accepted.

The personal history of Tomori was a most picturesque one. As a young man he was a capable military leader, but due to a personal tragedy, after losing successively two brides, he retired from the worldly life to a monastery where he intended to spend the rest of his days as a humble friar. However, since he was the most promising leader of the kingdom's forces, the king raised him from the status of an ordinary friar to that of the Archbishop of the southern regions of the kingdom.

So he at first assumed the defense of the borderland fortifications such as Petrovaradin, Slankament and others since the Turks were already banging at this line of defense. With every coming month the statesmen of the kingdom became more and more restless at the news that the Turks were preparing for new campaigns against Croatia and Hungary. The foreboding of the coming disasters was intensified especially after the unfortunate campaign of 1521, when the youthful sultan Suleiman sent his two armies for the conquest of Belgrade and Shabats, a Serbian stronghold on the banks of Sava River.

These two important bordertowns, although they were exposed in the past to repeated attacks, in 1521 were entirely unprepared to resist. However, the Hungarian Diet (convoked on the 24th of April) was not entirely indifferent to their fate. In order to make an effective decision, the Diet summoned the bani of the Shabats' stronghold, with Francis Hedervary, who took care also of the administration and defense of Belgrade (Nandor-Fehervar). The Diet prompted them to cede these strongholds to the royal troops, which would be more efficient in their defense. The bani agreed to this offer under the condition however that they would be reimbursed by the royal Treasury for all the expenses they incurred for the support and defense of said strongholds. In the meantime the pay of the garrisons and especially of the 1,000 Danubian sailors was long overdue, and they would not return to their defense posts unless they were provided with sufficient funds to satisfy their troops.

But since the royal Treasury was empty and could not provide them with necessary funds, the bani did not return to their official posts, and left the defense of the badly neglected strongholds to their subordinates.

Thus the defense of Belgrade was left to Blaise Olah and Michael Morey, minor military officers, and that of Shabats, to vice-bani Simon Logodi and Andrew Torma. The latter two, even though realizing their hopeless situation and the approaching doom of their defense post, refused to evacuate Shabats and in a flush of patriotic duty, they decided the self-sacrifice, and persuaded the whole garrison to follow their examples.

In the meantime Suleiman accelerated the course of events. Bringing his troops to the vicinity of Sophia[1] he split them into three sections: he sent its right wing under Mihaloglu to Transylvania, the left wing under Ahmed pasha to Shabats, while the main force under Piri pasha moved toward Belgrade itself. Suleiman himself followed the forces of Ahmed toward the stronghold of Shabats. By the end of June the Turks were at the fortified defense line south of the Danube and Sava rivers.

Ahmed pasha surrounded the city and stronghold of Shabats on the 20th of June. The outer

[1] Capital of Bulgaria.

defenses of the city were captured by the Turks in a few days. The garrison in the stronghold withdrew to the hilltop, and continued its heroic resistance. Even though its gunpowder supply was all spent, the garrison refused to save itself by crossing the Sava river (July 7). Reduced to a number of sixty fighters the garrison made its last stand at the main square of the city, and was killed to the last man. In the meantime the enemy crossed the Sava, and on its left bank occupied the towns of Kupin and Mitrovitsa.[2] Furthermore, the Turks occupied the stronghold of Zemun, opposite Belgrade.

In Belgrade things shaped themselves differently. For two months its garrison warded off the enemy's attacks. Even though its garrison, too, took oath to defend the fort to its last man, their commander, Michael Morey, became a traitor, deserted into the enemy camp, and betrayed the weak points of defense. The plight of the civilian population also became desperate and it was inclined to surrender the city. Finally, over the protests of Blaise Olah (the lieutenant of the forces), the garrison, which melted down to seventy-two fighters, decided to surrender. In spite of the promise of a free withdrawal of the garrison, the Turks massacred it to the last man. Thus the strongest stronghold of Christianity fell into the hands of its age-old enemy on the 29th of August, 1521.

The sad fact of the situation was that the great forts of the southern defense line: Shabats, Belgrade and Zemun had fallen into the hands of the enemy, without a single man of the royal forces participating in the spectacular struggle. In the meantime Suleiman, considering his task for the year accomplished, returned to Constantinople in triumph. Naturally he left a strong garrison in the newly conquered cities, with two hundred guns in Belgrade, fifty guns in Smederevo (Semendria) and twenty guns in Shabats.

In spite of the painful lesson of the loss of Belgrade the chief stronghold of Christendom, the political quarrels in Hungary continued unabated. The court party was tangling with the gentry party of Werboczy and Zapolya in a contest for power. In the meantime disturbing news of the preparation of the Ottoman empire for conquest of Hungary came from all sides. This information was clinched in November, 1525 by

a Turkish refugee, Paul Bachich, who was secretary of Suleiman's brother-in-law, Ferhad pasha. After the execution of Ferhad, Bachich also had reason to fear the sultan's wrath and fled, with his family, to Hungary. Bachich's story was confirmed by the Polish ambassador who arrived shortly after Bachich from Constantinople. This caused consternation in the royal council, and the king sent pleas for help to the Pope and the courts of Europe, but no effective succour came from anywhere.

With laurels still fresh from his triumph of capturing Belgrade and Shabats in the summer of 1521, the young and impetuous sultan sought new glory with the siege and capture of Rhodes island, the age-old possession of the Knights Hospitalers of St. John of Jerusalem. After a long and heroic defense of the stronghold by the members of the Order, the Grand Master of the Knights surrendered the island to the Sultan, on December 21, 1522.

After this momentous victory, which was denied his father Selim Yavuz (Selim, the Fierce), Suleiman decided to rest for a while on his laurels, indulging in pleasures of chase and sensualities. But martial inactivity aroused the anger of his most warlike troops, the Janissaries. They craved action, glory and plunder, of which they were deprived for the time being by inactivity of their Lord master. In fact a mutiny of Janissaries broke out in which Suleiman nearly lost his life, but by bloody repression and largesse in compensating the rank-and-file of Janissaries, he managed to quell the rebellion.

Yet it was a stern lesson to him that new paths to glory and wealth had to be sought by feat of arms. Besides the general policy of aggrandizement of the Empire, zealously pursued by his ancestors, he had reasons of his own to cast his glances north toward Hungary. Namely, ever since the capture of Belgrade and Shabats, hostilities between Hungary and the Turks had never ceased. Even though the Sultan himself was occupied with other affairs, his provincial governors (sanjakbegs) continued to harass their enemies and succeeded in taking a number of fortresses. In these engagements the victory was not always on the side of Turkish invaders. So in 1524 a 15,000 men strong akinji army (cavalry troops supported exclusively by plunder of Christian countries) was defeated in Sirmium by the forces

---

[2] The ancient capital of Sirmium.

of Paul Tomori, Archbishop of Kalocha, an excellent military leader and defender of the southern borderline of the kingdom. In the following year Kersto Frankapan, a Croatian magnate, relieved the besieged Bosnian stronghold of Yaytse amid the jubilation of the Christian world. Some strongholds in Dalmatia had also warded off the Turkish attacks. Thus Suleiman had ample motive to declare war on Croatia and Hungary whenever he was prepared for the campaign.

During the Fall of 1525 Suleiman studied a new campaign against Hungary with the members of his Divan (Imperial Council) and the total annihilation of that powerful country, which was a stumbling block to further expansion of the Ottoman Empire in northern and western Europe. The invasion of central Europe was indicated by flatlands bordering the tortuous course of the Danube and its tributaries, Sava and Drava. From a strategic point of view no better plan of invasion could be conceived, even though at that it was a risky undertaking which could have turned into the holocaust of Turkish forces, as it did in 1683 before the walls of Vienna.

In the meantime things went from bad to worse in Hungary. In spite of ample intelligence pouring from all sides, the Royal Council could not realize the magnitude of the impending peril. That moved cardinal Burgio, the statesman-like nuncio at the court of Buda, to outpour his despair in a number of reports to Rome. In one of them dated January 18, 1526, his despair rises to a climax. He writes: "This country cannot defend itself and depends upon the good graces of the enemy. Since it cannot provide the garrisons of the border places with pay, how can anyone expect that they would wish to come to blows with the entire power of the sultan. The king is so poor that frequently he himself lacks food supplies. The magnates are continually quarreling and antagonizing each other while the nobility is divided into parties. But even where there would be an agreement in their circles, they cannot get anywhere without military preparations. They could fight a battle, but if they lose it, there is not a single stronghold where they could retire while waiting for relief. But where could they get any aid? Germany is in the state of troubles and is the natural enemy of the Hungarian nation: Poland, on the other hand, has made peace with the Turks. I have very little

experience in military matters, but that little amount is sufficient to recognize that if the sultan comes with a strong army, there is no hope for the salvation of the country."

In the midst of these internal difficulties the news came that the sultan had already set out from Constantinople to conquer Hungary and its associate countries. Upon receiving this news Tomori hastened to Buda and from Buda to Esztergon where he found the king having a good time. He convinced the king that he should return immediately to the capital. Here consultations were started. The first factor was to bring Petrovaradin, a powerful stronghold, into such a condition that it could stop the progress of the Turkish army. The papal nuncio immediately placed 500 foot-soldiers and 200 cavalrymen with 36 small artillery pieces at the disposition of Tomori. At the same time, the silver coffin which Queen Anna had made up to keep the relics of St. Gellert in, was sent to the mint and the money minted from this silver mass was turned over to the Archbishop. The Royal Council provided 25,000 gulden for the benefit of the Archbishop. Tomori set out on the 25th of April for Petrovaradin, whither he arrived soon enough to persuade the residents of the city and the area, who in their terror were ready to flee, to stay in their homes.

Sultan Suleiman set out on the 23rd of April from Constantinople with more than 100,000 men. When he arrived in Bulgaria, he sent the Grand Vizir Ibrahim with 40,000 men ahead of the main forces to besiege Petrovaradin, which after the fall of Belgrade, was the key fortress of central Europe. At the northern end of the Frushka Gora Mountains, on a steep 200 foot high escarpment around which the Danube flows in a wide arc, stands the stronghold of Petrovaradin (in ancient times Cusum).* Here Tomori established his headquarters and fortified the position. Here also he assembled the rivermen (shaykash) who in the past had fought the Turks under the walls of Belgrade. They numbered about 1,000 men, some of them Serbs from the middle course of river, and some from the lower Danube area who had been collected and organized by Tomori into fighting units.

As the enemy was approaching, Tomori retired

* In German: Peterwardein; in Hungarian: Petervarad; in Turkish: Varadyn.

to the left bank of the Danube and pitched camp in the flatlands where now stands the city of Novi Sad, while the defense of Petrovaradin itself was left to an able commander, George Alapi.

The Grand Vizir, Ibrahim, followed by a considerable fleet, reached Petrovaradin on the 12th of July. Tomori had great confidence in the outcome. He wrote the king that according to his informers, Ibrahim had said that the stronghold would be but a small bite for him, not enough for a breakfast; so now if the king and the diet would properly assist him the Grand Vizir could take his "lunch and supper also under the walls of the stronghold." On the 15th of July the Turks made their first storm; but they were repulsed by the garrison. At the same time the Danube rivermen, supported by the guns of Tomori attacked the Turkish fleet and inflicted great damage. The next night the Grand Vizir sent a part of his army to the opposite bank of the Danube, and the following day the fight was resumed both on land and water, continuing until nightfall without decisive result.

At this point Tomori called his Lieutenants into council. Left to themselves, he said, they could not resist the numerous and constantly growing Turkish forces so that in the uneven struggle they were facing certain destruction; should they retire, however, and await the support that was to be sent by the king, a battle could be fought later with some hope of saving Petrovaradin. This meeting resulted in an agreement to withdraw upriver to the town of Bach. From here Tomori sent the Bosnian bishop to the king with the message that Petrovaradin could hold out for another eight or ten days at most but with reinforcements he could return and renew the battle. He had high hopes for this message, and awaited a reply impatiently but in vain.

Even after the retreat of Tomori and his forces the garrison of Petrovaradin kept resisting the Turkish onslaught, and on the 17th of July it repulsed the enemy for the second time. The Grand Vizir at this turn decided to resort to the ordinary siege procedure. He bombarded the city from his guns for several days without stopping. Although in town the greater buildings were turned into rubble and the walls were full of wide holes, the garrison repulsed two new storms. On the 28th of July two mines exploded which caused great destruction in the citadel

and set the garrison into confusion. Taking advantage of this moment the Grand Vizir ordered the general storm. Then the defenders, after terrific losses, could no longer prevent enemy penetration. Ninety of them retired into a tower and continued the resistance for a while, but the Grand Vizir offered them withdrawal if they would surrender. Trusting his promise they gave up the struggle. The sultan himself was an eye witness to the fall of the city and citadel, for precisely on that day he arrived at Petrovaradin. Yet Suleiman's diary indicated that 500 defenders were put to sword, while 300 of them were enslaved.

Eight days ahead of this date King Louis set out from Buda. The troops he led were hardly 4,000 strong. He advanced very slowly in order to give time to the troops (banderia) of the magnates and the counties (varmegye), as well as those reinforcements which were to arrive from the neighboring provinces (Transylvania, Slavonia and Croatia) to join him.

On the 4th of August in the town of Paksh, Louis was informed of the fall of Petrovaradin. Upon this tragic news, messengers, carrying a bloody sword, were sent throughout Hungary, Transylvania, Slavonia and Croatia notifying the Estates that the final peril had arrived, and that they should arm each and every one of their serfs. Upon this tocsin of peril the troops of magnates and higher clergy, including those of George of Zapolya, bishop of Eger (Erlau) and Nagy Varad (Gross-wardein) (Upper Hungary) assembled in the town of Tolna. On the other hand, the counties were very slow in sending their own troops.

The king arrived on the 6th of August in the camp of Tolna where conferences were started to set up the plan for the campaign. Most members of the royal council wished to proceed to the Drava River and there to engage in a battle. They minimized the power of the enemy and overestimated their own force. "You think that you can fly, but you have no wings" Chancellor Brodarich warned them. He suggested circumspection and recommended that the king remain at Tolna, while the Palatin (vice-roy) should proceed south to Drava in order to attempt to check the progress of the sultan's forces. But promptly they declared him a scary cat, a coward, and no one in the Council had the courage to espouse his advice. Thus they decided that the vice-roy (Nador) should advance to the Drava river and the king should follow him a few days later.

But the vice-roy did not comply with the orders. The magnates and the noblemen who had joined him declared that, by their ancient privileges, they would move against the enemy only under the personal leadership of the king. This message was passed on to the king, from whom they insisted on an answer. They wanted to be assured whether or not he was prepared to engage in battle with the enemy; "if he is not inclined to do that, then we ourselves will take care of the defense of the country." The king replied with an irritated voice "I see that everybody seeks excuse and safety behind my back. For the good of the country I shall expose myself to any danger so that no one can cover up his cowardice and shift the responsibility on my shoulders. With the aid of Almighty I shall set out tomorrow and I shall go precisely to such spots, whither without me, they are not willing to go."

True enough, on the 24th of August, the king set out from Tolna to Szegszard and from there to Batta, where Tomori, with several southern magnates, joined him. It was obvious that in a few days they would have to face the enemy, and therefore the orders of the Supreme Commander could no longer be postponed. This matter had worried the king and the magnates for many months in the past but they were unable to come to a final agreement. From the group of worldly magnates the only one who had some experience in the leading of large-size troops was John Zapolya; but the court, because of its lack of trust in him, chose to ignore him. In the first place they sent a message to Nicholas von Salm, the famous imperial general, offering him Supreme Command; but his answer was negative. Then they turned to Nicholas Frankapan, the great Croatian leader, who likewise refused to accept the responsibility for the difficult task. By the end of July in the camp at Ora a plan emerged in which the army was to be commanded by three chief captains: Archbishop Paul Tomori, the vice-roy Bathori and John Zapolya. These three should lead the army. Now in the camp of Batta the king summoned the magnates to get their personal opinions. The great majority agreed that the chief leadership should be entrusted to Archbishop Paul Tomori and George Zapolya, the latter being regarded as representative of his older brother (John Zapolya). But no one thought of the palatin Bathori, who by his official position, was entitled to the leadership of the country's armed forces, because in the last few days he noticeably betrayed his incompetence.

When the king, in accordance with the vote of the majority, expressed his agreement, Tomori pleaded with the king and the council, not to place on his shoulders the burden of responsibility for the discharge of an office for which he was not qualified.

However, the king stood pat by his decision and Tomori had to bow before the will of the throne.

The first tasks of the commanders in chief was to select a place where they could assemble the military forces of the country, and wait for the enemy. Since the area of Batta was not large enough for the convenient deployment of large forces, they agreed that the best place would be the plain of Mohach, with its wide expanse.

Then the army of Tomori was joined by the troops of Peter Perenyi, governor of Temesh, with 6,000 men, which was already encamped near Baranyavar, about 24 kilometers south of Mohach. Here the orders to withdraw towards Mohach were executed with great indignation. The reason for this withdrawal was the false news they got from informers and refugees from the Turks that the greatest part of the Turkish army was an undisciplined mob and that hardly every 10th or 20th man was armed, while the artillerymen were Italians and Germans who in the decisive moment of battle would turn their guns against the Turkish troops. This news was accepted as authentic and stirred up an impatient desire for battle. Tomori's soldiers spoke with contempt for the Turks over whom it would be easy to win a victory and for this reason they urged to be led as soon as possible into battle. Furthermore, when they were ordered to pitch camp at Mohach, the impatient troops saw deceit and a trap. "They want to keep us away from the enemy—this was their grouching complaint—but we should go against him; the magnates who were used to a life of ease and inactivity are thinking of flight, not of the battle; let the king come to us so that we may engage in battle as soon as possible." They were besieging Tomori with requests that he should snatch the king "from the hands of the helpless priests and the idle magnates, who were afraid of the battle" and bring him in their own midst.

This fighting spirit induced Tomori to make a bold move. Perhaps he flattered himself with the hope that, as in the past the troops of John Hunyadi and John Capistrano, by completely ignoring the rules of strategy and tactics but with a great display of enthusiasm, won miraculous results. Even now, perhaps, it would be able to hold up, with heroic effort, the huge masses of the enemy, and would give the king more time to assemble the troops which were now moving from all parts. Therefore on the 18th of August he galloped south with 5,000 cavalrymen towards Drava river in order to prevent the sultan from crossing the river. But in the vicinity of Osijek (Eszek) he was informed that he came too late, since the great part of the Turkish army was already on the opposite banks of the Drava river. Thus, by force of circumstances he returned to his camp at Baranyavar and now no other choice was available but to match his forces with those of the enemy in an open field battle.

On the 25th of August, the king summoned Tomori and the magnates for a new war council. The question was discussed whether they should accept the battle as soon as the enemy appeared, or should they rather retreat for a while and later engage in battle in some other place. Headed by Tomori the great majority expressed itself against further delay.

The Battle of Mohach

The Slavonian troops—more than 4,000 men strong, arrived the next day at the Mohach camp. The Hungarian army in the next few days increased to 28,000 men. This number compared to the manpower with which King Mathias used to go to battle, but on this occasion it was too small and insignificant beyond comparison.

However one should note the large number of magnates which appeared in the king's camp. The Archbishop and the Bishops were all there, with the exception of two of them. The Bishop of Veszprem was sent from Erd to Buda by the king with the assignment to stay at the side of the Queen, while Paul Vardai, the Bishop of Eger (Erlau) had been sent from Batta to Beszterczebanya on the 19th of August, in order to investigate a case where several treasury officials were accused of embezzlement. But before setting out, upon the order of the king, he declared that he was leaving the camp "against his will."

The military leaders, from the most distinguished families, joined the king, almost in their full number. Even though the magnates failed to display evidence of sacrificial effort, the spirit of their personal courage was not lacking.

At the time of extreme danger it is not surprising that the magnates of Croatia realized that the fate of their fatherland was closely knit with the fate of Hungary. The first order of the king, in which he summoned the estates of Croatia to appear, together with their armed serfs in the camp of Tolna, was not well received. The magnates and lower nobility (gentry), in spite of the protest of Nicholas Yurishich the future heroic defender of Gunz (Kiseg, Koszeg), declared that they would stay at home to defend their fatherland, and they could send only the troops paid by Archduke Ferdinand with his consent, to Tolna. Upon the tragic news of the fall of Petrovaradin, Count Christopher Frankapan, nobly disregarding the insults he suffered in Buda, set out in the company of several Croatian magnates at the head of considerable forces toward the king's camp, whither he was no longer able to arrive.

In the meantime, the Sultan who led his forces across the Drava river between the 14th and 17th of August, proceeded very slowly because continuous rainfalls made the roads impassable. On the 26th of August he arrived at Baranyavar where he spent two days to rest up his troops.

At that point the two camps were separated from each other with no more than a distance of two miles. On the 28th of August, the Supreme Command in the Hungarian camp was informed that the Turks would definitely advance the next day so that the battle could no longer be postponed. Therefore Paul Tomori and George Zapolya moved their troops on the 29th of August in the early hours of the morning to the plain extending south of Mohach at the location occupied by the towns of Kolked and Nagy-Nyarad. There they arrayed their forces in battle lines. Upon this the king asked the Archbishop "what is your appraisal of the numerical strength of the Hungarian army and that of the enemy?"

"In my opinion"—replied the Archbishop—"in the camp of your majesty and in my own camp there are hardly more than 20,000 armed fighters;

however the army of the enemy consists almost of 300,000 men. We should not be scared, however, by their large numbers since the greatest part of them is a cowardly mob." The king was not satisfied with this answer and further inquired, "What can be the enemy's well armed and disciplined force?" "I place it at 70,000" replied Tomori.

A delegation came from Tomori's camp while the war council was still in session. Its speaker begged the king and the magnates "not to oppose the acceptance of the battle." "The victory is in our hands"—the speaker said, "only let us take advantage of the good fortune which Almighty offers to us with grace. Let his Majesty and the magnates come with their manpower to our camp, which is located closer to the enemy and is more convenient for attack. Whoever advises in opposition, is the son of death." The threat benumbed even those who were not in favor of such hazardous tactics. A unanimous decision was made that they should engage in battle with the enemy on the plain of Mohach. At this moment the talented and witty Bishop of Varad, Francis Perenyi, turning to the king, made this facetious remark: "Your Majesty would do well to send the Chancellor right now to Rome and ask the Holy Father to insert in the calendar the date of the battle as the feast of 20,000 Hungarian martyrs." But in the camp of Tomori the royal decision was accepted with elation and its troops promptly proceeded to unite with the forces of the king at Mohach.

The king then ordered the commanders of all the troops to appear in the camp of Mohach with the greatest possible haste. One of these orders, which he sent to the Croatian Banus who was advancing toward Pechuh, to the Bishop of Zagreb, and to the other "Magnates and Estates of Slavonia" written by him personally in Latin, has been saved to this day, and reads as follows:

"Louis by the Grace of God King of Hungary and Bohemia, etc. Most Reverend, Magnificent, excellent and sincerely beloved faithful! Today we have already written to you and sent to you one of our court messengers with the request to hurry and join up with us. Now again we warn you and order you to hasten to us with the greatest dispatch. The enemy is turning our country into flames under our very eyes. We are waiting only for you. And as soon as you arrive,

we shall immediately start the battle with the aid of Almighty. Therefore hurry the fastest possible. Written in our camp at Mohach on Saturday the day of the Feast of Saint Bertalan, in 1526."

Under the effect of false news and information about the Turkish army, they thought that a courageous decision and display of moral bravery would secure the victory for them, and consequently, that the first powerful storm would decide the fate of the battle. Therefore their greatest worry was to have the army attack the enemy in a long line of battle (which naturally thinned out their ranks).

They divided the armed forces into two battlelines. The first one consisted of 10,000 footsoldiers and 4,000 cavalrymen. The right wing was commanded by Francis Batthyany, the palatin, and John Tahi; the left wing was under the command of Peter Perenyi, while the center was led by Paul Tomori and George Zapolya, the supreme commanders. Eighty guns were set up before the battleline and among certain army divisions.

The second line consisted of 10,000 cavalrymen and 2,000 footsoldiers. The cavalry forces were set up in four divisions commanded by Tarczoi, Korlatkovi, the Bohemian Trepko and John Dragfi, a member of the Supreme court. However, 2,000 footsoldiers were left for the protection of the camp. The last cavalry division was assigned to the king, who was surrounded by the Archbishop of Esztergom (Ostrogon), and the Bishops of Zagreb, Varad, Pechuh, Nyitra, Gyor, Vacz, Sirmium and Bosnia. Furthermore, the king was surrounded by the immediate forces of the vice-roy and several worldly commanders.

When the army divisions had occupied their positions, the king rode out before the army lines. The palatin followed him and he addressed the heroes with some inspiring words: "Behold"—he said—"the majesty of the king is here among us; he is ready to die together with us for the faith of Christ, for the fatherland, for your wives and children. Remember that you are Hungarians, grandchildren of those who earned so many triumphs over the enemy you are facing now. The victory will be won by heroism, not by multitude. Have faith in God, who will not abandon the fighters who defend his holy faith." The king, too, expressed in places several encouraging words.

The Hungarian army, thus set in fighting position, was impatiently waiting the appearance of the enemy for hours. The rising hills on the south-west blocked the view to Baranyavar, and the troops were left for a long time in uncertainty whether the Turks had set out from their camp, or not. The sultan, after his morning prayer, set out from Baranyavar but not having the intention to engage in battle on that day, he proceeded very slowly.

His front troops, about 5,000 horsemen, were commanded by Bali Bey, the commander of Belgrade. He was followed by Husref pasha, with his Bosnian troops, then the Grand Vizir, Ibrahim, with his Roumelian (European) forces, then Bahram pasha, with his Anatolian troops and 300 guns. Finally the sultan proceeded surrounded by heavy bodyguards. The full force of the Turkish army cannot be certainly or reliably determined, but it could be placed at 70,000 fully equipped fighters.

About noontime the Hungarians noticed the Turkish front troops. But Tomori did not plan to attack them immediately and to prevent the deployment of the enemy army. According to the strategic concepts prevailing at that time, it was proper to wait for the full deployment of the enemy. But in the first afternoon hours the Hungarians were facing only a part of the Turkish army, which they could have easily wiped out.

About 4 o'clock in the afternoon Tomori noticed that from the right-hand direction, where nowadays the locality of the Nagy-Nyarad stands, a Turkish army was advancing. This was Bali Bey, whose troops had the assignment to swoop at the flank of the Hungarian army in case of the deployment of the battle. The Archbishop, in fear of disorganizing the battle array, sent the captains Gaspar Rathai, Balint Torok and John Kallay with their troops, who were guarding the person of the king, to hold up the Turkish troop, and check its advance.

Soon after the larger masses of the enemy appeared against the center of the Christian troops on the top of the opposite hills. Then Tomori gave the signal for attack and amid the firing of the guns, stormed against the Turks with the first battleline. Without difficulty he pushed back the army division led by Ibrahim which was not yet fully prepared for battle. Now he rushed against the second battleline of Turks, while Andrew Bathori hopped to the king with the summons that he lead also the second battleline into the battle for the purpose of securing victory. The king immediately sped to the battlefield where in the meantime the Turkish guns had caused tremendous devastations to the lines lead by Tomori and Zapolya. The Turkish troops, in the meantime, surrounded these second battleline Hungarian troops, which came later from all sides, and after a fight of one and a half hours simply annihilated them.

About 24,000 Hungarian fighters covered the battlefield. Among them were the two supreme commanders, the Archbishop of Esztergom and five bishops, John Dragfi; member of the Supreme Court, Gabriel Perenyi and a large number of the country's grandees.

Hardly more than 4,000 men could save their lives. Among them were the troops of the palatin Stephen Bathori, Francis Batthyany, the Croatian banus, those of Peter Perenyi, the guardian of the Crown, and the Zagreb, Senj and Sirmium bishops. King Louis had fortunately extricated himself from the maelstrom of the fighters, followed by his courtiers. But when he reached the Chellay Creek on the road leading toward Buda, his wounded horse failed to climb up the opposite bank and dropped into the center of the creek and buried his master in the slimy water. An attendant of the king, Stephen Aczel, jumped into the creek to save his master, but he also drowned in the water. And another one, Ulrich Czettrich, witness of the tragedy, charged further and brought the news to Buda that the country had lost the battle and that its ruler had lost his life.

On the trail of his report the papal nuncio reported the tragic event to Rome. In addition he reported that King Louis had taken part in the battle and was fighting as a true hero. About the battle itself the nuncio could write only that it started at 4 o'clock in the afternoon. The Turks sent forward 10,000 horsemen who, after a brief engagement, were chased backward and persecuted by the Hungarians. But when they came to the edge of the forest, the gunfire from the guns cleverly hidden by the Turks, had caused so much devastation and scare among the Hungarian troops that they were unable to further continue the resistance. The battle in which

25,000 or 30,000 men found their death lasted not fully 90 minutes.

None of those who fled from the battlefield could later provide a clear enough picture of the event to report it. However, one of them, Stephen Brodarich, the Bishop of Sirmium and royal Chancellor, described the tragic campaign with some detail. The episodes dealing with the battle itself are described as follows:

(Brodarich's description of the battle). "We spent the greater part of the day waiting for the enemy. The enemy settled down between the dunes (hills) and sent out only a small force to engage in an insignificant skirmish with our forces. We were wondering whether the enemy wanted to entice us to a more narrow place or perhaps delay the battle until the next day while at night he would surprise us in our camp and destroy us; or finally, by delaying the battle engagement, he intended to tire us out. About the true intention of the enemy I could never get a reliable report. However, one thing is certain— the enemy kept us in suspense almost all day. Finally, as the day turned toward sunset a division of enemy forces appeared in a valley behind a range of hills advancing quietly so that only the peaks of their spears betrayed their movements. Tomori was of the opinion, which turned out to be right, that this echelon either wanted to capture our camp or wanted to surround us. Therefore, he rushed from the first line of battle to the king, and ordered Gaspar Rashkai and two other magnates, who have been assigned to the protection of the king's person, to immediately find out the intention of the enemy, and, if possible, to thwart it. In view of his assignment to defend the person of the king, Rashkai attempted to decline this task with polite words. However, upon the insistent demand of the commander-in-chief, and since the king himself did not object to Tomori's order lest he attract upon himself the suspicion of cowardice or scare, Rashkai spurred his horse and, with his two companions, promptly dashed at the head of the cavalry under their command whither they had been sent. He hoped that he would return by the time the king needed his services. Then about 3 o'clock in the afternoon, it was not certain whether or not the enemy would accept the challenge for battle.

"By this time quite a few members of the high command, disgusted with long waiting, suggested that they should return to camp. Informed of this turn, Tomori again galloped to the king, accompanied by his partner in the high command, and insisted that they should not, under any circumstances, delay the battle, for it is more profitable to fight one portion of the enemy's armed forces than to fight his entire army the next day. He said that the victory at this time was quite certain. Upon this the king immediately gave the signal for attack. Among the sounds of horns and trumpets the ancient exclamation 'Jesus' was heard.

"At this time we saw the huge masses of the enemy forces slowly descending from the hill opposite us, on which the Turkish emperor took his position. A helmet was placed on the head of the king and as if in premonition of the impending disaster his face became pale. After the signal was given for the attack, those who had been stationed in the first battleline, rushed into the battle and fought the duel with the enemy like heroes. Our guns too began to fire in full force, but caused little damage to the enemy. As one could expect from the small number of our troops, the struggle became evermore embittered. More of the enemy fell from their lines than from our own. Finally, while our men continued a heroic fight, the enemy began to retreat, either by yielding to the pressure of our soldiers, or in order to trap our troops before their guns. At this moment Andrew Bathori galloped to the king and reported that the enemy was retreating, that the victory is ours and now we should give aid to our troops, which were persecuting the enemy.

"Upon this they rushed forward. The places, where shortly before the battle was fought, were covered with corpses of many Hungarians but still more of Turks; among them a few wounded lay. In the meantime, while our troops were heroically chasing the enemy and the king's echelon rushed there with as much speed as the heavy armour permitted, our right flank began to waver and many from that flank took to flight; in my opinion this scare came as the result of the enemy's gunfire. The thickly ranged guns were aimed at the king's troops and even though the shells were flying over their heads, they caused a general panic. At the same time the king disappeared from our lines; either he charged in front of the battleline fighting the Turks (for in the preliminary plan of the battle it had been decided that the king should not stay immobilized anywhere), or those who were stationed behind him had removed him from the turmoil of the battle. Both cases are possible. There are those who assert that preceding the lines of his echelon, the king placed himself at the head of his troop and heroically fought the enemy. I dare not confirm or deny this belief.

"But I know for certain that when the firing of the enemy guns and the flight started on the right flank, the king could no longer be seen in our lines at the place assigned for him. Almost at the same time the Archbishop of Esztergom (Ostrogon) and others who had been in the immediate vicinity of the king, vanished as well. I do not want to blame those who were called to see to his safety nor those who perhaps took him out prematurely from the battle for the loss of the king. Our tragic fate brought it with itself that we should not only take crushing blows from the external enemy, but also to suffer from internal dissension. The king's army, even though in panic, thought of flight but they fought on for a long time; not any more on the wide plain, but right in front of the guns from which we stood hardly ten steps away. Finally, when panic and smoke from the artillery fire filled the air to such an extent that one could not see anything, a great portion of the army was forced to descend into the valley adjacent to the swamps. On the other hand, many of them still fought heroically right in front of the guns. Furthermore, even those who descended into the valley returned to the battlefield and renewed their duel, but when they were no longer able to withstand the firing of the guns and their smoke, and since a great part of the army took to flight, they were also forced to flee. Therefore all of them fled for the most part in that direction from which a while ago we came with high hope of victory in our souls, and toward the camp which the enemy had first plundered and demolished, and which was covered with the dead bodies of those Hungarians who were stationed there. The enemy, upon seeing the flight of our troops, either suspected some stratagem or was so tired out in the battle, that it did not move out from its position and refrained from persecuting our men. Many owe their safety to the approach of night as well as to torrential showers which just then started. The battle lasted one hour and a half."

Suleiman was under the impression that he had been in an engagement with only one part of the Hungarian army and was expecting another attack. So he wisely refrained from persecuting the routed Hungarian troops and his army remained in fighting readiness throughout the night. Only the next morning was he convinced that he had won a decisive victory. Then he set up camp on the plain of Mohach and stayed for five days. From there he set out with his entire army towards Buda, the capital of the country. On the 12th of September he made his entry into the Hungarian metropolis. No one made an attempt to prevent his progress. When the Queen heard the news of the disaster at Mohach in the evening of August 30th, she fled to Pozhon (Pressburg) whither she was followed by Buda's wealthy residents and the city remained without any garrison.

On the day of the battle at Mohach, John Zapolya stopped over in Szeged with his Transylvanian troops. There he boarded a carriage so that he could see the king as soon as possible in order to suggest delaying the battle. But on his way he was informed of the catastrophe at Mohach so he returned home and became an inactive witness to the events. At the same time Christopher Frankapan and the Croatian magnates who joined him in Zagreb were informed of the tragic issue of the battle, and in the hope that the war did not end with this, they proceeded in fighting order to Szekesfehervar; but being detached from the main forces they did not consider themselves, in their isolation, strong enough to engage in battle with the Turks.

Only Paul Vardai, the Bishop of Eger (Erlau), John Bebeck of Pelshots, and the nobility of the counties west of Tissa river, were thinking of resistance. On the 15th of September they decided at their convention in Mishkolts, to descend to camp as soon as possible and summoned John Zapolya and the neighboring cities to join their forces, but it was already too late. Suleiman did not intend to make a permanent conquest of Hungary. Even then he was afraid that the Christian powers would get together against him, and that the Hungarian people, properly organized and well led, would administer heavy blows against him during the winter. Therefore he sent his troops in all directions for plunder, arson and murder in the open places. They were also permitted to drive the population into slavery and get all the booty they could. He himself left Buda on the 20th of September, after he looted a great part of the art treasures of the Royal Palace, and returned with his whole army.

He made his way now on the left bank of the Danube. He set Pesht on fire and put to sword and flames all of the country between the Danube and Tissa through which he had passed. The city of Szeged became the victim of flames. However the inhabitants of the city of Subotitsa (Szabadka) successfully warded off the attacks of the Turks. Suleiman left garrisons in Ilok and Petrovaradin. He crossed the Danube at Novi Sad over a bridge he had built to reach Petrovaradin on the right bank of the Danube. He left Hungary on the 12th of October, 1526, and even though he did not at this time occupy Hungary, he devastated it, and destroyed 200,000 poor defenseless people of the open country.

Internal Conditions in the Croatian Kingdom (1102-1526)

The diplomatic name of the Croatian Kingdom continues under the label: "regnum Croatiae et Dalmatiae," designating the political territory between the Drava river and the sea. Besides the title "rex Hungariae" the king carries also that of "rex Croatiae et Dalmatiae." But besides these two names, from the end of the 12th century on, also the name of Slavonia is current as applied to all the Croatian lands from the Neretva (Narenta) river and the sea up to the Drava river. In such acceptance this name is used not only in Hungary, and along the sea coast, but also in Venice, Naples, and Rome. However, the kings before 1526 never used the title "rex Sclavoniae," but the dukes and bani used "dux Sclavoniae" and "banus Sclavoniae" for the designation of their own office since the end of the 12th and beginning of the 13th century.

At this time (12th and 13th century) the once united Croatian kingdom split into two separate territories: Croatia with Dalmatia and Slavonia. Dalmatia consisted at first of the islands of the coastal archipelago and coastal towns, while Croatia included all the lands between Neretva (Narenta) river, Verbas (river), Gvozd mountains (Alpes Ferreae), Kupa (river) from the town of Tersat (Tarsato) in the north to the Neretva estuary in the south. However, since the 13th century, that part of the Croatian lands was designated by the name of Slavonia, which extended from the Gvozd mountains to the Drava river and along the lower course and estuaries of Una, Verbas and Bosna rivers. This area was called intermittently a banate (banatus) and duchy (ducatus), and since the middle of the 13th century a kingdom (regnum). The territorial integrity of the Croatian State was finally split up by King Bela III (IV) who appointed in 1260 one banus (vice roy) for Slavonia and another for Croatia and Dalmatia.

Thus since the beginning of the 14th century three different names were applied to the sections of the old Croatian kingdom, but they still meant the same thing: the Croatian State. Furthermore, readjustment took place in each separate area. So the original Croatian cities of Shibenik (Sebenico) and Nin (Aenona) were included in Dalmatia obtaining from the kings Stephen III (IV) and Andrew I (II), the same privileges as were given by King Koloman* to Dalmatian towns Zadar (Yadera), Trogir (Tragurion) and Split (Asphalaton). Likewise the islands of Brach (Brazza) and Hvar (Pharos, Lesina) were considered Dalmatian ever since they came under Venetian authority. With the growth of Venetian power along the eastern Adriatic Coast the name of Dalmatia was applied to a wide area, restricting by that much the compass of the Croatian territory. On the other hand, north of Gvozd mountains the name Croatia gradually spreads over the territory formerly known as Slavonia. The area of Zagreb, with its hinterland, was known in the middle of the 15th century as Croatia, and has retained this name to this day. Furthermore, a number of towns (Bihach, Kostajnica, Zrinj, Topusko, Dubitsa, etc.) known in the first half of the 15th century to belong to Slavonia, were subject to Croatia towards the end of that century. Coincidental with the change of political territory is the change of population for masses of Croatian population, together with their nobility, migrated north due to the pressure of Venice, Bosnian-Herzegovinan grandees and especially Turkish

---

* Hungarian form Kalman probably comes from the Latin word "Calmus," "quiet, placid," cf. Almericus, Hung. "Imre"; Croatian "Mirko."

invasions along the southern borders of Croatia proper.

The frontiers of the Croatian political territory changed frequently. In the course of the 15th century, Croatia lost all her coastland for the benefit of Venice, with the exception of a strip between Rijeka (Fiume) and the island of Pag, including all the islands of the Adriatic archipelago. Even before the battle of Mohach the Turks seized all of Sirmium and Slavonia up to the Gvozd mountains, with the exception of a few strongholds. The banate of Yaytse (Jajce) in the northern part of Bosnia, surrounded on all sides by Turks, was a true Christian island in the sea of Islam which was soon to be submerged in the depth of the sea. Already in 1525 the once extensive Croatian kingdom is restricted to an area, the parliament of which claims as its constituents: "comites et reliquiae nobilium regni nostri Croatiae" ("Princes and remains of nobility of our Croatian kingdom").

Population: In spite of political changes throughout the Croatian territory, the chief ethnical element in the whole area from the Drava river to the sea, has been the Croats. In the Dalmatian cities and on the islands besides them, lived the Latins, i.e., romanized Illyrians, who became Italians when Venice consolidated her power in their territory for many centuries. In some cities of Slavonia, notably in Zagreb, Virovitica and Vukovar, German artisans settled in the 13th century, while Hungarians settled down preferably along the banks of the Drava and the Danube. (Belovar, Daruvar, Vukovar, Ilok (Ujlak), Benoshtor (Ban Monostor), Ujvidek, etc.) As refugees from Turkish inroads, Serbs came to southern Sirmium and settled there. Another important element of foreign blood and tongue were the Wallachians (Vlasi, Morovlasi, Morlaki-Nigri Latini) probable descendants of Roman colons or romanized Thracians. They became an important factor in overland trade of the medieval Balkans by transporting merchandise in horse-and-mule caravans. In the Slavic regions they spoke Slavic besides their native Roman tongue, but after settling in Croatia they gradually forgot their native speech and merged with the Croatian population. Besides their practices in overland trade, they engaged in sheep-raising and were known for their products of cheese, butter and wool. Occasionally, Italian and French merchants and men of the medical profession settled down in these cities.

Social structure. The society in this period was divided between the free and attached men (serfs and slaves). To the former belonged the ecclesiastic grandees, the prelates, the secular higher nobility (magnates, comites, barones), the lower nobility (servientes, nobiles), the burghers (cives, patricii), free peasants (liberi) and emancipated serfs (libertini). The attached classes consisted of the serfs (coloni) and slaves (servi, manucipia), in Croatian called "Sebri, robovi."

In comparison with the times preceding the enthronement of the Arpad dynasty, the social organization still followed the Croatian tribal patterns. However, in Slavonia, the tribal organization gradually yielded to the western-European feudal system and its institutions. This change induced numerous Hungarian noblemen to settle down with their families in Slavonia, which gave the country for some time the appearance of a Hungarian province. The townspeople had their own privileges, while officers of the royal court settled down on the king's lands. Other noblemen, again used the church lands (both bishop's and pastor's lands, praedium). The serfs cultivated the noblemen's lands; the slaves did not till the soil of their masters, but supplied them common labor and artisans' skill. The serfs or slaves, emancipated by their masters, enjoyed the privileges of libertines, whether in pursuit of some trade or moderate land ownership.

Croatian Church. In ecclesiastical affairs, as in the political domain, the Croatian kingdom was disintegrated. All of Croatia was subjected to the authority of the arch-diocese of Split, which consisted of ten dioceses to include that of Knin, extending to the towns of Bihach on the Una river, further that of Trogir, Nin, Kerbava, Skradin (Scardona), Shibenik, Senj, Makarska, Duvno and Hvar. Toward the middle of the 12th century the Venetians established in Zadar, which at that time was under their authority, an archbishopric, with the authority over suffragan bishops of Kerk (Veglia), Rab (Arbae) and Osor (Apsera). Under the Hungarian archdiocese of Kalocsa, Slavonia had three bishoprics which included Zagreb, Pechuh and Sirmium, with extensive territory attached to each. Besides this, the town of Djakovo in Slavonia was the seat of the Bosnian diocese.

The archdioceses and bishoprics were divided into archdeaconships, and the latter into parishes. Of especial significance to the cultural life of the Middle Ages have been the Chapters as the centers of religious life and schools for education of the priestly orders. Besides this the Chapters engaged, ever since the end of the 12th century, also in legal practices, performing the functions of Archivists and recorders of deeds, issuing on request also verified copies of a document. In Croatia and Dalmatia the Chapters of Split, Nin (Aenona), Knin and Senj, and in Slavonia the chapters of Zagreb, Chazma, Pozhega and Djakovo were engaging in such legal activities.

In addition to the income from their lands, the bishoprics and Chapters collected the church tithe, both in field produce and cattle, from which no one was exempted. From their combined income the bishops and Chapters supported their schools. In Dalmatia, through all this period, the bishops were elected by the clergy and laymen of their towns. However, in the 14th century the popes appointed the bishops, but in the 15th century this prerogative was transferred to royal authority, while the popes merely confirmed the king's choice.

Besides numerous clergy there was a large number of monasteries throughout the Croatian kingdom. After the establishment of the Benedictines, and since the 13th century, the order of Cistercites began to spread throughout Croatia. Their seat was in Topusko where they built a beautiful cathedral in Gothic style. The orders of Dominicans and Franciscans were introduced especially in Bosnia and southern Croatia, with the task of combatting heresy. The orders of Templars and Paulites were also conspicuous by the wealth and efficiency of their monasteries. Some other orders were also introduced, but they left the country after a short period of unsuccessful activity.

This period of ecclesiastic life was not without friction and debate in the ranks of the clergy. The Croatian glagolitic clergy, which insisted on the Slavic liturgy, had to ward off the attacks of the Latin clergy, which did not want any language but Latin used in the church services. In spite of all these difficulties, the Slavic liturgy and the glagolitic writing in the church books were preserved in the Senj, Kerk (Veglia) and Kerbava dioceses and locally throughout the

Split archdiocese. With the flight of the Croatian population before the Turks, the Slavic liturgy was introduced also in the Zagreb diocese, and in the 14th century also in a few monasteries in Bohemia and Poland.

Constitution and jurisdiction: In 1102 the Hungarian king also became the king of Croatia and Slavonia. Yet through this event Hungary and Croatia did not become a united kingdom in their internal administration, but each component of this alliance acted as a separate political, territorial and national unit. The only ground for common action was in the field of foreign policy, which was directed by the king himself. Up to Andrew I (II) and Bela III (IV) the kings were crowned separately as kings of Croatia and Dalmatia, but later the two coronation procedures were merged. However, the kings issued on that occasion separate writs of loyalty to the Croatian and Hungarian states.

In Croatia the king was replaced, whenever it was possible, by an independent duke of equal rank with the king, usually a member of the royal family. His usual title was "his ducal majesty" (ducalis maestas) enthroned by the "grace of God" (dei gratia). The duke usually resided in Zagreb, Knin and Zadar. Later he established his residence also in Bihach on the Una river. He kept a brilliant court, with a special chancellery, headed by a chancellor. The duke performed all the royal prerogatives such as appointing the bani (vice-roys), calling the diets, issuing patents of nobility to brave fighters, leading the armies in the time of war, confirming the ancient royal patents and privileges issued to various cities and noblemen (magnates) and by minting his own coins.

In the absence of dukes, the kingdom was governed by bani, with almost the same power and authority. At first there was only one banus, but at the time of King Bela III (IV), two banates were established; one for Croatia and Dalmatia, and another for Slavonia. During the reign of Mathias Corvinus, the two were merged into one office with the title; "Banus of Croatia, Dalmatia and Slavonia," a title preserved until the end of the first world war. The bani were usually selected from native nobility or such foreign magnates who owned land in Slavonia. Each banus could appoint from the members of the diet a vice-banus; one for Croatia and one for Slavonia. In addition to these dignitaries there was a prothonotary elected by the members of the diet who was guardian of the king's seal, and later represented the banus in higher courts.

The duke or banus called the diets in session upon the order of the king. Because the kingdom, since the second half of the 13th century was divided into two separate units, the Croatian diets (generalis congregatio regni Sclavoniae or regnorum Croatiae et Dalmatiae) met separately in the town of Krizhevtsi, in Zagreb or in Chasma for Slavonia, and the other in Knin, Nin, Bihach on the Una river, and later also in other places, for Croatia and Dalmatia.

These sessions took several days and were attended by the Prelates of the church and the members of higher and lower nobility, together with the representatives of the cities. Only on occasions of extraordinary importance did the two Diets meet together. In this case they were presided over by the dukes, bani or the king himself. In the absence of the king he sent his representatives (oratores) to advise the national assembly of his desires and proposals (propositiones regiae), which later came up for deliberation by the assembly and for its decisions. The Diets took action on all the basic problems of administration, such as taxes, national defense, military affairs and internal policies of Croatia, respectively Slavonia. Another important duty of the Diets was hearing complicated civil suits, i.e., administration of justice, in addition to legislative activity.

Toward the middle of the 15th century the Slavonian Diet sent its first representative and trusted men (nuncii regni Sclavoniae; oratores regni Sclavoniae) to the Hungarian parliament, and continued this practice until both countries were overrun by the Turks. The Croatian Diet, on the contrary, refrained from this practice, even at the behest of the king himself.

Both Croatia and Slavonia were divided into numerous counties, which, because of their small size, finally emerged as seven counties for both Croatia and Slavonia. After the expulsion of the Turks and the demilitarization of the defense zones, this situation prevailed until the end of the first World War. Because of a multitude of geographical names, otherwise inactive in the unfolding of historical events, we can pass up these details without prejudice to our main subject.

The center of each county, both within the jurisdiction of the banus of Croatia or Slavonia, was a fortified town from which the county itself, in most cases, drew its name. It was administered by the county chief (Zhupan), with the assistance of a castellan. This official was in charge of the royal servants and the townsmen (Castranses; servientes). With the passing of time, cities or villages were founded at the foot of the hills adjacent to the fortified towns. With the increase of population and their significance, such municipalities were finally granted the privileges and status of free royal cities.

On the other hand, by the end of the 12th century the kings started to grant land estates, of the size of one or several counties, to the members of higher aristocracy for loans of money or other significant services. Thus the Kerk princes (Krchki knezovi) came in the possession of the county of Modrush, Vinodol and Gat, while the princely Bribir clan got the Bribir county, and the powerful Nelipiches became the masters of their extensive Tsetina domain.

In the regular course of things the county chief (Zhupan) was the chief magistrate of the county and was assisted in the discharge of his duties by a vice-count (podzhupan). However, from the 14th century on, the royal towns were placed under the authority of the castellans who ruled supreme over the townspeople and the royal servants, whether noblemen or libertines.

The town's nobility met in assemblies which were called and presided over by the counts and frequently by the banus himself. They occupied themselves with the administrative affairs of the county, with collection of taxes and the establishment of military units in compliance with the king's orders, and also with judicial matters.

Courts: The administration of justice was substantially the same, both in Croatia and Slavonia. The supreme arbiter or Chief Justice was the duke or banus, who was substituted by the vice-banus (podban), and in Slavonia also by the prothonotary. In Slavonia certain periods have been designated for the regular banal court. At first they met twice, and later on four times a year, and always on the 8th day after the following feasts: At Epiphany (6th of January); feast of St. George (24th of April); St. Jacob's day (25th of July); and Michaelmas (29th of September). For this reason the regular banal courts were also called eight day courts ("judicia octavalia"). These banal courts were presided over by the banus himself (or his substitute), and attached to him were the assistants (Assessores) selected by Parliament.

A written order or decision bearing the banus' seal was issued with respect to the decision, and filed in the prothonotary's office. The affected parties could appeal the decision of the banal court both in Croatia and Slavonia to the Royal Court, or to the Chief Justice at the royal court (Judex Curiae regiae). The banal court in Croatia was held regularly in Knin, and in Slavonia at Krizhevtsi or Zagreb, but frequently cases were tried by the banus or his substitute while traveling throughout their territory.

Both in Croatia and Slavonia the county courts functioned in the capacity of the lower courts because at that time the administration of civil affairs was in close connection with the administration of justice. The county court was presided over by the Zhupan or count (or else by a vice-count) and attached to him as adjuncts were four (or more) judges who disposed of cases involving nobility (Judices Nobilium). They were selected from each district of the county. Finally two bailiffs, who saw to the execution of the decisions of the county court, completed the list of court officials.

Among the lower courts in Croatia we find the tribal courts for single tribes (so for the tribes of Mogorovichi, Shubichi and others), which lived within the confines of the newly established counties, with arrangements similar to those had by the county courts. In the free royal cities the municipal judge (Judex), as the court of the first instance, was trying both civil and criminal cases. He was assisted by assessors enlisted from the civilian population. Appeals were brought before the Tabernical Court as a higher instance court established in the royal palace.

The bani never administered justice in the cities except when specifically ordered by the king. The serfs were tried without appeal by their estate holders. In Croatia, cases were tried by the custom law (iuxta consuetudinem regni Croatiae), that is by Croatian justice and law. In addition, also the Hungarian customs and laws were used in adjudication of cases in Slavonia.

Statutes: From the 13th Century on, the maritime cities began to introduce written statutes patterned chiefly after Venetian. Thus Split introduced such a statute about 1240, Dubrovnik about 1272, Trogir in 1291, and Zadar in 1305. Almost at the same time private estate holders followed suit. In this way the law books of Vinodol were drawn which dated back to 1288, making them the oldest Croatian legal document. The population of Vinodol used to pay in the old times a certain tribute to the king, but when King Andrew I (II) assigned the county of Vinodol to the Princes of Kerk, the citizens of Vinodol became a sort of Prince's serfs and had to pay various taxes and tributes to their princely masters. Since the Princes of Kerk tried to make most of the situation, while the people of Vinodol were anxious to pay as little as possible, certain frictions took place which, from time to time, broke out into the open and made it necessary to find, once and for all, a proper solution.

Thus, both parties agreed to put in writing and confirmed "all the good and well-tried old laws in Vinodol." This event took place on the 6th of January, 1288, when the representatives and the community leaders of nine Vinodol towns met with Prince Leonard of Kerk to set up the much desired laws. So in the Prince's large hall the "collection of laws of Vinodol" with its 77 provisions was accepted and confirmed. In this code the provisions were based, in a majority of cases, on equality of rights. Very little interest is shown for civil suits even though there are provisions among them for criminal offenses. Litigations of this type were decided among the peasants themselves. Otherwise, the prince retained the right to control and supervise all the communities. Without his permission no meetings could be held, and in defiance of his decree the participants of the meeting could be punished with confiscation of property. Disloyalty to the prince was considered high treason. It is especially significant that the code of Vinodol did not provide for such cruelties which are on record in similar documents of other countries at that time. Judging by the standards of medieval law this code was outright humane, and provided severe punishment only for fortune telling and those guilty of arson.

There were several grave cases, with penalty not provided for by law, but by the will of the prince. The Vinodol Code did not contain provisions for torturing to extract confession from the accused. On the other hand, the law provided that the owner may kill the wrong-doer for the damage done if he has surprised him or seen him on his property. The court by its authority could not act, because the parties had to come before the prince in person and submit the complaint to him. The parties to the lawsuit could use the services of a "court lawyer." The testimony of witnesses was taken under oath. Excluded were the ordeals or trials by fire, boiling water, red-hot iron or court duels, which were customary at that time in other countries. As we see, the Code of Vinodol is not only the oldest written monument of the Croatian legal practice, but also an especially important cultural document. Chapters were also setting up their own legal provisions into codes. So the Canon of Zagreb, John, Archdeacon of Goritza, had set up (between 1334 and 1354) his famous legal code entitled "Statutus Capituli Zagrabiensis" which was a legal guide of that diocese for many generations.

Financial Affairs and Weapons. The dukes or bani could mint their own coins. This practice was introduced by Duke Andrew (about 1197-1203), and was maintained as a ducal privilege up to the reign of Queen Mary toward the end of the 14th century. This kind of money was usually called Moneta Banalis (banovac, banica), and was minted either in the ducal or banal mint, called "camera." The oldest mint was in the town of Pakrats, but in the 14th century it was transferred to Zagreb. The coins were minted from silver, with some copper alloy. Denominations varied. The unit was the "denarion," and was raised in value up to 200 denari.

Among various designs as emblems the most frequent was the likeness of a weasel running between two six-pronged stars. On the opposite side there was the likeness of a crescent. Only in the second half of the 15th century does the emblem of Croatia appear which consists of rows of red and silver squares. The emblem of Dalmatia appeared for the first time in 1406 on a seal carrying three leopard heads. These emblems are carried to this day and expanded by the emblem of Bosnia and Herzegovina, and Istria.

Taxes. There was a great difference in taxation between Croatia and Slavonia. Since King Koloman exempted the Croatian nobility from payment of the land tax in 1102, it was assessed and collected only in Slavonia in the amount of 12 denars a year. However, in the course of centuries the kings exempted many magnates, and entire corporations from this tax. For instance, King Andrew I exempted the Chapter of Zagreb of this tax in 1217. In addition to the land tax (also called a weasel tax or marturina), Slavonia was paying also a tax on the profits of the mint (lucrum camerae). In an older period the coins were minted every year to replace the old ones, but in such a way that the owner received only two equivalent coins newly minted for three old coins.

During the reign of Béla III (IV) this indirect taxation was converted into a permanent tax to the extent of 7 denars per year. However, Louis I attempted to abolish it in 1351 and introduced an annual tax of 18 denars from each gate (sorta), through which a fully loaded cart of wheat or hay could pass. The proceeds from this tax had to be delivered to the royal treasury, instead of the treasury of the banus (vice-roy). Furthermore, this tax had to be paid without exception by all the noblemen. This reform, however, could not take effect. Not even King Mathias Corvinus could succeed with his taxation reforms, and the Slavonians kept paying the weasel tax up to the battle of Mohach, that is, 20 denars from each serf hamlet or a ducat for 5 serfs' hearths (smoke stacks).

Yet the continuous and costly wars with the Turks in the 15th century brought about considerable fiscal changes including the introduction of extraordinary war tributes (contributio, dica). But this tribute could not be assessed or collected without especial consent of the Diet of Hungary or Slavonia, and only in such cases when the Estates considered it necessary. Moreover, the Estates themselves determined the rate of this tax in each particular instance. This extraordinary tax was paid not only in Slavonia but also in Croatia, until King Ladislav II fully exempted the latter from this impost. But somewhat earlier Slavonia obtained the privilege (1472) of paying only half the amount of the war tax which was assessed in Hungary, namely from each serf hamlet (porta, fumus) only a half ducat. Meanwhile in Hungary a whole ducat was collected under the title of this tax. This tribute was authorized by the Diet of Slavonia, and collected by the banus through his county organs (dicatores). But soon not only all of the church estates (those of Bishops, Chapters, Monasteries and Parishes), were exempted from this tax, but also those of the Government officials such as duke, banus, vice-banus, county chiefs and judges, in addition to some influential overlords. Thus the full load of war-taxation was laid on the shoulders of the small land-holders and their serfs, while the yield of this tax was continuously shrinking. Besides these general taxes, other revenue was collected from the mints, salt trade, port duties, custom receipts and the like.

Besides the taxes "the honor gift" also had to be delivered. When the king and his representatives, banus or duke, were travelling, it was customary that the nobility and citizenry give them a solemn welcome and treat them as guests. This was called the guest tribute (descensus), and was one of the most unwelcome taxes, since kings and bani and especially their officials, who were also benefited by these regulations, were always travelling. Naturally, the kings could dispense with the payment of these taxes, not only to the individual magnates and noblemen, but also to the ecclesiastic corporations and the free royal cities. So the king exempted them either from the full or partial payment of such tax, by restricting it only to hospitalization or to the delivery of food supplies. So a community near Zagreb was under obligation by the terms "of the golden bull" issued in 1242 by King Béla III (IV) to treat the king whenever he came by, with a dinner of 12 oxen, 1,000 loaves of bread, and 4 barrels of wine. If a duke of royal family arrived in the town, they had to provide half that amount. A banus was not usually treated so lavishly on his cross-country tour. However, when he set up his office in a town, the town folk had to provide one ox, 100 loaves of bread and one barrel of wine, for the use of his official retinue.

The Army and Navy. At this time important changes took place in the Croatian army (exercitus croaticus). During the first successors of Koloman the armed forces were maintained on the tribal basis as under the national dynasties, but the kings of the Anjou dynasty were eager to introduce a strictly feudal administration. Thus, the old tribal troops were replaced with the banderia or troops of magnates, while the banus and the nobility had to support them. Likewise, the ecclesiastic dignitaries and corporations (Chapters and Abbeys) as owners of extensive land estates, were under obligation to maintain impressive cavalry and infantry forces. This explains the fact that in the Turkish wars the bishops and abbots fought at the head of their troops. The courage and generalship of some of them aroused the admiration of their contemporaries throughout Christendom.

The royal free cities and towns, in return for their privileges, also had to maintain troops.

At the head of the Croatian army was usually the banus as its commander-in-chief (Capitanus). He was selected for this purpose by the Diet, but the estates could, by the privilege granted to them by King Mathias (in 1477) elect also any other person who they knew was better qualified for the duty. Such was the case, especially on the occasions when the office of the banus was vacant.

The navy had been considerably reduced ever since Dalmatia got into Venetian hands. It was at the climax of its strength during the reign of Louis I, who appointed an especial Croatian admiral (Admiralis regnorum Croatiae et Dalmatiae). The admiral was usually also the commander of the Islands of Hvar, Brach and Korchula where he could easily enlist the most skillful and courageous seamen. Besides the admiral, the Vice-admiral appears in the documents as his deputy. All the seacoast cities had to contribute funds for the support of the navy. This usually amounted to one galley or its equivalent in funds, and those towns which did not give a galley were bound to provide a small boat, a brigantine or a caravel. Thus, at the time of King Louis I, the navy consisted of 12 to 13 galleys and a large number of small boats. They were stationed along the coast in the protected coastal areas, but also participated in offensive wars. However, after Dalmatia came under Venetian rule, the navy started to disintegrate and finally vanished. By the end of the 15th century only a few vessels remained in Senj, commanded by captains of Senj. When also the

Island of Kerk fell to Venice, the Croatian navy disappeared altogether.

Naval forces were introduced on rivers and larger streams for the defense from the Turks, and especially in the time of Mathias Corvinus. Their center was in Petrovaradin. During the reign of Mathias there was a protective force of 364 ships. A part of these were large galleys with guns and siege instruments.

The Towns. There were two types of municipal government. The Dalmatian cities had been carrying on after the old Venetian pattern, while the Slavonian towns, such as Varashdin, Zagreb, Krizhevtsi, and others, were shaped after the German patterns as royal free cities. At the head of a free city was a judge, assisted by an elective city council. The city council could freely elect the judge and the parish-priest. Its duties were to safeguard and promote the city's interests, and especially those of trade and commerce. The city judge and other municipal officers were elected every year. In addition to that the citizens felt free to dispose of their possessions and arrange for city fairs. They also had to send a group of well-armed soldiers to the king in times of war providing he led the army to the battlefield.

Trade. The commerce consisted of both domestic and foreign trade. Slavonia had commercial relations with Hungary, Styria, Carniola, Croatia and Bosnia. On the other hand Croatia and Dalmatia were trading with Bosnia and Serbia. On the sea they entertained intense trade relations with Italy and especially with Venice. The coastal trade was carried on by numerous merchant ships of the Dalmatian cities while the land commerce was promoted by river navigation and highways. A network of important highways connecting Slavonia with Croatia continued over mountainous terrain to the seacoast. A military highway connected the interior of the country with the city of Senj on the seacoast.

Trade was carried on by guilds, made up of artisans of the same occupation, while kings were eager at times to give them various privileges as incentive for their work. Commerce proper was promoted by markets and fairs, constituting royal privileges granted to cities and towns.

Culture. Construction and architecture was also rising with the general welfare and advancement of culture. In Dalmatia the romanesque style prevailed, with renaissance coming in at a later period. In Slavonia, the Gothic was the prevailing style in architecture. Thus, in Zadar, on the contrary, the Cathedral of St. Anastasius (Stoshiye) was built in the Roman style (in the 13th century), while in Shibenik the Cathedral of St. James was erected in the renaissance style (in the 15th century). In opposition to this trend the Cathedrals of Zagreb and Topusko, built in the 13th century, were becoming the models of Gothic architecture. Likewise the arts of goldsmithing, sculpture and painting were cultivated throughout the country, and especially in Dalmatia.

Kings from the Hapsburg and Hapsburg-Lotharingian Dynasty

Ferdinand I, and Ivan Zapolski (1527-1564)

Election of two kings. The disaster on the field of Mohach was by itself only a lost battle, less bloody than so many others fought before and still many more recorded after. But the sudden death of the youthful King Ludwig II, who left no legal heirs, made it especially disastrous. Besides that, party strife did not cease. Moreover the factions, instead of seeking the salvation of their country by joining hands and striving for unity, they viewed the fatal event at Mohách through the eye-glasses of their factional interests, and fought each other with that much more bitterness. The National Party headed by Ivan Zapolski (Zapolya) and Stephen Verboczy, escaped the Mohách slaughter and remained the strongest on the scene. The party leaders saw in the national disaster only the defeat of the Court Party and its policy of fawning before foreign governments. Induced by the course of events, it now bent every effort to put through the Diet enactment of 1505, by which every foreigner was barred from the Hungarian-Croatian throne.

The Court Party again saw the Turks as a formidable enemy, and strove with that much more determination to tie up the country still more closely with the west. It was convinced that the national forces of Hungary and Croatia were not sufficient to successfully defend them in their struggle with the Ottoman Empire, which rose with the victory at Mohách to the rank of a great power of the first magnitude. Therefore, it was clear that the two parties, excluding each other on vital issues of national policy would also split in the election of a new king.

When early in September 1526, the first reliable news reached Zagreb about the Mohách disaster, all Slavonia was seized with panic and everybody was thinking of fleeing to safer parts. The real leader of the Croatian people, Prince Kersto Frankapan, arrived at that time, with his party to Zagreb. With his courageous words and reassuring public manifestos, he managed to calm down the people. He sent a troop of his horsemen across the Drava river to watch the movements of the Turks and report on them. At the same time he called the Estates to the Diet in Koprivnitsa for the 23rd of September.

In the meantime, the Diet of the Slavonian Estates met in Koprivnitsa and unanimously proclaimed Kersto Frankapan "governor and defender" of the kingdom (tutor protectorque regni Sclavoniae). Then the Estates selected and sent an embassy to Vienna to consult Archduke Ferdinand about an agreement in regard to their own needs and those of the kingdom. Then the Archduke effectively aided by his sister, dowager Queen Maria, ordered some of his influential supporters to contact the Hungarian and Croatian nobility. He was hoping that the crown of St. Stephen would come to him on the basis of the old treaties (of 1491, 1505, and 1515), without any difficulties, and even without any elective Diet. However, he quickly discovered that the situation did not favor his hopes. The Czechs unanimously elected him their king (23rd of October), but in Hungary, Croatia and Slavonia, things took a different course. For when they found out that the Turks had retired from Hungary, the majority of the Hungarian Estates, befriending the "National Party," met in the Diet arranged in Stolni Biograd (Székes Fehérvár). Here they elected and crowned (on the 11th of November) John Zapolski as their king, justifying their action with reference to the law of 1505 enacted and promulgated in the assembly at Rákas field (Rákos mezo) near Budapest. Nonetheless the minority Estates, belonging to the Court Party, met in a Diet in the city of Pozhun (now Bratislava), and on the 16th of December, 1526 elected Archduke Ferdinand of Austria their king.

By the analogy of the Hungarian kingdom also the Croatian kingdom split into two factions. The Croatian Diet met in October to deliberate on filling the vacancy on the throne. The diet was attended by Nicholas Yurishisch and Ivan Pichler as the trusted men of Ferdinand, but the Estates declared that they would attach certain provisions to their selection of the king. For this reason they sent their envoys to Vienna and when Ferdinand accepted their terms the Croatian Diet met again in the Franciscan Monastery in Tsetin on Sylvester Day, 1526. Present at the Diet were the titular bishop of Knin and abbot of Topusko, with the flower of the higher nobility of Croatia. The emissaries representing Ferdinand at the Diet were Captains Nicholas Yurishisch, Ivan Pichler, and Ivan Katzianer with Paul Oberstein, the mayor of Vienna. These envoys summoned the Croatian Estates to elect Ferdinand as their legal sovereign on the basis of his inheritance rights derived through his wife Anna and old treaties. At this the Estates withdrew to examine and discuss the rights of Ferdinand to the crown of St. Stephen. Later that day they sent a message to the emissaries that they had established the constitutional right of Ferdinand and his wife Anna to the crown of Hungary. The next day on the new year (1st of January, 1527), the second meeting took place, at which time the terms of the assembled Croatian Estates submitted to Ferdinand, were discussed. The debate continued until late afternoon. The uppermost problem in the mind of the assembly was what aid Ferdinand could furnish the Croatians in their struggle with the deadly foe. Finally, the Estates made an agreement with Ferdinand's envoys to bind himself to maintain for the defense of Croatia a force of 1,000 cavalry men and 2,000 foot soldiers, among which 800 cavalry men will be distributed among the magnates present in the Diet. Furthermore, Ferdinand bound himself to maintain a large force in Carniola (Slovenia) for the defense of Croatia. Finally, he reaffirmed all the ancient rights and privileges of the kingdom. Being satisfied with these conditions the Croatian Estates elected in full freedom and without anybody's interference, Ferdinand I (1527-1556) "the king of Bohemia and Archduke of Austria," king of Croatia.

As soon as the election was over, the Estates took the oath of allegiance to the new king administered by the Viennese prelate, Paul Oberstein. Messengers were sent in all directions to announce the glad news. A solemn "'Te Deum" mass was celebrated in the monastery's church, amid the ringing of bells and shooting of mortars.

The elective Diet of Tsetin is one of those important events in the past for the Croatian people, with which an old epoch is ended and a new one begins. Politically it is a powerful expression of the fact that the Croatian people, under the pressure of important historical events, had determined the most important constitutional problems, considering themselves and their fatherland a separate political nation and separate political territory, independent from Hungary.

At the same time, in Slavonia, things took a different course. After the election and coronation of Ivan Zapoljski, the leaders of the Slavonian Estates such as Prince Kersto Frankapan, Simon Erdody, bishop of Zagreb, took the oath of allegiance to the new "National" king. Then King John appointed Kersto Frankapan banus of Croatia, while he promised the office of the Chancellor of Kingdom to bishop Erdody. After the example of these two grandees, the major part of Slavonian nobility followed suit, including the Diet which met on the 6th of January, 1527 in the town of Dubrava, not far from Chazma. The Diet accepted as its legal sovereign the already crowned King Ivan (1527-1540), basing its decision on the law enacted in 1505. However, being afraid of civil war, the Estates of Slavonia empowered banus Kersto Frankapan to make an attempt at bringing about a conciliation between the two rival kings and their parties as soon as possible.

The Civil War and the Fall of Yaytse

At first the situation was decidedly in favor of King Ivan, not only because the majority of Hungarians and Croatians took him for their lawful king, but also because he found recognition abroad. So he was recognized by the Pope, France, Poland and Venice, while Francis I, King of France, promised him aid against Ferdinand. At the same time Ferdinand's position was weakened by the lack of funds, making it impossible for him to carry out his promises made to the Hungarian and Croatian nobility, although he had only a narrow strip of land along the western Hungarian border under his authority, including the cities of Shopron and Pozson (Pressburg,

Bratislava). In addition, his authority extended over most of Croatia from the frontiers of Carniola down to the stronghold of Klis. In his adversity, Ferdinand was deserted by many of his former supporters both in Hungary and Slavonia. Moreover Ivan Tahi, governor of the Vrana district, abandoned him and even Francis Batthyany, the banus of Croatia, was wobbling in his allegiance to Ferdinand, before the king reappointed him banus of Croatia (March 9, 1527) in opposition to Kersto Frankapan, appointee of King John.

The advance of King Ivan forced Ferdinand into decisive action. Knowing the lack of Ivan's preparation and his indolence, he, all of a sudden, broke into Hungary in August 1527 at the head of a strong German and Bohemian army. The key cities, Budavár and Székes Fehérvár, were easily taken, while King Ivan himself was defeated in the battle near Tokay. So he was forced to withdraw, at first, to Transylvania and after new losses, to flee to Poland. At the same time banus Kersto Frankapan was fighting for his King in Slavonia, but the very day that King John was defeated near Tokay, he died from wounds he got while laying siege to the town of Varashdin (27 September). The defeat at Tokay and the death of banus Kersto Frankapan considerably weakened King John's faction in Slavonia and Hungary. So the Slavonian nobility recognized Ferdinand as their king at its Diet in Krizhevtsi on the 5th of October, while Hungary crowned him on the 3rd of November at a Diet in Székes Fehérvár.

The chief beneficiaries of this civil war were the Turks, so much the more that nothing came out of that auxiliary army promised by Ferdinand the day of his election at Tsetin. The Croatians immediately caught sight of the impending peril and at a new Diet called in Tsetin (28 April 1527) they reminded Ferdinand of his pledge and urged him to act. That was their only hope since they had been deserted both by the Pope and the Venetians and their brothers in Slavonia. "May your Majesty know"—that was the message of the Croatian Diet—"that there is no record to the effect that any sovereign had ruled Croatia by force since after the death of our last king of blessed memory, Zvonimir. We have joined of our free will the holy crown of the Hungarian Kingdom, and then your own Majesty."

Yet the message was left unheeded and the Turks occupied the town of Obrovats on the Zermanya river late in March and Udbine in April. Furthermore, by the end of 1527 or early in 1528, they captured the stronghold of Yaytse and Banyaluka, and broke through on one hand up to Senj, and further south to Klis. At this time also Lika and Kerbava with the coastal line fell into the Turkish power. Thus the connection between southern and northern Croatia was broken. Only the strongholds of Klis in the south, Senj in the north and Bihach in the east still remained free, as the bridgeheads of the hopeless struggle against the Ottoman might.

The Alliance of King Ivan with Sultan Suleiman. The success of Ferdinand and the loss of his throne had dumbfounded King John. Thus, deserted and exiled from the very center of his state he could not of his own power, achieve anything in order to recover his loss. He was also haunted by the specter of the Turkish invasion, for the Turks certainly would exploit his disasters even more relentlessly than their policy of conquest.

True enough, the High Porte (Turkish government) had been planning for some time to occupy all of Hungary, and only upon the protests of Venice and France, did the Sultan postpone the execution of his plan for better times. These states, however, urged Suleiman to attack Ferdinand, but they did not want Hungary to fall entirely under the Turkish Sovereignty. For this reason a secret messenger of the Grand Vizir Ibrahim came to Ivan Zapolski and persuaded him to sue for Turkish aid. The decision of the exiled king was contrary to the traditions of Hungary, but in order to save his throne he decided to take the fatal step. Therefore, when his emissary Yerolim Laski, a Polish baron, came to Constantinople at the end of 1527 and made the suggestion of an alliance, he found the ground well prepared. At the end of January, 1528 Sultan Suleiman declared in a solemn audience to Yerolim Laski that he would give aid to King John and turn over to him all of Hungary without any counter service. This alliance with the Sultan, indeed, quickly deprived Ferdinand of the fruits of his victories, for he could hardly resist the huge war preparations of the Sultan with the

few thousand soldiers at his disposal. Thus, the Hungarian and Slavonian adherents of Ferdinand lost their faith in his fortunes.

Moreover, the friends of John again came out into the open and organized groups in support of the national king. They were especially emboldened when the Sultan turned over Budavár, with the crown of St. Stephen, to King John (September 1529), and moved on to Vienna where he laid siege to it. However, the infuriated Turkish attacks were frustrated by the courageous resistance of the population and the garrison of Vienna. Thus, the Sultan had to return (October 1529) without achieving his cherished ambitions.

At the same time a civil war was at its height in Slavonia. After the death of Kersto Frankapan, Simon Erdody, the leader of King John's party, became the bishop of Zagreb. In the Spring of 1529 the faction of King John Zapolski held sway over almost all of Slavonia. This prompted Ferdinand to send a large force of Carniolan cavalry and Spanish footsoldiers to the rescue of his adherents. Zagreb suffered bitterly at their hands, and especially the Chapter, the Bishop's town, and the cathedral itself, in this contest between the "Turkish" or "John's" and "German" or "Ferdinand's" factions. But finally the faction of King John carried the day, after which King John appointed Bishop Simon Erdody, banus of Croatia, and as such he was accepted also by the Diet of Slavonia, which met (early in 1530) in Krizhevtsi. After repeated bloody fighting the nobility of Slavonia effected (in October 1530) a "conciliation and alliance," with Ferdinand's faction and thus, by its own decision put an end to the civil war.

A New Campaign of the Sultan; Heroism of Nicola Yurishisch; Pozhega and Klis. In the meantime, both kings attempted to effect a compromise, but their negotiations did not bring about any positive results since neither of them wished to renounce to the Croatian crown. Upon this, Suleiman took (in the summer of 1532) to field in the 4th campaign against Hungary with the intention of reaching Vienna and taking it. But this plan was thwarted by the courageous and brave Croatian captain, Nicola Yurishisch, who blocked the advance of the huge Turkish army under Kisseg (Koszeg), not far from Szombathely in western Hungary. The siege was begun in August by the Grand Vezir Ibrahim, since Yurishisch refused to surrender the town with his small garrison of about 700 men. But when after 25 days of siege all the Turkish storms proved futile, the Grand Vezir started to negotiate with Yurishisch in the name of the Sultan.

In a personal interview in Ibrahim's tent the Grand Vezir told him that the Sultan "is giving him the town of Kisseg as a gift." As a result of this interview a Turkish guard was placed before the city walls, while Turkish flags were hoisted on its walls. When, later on the Sultan was informed that the town had allegedly surrendered, he issued an order to return (30 August).

As a reward for his valor, Captain Yurishisch obtained the town of Kisseg from King Ferdinand and at the same time he was raised to the rank of baron. He was buried in the town church in 1543.

On his way back the Sultan did not take the same route by which he came, but broke in through eastern Styria into Slavonia near Vinitza on Drava. From here he by-passed Varashdin and came to Rassinye, where the Turkish army split into two branches: the Sultan proceeded through Koprivnitsa and Virovititsa, along the bank of Drava, while the Grand Vezir took the route through Krizhevtsi and Chazma along the bank of the Sava. Near Belgrade the two branches of the army met, both of them loaded with rich booty and dragging along masses of enslaved prisoners.

This was the only time in the Ottoman history that a Sultan at the head of an army, with the exception of Sriyem (Sirmium), went through Croatian lands, and the eastern Slavonian parts, which were at this time considered as Turkish "imperial lands."

In the meantime, Charles V, with the aid of his brother, organized near Vienna an army about 100,000 men strong. But after the retreat of the Sultan's army, he did not undertake any military moves. Instead, he again attempted to make peace both with the Sultan and King John. However, the favorable outlook after a short-lived truce, made in the summer of 1533 with the Turks, gradually dimmed. After lengthy negotiations with King John were shattered the Turks again broke in from one side into the present day Slavonia and captured (the 15th of

January 1537), the town of Pozhega, and from the other side into Croatia, where they took the stronghold of Klis (12 March 1537). At the defense of this stronghold its brave defender Peter Kruzhich lost his life. With Klis lost, soon all of southern Croatia (at present Dalmatia up to Neretva) fell into Turkish hands. Only the Venetian coastal towns and adjacent islands were spared.

The Campaign of Katzianer and Peace of Nagyvárad. Death of King John. The Turkish pillaging and plundering and especially the fall of Pozhega and Klis painfully affected the people of Croatia and Slavonia. Indeed, it was small wonder that the lower nobility was clamoring in public that it was immaterial who was the master, Ivan or Ferdinand, and that they would submit to the one who would effectively aid them. But the fall of the two cities made a deep impression upon Ferdinand himself, and for this reason he hastened to bring aid to the Croatians, fearful of troublemaking and agitation by the faction of King Ivan, which was still strong amongst them. In order to raise depressed spirits especially in Slavonia, he appointed as commander-in-chief against the Turks, General John Katzianer, and ordered him to start a campaign with the forces at his command, at the earliest date. The objective of the campaign was to recapture the city of Osiek and liberate eastern Slavonia from the Turks. This campaign ended in failure because the army scattered due to lack of provisions, and finally the Turks simply rubbed out those parts of the army which remained together at the town of Goryany, while Katzianer himself fled, even before the battle took place (in the night of October 9 and 10, 1537).

With the defeat at Goryany the Turkish power was consolidated in present day Slavonia. The unsuccessful campaign of Katzianer caused consternation in Croatia and Slavonia. Thus Ferdinand appointed as his commander-in-chief in Slavonia, Nicola Yurishisch, while Katzianer, who came to justify himself was thrown into prison. In addition to Yurishisch the king appointed two more Bani, Peter Keglevich (1537-1542) and Thomas Nadashdy (1537-1540). They called the Diet in Krizhevtsi (January 6, 1538) in which the assembled nobility discussed chiefly the problem of the defense of the country. In the meantime the imprisoned General Katzianer managed to escape from prison in Vienna and took refuge in Susyedgrad. When Ferdinand heard of this, he issued a pursuit warrant against him and offered a monetary reward to anyone who would seize him, dead or alive. But Katzianer, far from being afraid of this decree, went straight to the Croatian nobility by whom he was gladly received. In Gvozdansko he had secret trysts with the disaffected nobility in an attempt to win them over to King John. His intriguing soon became very serious and especially since he sought connection with the Turks. In spite of the fact that the bani exerted all efforts to seize him they failed, until finally he was apprehended by Nicola Zrinski who had him beheaded in Kostaynitsa (October 1539).

Impressed by the failure of Katzianer's campaign, Ferdinand tried to come to some understanding with King John as soon as possible, and so much the more as John himself wished to have peace. He decided to marry Isabel, the daughter of the Polish King Sigismund I, but was refused by him until Ferdinand recognized him as a king. And thus through mediation of Emperor Charles V, a peace treaty was made in Nagyvárad (Oradia Mare) on February 24, 1538 by which Ferdinand recognized the royal title of John. Further, John was recognized also as an effective sovereign in that part of Hungary which at that time was in his hands. On the other hand, John renounced his claim to all of Slavonia and Croatia with Dalmatia. After John's death his part of Hungary would again fall to Ferdinand. Moreover this peace treaty had to remain a strict secret. Soon after this arrangement Ivan died (July 18, 1540) leaving behind an infant son. On his death bed John bequeathed all his royal rights to his minor son, Ivan Sigismund, to whom he appointed as guardian George Utyeshenich, bishop of Nagyvárad, a Croatian by birth.

Ferdinand Reigns Alone. With the death of King John, Ferdinand remained, true enough, the only Hungarian-Croatian king, but he could not extend his authority the way he had hoped. Immediately after the burial of King Ivan Yuriy Utyeshenich had the assembled nobility proclaim the young Ivan Sigismund King of Hungary, on the Rákos field near Budavár, and placed him at the same time under Turkish protection. With this act the court of Budavár gave the most effec-

tive answer to Ferdinand, when he summoned the Dowager Queen Isabel to keep the terms of the peace treaty of Nayvárad. In such circumstances Ferdinand had only one recourse, namely to force the respect of his rights, but thus he provoked Sultan Suleiman to the fourth campaign against Hungary (1541).

With this campaign, the Sultan hoped to carry out his long cherished plan to have Hungary entirely in his power and to claim his right to rule over Hungary through his victory in the battle of Mohách (1526), alleging that he had conquered that country by the might of the sword. Therefore, arriving at Budavár he proclaimed the whole country between the Balaton Lake and Tissa (Theiss) and from Budavár to Sava, that is, including the present eastern Slavonia, with Sriem, a Turkish Pashalyk, or a Turkish province subject to the authority of the Sultan. On the other hand he assigned the territories along the eastern bank of Tissa and Transylvania to the youthful John Sigismund in sovereign possession. Thus, Ferdinand retained only western Hungary with Pozhon as the main city, while the remainder of Croatia and a part of Slavonia also remained under his rule.

Hence the legacy of King Louis the Second, broke into three parts (by the end of August 1541). Isabel, with her son and her chief advisor, George Utyeshenich, had to leave Budavár, which became the center of the pasha of "Three Horse Tails," and retired into Transylvania. From this time on, Transylvania became a separate political territory, and it is here that the independent Hungarian national life boils for over a century, but always under the same Turkish protectorate until 1690. In the meantime Budavár, the beautiful Hungarian capital and seat of the brilliant court of Mathias Corvinus, became the center of the Turkish dominion in Hungary for nearly 150 years. The pashas of "Three Horse Tails" ruled Hungary from now on in the name of sultans.

New War with Turks. But two years later (1543), the Sultan set out on his fifth campaign against Hungary, in the course of which he seized the Slavonian towns Valpovo, Orahovitsa, and Pakrats, while in Hungary proper he captured the cities of Pechuh (Pécs), Stolni Biograd (Székes Fehérvár) and Ostrogon (Esztergom). Having divided the occupied country into Sanjaks (military districts), he returned to Constantinople. Being unable to stand the onslaught of the irresistible Turkish power, Ferdinand now tried to effect a peace or at least a lengthy truce with the Sultan. Thus, in the year 1547, a five-year truce was concluded, by which Ferdinand bound himself to pay a yearly "gift" in the amount of 30,000 ducats, but otherwise he could retain anything that he still owned in Hungary and Croatia. With this truce, which became the foundation for further ones, Ferdinand finally, after 20 years' warfare, saved for himself and his dynasty, the authority of the Hungarian-Croatian king, and also the remains of Croatia and Hungary from complete disaster.

In the meantime developments in Transylvania, in the course of which Yuriy Utyeshenich lost his life (in 1551), the "wisest Hungarian statesman of all times," as the modern Hungarian historians call him, provoked some new conflicts with the Turks. As a result of new Turkish attacks Croatia lost Virovititsa (early in 1552), Chazma (in August 1552), and Kostaynitza in July 1556, all of them famous outposts of Christendom. In spite of the prolonged truce on the basis of the agreement of 1552, all these towns remained in Turkish power. Moreover, in Chazma a new sanjakate was established.

Nicholas Zrinjski was banus of Croatia (1542-1556) in the period of the latest Turkish campaigns. On the title of back pay for the support of the army and also for many deeds of valor, Zrinjski was given by Ferdinand the whole territory of Medjumurye, an enclave formed by Mura and Drava rivers. The decree of this grant was signed on the 12th of March 1546. Thus the center of the family fortunes of the Zrinski clan was transferred from the stronghold of Zrinj to the town of Chakovats (Hung.: Csáktornya). When Zrinjski resigned to his Office of Banus, he was appointed, by Ferdinand, captain (military governor) of the Sziget (Hung.: Szigetvár "island city") district. In place of Zrinjski, Péter Erdody was appointed banus of Croatia and had the tragic distinction of calling the last extraordinary Croatian Diet in the town of Stenichnyak (July 1558).

Although Ferdinand knew well that Bohemia, Hungary and Croatia, together with the inherited Austrian provinces, entered only into a personal union, he nonetheless strove to have all these countries centralized in order to make a tight political union out of a personal union with the passing of time. Making the most of the miserable conditions prevailing throughout the period of continuous Turkish wars, he first attempted to introduce a parliamentary system uniting all the sections of his political domain. Specifically, Ferdinand demanded that each of his kingdoms and provinces send representatives to his court so that all of them might deliberate in the matters of common interests. But this plan failed since neither Hungarians nor Croatians wished to deliberate about the affairs of their countries outside of their own lands. Confronted with this resistance, Ferdinand resorted to administrative subterfuge by establishing some control offices at his court in Vienna. This was the imperial war council, secret council, court chancellory, and the court chamber. These offices were made up chiefly of Germans who submitted proposals dealing chiefly with military and financial affairs to the king. With the passing of time, however, the importance and power of the imperial government tended to eclipse the rule of the Croatian and Hungarian Diets, which caused much misgiving and opposition among their respective Estates.

Ferdinand I died on the 25th of July, 1564. At his death his sons divided the state among themselves, guided by the provisions of their father's testament. The oldest son, Maximilian, whom the Croatians and Hungarians crowned their king while Ferdinand still lived (September 8, 1563), obtained Bohemia, Hungary, Croatia and both Austrian provinces (upper and lower Austria) with Vienna. Ferdinand's share became Tirol, while Charles obtained Styria, Carinthia, Carniola (Slovenia), Goritza, Trieste and Istria with Rijeka (or Fiume).

MAXIMILIAN (1564-1576)

Maximilian ascended the throne as a mature man. At that time he was 37 years of age. Croatians, Hungarians, and Germans greeted him with enthusiasm, inspired with the hope that he would meet their desires. But soon it transpired that he was the true son of his father. Moreover, during his reign began the struggle of the Croatian and Hungarian Estates for the protection of their respective constitutions from the encroachments by the Viennese central government.

Nikola Zrinsky and the Siege of Sziget. As soon as Maximilian ascended the throne, he made an attempt at a compromise with Ivan Sigismund Zapolski, the duke of Transylvania. But since the latter refused to renounce his Hungarian-Croatian royal title, negotiations were soon called off. Moreover, they became the cause of a new Turkish campaign. This quarrel fitted well into the contemporary Turkish concept that with the death of Ferdinand the recently made truce (1562) had expired. And thus, Suleiman in the 75th year of his life decided to undertake his sixth campaign against Hungary with the intention of capturing Vienna. He may have been induced to carry out this ambitious project to compensate for the lost prestige of his power through failure of his campaign against the Maltese Knights the year before. In addition he was egged on to this war especially by his Grand Vezir, Mehmed Sokolovitch. Shortly before this great campaign the Turks broke (in the summer of 1565) into Croatia and captured Krupa on the Una River which was defended by a small group of Croatians. The banus Peter Erdody, whose forces were under the command of Matiya Bakich, gave the Turks a crushing blow near Obreshka, not far from the town of Ivanich. Due to this exploit, King Maximilian raised the banus to the rank of a hereditary count. This was the first Croatian-Hungarian family to receive that title (11, October, 1565).

In May of the next year (1566) Sultan Suleiman himself, together with the Grand Vezir, Mehmed Sokolovitch (Turkish Sokolli), started, at the head of an army 150,000 strong, and a large number of artillery pieces, on the new campaign. Having crossed Drava near Osiek by the middle of July, he turned with 15,000 men and 300 artillery pieces against Sziget (between Barch and Pechuh), where the former banus, Nicholas Zrinsky was in command of the stronghold. Based on his fortress of Sziget, Zrinsky frequently raided the Turkish positions around the Balaton Lake (Blatno Jezero: Muddy Lake). In addition, he was known all over the Orient as the sworn enemy of the Turks. For this reason the Sultan made up his mind to severely punish him. In the meantime, Nicholas Zrinsky found out what was in store for him even before the coming of Suleiman's host. Consequently he provided Sziget with provisions and ammunition,

and gathered around himself a brave host, mostly Croatians with some Hungarians, all in all about 2,500 men. He did so with a firm decision to keep the Sultan busy before the city until the promised aid from King Maximilian arrived.

Early in August 1566 the Sultan surrounded Sziget from all sides and began to bombard the suburban area with his heavy guns, so that within a few days of ordeal Zrinsky was forced to withdraw inside the walls of his stronghold.

At this turn the Grand Vezir, who was in charge of operations under Sziget, promised Nicholas all of Croatia, if he would surrender the town. But Zrinsky rejected this offer with contempt. After that the Turks began to storm the city but Zrinsky repulsed them and moreover, with daring sallies, he caused them considerable damage. Being helpless in open engagements, the Turks decided to dig subterranean channels and blast the walls of the city enabling them to break into the town. And indeed when they succeeded in destroying a chief part of the city walls, Zrinsky had no other choice but to surrender as a coward, or die as a hero. On the 7th of September he broke out at the head of the remaining garrison from the town and perished in this engagement as "the new Leonidas."

But the Sultan never heard the glad news of Sziget's fall, because he died on the 4th of September in his own tent. The Grand Vezir cleverly kept the padishah's death a secret, for fear that the Turkish force would scatter. With this clever trick, Mehmed Sokolovitch saved the glory and the force of the Empire. He sent at the same time a special messenger to Sultan Selim, his son-in-law, to greet him first as the new Padishah. The heroism of Nicholas Zrinsky caused admiration in all Christian Europe. In spite of the fact that the Turks had captured Sziget, its fall marked the ebbing of the huge Ottoman power, undermined by the failure of the Maltese expedition and the sixth Hungarian campaign to suffer a crushing blow at sea four years later at Lepanto.

Immediately after the Turk's retreat, Maximilian began to negotiate a truce. After some bickering the truce was concluded on the 17th of February, 1568, in Adrianople for a period of eight years under the terms similar to those granted in 1547. This forced John Sigismund Zapolsky to open negotiations with Maximilian. He renounced (1570) his royal titles, keeping only that of the "Duke of Transylvania." On the other hand Maximilian bound himself to permit the Transylvanians to freely elect their own new duke at Zapolsky's death. Young Zapolsky died from the life of extravagance and debauchery the next year (1571), and with him the whole Zapolsky clan died out.

Maximilian and the Croatian Estates

After the death of banus Peter Erdody (26 April 1567), King Maximilian appointed two bani, the Bishop of Zagreb Julius Drashkovich and Francis Frankapan of Slunj, both of whom the common Croatian-Slavonian Diet (21st of September, 1567) solemnly and gladly confirmed. But the new bani were confronted with many grave problems and trials. Dissatisfied with the insignificant income from the Slavonian taxes, the Hungarian chamber (residing in Pozson), advised the king to abolish some of the past privileges of the Croatian nobility. Accordingly, also the areas on the other side of the Kupa river (at that time called Croatia) were forced into payment of a war tax (dica) although they had been exempted from such payment back in the time of King Vladislav II. Likewise, the Chamber of Pozson urged the Proto-Notary to have taxes collected also from the Vice-banus, Vice-counts and Tribal Judges of Slavonia as well as from the Chapter of Zagreb, which from 1544 on applied its tax exemption privileges for the construction and fortification of Sisak, and also of the remnants of the county of Krizhevtsi. All this was in violation of the old Constitutional rights and customs. So, when Maximilian's delegates appeared before the Croatian-Slavonian Diet with these royal proposals, the Estates rejected them insisting on their old privileges. Moreover they enacted pertinent provisions, which they sent to Maximilian in Vienna with the request that they be confirmed.

Now again the Hungarian Chamber advised the king to refuse confirmation of these acts. He changed them in accordance with the advice of the Hungarian Chamber and sent them back to Zagreb. For this reason a tension set in between the king and the Croatian Estates. This tension continued for a number of years, but finally the Estates yielded and satisfied, at least in part, the king's demands. Besides this, the bani were preoccupied with the defense of the country, to

which they devoted themselves with such zeal that "the frontiers of the kingdoms (Croatia and Slavonia) were preserved intact"—as we read in the acts of the Croatian Diet of 1572. "Furthermore—the Diet records—during their tenure of the Banus' Office, not one castle was yielded to the Turks, not even the least significant of its bastions, but they all were defended and retained." As compensation and in recognition of his services the banus Drashkovich was given the authority over the town of Trakoshchan (1569) but later, King Rudolph granted this town to the Drashkovich family for permanent keeping (1585). But the young Frankapan of Slunj suddenly died (2nd December 1572 in Varashdin). His death was mourned as a misfortune of the Croatian kingdom. With the death of Francis Frankapan, the family of Frankapans of Slunj died out. Thus the Office of the banus was carried on for the next two years by Bishop George Drashkovich alone.

Peasants' Rebellion

Matiya Gubets—The Peasant King

Soon new troubles in the country were added to the old ones early in 1573 when a peasants' rebellion broke out in the regions surrounding Stubitza and Susyedrad in the Zagreb area. This fatal event was provoked in the first place by the magnate Francis Tahy, a baron of great wealth and owner of the Susyedgrad area. In addition, Tahy was a man of violent temper, haughty and greedy. While his serfs carried on a miserable existence, other peasants of the area fared no better. Describing the lamentable lot of the peasants, the Archbishop Anton Vranchich, Archbishop of Ostrogon, reported to King Maximilian that "the estate holders in Croatia treated the peasants worse than cattle." However, the rebellion did not break out suddenly. Only when the oppressed peasants saw that their grievances had no effect, and when the Croatian Diet proclaimed them "traitors of the fatherland" because of their resistance to the violence of Tahy, they had taken up arms. According to their own depositions in court after the suppression of the rebellion, the peasants took up arms "for general liberty and equality of social ranks," that is, for abolition of feudalism, and then "for general payment of tax and general duty for the defense of the country, likewise for abolition of the customs duties and tariff in favor of free commerce and trade." They aimed also to extend these reforms throughout the country to the seacoast. Their watchword was "for the justice of the old." Thus, during the investigation proceedings one of their leaders (Ivan Sverach from Pushcha) said: "Had we defeated the nobility, we would have established a separate imperial government in Zagreb; here we would collect the taxes and tributes and we, ourselves, would take care of the defense and protection of the frontiers" (from the Turkish inroads). They remained loyal to Maximilian, but refused to serve anybody else.

The seat of the peasant "government" was Dubitza, where Matiya Gubets carried on as the supreme judge. In command of the troops was Ilia Gregorich of the town of Berdovets. He was quite an expert in military affairs of that time. Gregorich's plan was to arouse the serfs of the Erdody estate in Yastrebarsko and Tsesargard on Sutla river. Then the Uskoki (see section VI of this book) of the coastland, and the peasants of the neighboring Carniola and Styria would attack Zagreb and force the nobility to accept their own terms of peace.

In execution of this plan he first broke (early in February 1573) into southern Styria, but the Styrian nobility decisively defeated him in a few days and routed his troops (8th of February 1573) even though his forces were joined by many Styrian peasants.

Gregorich himself fled but was seized in his flight and taken before the court in Vienna. There he was sentenced to death and finally beheaded in Zagreb. In the meantime banus George Drashkovich summoned the whole nobility to arms. Under the leadership of Vice-banus Gashpar Alapich the second branch of the peasant army, under Matiya Gubets, was defeated not far from Stubichke Toplitse (Stubitsa Hot Springs), on the 9th of February. In these battles many peasants were either killed or seized and later on put to death. Matiya Gubets, who was charged with proclaiming himself a "peasant king," was subjected to a terrible fate. After his condemnation he was tortured with white glowing tongs in the public square of St. Mark in Zagreb, and then the executioner crowned him with a red hot iron "crown."

After crushing the rebellion, Drashkovich re-

signed his office as banus, because he found it incompatible with his spiritual duties as a bishop. Moreover, he defended a part of the seized peasants but with little success.

Battle near Budachki

The unfortunate rebellion of the Croatian peasantry served as a signal for continued Turkish invasions of the Croatian territory with ever increasing vigor and determination. The Bosnian Ferhad Pasha, with his seat in the neighboring town of Banya Luka, was the initiator and leader of these inroads. Both the Croatian Diet and banus Drashkovich were unable to stem the Turkish tide. Emperor Maximilian tried to remedy the situation, first by appointing General Gashpar Alapich the second banus of Croatia, and second by sending him General Herbart Auersperg with a supporting army. The immediate objective of the campaign was to relieve the town of Bihach on the Una river, which still held out against a score of Turkish attacks as a Croatian island in the Turkish sea. That made Ferhad Pasha decide to capture the town at all cost. Apprised of the nearing rescue army of Auersperg, Ferhad, in a surprise move, headed off the enemy at Budachki near the confluence of Radona and Korana river, inflicting such a crushing blow on the Christian troops that General Auersperg himself fell in the battle (22 September 1575). This defeat had a distressing effect upon Maximilian, but before he could do anything about it, he died (12 October 1576). He was succeeded by his oldest son, Rudolph, who still during the life of his father (25 September 1572) was crowned Hungarian-Croatian king.

RUDOLPH (1576-1608)

The King's Character and Beginnings of his Reign

Rudolph was 24 years of age when he assumed the throne. As a young man he spent 8 years in the court of his relative, King Philip II of Spain, where he not only became an ardent Catholic, but also acquired much predilection and understanding for science and arts. Moreover, he was also versed in the astrology and alchemy of that time. Otherwise, he was restrained in speech, filled with Spanish dignity, but at the same time, timid and melancholic, which in time degenerated into an oppressive mental disarrangement. In connection therewith, Rudolph became more and more diffident and indecisive, all of which had fatal consequences for the direction and unfolding of his reign. Immediately at the beginning of his reign he retired to his Court in Hradchany, a stronghold of Prague. There he set up a real museum of antiquities and arts, turning over the administrative and political affairs in Hungary and Croatia to his brother Ernst, and military affairs to his uncle Carl of Styria. Thus, it so happened that the Croatians had at that time three masters, King Rudolph in Prague, Archduke Ernst in Vienna and Archduke Carl in Gratz (Gradets of Styria).

The bani George Drashkovich and Gashpar Alapich requested their release during the reign of Maximilian chiefly because they did not have sufficient financial means to cover the expenses needed for the defense of the country. But Rudolph summoned them to continue in their duties until the final decision. In such circumstances it is understandable that the territories of Croatia and Slavonia were reduced more and more by Turkish inroads. Thus, Croatia and Slavonia during Rudolph's reign were reduced in size to a mere token of their former territory (reliquiae reliquiarum, etc.) which encompassed a small area between the sea and Carniolan-Styrian borders, between Drava and Djurdjevats, between Chazma and the Sava river slightly below Sisak, and finally between the Kupa river and the Kapela mountain range.

In this hour of despair there was a desperate need to stop somehow the advance of the Turkish troops and the only effective remedy appeared to be the establishment of the military district (Voyna Krayina) along the Turkish borders. It was organized by Archduke Carl after the model of the Turkish sanjaks.

Beginnings of the Military District (Voyna Krayina)

The continuous and sudden inroads of the Turks from the Pashalyk of Bosnia, not only into Croatia and Slavonia, but also deep into the hereditary Austrian lands such as Istria, Carniola, Styria and Carinthia, forced the Croatians and their neighbors to establish a permanent army along the frontier garrisoned in various royal and private towns. Besides, the king had to provide means for the maintenance of this army as well as the local magnates who were owners of the individual cities. So the Princes of Blagay and Kerbava, Zrinskies and Frankapans were under obligation to support these troops. But through the loss and insecurity of their estates, the magnates themselves became impoverished and due to lack of funds they could not perform this service. The distress was still further heightened by the flight of the population from the areas either conquered by the Turks or adjacent to the border districts.

Ferdinand, still as Archduke of Austria, and during the lifetime of King Louis II, made some serious attempts to establish the Croatian military districts and to defend the same realizing that thereby he was defending his own territories. Furthermore the Carniolan Estates declared that it was better to defend themselves from the Turks in a foreign land than in their own country. Ferdinand's burdens were further increased when he bound himself as King of Croatia to maintain a good-sized army for the defense of that country. From the king's obligation and the worry of the Austrian Estates about their own safety, the military district was organized. It was not a separate territory but was merely defended by an army made up chiefly of native soldiers, Croatian magnates' private troops, of hired soldiers, and of Ferdinand's Austrian subjects. This military organization was further sub-divided into Captaincies (Kapetaniya), which were maintained chiefly by the Styrian, Carinthian, Carniolan, and Istrian Estates. These troops were under the command of an Austrian general.

About the middle of the 16th century two such military provinces were created: the Slavonian district (Krayina) consisted of a number of captaincies such as those of Koprivnitsa, Krizhevtsi, and Ivanich, while the Croatian district, extending from the Kupa river to the sea was made up of the Hrastovitsa, Ogulin, Bihach and Senj captaincies. But real garrison life began to take effect in the military provinces only when King Rudolph (25 February 1578) turned them over into the direct administration of his Uncle, the Styrian Archduke Carl, and subordinated to him all the local commanders. Moreover, the bani and the Diet of Croatia were obligated to him in military matters.

King Rudolph's drastic decision did not meet with the approval of the Croatian Estates, but in view of the distressing conditions the Croatian Diet in Zagreb (15 July 1578) passed the resolution that it must take cognizance of the king's order. But it added the specific provision that "Archduke Carl must cultivate true friendship and cooperation with the Banus of Croatia and Slavonia." Furthermore, "nothing improper, or contrary to the freedom of the kingdom should take place," because "our Banus shall not submit to any other captain by encroachment on his prestige or on our age-old liberties."

With the completion of the stronghold of Karlovats, Archduke Carl made up his mind to wage war against the Bosnian Turks. But the army, which was under the command of the Carinthian Captain, Julius Kevenhuller, together with the forces of the new Banus Kersto Ungnad (1578-1583), was given a crushing blow by the Bosnian Ferhad Pasha. This luckless war resulted in permanently shifting the defense line from the Una river to the banks of the Kupa, while Bihach still remained in Croatian hands as an isolated island in the Turkish sea. At this juncture Archduke Carl ordered a strong fortification to be built for the defense of the remaining Croatian territory. The Croatian Estates demanded that it be built closer to Sisak along the lower Kupa, but the Archduke's advisers selected as a more suitable place, a corner between the confluence of the Korana and the Mrezhnitsa Rivers near Kupa. The area was purchased from the princes of Zrinj and toward the middle of July 1579 the foundation was laid to the town of Karlovats, i.e. Charlestown, named so in honor of Archduke Carl. Characteristic of the psychology of the era, is the fact that, 900 Turkish skulls were laid in the foundation of the stronghold. With the building of Karlovats the Croatian military district obtained a permanent residence for its general, while Varazhdin became the seat of the military district of Slavonia. Thus in the turbulent times of the later part of the 16th century and at the climax of national distress, a new political territory was created in the Croatian kingdom, one that was removed from the authority of the banus and the Diet.

The Bani Kersto Ungnad and Thomas Erdody

For the present the stronghold of Karlovats stopped the Turkish inroads. But soon the Turks began again to break into the Croatian territory up to Kupa River valley and the Turopolye area. In this desperate plight banus Kersto Ungnad was quite helpless, since his own situation became worse every day as a result of violent conflict, not only with the magnates but also with the city of Zagreb. The citizens of that city were provoked by Ungnad's boastful assertions that he "is not only their banus and captain but also their king." Soon the banus engaged in a conflict also with some leaders of the military districts and the generals of his own troops to such a degree that his authority sank to a low ebb. Consequently he resigned his high office. King Rudolph then appointed his 26 year old son-in-law, Thomas Erdody (1583-1595) banus of Croatia and Slavonia, with full approval of the Croatian Estates.

The main concern of the young banus was the defense of the country since, in spite of the renewal of a truce by King Rudolph with the Turks, the fighting in the Croatian and Slavonian military district never ceased. So, in October 1584 the young banus defeated a large Turkish force near Slunj, and Ivanich (December 6, 1586). The brilliant victories of the Banus raised the spirits of the Croatian Estates and their despairing troops, but other clouds were gathering on the political horizon.

The trouble came this time from the commanding general of Karlovats, and his unruly German troops. The general not only refused to submit to the banus and the Diet, but also arrogated himself the right to sit in judgment over the Croatian noblemen by arresting them and seizing their property. On the other hand the German soldiers were molesting and robbing the population because they were unable to get their regular pay from Graz. Because of these distressing conditions, the Croatian Diet complained to the king and the Archduke in Gratz, but all was in vain. Soon after Archduke Carl (10 July 1590) died, and the administration of the military district passed to his son Ferdinand (later king). Since the young Archduke was still a minor, he was replaced in the first year by the Archduke Ernest (up to 1593), brother of King Rudolph.

Fighting Around Sisak

Just about that time the war-like Hassan Predoyevich came to the head of the Bosnian pashalyk (founded in September 1580). He was a personal friend of the Grand Vezir, Sinan-Pasha, the Albanian who was anxious to break off the truce made with King Rudolph. Apparently at his behest Hassan-Pasha broke into Croatia in August 1591. Advancing to Sisak he was forced into retreat four days later after a serious defeat. Then the banus Thomas Erdody went into pursuit of the Turks, in the course of which he recaptured some towns of Moslavina. However, he could no longer reach the Turkish troops. In retaliation Hassan Pasha set on fire and laid waste all of the area around Bozhyakovina and Verbovets, and then captured the town of Ripach on the banks of the Una, not far from Bihach.

About that time the Croatian Diet met (5th of January 1592) to deliberate on the country's plight. On this occasion the Diet made a memorable decision to raise the country to its feet by ordering a general insurrection for the defense of the fatherland. Likewise provision was made to supply the army with the necessities of life because the Estates were sure that Hassan-Pasha would make another incursion the next Spring. And indeed the Pasha set out in April with the intention of establishing some firm stronghold in the neighborhood of Sisak. He wanted to capture this town as a base for his further military advances in Croatia.

After the capture of the stronghold of Petrinya, the defense line went from Ogulin through Karlovats along the course of the Kupa to Sisak. After the fall of Bihach, Hassan-Pasha besieged Sisak for the second time. The stronghold was defended by a small garrison of Croatians headed by the canon of Zagreb and two companions. Having suffered tremendous loss, Pasha was soon forced to abandon Sisak, but on his return he laid waste the whole area from Turopolye and Okitch (in July 1592).

Thus in the year 1593, when the Croatians again expected the Pasha to come, the Banus and the Diet made preparations for a stiff resistance, suing the king and archduke Ernest for aid. In June, Hassan-Pasha came at the head of a strong army to Sisak, with the plan to attack Zagreb right after the fall of Sisak, and so to conquer the remaining portions of Slavonia. Banus Thomas Erdody came to the relief of the town followed by General Andrew Auersperg, commander of Karlovats, and the Styrian Colonel Ruprecht Eggenberg, with a force of 5,000 cavalrymen and footsoldiers. The combined Christian forces met the Turkish army on a field between the rivers Kupa and Odra and administered it a smashing defeat (June 23, 1593).

Hassan-Pasha himself, with two of the sultan's relatives and a number of Turkish grandees fell in the battle. The whole Christian world rejoiced when it heard the news of the victory. Appropriate memorial writings concerning the event were published and congratulations and gifts sent to the Banus. The battle of Sisak was an important military event, not only in Croatian history but also for the history of Europe. Under the walls of the stronghold of Sisak, the expansionist movements of Islam to the west of Europe were finally checked since the Turks could never cross the extreme northwestern boundary towards Italy. With this battle the century-old defensive struggle of Croatia (from 1493) is pushed in the background, and the country is set on the path of successful offensives which will finally deliver it from the Turkish yoke in less than a century (1683).

The Great Turkish War (1593-1606)

When the news of the defeat at Sisak reached Constantinople the Turks were stirred to a frenzy and under the instigation of the Grand Vezir, Sinan-Pasha, Sultan Murad III was moved to declare war on King Rudolph. This war was fought in Hungary and Croatia and lasted 14 years. In Croatia proper the campaign took another 2 years. Hungary was then the real battlefield, while Croatia provided only a secondary theater of war, although here, too, important events had taken place. Among these one should mention the victory near Petrinya (26 September 1595), with which all of the country north of Kupa was forever liberated from the Turkish inroads. But on the other hand, with the defeat of the Karlovats general, Yurye Lenkovich, under Klis (end of May 1596), hope had vanished that it would be possible to strike a lateral blow at the Bosnian Pashalyk by an invasion of same from this direction. In the meantime, Thomas Erdody resigned the office of banus because he did not receive funds regularly for the upkeep of his troops, and also because aliens were appointed army commanders in Croatia.

When the banus submitted these reasons before the assembled Estates in the Croatian Diet (1595), they turned to Archduke Maximilian with the petition that he plead with King Rudolph to appoint as soon as possible "native sons" of Croatia to the Office of Banus. Furthermore, the appointment should be given to a person fully expert in military affairs. "Hence, if the Estates cannot have their own banus, let your Highness know that for certain they will not submit to any general of alien nationality, nor will they ever set out in a campaign with him, even though all of us perish together with the fatherland; they will also undertake the extreme before their liberties will be curtailed in this respect."

Upon this, King Rudolph appointed as Bani, the Bishop of Zagreb, Gashpar Stankovachki and Ivan Drashkovich; but since the Bishop, who was sick, died in the same year, the office of banus fell exclusively to Ivan Drashkovich (1596-1609). During his tenure of office, peace was concluded with the Turks after long negotiation at the mouth of the Zhitva river at its confluence in the Danube not far from Komoran (Komárom), on the 11th November 1608. This document was made up of seventeen articles which provided that each party would retain whatever possessions that it had at the moment when the peace treaty was signed. Furthermore the plundering and inroads into foreign territory would be stopped and both parties would punish those outlaw bands which would refuse to uphold this agreement. Finally, the emperor and king would no longer pay yearly tributes, but would make a gift of 200,000 ducats to the Sultan, once and for all. The peace treaty concluded at the mouth of the Zhitva River, is the first one in which the Hungarian-Croatian king and the sultan appear as each other's equals. Now the chains of tributary submission were sprung, which from 1547 the king's ambassadors had to carry each year to the sultan, when they offered him the so-called "presents." Now, for the first time a real peace treaty was signed by the plenipotentiaries of the sultan. This peace was a clear sign that the Turkish overlordship had been repulsed and its ebbing was about to start.

The Rebellion of Stephen Bochkay

By the end of the "long" Turkish war, a dangerous rebellion broke out in Hungary. The causes of this rebellion included not only the tramping upon the Hungarian constitution by foreigners and the behavior of the German troops, but in addition to that, also religious controversies became violent and widespread. The violation of the constitution took place when the Court of Vienna refused to permit (ever since 1531) the vacancy of the palatin to be filled by election in the Diet. Furthermore, the Hungarians were irritated by the interference of the German royal advisers in Hungarian affairs, especially those of military and financial nature.

The religious controversies arose again because of mutual intolerance between the Catholics and the Protestants. Ever since the time of Ferdinand I, there were many adherents of Reformation in northern Hungary and their numbers steadily rose, especially among the nobility, and in the towns. Soon Protestantism became something of a national doctrine, in opposition to Catholicism, which allegedly was less patriotic. Since Rudolph, from his youth, was an ardent opponent of Protestantism, it was not difficult to persuade him to issue various edicts against the Hungarian adherents to this faith. This procedure rose to a climax when the king arbitrarily (motu proprio deque regiae suae potestatis plenitudine) added to the Hungarian Parliamentary acts of February 1604, also the article "22." By virtue of this article the king not only refused to comply with the petitions of the Hungarian Protestants, but also confirmed all the orders issued in favor of the Catholic Church ever since the reign of King St. Stephen. Finally, he ordered that those who would be in a mood to bring up religious problems in the Diet should be punished as initiators of disorder and dangerous innovations.

Upon this, an open rebellion broke out both in Hungary and Transylvania under the leadership of a Protestant nobleman, Stephen Bochkay, when his adherents, who were at the same time members of the Hungarian Diet, elected him the Prince of Hungary. Bochkay immediately entered into an agreement with the Turks, so that the court from now on had to fight on two sides. At the same time the newly elected prince summoned also the Croatians to recognize him as their sovereign but they denied him any such recognition. Moreover, the Croatian Diet accepted with enthusiasm (in Zagreb, July 5, 1604) the king's article "22," and decided that all the heretics (universi heretici) must be thrown out of Croatia. The Bishop of Zagreb, Shimun Bratulich, was entrusted with the execution of this act.

In the meantime Bochkay's army commander, Gregory Németh, set out towards Croatia. In their turn the Banus Ivan Drashkovich and the Estates decided to offer him resistance at the Drava River. But when Németh changed his mind about entering Croatia, the banus crossed the Drava and together with the king's troops, defeated Bochkay's forces.

In the meantime the sickly King Rudolph showed complete indifference to this dangerous rebellion. For this reason his brothers came to Prague and forced him to surrender the military and civilian affairs of Hungary and Croatia to his brother, Archduke Matthew. The new sovereign, knowing that he could not successfully resist two great enemies, Bochkay and the Turks, immediately engaged in negotiations with Bochkay and made a peace treaty in Vienna (23 June 1606), by which the Hungarian religious affairs were settled up to 1848. The peace treaty of Vienna provided that the nobility and citizens, who were town dwellers in Hungary proper (Infra ambitum regni Hungariae solum) might freely confess any religion of their choice, that is, both denominations became equal in rank, while article "22" of 1604, had been abrogated. Furthermore, a general amnesty was given and a promise made that the next Hungarian Diet could select a palatin, with whom the Archduke Matthew would consult and make decisions in the affairs of Hungary. The supreme treasurer, other dignitaries and military commanders in Hungary and Croatia might and could be exclusively native noblemen without regard to their religious faith.

Finally it had been agreed that Bochkay retain, as the Duke of Transylvania, also some neighboring Hungarian counties. Only after much hesitation King Rudolph, too, signed the peace treaty. But before the peace treaty was signed its draft was sent also to the Croatian Estates. The Croatian Diet, at its session of the 10th of April, 1606 in Zagreb, accepted essentially all its provisions but made a strong reservation against the exercise of religious freedom, and even expressed the desire to keep in force Rudolph's article "22" of 1604. Besides this, it was expressly stated that the king should see that "from now on and in the future he appoint to high offices and commanding military positions in Slavonia and Croatia only meritorious and loyal native sons, while the banus will be granted all his old privileges from Drava to the seacoast, that is, he will be at the head of the kingdom and its military districts."

The demands of the Croatian Diet were so strictly complied with that the freedom of religious faith was restricted, by the peace treaty of Vienna, only to Hungary. Somewhat later King Rudolph sanctioned the enactment of the Croatian Diet with regard to the exclusive recognition of the Catholic faith within the boundaries of Croatia and Slavonia (January 16, 1608), upon which it had been promulgated in the Diet as a law. Thus, the Croatian kingdom obtained its own special religious law, entirely in opposition to the Hungarian law.

MATTHEW II, FERDINAND II AND FERDINAND III
(1608-1657)

Rudolph and Matthew II

At the time Archduke Matthew negotiated with Bochkay and the Turks about a peace treaty, the state of Rudolph's mind went from bad to worse.

Living in isolation and away from the world in Prague in his palace at Hradchany, Rudolph was preoccupied exclusively with astrological forecasting and experiments in alchemistry. In this frame of mind he not only fully neglected the affairs of the state government, but he did not even permit anyone to come into his presence, not even his own brothers. So it happened that Rudolph, when they submitted to him the text of the peace treaty between Bochkay and the Turks for confirmation, refused for a long time to sign it.

As a result of this refusal a violent quarrel broke out between the two brothers, and when Matthew was joined not only by Hungarian and Croatian Estates but also by those of Bohemia and Austria, he entered Bohemia with an army. By a treaty signed in Liben, Matthew forced his brother to give him a suburb of Prague (24th of June, 1608) and to transfer the reins of government in Austria, Moravia, Hungary, and Croatia to him. Upon this he was crowned as Matthew II (1608-1619) in Pozhun as a Hungarian-Croatian king (19th November). Three years later King Matthew forced his brother to renounce also the Bohemian crown, and when Rudolph died (20 January, 1612) Matthew became, in addition, also the German-Roman Emperor.

Struggle of the Croatian Estates for the Military Districts. With the peace treaty concluded at the mouth of the Zhitva the Croatian Estates were of the opinion that the Croatian-Slavonian military district had become unnecessary. However, should it still be necessary, it should be returned to the mother country and placed under the supreme authority of the banus. But the Archduke Ferdinand not only turned deaf ears to that request, but also embarked on a course of subordination of the remaining civilian Croatia and Slavonia, to his own provincial generals and captains. This resolution became even firmer after Banus Ivan Drashkovich resigned at the Croatian Diet (in Zagreb 10th April, 1606). The Croatian Estates rose against that.

Before the crowning of Matthew in the Pozhun Diet, the Croatian Diet met in Zagreb early in September, 1608, for the purpose of selecting envoys to go to Pozhun with instructions to demand certain things from the new king. In these instructions the Croatian Diet demanded that all of the alien military commanders and alien troops be withdrawn from the Croatian towns, and especially from Varashdin as the center of the county, while the Banus should be invested with his ancient and exclusive authority from Drava down to the sea. But since the Austrian provinces, proper, financially supported the military district with their own funds, and because, therefore, the Archdukes were allowed to exercise some authority in the administration of the military districts, the Croatian Diet was of the opinion that in this matter King Matthew should make some arrangements with Archduke Ferdinand.

The military vacancies had to be filled under all circumstances by the meritorious native sons, since "the Croatian estates have decided sooner to die than to have henceforth, aliens rule over them or to have to perform any kind of service at the detriment of their freedom." King Matthew

II accepted the demands of the Croatian Diet, and even appointed the popular Thomas Erdody as banus (1608-1614). But in spite of all that, the situation which was causing so much dissatisfaction and protests among the Croatian nobility about the military provinces, remained as it was before.

The reason for this was Archduke Ferdinand's stubborn resistance. So all the embassies of the Croatian Diet, both to Graz and Pozhun were unsuccessful in their mission. In connection therewith the Croatian Estates declared in the Diet that (in Zagreb 20th April 1610) they were aware "that the king (Matthew II) is willing to fulfill their desires, but there is a certain person who is raising obstacles to such a move and dissuading the king from carrying out his decision. Consequently the mission of the Croatian embassies sent both to Pozhun and Gratz was frustrated." However, "if such a destroyer of the general liberties is detected, the hands of the whole kingdom, belonging to all estates and orders, will be raised at him." Who that person was, is not known with certainty, but very probably it was Baron Sigismund Trautmansdorf, general of Slavonia. Even though the Croatians rejoiced over the appointment of Thomas Erdody as their banus, they were painfully impressed by the king's reluctance to install him solemnly in the Diet, with the rites celebrated in accordance with the age-old tradition. This was also interpreted as the result of the intrigue and secret interference of the German officers of the military district. Thus the Diet complained on several occasions via the embassies to the king, but always without effect.

In view of this, Thomas Erdody resigned the banus' office in the Diet (Zagreb, 27th November 1614) for the second time, and only upon the pleading of the Estates, he retained the administration of the country until the appointment of a new banus.

Benedict Thuroczy of Ludbreg was immediately installed in the banus office (1615-1616) without military honors befitting the occasion and climaxed by receiving the royal flag as a symbol of supreme military authority in the kingdom. Furthermore, the banus was denied funds for the support of the native royal troops. The new banus died the next year (9th November 1616), upon which the king appointed

Nicholas Frankapan of Terzhats (1616-1622), who was solemnly installed into his office on the 6th December 1616. During his tenure of banus' office the complicated problem of the refugees (Uskoki) found its final solution.

Refugees (Annotation #1)
(Prebyegi and Uskoki)

After the fall of Bosnia (1463) and Herzegovina, (1482) a part of the population (chiefly of the Catholic faith), which was loath of submitting to the Turks, found refuge in neighboring Croatia and Slavonia. These refugees were called in the Slavonian areas usually "prebyegi or prebyezi" meaning refugees, and in the southern Croatian parts they were known as "Uskoki" or fugitives. There was a number of such refugee groups but the best known is the one which began to assemble in 1530, around the stronghold of Klis near Split. Here Captain Peter Kruzhich of Senj received them in the service as hired soldiers since Klis belonged to his command. These groups naturally came from Bosnia and Herzegovina. From Klis the Uskoki made more and more frequent raids into the neighboring Turkish regions, and for this reason the Turks were determined to capture the city which they actually did on the 12th of March, 1537.

At this turn the Uskoki migrated to Senj, the center of the captaincy, under which they settled down. So at this time the name of "Uskoki" was applied to all the soldiers of Senj captaincy from the banks of the Ryechina (Fiumara) to the mouth of the Zermanya on the seacoast and to Brinje and Otochats in the interior. The position of Senj, with its mountainous background and island promontories and moreover with its famous bura storm, was such that it was not an easy job to capture it either from the seaside or inland. At that time (1537) Senj was under the command of the war council of Lyublyana. Later on (since 1564), it was under the authority of the court of Gratz which was the administrative center of the captaincy of Senj as a constituent part of the Croatian military province. By this arrangement the Uskoki became soldiers in the Croatian military province and, with their descendants, they were in charge of the city garrison for more than eighty years. The garrison was divided into four companies, headed by their native chiefs (voyevodes).

Little by little, frequently under the threat of some punishment, a large number of refugees from Venetian Dalmatia joined these Uskoki in Senj. For this reason the Uskoki were not a uniform ethnic group, since, besides an overwhelming majority of Croatian Catholics, the Orthodox Serbs and some Italians (called Venturini) composed the city population. The Uskoki were a very daring lot, armed with gun and hatchet and sometimes also with a dagger. They could bear privation and all kinds of hardships. Besides this, they knew every corner, both in the Velebit ranges, at that time occupied by the Turks, and on the islands. They were entitled to a monthly pay, but rarely received it. Thus, by the force of circumstances and since the vicinity of Senj bore no produce or crops*, the Uskoki had to support themselves by plunder and looting. The Croatian military district was in continuous warfare with the Turks so the Uskoki most frequently seized Turkish food supplies both on land and sea. On land they foraged the Turkish Lika and Dalmatia, which at that time was for the most part in Turkish power.

It stands to reason that because of the continuous "small" wars in the military province, no one ever thought of preventing the Uskoki from fighting the Turks. Even Venice aided them when she was at war with the Turks, permitting the Uskoki to pass through her own territories into Turkish lands. But when Venice made peace with Turkey (1540), the High Porte insisted that Venice stop giving aid to the Uskoki since they usually attacked and seized the Turkish vessels in the Adriatic Sea. In order to comply with Turkish demands the Venetians undertook to carry the Turkish goods in their own vessels. But then the Uskoki arrested the Venetian vessels, demanding that they turn over the Turkish cargo to them. Now Sultan Suleiman informed Venice that, since the Venetians were not able to maintain order in the Adriatic Sea, he would dispatch his navy in order to capture Senj and eradicate the Uskoki. But the Venetians would not permit the Turkish navy under any circumstances to enter allegedly "their" sea, the "Gulf of Venice" so the conflict between the Uskoki and Venice became inevitable.

* Similar was the case of the German garrison of Karlovats. Since the soldiers did not get their pay and supplies, they were forced to plunder the nearby Christian population.

The first conflicts are recorded already in the year 1557, when the Venetian navy for the first time blockaded the port of Senj. Yet when Venice again engaged in war with the Turks (Cyprus war) from 1570-1573, the Venetians again renewed their friendly ties with the Uskoki, but immediately after the conclusion of the peace treaty with the Turks, they again broke them off. However, the real bitter conflicts between the Uskoki and the Venetians took place after the battle of Klis (1596), in which the Venetians aided the Turks. In the same way as the brave Narentians (Neretvlyani) during the reign of the National Dynasties, so also the Uskoki, with their bold attacks, interfered or prevented the free navigation of Venice in the Adriatic Sea. They were attacking the Venetian ships and confiscating their cargo with such success that all of the Venetian power was not able to cope with them.

This long and spectacular struggle breaks into two periods. The first period ends with the assassination of General Joseph Rabatta (31 December 1601) who was sent to Senj with the mission of restoring peace and order, in which he completely failed. With his cynicism and cruelty he stirred up a rebellion in the course of which he lost his life.

The second period continued to the so-called Uskoki War (1615-1617) and peace treaty of Madrid (1617). Throughout this time Venice was negotiating with Archduke Ferdinand in Gratz and Kings Rudolph and Matthew II. But all her moves were of no avail since the court in the clutches of general destitution and distress could not regularly pay the Uskoki and support them. The result of all this was an open war between the Uskoki and Venice, while fighting on land was carried on around the cities of Goritsa (Gorizia) and Gradishka on Socha (Isonzo river). After two years of stubborn fighting a peace treaty was signed in Madrid through the mediation of Spain and France. According to the provisions of this agreement, Archduke Ferdinand bound himself to move the Uskoki from Senj somewhere in the interior of the country, to set their ships on fire, and to garrison the city of Senj with German troops. The Uskoki then were transferred to the Zhumberak (Schonberg) area on the Istrian coast and nearby islands. During 30 years of fighting the

Uskoki it cost Venice 20 million ducats through the loss of shipping and bearing the expenses of the war.

In the meantime the Uskoki gradually merged with the native population of their new homeland, leaving behind only legends of their warlike exploits.

Election and Coronation of Ferdinand II

At the time the sickly Matthew appointed Nicholas Frankapan of Terzhats banus of Croatia, he had for some time planned to bequeath all his dominions to his nephew Archduke Ferdinand of Styria, since he himself had no children of his own. For this purpose he called the Hungarian Diet by the end of 1617 to Pozhun in order to elect and crown the king of Hungary and Croatia. The Archduke by that time had already been elected and crowned king of Bohemia and Moravia (June 1617). Before the Hungarian Estates met in Pozhun the Croatian Estates were called to the Diet in order to elect their own envoys who were to be sent to Pozhun. On this occasion Nicholas Frankapan was solemnly installed in his high office with full military honors and the royal banner (banderium). In the meantime the Diet of Pozhun met, because of the king's illness in March of the next year, and after protracted negotiations elected Archduke Ferdinand to the throne by the middle of May. Yet it took another six weeks for the coronation exercises because the Diet was bent on discussing its grievances to make sure the new king would remedy them.

The Croatian envoys renewed their complaints in view of restoring the banus' authority which should extend also to the military provinces. Furthermore, since the general of Karlovats, Count Adam Trautmansdorf died in 1617 and left his place vacant, they requested King Matthew to appoint Nicholas Frankapan of Terzhats also the general so that the Croatian military province might again be subjected to the authority of the banus. Finally, the elected King Ferdinand guaranteed, in a special inaugural decree to the Croatian kingdom, that he will fulfill all the desires of the Croatian kingdom when he ascends the throne (June 17, 1618). He was crowned Hungarian-Croatian king on the 1st of July, 1618 and on this occasion the Banus Nicholas Frankapan carried the royal scepter, the younthful Count Kersto Erdody carried the banner of Slavonia while Count Julius Zrinski carried the banner of Croatia. Soon after this King Matthew died (28th March 1619). He left to his nephew in heritage the throne and the 30 Years War, which broke out at the time of the Pozhun Diet because of religious strife in Bohemia.

Ferdinand II (1619-1637)

The reign of Ferdinand II is filled with continuous struggles not only in Bohemia and Germany but also in Hungary with the Transylvania, i.e. Duke Gabriel Bethlen whom the Hungarians proclaimed as their king while the Turks supported the move. The Croatians participated in both these wars as light cavalrymen, usually called arquebusiers, who would always start and finish the battle on their small but swift horses. In the army of Wallenstein, the Croatians were led by Julius Zrinski (1622-1626), father of brothers Nicholas and Peter. He died suddenly during his campaign against Mansfield (in Pozhun, 18 December 1626) in his 28th year.

After him, the Croatians were under the command of various imperial generals (Count Ivan Isolano, Count Ivan Werth and Walter Leslie), who distinguished themselves in all the more important battles. It is said that in the battle of Luetzen (16 November 1632), the Swedish King, Gustavus Adolphus, fell exactly from their hand; while in the famous imperial victory near Noerdlingen (September 7, 1634) their courage contributed a great deal to the issue of the battle. During the 30 Years War (during the reign of Ferdinand III, son of Ferdinand II) both brothers, Nicholas and Peter Zrinski, distinguished themselves in many battles and engagements.

Problem of the Military Districts

In spite of their meritorious service and heroic exploits in the long campaigns, the central imperial government denied the Croats their requests which had been approved by royal decree to have the military province subjected to the banus and the Diet. Moreover, precisely during the reign of Ferdinand II, who issued the solemn decree to have the wishes of Croatia fulfilled, the internal organization of the Military Province was consolidated. From that time on that province was split into two generalships; one governed from Karlovats, extending over the Croatian Province; and the other from Varazhdin, including the Slavonian Province.

Furthermore, since these areas had been depopulated as a result of continuous warfare, the German generals sought to attract the orthodox Serbs or Wallachians with various privileges from the Turkish border area. They also protected them from the Croatian land nobility which demanded in the Diet to use the newcomers as serfs since they had settled on their property. They also insisted that the Turkish settlers pay a tithe to the Catholic bishops. Because of these differences sharp conflicts arose between the Croatian Estates and the central government in Vienna.

The disputes were ended by a decree of Ferdinand II issued on October 5, 1630 to the immigrants. The decree provided that they would not be the serfs of the Croatian estate-holders but merely perform military service in the district. They also could freely elect their village chiefs who in turn would appoint their own judges. With this unconstitutional act Ferdinand II established in the military districts a separate territory removed entirely from the authority of the banus and the Diet. This further mincing of the disastrously reduced Croatian land moved the Croatian Estates to strengthen their ties with the Hungarians for the purpose of common defense.

Ferdinand III (1637-1657)

To the problem of territorial integrity was joined also the problem of survival of the constitution after the death of Ferdinand II (15 February 1637), and during the reign of his son and successor Ferdinand III.

After the peace of Westphalia (1648) it was seriously planned in Vienna to place Hungary and Croatia on the same level with the Austrian lands, that is, to reduce them to the status of provinces. This plan was patterned after the case of Bohemia, which was reduced to the level of a province after "Belohorska (White Mountain) battle" in 1621. For this reason the banus, Nicholas Zrinsky (1647-1664) had to fight with determination for his judicial authority, while his effort to obtain the generalship of Karlovats was entirely unsuccessful. Moreover, it was not looked upon with favor in Vienna, that the brothers,

Nicholas and Peter Zrinsky had bravely repulsed the Turkish inroads into their possessions (which continued unchecked regardless of the peace at Zhitva) especially near Kostaynitsa (in August 1651). These developments resulted in a tense situation between the Croatian Estates and German Officers, who preferred comfort to military exploits, but made themselves conspicuous with their frivolity and arrogance. This unfortunate situation led to disaster with fatal consequences after the death of Ferdinand III (April 2, 1657).

THE REIGN OF LEOPOLD I UP TO THE GREAT WAR FOR LIBERATION (1657-1683)

The First Turkish War

Ferdinand IV, the eldest son of Ferdinand, was crowned during the lifetime of his father as Hungarian-Croatian king (16 June 1647) but died even before the death of his father (9 July 1654). He was succeeded by his younger son, Leopold I (1657-1705). The young king was of weak bodily constitution, silent and indecisive. But otherwise, he was distinguished by sincere piety and modest mode of life. He had no power of independence and listened to his advisers concerning every matter and approving always of their proposals. Of course there is nothing wrong in that. However, Leopold I unfortunately was surrounded by weak and sometimes vicious individuals, some of whom were under foreign influence, especially that of the French king Louis XIV, the great enemy of the Hapsburg House. But as if in compensation, the Providence made him beneficiary of a series of glorious generals who exalted his name and extended the frontiers of his dominion.

In the meantime the conditions in Transylvania became embroiled. There the Austrian faction elected John Kemenyi as their duke, while the Turkish faction raised Michael Apafi to the ducal throne. Because of his interference in the affairs of Transylvania, Leopold, soon after his ascension to the imperial throne, became entangled in the first Turkish War (1663-1664), against his will. In Hungary the main imperial leader and chief commander was General Montecuccoli, while in Croatia and southwest Hungary, banus Nicholas Zrinski and his brother Peter commanded the imperial troops. The two brothers welcomed the war since they saw in the armed struggle a promise of salvation for Croatia and restoration of her pristine power. Still in 1660 Nicholas Zrinski wanted to attack the Turkish Kanizha, but the war council of the court prohibited that. He submitted to this order but in the next year he built at the confluence of the Mura and Drava Rivers a powerful stronghold to which he gave the name of Novi Zrinj. During the great war he successfully smashed at Mura River, with a force of 300 Croatian cavalrymen, 2,000 Tartars, as they were attempting to break into Styria (November 1663). Almost at the same time, his brother Peter destroyed near Otochats, with a force of 2,500 men, the army of Ali Pasha Chengich, 10,000 strong, as it was making ready to break into Carniola and Istria. At the beginning of 1664 (from the 13th of January to 15th February), Nicholas Zrinsky broke into the south Hungarian Drava valley, captured Bobalishche (Babocha) and Pechuh, reaching down to Osiek where he set on fire the famous bridge of Suleiman which spanned the Drava river. The bridge was four miles long and about 50 feet wide. Its construction took six years (1529-1535) with a force of 30,000 workmen.

All of Europe admired the war fortunes of the two Zrinski brothers. For this reason the Grand Vezir, Ahmed Koeproeli (Chuprilich), set out at the head of a huge army to attack Nicholas. He laid siege to Novi Zrinj and took it on the 30th of June, through the fault of General Montecuccoli, a personal enemy of Nicholas Zrinski, who refused to come to the aid of the town although he was stationed in the neighborhood of Zrinj. After the capture and destruction of Novi Zrinj the Grand Vezir turned north toward Vienna. But on the first of August, 1664, his troops were met near St. Gotthard on Rab (Raab) River by the forces of Montecuccoli and an auxiliary French troop, who fully annihilated them.

This was one of the most brilliant Christian victories and the beginning of a series of successful wars which repulsed the Turkish tide. But the indecisive imperial war council, instead of prosecuting the war with more vigor and annihilating the enemy, hastened to offer peace, which was concluded in the near-by city of

Vasvár (Iron City) for a period of 20 years. By the terms of this treaty the Turks not only retained all their possessions owned at that time, but were paid 200,000 Austrian thalers by Leopold as war indemnity.

Annotations to Battle of Kossovo

The Battle of Kossovo (Blackbird field)

The following article is taken from the book of Stanley Lane-Poole entitled "Turkey," page 42-22.

"It was a bloody battle, one of the bloodiest battles between the Crusaders and the Moslems in history.

"Sultan Murad's general, Ali Pasha, crossed the Balkan by the Derbent Pass, descended upon Shumla, seized Tirnova and brought Shishman, the king of Bulgaria to his knees. Besieged in Nicopolis, the prince surrendered, and Bulgaria was immediately annexed to the Ottoman empire, of which the Danube now formed the northern frontier.

"Lazarus, the Serbian, though deprived of his Bulgarian ally, was not yet daunted. He challenged Murad to the battle, and the opposing forces met (1389) on the plain of Kossovo by the banks of Sitnitsa river. Serbs, Bosnians, Skipitars (Albanians), Poles, Magyars, Vlachs were massed on the north side of the stream. The Ottomans, under Murad himself, were on the south side supported by his vassals and allies of Europe and Asia. The sultan spent the night before the battle in prayer for the help of God and a martyr's death, for like all true Moslems, he coveted the crowning glory of dying in fight with the Infidels. In the morning he saw the answer to his petitions in the rain which laid the clouds of dust that were driving blindingly in the faces of the Turkish troops. When the sky cleared the two armies came forward and were drawn up in battle array.

"Lazarus commanded the center of the Christian line, his nephew Vuk Brankovich, the right; Vlatko Vukovich, the lieutenant of Tvartko, King of Bosnia, the left. On the Turkish side Murad himself was in the center, his sons Bayazid and Yakub commanded the right and left wings, and Haydar ranged his artillery on the brow of the hill behind the main body.

"The battle was long and obstinately contested. At one time the left wing of the Turks wavered, but its courage was restored by the charge of Bayazid whose rapidity of action had earned him the name of Yildirim (thunder bolt). He raged through the ranks of the enemy, brandishing a mighty iron mace, and felling all who came in his way. He renewed his fight with such fury that the Turks, who before were so discouraged that they fled in the left wing, began to turn again upon their enemy; and the Christians, thinking that the victory was already theirs, were to begin a great battle in which many thousands fell on both sides. The armor and weapons were as bright as lightning; the multitude of the lancers and other horsemen's staves shadowed the light of the sun, arrows and darts fell so fast that a man would have thought they had poured down from heaven; the noise of the instruments of war, with the neighing of the horses and the outcries of men, were so terrible and great that the wild beasts of the mountain were astonished therewith; and the Turkish histories, to expose the terror of the day, vainly say that the angels in Heaven, amazed with that hideous noise, for that time forgot the heavenly hymns wherewith they always glorify God. About noontide of the day, the fortune of the Turks prevailing, the Christians began to give ground, and at length betook themselves to plain flight; whom the Turks, with all their force, pursued and slew men down without number or mercy." The field, says the Turkish chronicles, was like a tulip bed, with bloody severed heads and rolling turbans.

Annotation No. 2

Sultan Bayazid's Testimony

The text below is taken from Sultan Bayazid's firman (imperial order) to the Kadhi of Brussa, Suleiman-Beg, dated the month of Shaban 791, that is 1389. This firman is preserved in Constantinople in the Archives of the State.

"When this firman comes into your hands (wrote the sultan) you ought to know that there was, in accordance with Allah's will, a battle on the field of Kossovo. My father, Sultan Murad, whose life had been happy and whose death was that of a martyr, prayed after a vision in a dream, to Allah to make him worthy of martyrdom. The battle being ended, he returned unhurt in his full health from the battlefield to the tent, which was elevated towards the heavens. And while we enjoyed the greatest pleasure, in seeing how the cut heads of the Christian dukes rolled under the horses' feet, and how many of them with tied hands and others with broken legs stood, suddenly there appeared a fighter by the name of Milosh Obilich. He came perfidiously saying that he accepted Islam and asking that he might so be ranked in the victorious army. And when he, after his own wish was allowed to kiss the feet of the illustrious Sultan, he drew a poisonous hanjar (dagger), hidden in his sleeve, and boldly thrust it into the body of the Sultan, sorely wounding him. Well, he caused the illustrious Sultan to drink the sherbet of martyrdom. After Milosh finished this deed, he tried to escape through the soldiers who shone like the stars in the sky, but by them he was caught and cut in pieces.

"Having been informed about this event I came to the martyr's bed but I found the Sultan dead. At the same time, it happened that my brother, Yakub, departed into eternity. I am sending the shining body of my father there (to Brussa) to be buried. When the corpse arrives you are to bury it in secrecy without informing anybody about the real event."

Annotation No. 3

Another description of the situation between the battle on the Maritsa river and the Kossovo (Blackbird) plain.

This is from W. Miller's description, "Balkans," page 283 and the following:

"The Turks, under the able leadership of Murad I, one of the greatest generals of his time, continued their career of conquest. Their advance in the direction of Serbia aroused Vukashin's fears for the safety of his throne. Summoning the chieftains together, he implored them to forget their dissensions and join him in a campaign against the Turkish conqueror. An army almost as large as the one which followed Dushan on his last expedition (toward Constantinople) was collected, and Vukashin believed himself to be the leader of a new Crusade. At first his efforts were successful and Murad received a severe

check on the spot, where a few years earlier the Serbs had been routed with such loss. But in the dead of the night Murad surprised the Serbian camp and completely destroyed the Christian army.

"The news of the Serbian defeat excited the greatest alarm all over Christendom. The Pope lamented loudly that nothing could withstand the onward march of the Turks. The Serbs thought that the sole chance of their safety lay in the election of Lazarus, a connection by marriage with Dushan's dynasty, in whose wars he had served with great distinction.

"Lazarus, the last of the Serbian tsars, ascended the throne in 1371 under gloomy circumstances. He did not deem it prudent to attack the victorious Turks until he had time to recruit his scattered forces, and so quietly looked on while Macedonia gradually fell into their hands.

"But at last the Christian States of the Balkans discovered too late that they must unite against the Ottoman power.

"In the fastness of the Black Mountain (Montenegro), where the Turks were in the coming centuries to see so many fatal reverses, a body of Serbs and Albanians utterly routed the Ottoman force. Murad I, who was celebrating his marriage in Asia-Minor when the news reached him, vowed vengeance. Hurrying back to Europe he collected an enormous army and marched against the Serbs."

"The battle, which was to decide for five centuries the fate of the Balkan Peninsula, was fought on the plain of Kossovo, the "field of Blackbirds" as it is called in Serbia, from the flocks of those creatures which frequent it.

"Shut in by a chain of mountains, and a vast extent, the plain seemed intended by nature for an Armageddon of nations. Around this spot, the Waterloo of Balkans' freedom, clusters a whole literature of patriotic ballads, from which it is no easy task to discern the true story of that fatal day. The Serbs, Bosnians and Albanians were banded together in the common cause under Lazarus' leadership.

"On the morning of June 28, 1389, the battle of the Dervishes began. Murad had perished."

Croatian-Hungarian Kings, after the extinction of the Arpad Dynasty (from 1301 until 1918)

1. Vencel (Czech) 1301-1304
2. Otto (Bavarian) 1304-1308
3. Charles-Robert (Angevine) 1308-1340
4. Louis the Great (Angevine) 1340-1382
5. Maria (Angevine)
                   1382-1385 and 1386-1395
6. Charles of Durazzo (Angevine) ... 1385-1386
7. Ladislaus of Naples (Angevine) ... 1396-1409
8. Sigismund of Luxemburg 1410-1437
9. Albert of the Habsburg House 1438-1439
10. Vladislav I Yaghellonian 1440-1444
11. Ladislaus IV (V) 1445-1457
12. Governor John Hunyadi (effective
        ruler) 1446-1452
13. Mathias I. Corvinus 1458-1490
14. Vladislav II 1490-1516
15. Louis II 1516-1526
16. John Zapolski 1526-1540

Habsburgs

17. Ferdinand 1527-1564
18. Maximilian 1564-1576
19. Rudolph 1576-1608
20. Mathias II 1608-1619
21. Ferdinand II 1619-1637
22. Ferdinand III 1637-1657
23. Leopold I 1657-1705
24. Joseph I 1705-1711
25. Charles III 1711-1740
26. Maria-Theresa 1740-1780

Lotharingians

27. Joseph II 1780-1790
28. Leopold II 1790-1792
29. Francis I 1792-1835
30. Ferdinand V 1835-1848
31. Francis Joseph I 1848-1916
32. Charles IV 1916-1918

Kings of Yugo-Slavia

1. Alexander I 1918-1934
2. Peter II (minor) 1934-1945

Plate 5.

A. The view of the mosque in Banya Luka. *B.* A mosque erected by the Government of the Independent Croatian nation in spite of its division into Catholic, Orthodox and Moslem denominations. One of the first acts of the Communist government was to raze the minarets and turn the mosque into an office building.

(Engraving by courtesy of Mr. Stanley Boric.)

Section II

BOSNIA AND HERZEGOVINA FROM ANCIENT TIMES UNTIL THE END OF THE CRETAN WAR (1669)

TO which race the inhabitants of Butmir, Glasinats, Yezerine and other settlements of the stone, bronze, and iron ages belonged, cannot be guessed, and their tribal relationships will in all probability remain unknown forever. But the first known inhabitants of Bosnia were the Illyrians who settled there in La Téne period, and whose present-day descendants are perhaps the Albanians or Shkipetars. By the end of the 5th century, B.C., two Illyrian tribes are mentioned as the masters of the country: the Ardians and Autariates. The Ardians lived east of Liburnium (in other words on the present Croatian coast of the North Adriatic), a hard drinking people who owned slaves and were known as fighters. The Autariates lived in the southwestern part of Bosnia and Herzegovina. West of them, around the estuary of the Neretva (Narenta) and opposite the islands of Brach (Brattia) and Hvar (Lesina), lived the Nestians and Manians, two small tribes.

Around 380 B.C. the Celts swooped down on the Balkans and occupied the Morava valley, driving a wedge between the Illyrians and Thracians. Twenty years later they struck at the Ardians and drove them south to the mouth of the Neretva. Next they attacked the Autariates and temporarily drove the Illyrians from ancient Bosnia. After this for nearly three centuries we have no report, either from Bosnia or the nearby lands. During the Roman invasions of Dalmatia the hard-pressed Illyrian tribes returned to the western mountains of Bosnia. The mountain people joined with them and in 170 B.C., the natives of Dalmatia, Liburnium and western Bosnia made a defensive alliance against the Romans in the town Delminium, near the Bosnian frontier.

The Roman Authority and Civilization

During nearly a century of fighting the Romans conquered not only Dalmatia, but also Bosnia and Herzegovina, extending their power to the Drina river in the east, the Sava in the north, the Drim in the south. In 87 B.C. they incorporated all this territory into the Roman province of Illyricum. However, neither the Illyrian nor Celtic inhabitants had been fully subdued, and in 6 A.D. a powerful uprising broke out in Illyricum and Pannonia under the leadership of Bato and Pines. The rebels destroyed the capital of Sirmium and laid siege to Salona, capital of Dalmatia. The uprising was eventually crushed, but not until three years of struggle had laid the country in ruins. Later when the Romans moved their frontiers east and north, the enlarged territory was divided into three administrative areas or provinces: Dalmatia, Pannonia and Noricum. There was no special administrative unit for Bosnia and Herzegovina; the larger part of the country was attached to Dalmatia, and the northern strip to Pannonia.

In Roman times, Dalmatia itself was divided into three administrative districts, the northern, with Scardona as administrative center, the central, with Salona as the capital, and the southern governed from Narona. Thus Bosnia belonged to Salona, and Herzegovina, together with Montenegro and northern Albania, to Narona. According to Roman and Greek writers, Bosnia was inhabited by the Delmati, Ceraunii, Dindarii and Daesitiates, all small, but brave native tribes.

The known inhabitants of Herzegovina were: Ardians, Daorsi, Naresii and Deramestae.

After pacifying the area, the Romans turned with zeal to the task of civilizing the country, and improving it throughout. They built highways, spanned the rivers with solid bridges, some of which are used today, fortified towns, built strongholds, developed trade, encouraged crafts, opened up gold and silver mines, and eventually elevated both the culture and prosperity of the country.

Numerous inscriptions, ruins of temples and public buildings bear testimony to the efforts of the Romans to make the country strong and prosperous. Bosnia was both of economic and strategic importance: through it the Romans could reach out for the central and lower Danube, and eastward through Moesia to the Black Sea. The Roman roads in Bosnia played a most important role during the migrations, for the Barbarians from the north and east used them in advancing to the Adriatic. Some of them are still preserved.

There are no reports on the introduction and diffusion of Christian doctrines in Bosnia and Herzegovina. However, we may guess that the development of early Christianity in Dalmatia proper was paralleled in Bosnia and Herzegovina, the nearest administrative districts of that Province. By the 6th century of our era several bishoprics, among them the diocese of Bistue, had been established in Bosnia under the authority of the archbishop of Salona.

Barbarian Inroads

After the downfall of the western Roman Empire (476 A.D.), Bosnia and Herzegovina went through an ordeal of invasion and conquest as did Dalmatia and Pannonia, of which they were components. First came the Ostro-Goths under Theodoric in 493, to hold sway until 535 A.D. when the Byzantine Emperor Justinian engaged them in a war of twenty years which left the country prostrate.

In the course of this struggle the Slavs appeared in the area for the first time. After a first incursion in 548 A.D., they returned in 551 and 553, apparently as allies of the Goths against Byzantium. The Goths suffered a crushing defeat and in 555 Bosnia and Herzegovina submitted to Byzantium. But the might of the emperors could not stop the barbarian invasions for long. The Slavs came back, at first apparently alone, later in the company of the Avars. Their joint campaign of 598, when they broke out from Sirmium and forced their way through Bosnia and Dalmatia proper, again brought devastation to the province. Forty strongholds were taken and demolished and the invaders ravaged the country without mercy. In 617 they destroyed the Dalmatian capital Salona, together with a number of flourishing towns.

Toward the middle of the 7th century the Croats appeared in Dalmatia, having been invited by Heraclius, Emperor of Byzantium.

(For Roman antiquities in Bosnia and Herzegovina, see: Arthur Evans, "Through Bosnia and Herzegovina," London, 1876.)

Bosnia: Place Names: Kinship of Croats and Serbs

The name Bosnia represents an instance of geographic and ethnographic extension of a place-name south of the Sava and north of the Piva, Tara, and Lim rivers. The origin of the name is prehistoric; it is certainly neither Croat nor Roman, and its significance is unknown, although it could have meant something in the nature of "clear water." This name did not spread east of the Drina or west of the Neretva (Narenta) rivers although the upper reaches of both rivers are in places within 15 miles of each other.

The territory embraced by the winding course of the Neretva was called Hum (old form Hulm), meaning "hills, highland" or "Zahumlye," literally "Tramontane; land beyond the hills." In general, the Slavs are fond of designating their countries or local areas by names of mountains, rivers, or fields. So we have Crna Gora "Montenegro," lit. "Black mountain," but formerly Zeta from the river of the same name. "Polska," Poland, literally, "Field-country." In Dalmatia we have "Zagora," in Croatia "Zagorye," literally "Tramontane." Further: Posavina meaning "Sava"; Podravina meaning Drava; Podunavlye, or "Danube"; Pokuplye, "Kupa"; Podrinye, meaning Drina-valley, etc. Later in the 15th century the country was given the political name of "Herzegovina," lit. "Duchy of St. Savvas," which it keeps up to the present.

In Roman times the name "Bosnia" was not used for the country south of the line of Zvornik, Maglay, Banya Luka. The land was called Dalmatia, and north of it Pannonia. The only reference from this period is the name of a town "Ad Bassantes," which according to some was located at the mouth of the Bosut river and, according to others, at the mouth of Bosna river, in Pannonia proper. The name could well have been spread southward by the movement of the people along the Bosna river valley.

The chronicle of the Priest of Dioclea indicates that Bosnia originally belonged to Croatia. The Banus of Bosnia was a vassal of King Tomislav and paid his debt of allegiance to his sovereign at the latter's coronation—as did the princes of Trebonia (Herzegovina) and Dioclea ("Red Croatia," later "Montenegro"). And Tomislav's large army of 40,000 horsemen and 100,000 footsoldiers would not have been recruited at that time without the manpower of the Bosnian and Herzegovinian lands. (W. Tomaschek. Die vorslavische Topographie der Bosnia-Herzegovina, etc., 1880.)

It is not known that Tomislav or any of his predecessors had waged war against these provinces, therefore, their attachment to the King of Croatia must have been the result of consanguinity and tribal organization. During a dynastic strife, Dioclea later drifted away from the Croatia in order to become, under the name of Zeta, the organizing center of the Serbian State. Relations between the Bosnian and Serbian ruling families were friendly and intimate as were those between the Croatians and Serbs until in later times when the Croatian State effected a personal union with the Royal House of Hungary. Even then intermarriages between the Serbian and Croatian princes were frequent.

The difference between Serbs and Croats before their conversion to Christianity and up to the separation of the Churches was negligible, if at all discernible. The bitterness and provocation of the strife between Rome and Constantinople, plus the dissension introduced by the Bosnian sectarianism and later Islam, left such deep traces in the lives of Serbs and Croats that the split between them constantly widened, and the breach was never healed.

In the course of time and under the stress of the stormy episodes of Bosnian history, the ethnical character of its population underwent some changes. Yet from the purely ethnographic point of view, the population of Bosnia and Herzegovina is still substantially Croatian, although modified by later migrations from Serbian areas, and by the many nomadic elements that wandered in during the Turkish rule from the East, or were forcibly imported by the Sultans as farm-hands, and attached to the estates of the Mohammedan nobility.

Slavic Settlers and Beginnings of the Bosnian State

In the twilight of the 7th, 8th and 9th Centuries the small and scattered Slavic clans maintained themselves in the new country, and assimilated the remnants of the ancient native populations. Gradually the clans became grouped locally and regionally into larger districts (Zhupa) controlled by an administrative head called Zhupan (Gothic

Siponeis). The more influential Zhupans gradually brought the several administrative districts under the supreme authority of a banus.

The banate of Bosnia was from the beginning a member of the Croatian tribal confederation, and only second in importance to the banus of White Croatia. Moreover, as elector of the Croatian Kingdom, the Bosnian banus was eligible to the Croatian throne. In the reign of Zvonimir the Bosnian banus was an opponent of the king who in exalting his own power, tried to curtail that of the bani. After the disaster of Peter Svachich, the banus of Bosnia remained the only champion of Croatian independence ready to cross his sword with that of king Koloman. The power and prestige of the Bosnian banus was enhanced through the retreat of the Croatian national party to the mountains of Bosnia, a political migration that continued for nearly a generation. There the Croatian nobility, with its national traditions, equally adverse to Latins and Hungarians, reestablished its skill and energies to the development of Bosnia.

Thus, Croatia's loss in the coastal area and along the Drava river, was a gain to the mountain ranges of Bosnia where a strong political power and national church organization arose to give anxiety both to the Roman Church, which was still adverse to the Croatian liturgy, and to the kings of Hungary who needed Bosnia for the territorial continuity of their dominion between Hungary and Dalmatia.

Some Early Records

In 955 Bosnia was invaded by the Hungarians under the leadership of Prince Kes but the Serbian Prince Cheslav defeated them at Tsvilina on the uper Drina. According to Porphyrogenete, the Hungarians lost nearly all their men on the field of battle.

In 968 Kreshimir of Croatia defeated the Bosnian banus. In 1019 Bosnia and Serbia both were occupied by the Byzantine Emperor Basilius II, Bulgaroctones ("Destroyer of Bulgars"). But after the death of Basilius Bosnia regained her independence and carried on under her own native Bani.

In 1082 the king of Dioclea Bodin subdued both Bosnia and Serbia and reigned over them through his Zhupans.

On the 15th of June, 1103, king Koloman in

a patent issued to the city of Split, assumed for the first time the title of king of Bosnia (. . . rex Ramae), along-side his titles: king of Hungary, Dalmatia and Croatia.

The Bosnian bani, due to their exalted position, became the leaders of Croatia and by defending their own rights emanating from pacta conventa,* they defended the rights of Croatia stemming from the same source. Thus, in union with Hungary the constitutional relationship between Croatia and Bosnia was tightened and the two often appeared together either as allies or opponents of Hungary. So under banus Borich, Bosnia and Croatia fought beside the Hungarian King Geza II and his Serbian allies in the struggle against Byzantium, of which Emmanuel Komnenos was then emperor. Komnenos defeated the Serbs in 1151 on Tara river, and drove the Hungarians from his province Sirmium. Later when the Hungarians laid siege to Branichevo, a city on the lower Danube, Komnenos dispersed them, and sent one of his generals in pursuit of Banus Borich. This force was annihilated near Belgrade by the Hungarians, and Borich returned to Bosnia unharmed. Borich later played a part in the dynastic struggle which followed the death of Geza II. He sided with King Stephen IV, the eventual loser, and was a member of his Crown Council. So when Stephen IV had been crushed, Stephen III sent a force against Borich. In 1163 the Bosnian banus was defeated, and probably fell in battle, for his name does not appear again.

Renewal of Pacta Conventa

After the death of Manuel Komnenos, both Croatia and Bosnia rid themselves of the Byzantine governors. In 1180 they both returned under the sovereignty of Bela III, yet with the provision of secundo-geniture, or permanent establishment on the Croatian throne of a lateral branch of the Arpad dynasty. This promise was never kept, for the elder members of the family were steadily after both crowns: that of Hungary and Croatia. In the meantime, the Bosnian State achieved political and economic ascendancy, which it did not relinquish in spite of temporary setbacks, until its fall in 1463. The first great Bosnian ruler was banus Kulin (1180-1204), whose memory is

* See volume I, p. 87.

still alive among the common people of all Croatian lands. Popular legends all recall the prosperity and prestige Bosnia enjoyed during Kulin's reign. A banner-crop still today is called "Kulin's crop," etc. The ruggedness of the Bosnian people and devotion to their country produced a wealth of farm-products and manufactured goods. Mining flourished and export was taken care of by Ragusans whom Kulin endowed with grants and trading privileges.

Banus Kulin (1180-1204)—Ecclesiastical Problems—The Native Church

Bosnia enters the field of modern history in the middle of an ecclesiastical dispute. In this wild mountain region, difficult of access whether one approached it from the cities of the Dalmatian coast or from the Hungarian capital in the north, there originally prevailed a localized form of Catholicism which although at times nominally adhering to Rome, had a native language liturgy and customs very similar to the native glagolitic church of Croatia. At about the same period there was arising in Bulgaria a Manichean cult, the Bogomils, so closely resembling the Patarenes of Italy that the two terms, Bogomil and Patarene, came to be used almost interchangeably in the judicial and ecclesiastical vocabulary of the area and time. Some historians have maintained that elements of these Bogomils, persecuted by the Byzantine rulers of Bulgaria, entered Bosnia and attracted to their side numbers of the people among whom they settled. On this point the evidence at best is vague. The probability is that around the end of the twelfth century there were three main religious elements, and perhaps a fourth minor one, to be discerned in Bosnia: 1) Roman Catholic properly speaking, with a Latin liturgy, supported from the Dalmatian cities and found mainly in the Bosnian court and among its followers, but not always even there; 2) the schismatic eastern or Greek Orthodox church; 3) the primitive popular form of Christianity to which the bulk of the population belonged, and which amounted to a "national" church, although lacking organization; 4) a fractional element of Bogomils or Patarenes who began combining with the larger group, perhaps modified it to some extent, and were eventually submerged in it, but not before they had given it, in western eyes, the name of Patarene.

The exact nature of the popular national or "Bosnian" sect is still in dispute among scholars. Some maintain that it was simply a glagolitic form of the Roman church, and there is much to support this view, particularly as it refers to Kulin's time; others that it was a nationalized form of the eastern Orthodox church; some, although on tenuous ground, that it was indeed the Manichean cult of "Bogomil" or "Patarene." The important point for our narrative is that in 12th century Bosnia there was already a large Christian community which, whether it was truly heretical or merely schismatic, was at any rate often termed "heretical"—although at this time divergence from Rome was not so marked as it later came to be, and reconciliation with the Vatican was, from the time of Kulin through at any rate the reign of Ninoslav, rather easily and frequently effected.*

In the year 1180 the new Banus of Bosnia, Kulin, received a letter from Theobald, legate of Pope Alexander III. From this it appears that Kulin was at first an adherent of the Roman liturgy who reigned peacefully and devoted his energies to the promotion of trade and industries. A trade agreement with the city of Ragusa, signed in 1189, identifies him as the sovereign ruler of his land, interested in encouraging commerce. He had connections with the Serbian ruling house through his marriage to Stephan Nemanya's sister.

At that time, the administrative offices in the Arch-diocese of Split (Spalato) were re-organized, and through the influence of the Hungarian king Béla III, the Diocese of Bosnia was attached to Split. Béla's friend Peter Ugrinus was appointed Archbishop, with the understanding that he would promote the interests of his sovereign in Bosnia. Kulin was outraged at the subordination of the Bosnian bishopric and in protest led his household and 10,000 of his subjects into the national church.

The Hungarian monarch now made preparations for a campaign against the "heretics." He died in 1196, however, before he could carry out the plan.

---

* One reason for the confusion is probably that the sect differed from valley to valley and region to region, resembling the Roman church along the Dalmatian border, and the Orthodox church farther east. Also the "Bosnian" church of the late 13th and 14th centuries is something other than the popular religion of Kulin's day.

Complications about the Bosnian Church

Upon succeeding to the throne of Hungary, king Emeric not only furthered the plans of his father to conquer Bosnia, but also attempted to impose his authority over Serbia and Bulgaria as well. The success of such a venture appeared promising since his brother Andrew, Duke of Croatia, had subjected the province of Hum (Herzegovina) to his power in 1198. The plan found favor with the Pope, then Innocent III (1198-1216), who ardently desired to bring all the Balkan peninsula within the fold of the western church. Thus, Emeric as the true son of the Church, would assist the Holy See in exterminating the "Bogumils and Patarenes,"* while advancing his own designs.

In furtherance of his plans, Emeric found an associate in the person of King Vukan of Dioclea, scion of the Serbian Nemanya dynasty. Vukan had his own designs upon Bosnia and Serbia, which he intended to rule as vassal of the king of Hungary. So he formally entered the Roman Catholic Church, and complained to the Holy See against Bosnia as a haven of "Patarene heretics." He charged that Kulin treated the "Bogomils" as true Christians, and gave refuge to heretics that had been expelled from Dalmatia or Serbia. These charges, supported by Archbishop Bernardus of Split, moved the pontiff to action.

In a letter of instruction (October 11, 1200), Innocent III summoned King Emeric first to demand of Kulin that he desist from protecting and encouraging the "Patarene heresy." Should the banus refuse to comply, then Emeric was to invade Bosnia, expel Kulin and the heretics and seize all their possessions.

When Emeric's summons reached Kulin in 1201, the banus replied with a defense of his people as true Catholics. Further, he proposed to send the more distinguished of the alleged "Patarenes" to Rome to explain their teachings, so that if they were found to be deficient in any tenet of the Church, they might be enlightened and live in accordance with the teachings of the Apostolic See.

Kulin kept his word, and in 1202 the Archbishop of Dubrovnik (Ragusa) and Archdeacon Marinus appeared in Rome, bringing with them

---

* The controversial terms "Bogomil" and "Patarene" are left here as they appeared in the original documents.

a few of the native Christians. Innocent III took Kulin's proposal seriously, and relegating Emeric's political ambitions to the background, appointed Archbishop Bernardus of Split and his Court Chaplain Johannes de Casamaris, Apostolic Delegates to Bosnia (Nov. 1, 1202) with extensive instructions.

Conversion of Kulin and His Court to Catholicism

In compliance with the Papal orders de Casamaris arrived at the Court of Kulin, converted him, together with his family, retinue and "Patarene" chiefs, to the Catholic faith, and made a report on their conversion. This document goes into great detail describing how the converts abjured their beliefs and practices, and what vows they assumed. In this impressive document there is not a word on Dogmatic difference between the Catholic doctrine and the native creed. Much is said on the other hand, about the upkeep of monasteries, functions of the monks, their dress and bearing, together with dispensation of rites to laymen, according to the calendar. This would strongly indicate that Kulin's deviation had been to a native sect not yet so widely separated from Rome as the two "Bogomils and Patarenes" already were, or as the "Bosnian" church eventually came to be.

Banus Kulin promptly sent two native chiefs, Lyubin and Dragota, in the company of the Apostolic Delegate, to the Hungarian Court, where they confirmed the conversion of the Bosnians. On the 30th of April 1203, in the presence of King Emeric, the Royal Council and the hierarchy of the Church in Hungary, Lyubin and Dragota swore on their own behalf and that of Kulin and his Court that they would abide by their oath of fidelity to Rome.

Johannes de Casamaris was overjoyed with the success of his mission. In his message to the Pope (June 10, 1203) he made various suggestions toward strengthening the influence of the Church in Bosnia. Since only one bishopric existed in Bosnia, he recommended that three or four more dioceses be established, and Latins be appointed bishops, because Slavs, in his estimation, were not reliable.

However, the real triumph was that of banus Kulin, who had checked the expansionist intentions of Emeric toward Bosnia.

The reign of Kulin is remembered both by the chronicle-writers and in popular tradition, as one of general welfare and prosperity. Later kings and dukes of Bosnia, in their negotiations with foreign courts, insisted on the boundaries and privileges enjoyed by Bosnia during Kulin's reign. No better tribute could be devised for ·this great ruler whose figure stands so clearly on the horizon of history.

Banus Stephen on the Throne (1204-1232)

Kulin was succeeded as banus of Bosnia by Stephen, probably his son. Stephen's reign was untroubled by foreign complications and the country enjoyed peace and prosperity. At this time the spreading of the "Patarene" cult through the Bosnian native Church was given momentum by the strife and disorders that burdened the reign of Andrew II in Hungary. Patarene influence was felt also in Croatia and Dalmatia, and the sect made inroads into Serbian territory. Finally, the Patarenes became so influential in Bosnia that they deposed Stephen, a Roman partisan, and placed at the helm of the State one of their own: Mathew Ninoslav.

Ninoslav (1232-1250)

A gigantic struggle between Bosnia and Hungary developed under banus Ninoslav (1232-1250), whose reign is significant because it was then that the Hungarian State-idea came for the first time into conflict with the national tradition and the Croatian State policy laid down in the pacta conventa.

Ninoslav appeared during the closing stages of the second Hungarian civil war, which ended with the second issuance of the Golden Bull (1231), and the grant of privileges to the Hungarian Clergy (1232). After restoration of order and peace in his kingdom, Andrew II made serious preparations for common action with his second son Koloman, Duke of Croatia and Dalmatia, against Bosnia.

About this time Jacob of Praeneste, the Papal Nuncio in Hungary, was conducting an inquiry into the conditions of the faith in Bosnia. He soon learned that the greater part of the Bosnian population now embraced the native faith, that the only Catholic bishop of Bosnia had become a "Patarene," and that the Archbishop of Ragusa was fully apprised of the bishop's deviation, and condoned it. Jacob of Praeneste promptly transferred the Bosnian diocese from the jurisdiction of Ragusa to that of the Archdiocese of Kalocha in Hungary.

But the main task of the Nuncio was to bring the banus Ninoslav and his family into the Roman church. In this he so far succeeded that Ninoslav donated funds toward the construction of a cathedral, and some of his courtiers followed suit. Pope Gregory IX showered the returning flock with benefits, declared Bosnia to be under the protection of the Papal State, and wrote Koloman of Croatia that the sovereign rights of Ninoslav to Bosnia were to be respected, and the seized lands restored.

However, this arrangement was not of long duration. By the following year (1234) the "Patarenes" were once more in the open, with more power than before. Ninoslav had either been insincere in his vows to the Nuncio or found himself unable to check the trend to heresy. The Roman Curia and Andrew II of Hungary now prepared for a campaign to eradicate the "Patarenes" and at the same time bring Bosnia within the Croatian dukedom.

First Campaign against the
Bosnian Church (1234-1239)

October 14, 1234, Gregory IX summoned Koloman of Croatia to a crusade against the heretics in Slavonia. Three days later he wrote twice to John, Bishop of Bosnia, in the first letter instructing John to proceed sternly against the heretics, and in the second, to give absolution to all who drew the sword in defense of the Church. On the same day he wrote Stephen II, Bishop of Zagreb, to the same effect, adding that Koloman and his possessions were to be under the protection of St. Peter for the duration of the crusade.

Andrew of Hungary now declared all Bosnia subject to the Duke of Croatia, an act which was solemnly confirmed by Gregory IX, in a decree of July 28, 1235. Ninoslav retaliated by openly joining with the "Patarenes," and made ready for the defense of his country.

For two years Ninoslav fought off the attacks of his neighbor. John, Bishop of Bosnia, lost hope in the victory of the crusaders, and resigned. But in 1237 Koloman gathered his forces for another effort and crushed the Bosnians. The following year he broke into Herzegovina. As an unchalleneged ruler of the two countries, Koloman now reorganized the hierarchy, established new bishoprics, built churches and strongholds. Meanwhile Ninoslav went into hiding. But hardly had Koloman and his crusaders left the country, then Ninoslav once more seized the power and soon everything was again as it had been before the crusade.

Invasion of Tartars

Ninoslav's opportunity was a byproduct of the great disaster that fell upon Hungary and Croatia at this time.

Since the year 1237 the Mongol horde had been methodically attacking the cities of European Russia. In the winter of 1237-38 alone they had taken and destroyed Ryazan, Vladimir, Moscow, then a small place of no importance, and twelve other cities. In 1240 they took Kiev, tore the beautiful city apart and left it lifeless. During these years great numbers of refugees streamed westward, and into Hungary there came 200,000 Kumanian tribesmen and many of the South Russian princes and their retainers, carrying a tale of ruined cities, burning towns, and large scale massacre.

In the winter of 1240-41 the horde broke through the Carpathians, and while the right flank swept into Poland, the left under Sabutai entered Hungary from the south and confronted Pest, where King Béla had assembled a magnificent force. Sabutai decoyed Béla out from the walls of Pest to the field where the Sajo river joins the Theiss (Tissa), and there, around the end of April, 1241, smashed the army of the Hungarians and their allies. Koloman of Croatia and many other famous dukes and knights of Central Europe fell on this day.

Béla IV fled to Dalmatia, and sought safety on one of the minor islands of the Adriatic while a division of Sabutai's army searched up and down the coast for him. The sudden plight of Hungary and Croatia was a blessing for Ninoslav and Bosnia. Now the Patarenes and Bosnians could breathe freely, and lick their wounds. Ninoslav and his aides did everything to restore the power and welfare of their country. When, in April 1242, the Tartars withdrew from the devastated Croatia, they moved east through Bosnia and Serbia.

Bosnia Exerts Influence Abroad

For the time being Béla IV was helpless, opening the way to Ninoslav for an aggressive foreign policy. The occasion came soon. In 1243 the Dalmatian cities, Split and Trogir (Trau) quarrelled over their marginal lands. Trogir was granted special privileges by the king, while Split (Spalato) incurred his wrath. So in the struggle of the two cities, Trogir was assisted by the royal faction, which made the residents of Split look for aid among the enemies of the king. They promptly found allies in banus Ninoslav, Prince Andrew of Herzegovina, and the City State of Polyitse. Ninoslav laid siege to Trogir. The citizens of Split proclaimed him defender of the city and gave him the title of the duke of Split. After devastating the fields of Trogir, Ninoslav returned to Bosnia.

Incensed over the temerity of Ninoslav, Béla IV set out in 1244 at the head of an impressive force to bring him to account, at the same time sending a body of troops under the Croatian banus Dionysius against Split. Dionysius took Split on the 12th of July 1244, but all the efforts of the king against Ninoslav were ineffective, and the quarrel was ended with a treaty before the year was out. For two years thereafter Ninoslav and his followers remained quiet, probably gathering momentum for a new action. The occasion came when Béla IV became embroiled in the west with the Austrian Duke Frederic II. Banus Ninoslav and his "Patarenes" rose again against the king. The bishop of Bosnia, Ponsa, frightened by the uprising, sought aid both from the Pope and the archbishop of Kalocha.

Since this Archbishop had been entrusted in the past with organizing and carrying out a crusade against Bosnia, Innocent IV ordered him (August 3, 1246) to proceed with a new crusade against the heretics. Little seems to have been done, for six months later (January 20, 1247) the pontiff summoned Béla IV to a decisive struggle against the "Patarenes," offering in return not to intervene in Bosnian matters without Hungarian advice and approval. But the king was not persuaded, and the Vatican again turned to the Archbishop of Kalocha, on August 20, 1247 transferring the Bosnian bishopric from the Archdiocese of Ragusa to that of Kalocha. The Bull justifies this disposition by the assertion that "Bosnia will never return to the true faith of its

own accord, and that only the Archbishop's crusaders could restore order. And the Prelate is urged to undertake a new campaign against Bosnia."

When Ninoslav heard of this, he promptly protested, informing the Vatican that ever since his conversion in 1233 he had remained loyal to the Church, and that he had used the Patarenes in the crusades of Koloman and the Hungarian kings only to save his country from invasion. Ninoslav's protest had a tremendous effect in Rome. The Vatican now turned away from the Hungarian prelate to seek information and advice on Bosnian matters from Croatian bishops, and notably from the bishop of Senj (Segna). To show his good will toward the Croats, the Pope issued a Bull (March 29, 1248) by which he authorized the use of the glagolitic script and Croatian language in the Catholic liturgy and scriptures throughout Croatian territory. Thus was ended the persecution of the Croatian ritual which for almost a century had been such a powerful stimulant to the spread of the "Patarene" sect.

The last year of Ninoslav's reign was attended by peace and prosperity throughout Bosnia. Despite three crusades against him and the depradations of the Tartars, he had maintained the borders of his country as he had received them from his predecessors. In the year 1250, he died after a reign that had seen much struggle, but also much good fortune.

NINOSLAV'S SUCCESSORS AND REIGN OF STEPHEN KOTROMANICH

Dynastic quarrels and religious strife came in the wake of Ninoslav's death. Priyezda, a relative of Ninoslav, first seized the power. A Roman Catholic and partisan of the King of Hungary, Priyezda incurred the enmity of the heretics who deposed him. This gave the occasion to King Béla for intervention and a new crusade followed. By the end of 1254, both Bosnia and Herzegovina had been conquered by the Hungarian king.

Dismemberment of Bosnia

With a view to strengthening his hold on the conquered provinces Béla IV divided the country into two parts. The administration of upper

Bosnia and the regions (Dolnji kraji) was left unchanged while the provinces of Usora and Soli were detached from the rest of the country, to form a new banate. East of Drina and along the course of Kolubara river another banate was set up, that of Machva (Machova), coinciding with the present day northwestern Serbia. Out of these banates Béla formed later (1264) the duchy of Machva-Bosnia. In 1272 in Bosnia proper, banus Stephen ruled as a vassal of the king. This is the banus Stephen Kotroman, founder of the dynasty which for a century and a half gave Bosnia its bani and kings. Up to 1280 Stephen ruled the Upper Bosnia and Lower Regions (Dolnji Kraji) under the direct authority of the king. From 1280 until 1282 he was subject to Elizabeth, duchess of Machva-Bosnia. After her death the same relationship continued under Stephen Charles (Styepan Dragutin), ex-king of Serbia and duke of Machva-Bosnia. Stephen Kotroman married the duke's daughter Elizabeth, and the ties between the two houses became intimate. Banus Stephen was a zealous Catholic and persecuted the "good Christians," i.e. members of the native Bosnian Church.

Rise to Power of the Shubich Family

During the wars of succession, which broke out in Hungary and Croatia after the assassination of king Ladislaus IV the Croatian banus Paul Shubich and his brothers rose to power. Both the Frankish and Hungarian courts vied for the friendship and support of the Shubich family, showering them with gifts and grants. In 1298 Bosnia was added to the domains of Paul Shubich, and in an edict issued on April 7, 1299, Paul signed himself: "Banus of Croatia and Dalmatia, and Lord of Bosnia."

Paul Shubich took Bosnia from Stephen Kotroman, thus suppressing the over-lordship of Duke Stephen Dragutin. At the same time in the Lower Regions, Prince Hervatin appears, founder of the Vukchitch dynasty. As a relative of Paul Shubich, Hervatin was the supporter of the Anjou dynasty, and the grateful king Charles II donated to him and his family the Bosnian Lower Regions "for all time to come." Because of his extensive dominions Paul Shubich could not administer Bosnia himself, but appointed his son Mladen to govern the country with the title of banus.

Mladen Shubich (1302-1322) ruled for twenty years in Bosnia. He brought it peace and prosperity. He made commercial treaties with Split and Dubrovnik (Ragusa) with a view to promoting trade and crafts. In 1312 his father Paul died leaving him vast possessions. In 1314, after the death of duke Stephen Charles, he conquered the banate of Usora and Soli and took the title of the banus of Croats and of all Bosnia. Meanwhile he effected a conciliation with Stephen Kotroman, the former banus of Bosnia, and after Stephen's death became the guardian of his three sons.

In 1314 Mladen Shubich was at the zenith of his power. Since he could not govern alone the vast territory under his command, he entrusted his youthful ward, Stephen Kotromanich, with the administration of Bosnia. He himself retained the title of banus of Bosnia and supreme authority over that country, but he gave full support to his youthful appointee on every occasion.

Fall of Mladen Shubich

In the meantime the situation bearing on the native sect in Bosnia grew from bad to worse. In 1319 Pope John XXII summoned Mladen Shubich to act against the heretics in Bosnia, "for only then will he be able to win over his opponents." Indeed, Mladen Shubich had many enemies who envied his power and worked for his downfall. His brother Paul was one of them. Among others were the princes Kuryakovichi of Corbavia (Kerbava), the banus of Slavonia (Babonich, with his clan, and Stephen Kotromanich, the youthful appointee of Mladen, with a number of Bosnian magnates). This group of conspirators made thorough preparation for the defeat of Mladen Shubich. First they tried to murder him, and when the attempt had failed, the Slavonian banus Babonich moved against him at the head of a large army. Babonich was defeated, however, and pressed hard, so that he took refuge in his stronghold of Klis (Clissa). Here he sued for aid to king Charles Robert who was indebted to him for former support. The king himself feared Mladen, and arranged to have him seized and sent to Hungary where he was either murdered, or died in prison.

Thus the youthful Stephen Kotromanich was liberated from the tutelage of his guardian, and grasped with a firm hand the helm of the State.

Reign of Stephen Kotromanich (1322-1353)

In the first years of his reign Stephen Kotromanich stood by his benefactor, King Charles Robert, who had promptly named him Banus of Upper Bosnia and Lower Regions, Usora and Soli, thus uniting the entire Bosnian territory under a single authority. This attachment not only saved him from the rising power of the Serbian King, Stephen Urosh III, but also gave him the opportunity to interfere in the affairs of Croatia and Dalmatia, both of which went through the harsh experiences of a civil war caused by the strife and rivalry of powerful oligarchs.

After breaking the power of Mladen Shubich, Robert Charles thought that he would win over and subdue the oligarchs of Croatia, as he had those of Hungary. But the powerful barons and princes of Croatia united against the king as easily as against Mladen Shubich. Also they concluded a treaty of alliance with the Republic of Venice. Even after the elimination of Mladen Shubich, his younger brothers Paul, Gregory, and George still were the leading magnates of Croatia, with a number of strongholds so disposed that they could control all the larger cities of the kingdom. Next in power was the clan of the princes of Nelipichi who controlled eastern Croatia, the districts bordering on Bosnia, and the region of the river Tsetina, with a number of strategically situated strongholds. Overlords of the mountainous Corbavia (Kerbava) district were the princes Kuryakovichi while the princes Babonichi joined possessions in Croatia and Slavonia.

Foreign Policy of Banus Stephen

The position of Robert Charles was weakened by the designs of Venice, and the growing power of the kings of Serbia. Thus Stephen Kotromanich became the natural ally of Robert Charles, both against the Croatian barons and the king of Serbia. In order to raise the prestige of his dynasty Robert Charles married, in 1320, Elizabeth, daughter of the Polish king Włodzisław Lokichek, and in 1323 he arranged the marriage of Stephen Kotromanich with the daughter of a Polish duke related to the Queen. The glow of the Polish crown raised the prestige of both the king and the banus, whose alliance was shaping the course of events in the Balkans.

In the meantime the powerful Shubich clan engaged in a struggle with the princes Nelipichi over the possession of the royal stronghold of Knin. Both looked for allies, and the Bosnian banus sided with the Shubichi, his friends and benefactors. George Shubich commenced the hostilities by laying Siege to Knin, with his own troops, Bosnians and other allies. But soon prince Nelipich and his allies appeared at Knin and annihilated the Shubich forces. George Shubich and the other troop leaders were taken prisoner and Bosnians fled from the battlefield.

Struggle of War-lords and Bosnian Conquests

In a lust of revenge for the defeat of his Bosnian troops, Stephen Kotromanich declared war against prince Nelipich. The number of Nelipich's allies was increased by the forces of the city of Trogir (Trau), which joined the anti-Bosnian alliance. Although the details of this struggle are not known, it appears certain that prince Nelipich came out of it victorious. This made the Bosnian banus still more embittered against his enemies, and especially against the city of Trogir.

The struggle of the Croatian magnates convinced the Croatian-Hungarian king Robert Charles that he must proceed with energy in order to break the power of the warring overlords. He threw his authority to the support of Stephen Kotromanich, and in 1326 ordered banus Mikich of Slavonia against Nelipich. Even this campaign was unsuccessful and after some fighting, banus Mikich withdrew north and the Bosnian banus returned home without having done any appreciable damage to Nelipich and his party.

However, Stephen achieved signal success in the southwest, where he not only attached the region of Hum (Herzegovina) to Bosnia, but also occupied the rich and flourishing coast-land from the mouth of Neretva, south to Dubrovnik (Ragusa). He apparently acquired this province in 1325, whether through inheritance or conquest, is not known. But the coast from the Neretva north to the Tsetina river he seized by taking advantage of religious strife in the Makarska district. The Croatian districts of Hlivno, Dlamoch and Dumno situated between the coastland and Herzegovina, also came under his power. Encouraged by his easy success the Bosnian banus planned to extend his authority over the adjacent islands held by Venice. As a beginning, he hoped to conquer the island of Korchula (Curzola) separated by a sound from the peninsula of Pelyeshats (Sabioncello), but with no ships at his disposal, he had to abandon the plan.

Growth of the "Bosnian Church" and Local Crusades

Since the campaign of 1250 nothing had been done about the heretics, and the "Patarene" sect had been making great strides in Bosnia, Herzegovina, Croatia, Slavonia and Serbia. Its missionaries established themselves abroad, and the sect became known in western Europe under the name of "Ecclesia Sclavoniae" (Slavic Church). At the same time the Roman Catholic Church as a result of internal difficulties and the strife between the Franciscan and Dominican Orders, lost much of its influence in the country.

Apprised of this situation Pope Benedict XII decided to take stern measures against the heretics in Bosnia. Prince Nelipich offered his support and on the 22nd of May 1337, Benedict XII sent a message to all the Croatian magnates, calling on them to rally around prince Nelipich for the campaign against Bosnia. The Pope complained that not even his Franciscan and Dominican inquisitors could achieve anything in Bosnia, for the banus and the magnates protected and sheltered the "Patarenes."

So the struggle between Nelipich and Stephen Kotromanich was renewed, this time on religious grounds. Fighting went on for two years (1338-1340), in the course of which the Bosnian troops fought in Dalmatia and Croatia. Then the war was ended through the intervention of the Croatian-Hungarian King Robert Charles, Stephen Kotromanich agreed to rejoin the Catholic Church, but refused to persecute the "Patarenes" for fear that they might join the Greek Orthodox Church and have the powerful Serbian emperor Stephen Dushan for their protector. Furthermore, since the annexation of Hum (Herzegovina) to Bosnia the banus and emperor Dushan were not on friendly terms.

Banus Stephen in Opposition to Angevin Dynasty

After the death of Robert Charles (July 16, 1342) the Bosnian banus changed his policy of support to the Angevin kings. At first he had little use for the youthful Louis I (1342-1382), son of Robert Charles, and welcomed every opportunity to reduce his power. For this reason he sent an envoy to the Venetians, traditional enemies of the Croatian-Hungarian kings, offering them alliance. This alliance would be joined by the rebellious Croatian barons and king of Serbia, Stephen Dushan II. Obviously this combination was directed against King Louis I.

Venice was favorably inclined to the proposal of Stephen Kotromanich, for she had to fear the king's power, which jeopardized both her Dalmatian islands and mainland possessions. Further, the Venetians had been waging a hit and run war against Prince Nelipich, and found the Bosnian banus a convenient ally. So in 1343 the Grand Council of Venice induced its Dalmatian cities to negotiate an alliance with the Banus but only in their own name.

This affair did not make more headway, because in 1344, banus Stephen discovered that Louis planned to subdue the proud Croatian barons, to seize the Dalmatian cities from Venice, and to weaken the power of Stephen Dushan II, King of Serbia. This fully satisfied the Bosnian banus, for he equally feared the power of the Croatian overlords and that of the Serbian king, with whom the Croatian magnates had intimate ties. Therefore he once again allied himself with King Louis.

Alliance with King Louis I, the Great

In May 1344, Nelipich died, leaving his spouse Vladislava and his minor son, Ivan, in charge of a vast domain. King Louis found this occasion propitious for a show-down with his rebellious subjects. He mustered an army with which to subdue the Croatian magnates and seize their strongholds. The news of the impending campaign terrified not only the Croatian higher nobility, but also the Venetians who were certain that once the magnates had been defeated, the king would seize their cities in Dalmatia. So they made an alliance with the Croatian princes, supplying them with arms, money and troops.

In the meantime, the king sent the Slavonian banus Nicholas, with an army to the coast-land. Passing through the province of Corbavia (Kerbava), Nicholas laid siege to Knin, the powerful stronghold of the Nelipich family. Vladislava's defense was so formidable, however, that all the efforts of the royal army to take the city were in vain, and banus Nicholas returned with his forces to Slavonia.

King Louis was astonished at the victory of his Croatian opponents. He decided that he must undertake personally a new campaign against Croatia, and summoned the Bosnian banus to join him. On July 13, 1345, he set out in person at the head of an army, 20,000 strong. At the town of Bihach, on the banks of the Una, the royal army was joined by the Bosnian troops of Stephen Kotromanich, and other noblemen. There Louis pitched camp for three weeks, with an army now enlarged to 30,000 men.

As the news of the great might of the king spread, some Croatian barons decided to submit. Among the first were the princes of Corbavia, headed by the Kuryakovich clan. Vladislava followed suit. But the recalcitrant Shubich princes refused to surrender their strongholds. Satisfied with what he had achieved by a mere display of force, King Louis retired his forces to Hungary, while Stephen Kotromanich returned to Bosnia. A small royal garrison was left in Knin.

Heroic Defense of Zadar (Zara) and banus Stephen's treachery

The bloodless victory of the king in Croatia worried the Venetians greatly. They had obtained their authority over the Dalmatian cities and islands mostly by ruse, offering them protection without detaching them from their allegiance to the Croatian-Hungarian king. Now that the king began to show force, the Venetians feared that the cities and islands would return to the protective hand of their sovereign. This is exactly what did happen with the city of Zadar (Zara), which sent envoys to Bihach, with expressions of allegiance to the king. Lest this example become contagious, the Venetians decided to impose a heavy penalty upon Zadar. On the 13th of August 1345, they appeared with ten vessels off the island-city of Zadar, and held it under blockade until the 15th of December 1346 when the city finally surrendered.

Although the Zadrans sank the Venetian vessels, Venice sent a still larger fleet to renew the siege. In their distress the Zadrans turned to the king for prompt aid. Being unable to undertake the campaign in person, he commanded the Slavonian banus Nicholas, and the Bosnian banus Stephen Kotromanich, to hasten with their troops for liberation of Zadar. Already in November 1345, the combined Bosnian-Slavonian troops pitched camp near the town of Vrana, about twenty-five miles south-east of Zadar, preparing for action against the Venetians. In the meantime, the Venetians sent their envoys to negotiate a truce with the two leaders. According to some sources both Nicholas and Stephen Kotromanich accepted bribes, and obliged the Venetians by prompt withdrawal of their troops from Dalmatia, leaving the Zadrans to their bitter fate.

In their despair, the Zadar citizens sent another delegation to the king, complaining against the Venetians and the Bosnian banus. The king promised that the next year he would lead an army in person against the Venetians. The king kept his promise. Early in spring, 1346, he collected a huge army for his Dalmatian campaign. On the 27th of May he again pitched camp near Bihach, with an army of 100,000 men. Yet the Venetians did not give up their hope, and offered bribes to the leaders of the king's army, if they would desist from fighting, or return home. Moreover, they offered 100,000 ducats to the king, if he would sell them Zadar and other Dalmatian cities. They also offered the Bosnian banus and other generals 20,000 ducats if they would persuade the king to retire his force from Zadar. The king declined their offer and prepared for decision on the battlefield.

On the 1st of July 1346, the shameful battle took place. According to the plan of the battle, the Zadran infantry had to attack the Venetians, while the huge Hungarian-Croatian cavalry would rush to their support as the battle develops. When the Zadrans commenced the battle, and were promptly pressed back by the Venetians, the royal cavalry stood by idly, leaving the citizens to their fate. This despicable treason was again ascribed to the Bosnian banus. Embittered over this defeat, the king returned to Hungary declining the lucrative offer of the Venetians and spurning their advances. The king planned to undertake a major campaign against Venice at a later date and left the things in the balance. The Zadrans, left in the lurch by their friends, surrendered to the Venetians on the 15th of December 1346.

War with Emperor Dushan of Serbia

By his treacherous policy the Bosnian banus strove to strengthen his own ties with Venice, and turn that friendship into a profitable alliance. He eventually ironed out the unpleasant incident of Zadar with the king, so that he could keep the good will of both the king and the Republic of Venice. However, this was not a matter of vain ambition, but a policy of vital interest for himself and Bosnia. For dark clouds were gathering for both of them in Serbia. The Serbian king Stephen Dushan II managed to unite under his scepter: Serbia, part of Bulgaria and Greece, and was crowned in 1346, "emperor and autocrat of all Serbs, Greeks and Bulgars." Dushan could not forgive Kotromanich that he snatched away Herzegovina and the Adriatic coastland, which he claimed for his own account. In this quarrel between Bosnia and Serbia, Venice, too, was vitally interested. Venice had interest in the City of Dubrovnik (Ragusa) and surrounding territory, which lay between Serbia and Herzegovina. Therefore, if the war started between two so powerful rulers, it could be of disastrous consequences for the neighbors as well. Thus, Venice took pains to compose the differences and gave all her moral support to the Bosnian banus.

Yet all the mediation and good offices of Venice were fruitless. Banus Stephen Kotromanich, encouraged by king Louis invaded in 1349, with an army of 80,000 men the province of Travunya (Trebonia), that was under the suzerainty of emperor Dushan. Details of this invasion are lacking. It is certain, however, that the prince of Travunya suffered great damage from the Bosnian troops, for emperor Dushan in his message to Venice (April 30, 1350), insisted that banus Kotromanich repair the damage caused by his troops in Travunya. The emperor further complained that the Bosnian banus repaid with evil the friendship he extended to Kotromanichi upon recommendation of Venice. Therefore, he asked the most Serene Republic to impress upon the Banus that he should desist from disturbing the peace of his dependencies and restore to him what he unlawfully took away from Serbia.

Alarmed by the precarious situation, the Venetians assured the emperor that they would do everything to persuade the Bosnian banus to right the wrong. They also offered the Banus their services to reconcile him to the emperor.

But negotiations failed and Stephen Dushan broke at the head of a large army into Bosnia crushing the Bosnian troops. Banus Kotromanich withdrew with his troops in the thick forests of his mountains, waiting for an opportune moment to attack the invaders. In the meantime, emperor Dushan laid siege to the banal stronghold of Bobovats, but in spite of much bloodshed he could not take it. Soon he lifted the siege, devastated the country-side and left with his troops for Herzegovina. Details of this struggle are unknown, but the hostilities were ended in 1351 when Dushan's presence was needed in the east. The two opponents did not make peace, and banus Kotromanich rejected the emperor's plea to obtain the hand of his daughter Elizabeth, and the land of Hum (Herzegovina) as a dowry.

Last Years of Stephen's Reign and Marriage Tie with Angevine Dynasty

After his struggle with Serbia Stephen Kotromanich lived in peace for over two years. He gave his daughter Elizabeth in marriage to king Louis I. In summer of 1353 he attended in Buda-Pest the marriage ceremony of his daughter, who thus became the Queen of Croatia and Hungary, and also later of Poland, Lithuania and their dependencies. That made her the most powerful monarch of the XIV century in Europe. Stephen Kotromanich did not survive long the elevation to the Croatian-Hungarian throne of his daughter, but died on the 28th of September 1353, a few weeks after the marriage ceremony.

The policy of Stephen Kotromanich is open to criticism from many quarters. Yet, his was a policy of crass realism in an age when feud and dynastic interests were closely interwoven. Through his course of policy he not only saved Bosnia from dismemberment, but united it and expanded its territory, thus laying foundation for the dominant position of that country under Tvartko, the last Banus and first King of Bosnia.

CLIMAX OF BOSNIAN POWER

Stephen Tvartko, the First King of Bosnia (1353-1391)

Banus Stephen Kotromanich had no son to succeed him on the throne. His nearest relative was the youthful Tvartko, son of his brother Vladislav and Helena Shubich, the daughter of prince George Shubich of Klis (Clissa). In place of the minor Tvartko, his mother Helena held the reins of government. A woman's rule at a time when the great war between king Louis, Venice and emperor Dushan broke out, was a great misfortune for Bosnia. It also made the non-conformist magnates independent from the throne, and in asserting themselves they enlisted the aid of emperor Dushan of Serbia.

Forced by the circumstances and prompted by his ambitious mother, Tvartko engaged at an early age in armed struggle for the interests of his throne and family. In May 1355 he was fighting in Croatia and took the strongholds of some hostile Croatian princes. His position was strengthened by the death of emperor Stephen Dushan (December 20, 1355), who earlier in the reign of Stephen Kotromanich attempted to conquer Bosnia. Thus, the peril from the Serbian side ceased. Yet removal of this threat created another one. Contrary to the traditional policy of the kings of Croatia and Hungary, who sponsored the power of the bani of Bosnia, king Louis decided, after the death of Dushan and the down-fall of the Serbian empire, to reduce not only Serbia, but also Bosnia. He could not brook the formation of another great power at his southern frontiers. In addition, there was an element of personal feeling against Tvartko as banus of Bosnia, since he, as a son-in-law of Stephen Kotromanich, considered himself as the rightful heir of the Bosnian throne.

Louis' Interference in Bosnian Affairs

Louis I decided to force his will upon Tvartko. It is not known to what form of coercion he resorted, but the treaty issuing from his action shows complete submission of Tvartko to the king, and his acceptance of vassaldom. According to the terms of this treaty, concluded late in 1356, Tvartko was left in possession of Upper Bosnia, Lower Regions, Usora and Soli, but had to cede Hum (Herzegovina) and the coastland to the king, as dowry of queen Elizabeth, daughter of the late banus Stephen Kotromanich. Further, Tvartko had to commit himself to the persecution of heretics, further to provide, in case of war, troops for the king's army and to establish his residence at the Royal Court, either personally, or by keeping there his younger brother Vuk. Thus, Tvartko made himself not

only the vassal, but also, to a certain extent, hostage of the king.

Even this was not enough for the aspiration of Louis I, for he wanted to undermine the power of Tvartko in Bosnia itself. He established contact with the discontented Bosnian magnates and promised them protection, privileges and possessions, if they would break away from Tvartko. Chief among the malcontents were brothers Gregory and Vladislav Pavlovich (Hervatinich) who organized with their relations and friends, an open revolt against Tvartko mostly in parts bordering on Croatia. Yet the policy of Louis I was doomed to failure. Tvartko met the move of the king by giving grants and privileges to his own adherents and by dispossessing those who broke their pledge of loyalty to him. So he showered with gifts and privileges Vlatko Vukossavlevich, nephew of the two rebel leaders, Gregory and Vladislav. Other malcontents who considered themselves "peers of the banus," were glad to see Tvartko humiliated, but resented the encroachment of their freedom by a foreign ruler. So Louis' interference in Bosnian affairs resulted in a civil war in which the adherents of the Bosnian church came out on the top.

The sudden emergence of the heretics alarmed the Holy See, and the Pope, Innocent IV, began to plan in 1360 a new crusade against Bosnia. In a message sent on the 24th of April, 1360, the Pope instructed Peter, bishop of Bosnia, to seek aid from the worldly Power to eradicate the Bosnian heresy.

In the meantime, Louis I realized that he committed a grave error by his attempt to undermine the power of Tvartko, so he decided now to restore it and strike at the same time at the Bosnian Christians. He equipped two armies for this campaign. He undertook personal command of the forces, which were to break into the Lower Regions and Upper Bosnia, while the forces assigned to invade the Usora district he placed under the command of archbishop Nicholas of Esztergom (in German: Gran; in Croatian: Ostrogon), and the Palatin (Vice-roy) Nicholas Kont. This army proceeded to the town of Srebrenik, but after an unsuccessful siege and much loss ("cum magno damno personarum at rerum discesserant," Chronicle of Thurocz) in manpower and war material, returned to Hungary. Nothing is known about the accomplishments of the royal forces under Louis' personal command, but he may have had a measure of success, for the Council of Venice made in 1364 Tvartko and his family honorary citizens of the Republic calling him "powerful" and "banus of all Bosnia." This would indicate that Louis I restored the authority of Tvartko in this campaign.

Tvartko in Exile

In spite of this success the power of Tvartko did not last long. In 1365 the persecuted heretics rose against him and were joined by the disaffected peers of the land. Moreover, Tvartko's own brother, Vuk, joined the rebels. Tvartko was dethroned, and together with his mother, Helena, expelled from the country. They took refuge at the court of king Louis I who gave Tvartko a small army, with which to fight the rebels. In fact, he succeeded in recovering a part of the Lower Regions. Fighting was embittered and, according to a chronicle-writer of Split, the heretics set the forests on fire, in which men and beasts perished. Yet, Tvartko regained his full power in 1367, and his brother Vuk fled to Dubrovnik (Ragusa).

Tvartko Regains his Throne

In the same year Tvartko made a trade-agreement with the city of Dubrovnik (Ragusa), in which he confirmed all the grants, patents, agreements and privileges given to the Ragusans by his uncle Stephen Kotromanich. Since Ragusa came in 1358 under the sovereignty of the king of Croatia and Hungary, a new clause was inserted in the treaty specifying that "no action will be undertaken, which would cause dishonor or prejudice to the king of Hungary." On the 1st of June, 1367, Tvartko with his suite, was solemnly received in Ragusa. On that occasion he tried to obtain from the Ragusans extradition of his brother Vuk, but they refused to comply on the basis of the "sanctity of political refuge."

Developments in Serbia

By 1370 Tvartko managed to consolidate his power and was preparing for action abroad, and especially in Serbia, where conditions were favorable for his interference and intervention. Since the death of emperor Dushan II, things in Serbia went from bad to worse. A powerful oligarchy, greedy of power, pushed in the background the youthful Urosh IV (1356-1367), son of emperor

Dushan. Among the grandees who established unlimited power in their provinces, were the two royal brothers, Vukashin and Uglyesha, then prince Lazarus Greblyanovich, Vuk Brankovich, the princes Balshichi, prince Voyslav and his nephew Nicholas Altomanovich. Each of them had a territory of his own, and carried on as a true sovereign. Moreover, king Urosh IV was assassinated at a hunting party. Vukashin, alleged murderer of Urosh IV, now ascended the throne (1367-1371), trying to impose his authority on his rivals. But through events in the East his plans were thwarted and Serbia itself was brought to the brink of disaster. The overshadowing event was the rising power of the Ottoman Turks.

The Rise of the Ottoman Turks

East of the Caspian Sea, in the extensive steppeland or prairie country, known under the name of Turan or Turkestan, for many centuries various nomadic tribes, called comprehensively Turks, were living undisturbed. When Genghis Khan (Temudjin) founded his gigantic Mongolian empire, part of the Turkish population left early in the 13th century its country and migrated to Asia Minor. In this new homeland a tribal chief by the name of Osman (Ottoman), embraced with his people at the beginning of the 14th century, the Mohammedan religion, and declared himself a sultan, independent from any foreign power. By the name of their leader the people were called ever since Osmanli or Ottoman Turks. In 1326 Urkhan (1328-1359), established himself at Brussa, the first Turkish capital, extending his power to the shores of the Marmara Sea. Famed for their courage and martial qualities, the Osmanlis were frequently used by Byzantine emperors as auxiliary troops or allies against their domestic foes, and especially in their struggle with the Serbian king and emperor, Stephen Dushan. In 1352 Urkhan's son Suleiman crossed, with a small band of fighters the Dardanelles and by surprise captured the fort of Zimpi, close to Gallipoli. This was the first European place ever captured by the Turks. From that time on no one could expel them from there, and two years later (1354) they captured Gallipoli.

Being in need of fighting troops, the warlike but unpopulous Osmanli tribe resorted on an expedient that struck terror in the hearts of the Balkan Christians, and caused untold misery in this area through centuries. The barbarous practice consisted in snatching from their parents Christian boys, whenever the Turks broke into a Christian country or occupied it. Then the youthful captives were naturally converted to Mohammedanism, given military training and raised in the spirit of fanaticism directed against their Christian kin. This was the yenicheri or "new army" organization responsible for the worst "zulums" or atrocities among the Christian "rayah" or infidels. But for their fighting zeal and efficiency the yenicheri were unexcelled for centuries.

This kind of force sultan Urkhan left to his son Murad I (1359-1389), who further developed it. At his ascension to the throne, the Byzantine power was at its lowest ebb, and Murad had no difficulty in expanding his dominion throughout the Byzantine-held Balkan area. So, in 1363 he captured easily Adrianople, making it the first Turkish capital in Europe. With this event the Turks established themselves as a new State in Europe, eager of further conquests in the Balkans and Central Europe. No serious obstacle lay in their way, except the stubborn opposition of Serbs and Bulgarians. They were the only ones who possessed in that area effective striking power, and quite naturally Murad had to cross swords with his new neighbors.

Tragedy of Serbia

Luckily for him, and disastrously for the Serbian people, domestic strife and rivalry of oligarchs weakened the once powerful empire of tsar Dushan, in which respect Serbia resembled the agonizing Byzantium. Well-entrenched in Thrace Murad's troops raided Greece and Bulgaria, but carried their worst blows against disintegrating Serbia. In 1370 sultan Murad broke with 70,000 men into Serbia, devastating the country. King Vukashin drove them out, but they kept raiding the lands of his brother Uglyesha. Vukashin decided to expel the Turks from Europe altogether and in 1371 moved at the head of a large army against Adrianople. The battle was fought near the town of Chernomen (Tainaros) on the banks of Maritsa river. The Serbs won a decisive victory over the Turks. But at night the Turks suddenly returned and in a surprise attack destroyed the Serbian army altogether. King Vukashin and his brother fell in the carnage, with most other leaders.

The defeat at Maritza was a dreadful blow for the once powerful Serbia. The Serbian princes had to declare allegiance to the Sultan, and pay him tribute. Prince Lazarus Greblyanovich, who was elected king by part of the Serbians (1371-1389), became a Turkish vassal, and paid the Sultan a yearly tribute. Still worse, the same fate befell Bulgaria, whose Tsar Shishman also became a Turkish vassal. Lazarus Greblyanovich felt so weak and discouraged that he took only the title of prince, avoiding the title of king. This particular circumstance attracted the attention of Tvartko, banus of Bosnia, who intensely watched the episodes of the struggle in the east. With the death of king Urosh IV the male line of the Nemanide dynasty became extinct. On the other hand, Elizabeth, daughter of the Nemanide Serbian king Stephen Charles, was the wife of Stephen Kotroman, his grandfather. So Tvartko decided to unite all the Serbian lands around his person as the legal heir of the Nemanide dynasty.

The opportunity presented itself soon. When Prince Lazarus, a friend of Tvartko, became embroiled in disputes with other Serbian princes, Tvartko supported Lazarus. So the two sons of king Vukashin, Andreas and Mark, legendary heroes of the Serbian folk-lore, rose against Lazarus. In pursuit of his selfish interests Tvartko sided with Lazarus. Soon after Tvartko and Lazarus combined their forces in the fight with prince Nicholas Altomanovich, ruler of Trevunya (southern Herzegovina and Sanjak) and Morava valley, who made alliance with the princes Balshichi of Zeta (Montenegro). Tvartko and Lazarus defeated their opponents, while Tvartko took the province of Travunya, with the seacoast up to the port of Kotor (Cattaro). In the east he took a part of Serbia (Rascia) up to the town of Syenitsa. Thus, by 1375 and 1376 Tvartko had in his possession, a good part of ancient Serbia.

Tvartko, King and Autocrat of Serbs

Being at the zenith of his power as king of Bosnia, Tvartko found the moment propitious to achieve his ambition as autocrat and king of Serbia. In 1377, without informing of his intention, either prince Lazarus of Serbia, or king Louis I of Hungary, Tvartko had himself crowned in the monastery at Mileshevo, over the grave of St. Sabbas, Serbian national saint, king of Serbia, Bosnia and Coastland. Tvartko's coronation was promptly recognized by the Ragusans and Venetians, while king Louis I was too much pre-occupied with his Polish-Lithuanian affairs to worry a great deal about Bosnia and Serbia. Becoming a king Tvartko devoted his effort to raising the prestige of his court by glamor and pomp in the Byzantine style. At this point he collected tribute from Ragusa and Venice, both as a king of Serbia and Bosnia. He issued edicts, grants and charters under both titles. This became the established custom of all his successors until the fall of Bosnia (1463).

In his new position as the chief Christian ruler of the Balkans, Tvartko was forming new plans. In the first place he wanted to found a dynasty, and married Dorothea, niece of the last Bulgarian Tsar Shishman. In order to improve the military security of his realm, he built inland many strongholds and fortifications, while on the sea-coast he was longing for ports, and set his eyes on both Cattaro and Ragusa. Yet during the life time of King Louis I, such a plan would be doomed to failure and fraught with dire consequences. But on September 13, 1382, king Louis died and new perspectives opened for the ambitious policy of Tvartko. In the first place king Louis died without a male heir, leaving behind two daughters: Maria and Hedwig. Louis bequeathed his throne to Maria who was betrothed to prince Sigismund, son of the German emperor, Charles IV. But the Poles rejected Maria, and elected her younger sister Hedwig as queen of Poland. Moreover, a powerful party rose against queen-mother Elizabeth and Palatin Nicholas of Gara. It soon spread throughout the kingdom: in Hungary, Croatia, Slavonia and Dalmatia. The rebels looked for a king of their liking abroad, and a civil war broke out, which continued for nearly quarter of a century.

Tvartko Turns to the Coastland

All this favored the expansionist policy of Tvartko and he decided to turn the troubled situation to his best advantage. He realized quickly that without a powerful fleet he could not take the formidable fortification of Ragusa. On the other hand, he was also conscious of the fact that Ragusa lived from commerce and shipping and that he could bring this community to terms by an intense competition, and by blocking its overland trade. In pursuit of this plan he built at the entrance of the bay of Cattaro, a new port, which he named San Stephano, but later was renamed into Novi (Castelnuovo). He made it into an important trading center and opened a great salt-market, the chief commodity of the Ragusans. The Ragusans saw clearly whither Tvartko aimed and sent him a delegation reminding him of his obligations as king of Serbia. By the terms of the old commercial treaties with Serbia, Ragusans were protected from encroachment on their salt trade by an explicit prohibition of opening salt-markets in any new town or community. Tvartko admitted treaty-violation and promised the envoys that the port Novi in the future would not trade in salt.

On making this concession to the Ragusans, Tvartko made another move for a showdown with the Ragusans. He initiated negotiations with the Venetians for the purchase of two galleys and necessary munitions. The Venetians sold him immediately one galley, and permitted him to build in their dock-yards two new vessels. The news of this deal alarmed not only the Ragusans, but also queens Maria and Elizabeth who were alarmed at the prospect that the powerful king Tvartko might join the rebels in Croatia and Dalmatia. In order to win him over to their cause and reconcile him with the Ragusans, the two queens donated him the port and bay of Kotor (Cattaro). This gesture of the two queens solved Tvartko's problems on the sea-coast, and he restored his friendly relations to Ragusa.

The ease with which Tvartko obtained the all-important port and bay of Cattaro excited the anger of prince Balsha Balschich, ruler of Zeta (Montenegro) and its dependencies. Soon they engaged in a bitter warfare, in which the two old enemies were intent on destroying each other. In the first year of war Tvartko was victorious over Balschich, whose country he ravaged. But the closing period of war favored Balshich, and Tvartko in his predicament applied to Venetians for mediation toward conclusion of peace (1385). Even after these reverses,

Tvartko retained Cattaro, which was the crown of his achievements on the southern sea-coast.

The expansionist policy of Tvartko was favored also by the civil war raging in Dalmatia, Croatia and Hungary. The reign of the two queens and their advisor, Nicholas of Gara, caused great dissatisfaction in the country, which was suffering much from the wars and campaigns of the late Louis I. Even the close friends of the late king turned against the misrule of the queens. After efforts at conciliation, it came to armed clash with the rebels, in the course of which the ill-fated mother-queen Elizabeth was murdered, while her daughter, queen Maria, was thrown into prison in the stronghold of Novigrad in Croatia.

Tvartko's Intervention in Croatia

All this time king Tvartko carefully watched the unfolding of events west and north of his frontiers. At first he refused to side with either faction, but when the youthful queen was made prisoner, he threw his lot with the Croatian and Dalmatian rebels. His chief associate became John Palizhna, prior (mayor) of the town of Vrana, situated between Zadar (Zara) and Shibenik (Sebenico). This courageous magistrate was fighting the royal forces for years, and in spite of his occasional reverses, he became the leader of the rebellion in Croatia. In the meantime, the stronghold of Klis (Clissa) submitted to Tvartko, which gave him a key-position in the communications between Bosnia and Dalmatia. Moreover, it gave him control over the communications of the city of Split (Spalato), a staunch supporter of the queen. Further, the combined forces of Palizhna and Tvartko took the stronghold of Ostrovitsa and thus established control over the communications of the cities of Zadar (Zara) and Nin (Nona). At the same time the Bosnian troops were aiding the rebels in Slavonia and Machva (northern Serbia).

Impressed by the might of Palizhna and Tvartko, the cities throughout Croatia and Dalmatia began to waver in their loyalty to the helpless king. The example of Split (Spalato), whose suburbs and fields were being devastated for years, made even the most loyal communities wonder if their allegiance to the king of Hungary was a wise policy. The citizens of Trogir (Trau) joined up with Palizhna and the Bosnians. The other cities sent their envoys to king Sigismund, husband of queen Maria, for protection, but all the entreaties remained unavailing since the king himself was not sure of his own position. The most tragic was the plight of Split (Spalato), which through all its trials, remained faithful to the king. In a message sent on the 10th of June, 1388, to the king, the citizens of Split complained: "For more than three years the sword of the Bosnian king is striking at us. For eighteen years we suffered from persecutions of John Palizhna. Before, these enemies of our were plaguing us, each of them separately, but since the 18th of February of this year, they are oppressing us with their combined forces."

Serbian Catastrophe on Kossovo Polye (*Blackbird field*) (1389)

Although he had the situation in hand, Tvartko did not proceed against the recalcitrant cities with sufficient energy. The reason for this was the grave situation developing in the south through renewed Turkish attacks against Serbia. Tvartko remained on friendly terms with the Serbian prince Lazarus Grebelyanovich, with whom he was in alliance against prince Nicholas Altomanovich. Lazarus pleaded for aid against the Turks, and Tvartko sent him the necessary troops. In 1387 prince Lazarus defeated, with the aid of Bosnians, 20,000 Turks near Plochnik in Old Serbia so thoroughly that only one-fifth of the Turkish army was saved. Aroused over this defeat, sultan Murad I made preparations for a new invasion of Serbia.

Confronted with the new peril Lazarus sought aid from the Bulgarian Tsar Shishman, king of Hungary, Sigismund, and king Tvartko. Without delay king Tvartko sent Vlatko Hranich, one of his best generals, with an impressive force, to the aid of Lazarus. The decisive battle was fought near the town of Prishtina in Old Serbia, on the historic Blackbird Field (Kossovo Polye). The battle began on the 15th of June, 1389 and continued for three days. The battle ended in the worst disaster that yet befell not only Serbia and Bosnia, but also Hungary and all of Central Europe. It was not so felt immediately, and for a long time it was considered abroad as a Christian victory over the Turks.*

---

* See for the more detailed accounts of the battle of Maritsa and Blackbird Field the annotations.

Tvartko, King of Croatia

In the meantime, the forces of king Sigismund moved to Dalmatia, and under banus Ladislaus, laid siege to Klis, which John Palizhna could not defend, and in July, 1389, surrendered it. Also other strongholds were taken by Sigismund's troops. But early in Fall, Tvartko sent strong reinforcements to Palizhna who in a number of engagements, defeated the forces of banus Ladislaus. Now it was obvious that the Dalmatian cities could no longer escape submission to the king of Bosnia. On the 2nd of June, 1390, even the recalcitrant Split declared its allegiance to Tvartko. In June and July 1390, Tvartko became also King of Croatia and Dalmatia. Consequently, he took the title of the "King of Croatia and Dalmatia." Thus, he became the ruler of a great part of the lands, once the dominion of Zvonimir, the great Croatian King, and that of Tsar Dushan, the most powerful king of Serbia. He was the first in history to unite the Croats and Serbs under a single scepter. Bosnia, which had to lean in the past now on Serbia, now on Croatia, became the uniting center around which the remains of the fallen Serbian and Croatian States could gather.

In midsummer, 1390, king Tvartko was at the zenith of his power. But all this did not satisfy him, and he had already new plans for more ambitious and momentous undertakings. He wanted to make an alliance with Venice, and connect up, through marriage ties, with the Hapsburgs of Austria. These would be his first moves in a show-down with Hungary. But all these plans were voided by his sudden death on March 23, 1391.

DECLINE OF THE BOSNIAN POWER

Stephen Dabisha (1391-1395) and His Wife Helen (1395-1398)

The phenomenal rise to power achieved by king Tvartko was based chiefly on the weakness of the neighboring States, and on the prestige he enjoyed among his own people. Should the neighboring rulers recover from their temporary set-backs, and Bosnia itself fall prey to internal strife, the whole magnificent edifice of tri-unite Bosnia erected by Tvartko, was doomed to collapse. Especially acute was the problem of throne succession, which in Bosnia as well as in Croatia and Serbia, became conducive to national disasters. Moreover, religious conflict hastened along the inevitable doom.

A significant development of this precarious situation was the weakening of the central power and excessive growth of oligarchy, so that the king eventually became a puppet in the hands of the more powerful barons who carried on in their respective domains as actual sovereigns. Moreover, the possessions of the magnates extended over two kingdoms and they pursued their dynastic policies with the aid of two sovereigns (e.g., Hervoye Hervatinich and Sandal Hranich). Even emperors were eager to cater to their whims.

Tvartko's successor to the throne was Styepan Dabisha, a younger brother of his. Even though he was lacking the qualities of a ruler, the first two years of his reign were marked by success continuing under the momentum of authority created by his famous brother. As this petered out, everything went wrong.

The new king was promptly recognized by the Venetian Republic, which made him an honorary citizen of the Republic. (June 1, 1391.) The Republic of Ragusa (Dubrovnik) followed suit, and upon its promise to pay him the customary annual tribute, Dabisha confirmed (June 17, 1392) all the rights and privileges enjoyed by this merchant republic in his dominions. Even in Croatia and Dalmatia Dabisha was recognized as a king. In this capacity Dabisha issued a number of decrees in favor of the Dalmatian cities. Even the recalcitrant city of Zadar, which resisted the power of Tvartko, was won over to the side of the Bosnian king.

The success of Dabisha in Dalmatia and Croatia would have been consolidated, if not for the dark war-clouds which were hovering south-east of his dominion, and burst open in the form of a Turkish invasion in 1392 when sultan Bayazid engaged in a struggle with king Sigismund. A Turkish army broke on this occasion into south-eastern Bosnia, devastated the country-side and established itself for permanent stay in a camp near Glasinats.

Another source of worry for the king of Bosnia was the proclamation of Ladislaus, King of Naples, and son of Charles of Durazzo—the short-lived king of Croatia and Hungary—in 1387 by the Croatian revolutionaries, king of Croatia and Dalmatia. During the life-time of Tvartko, the youthful Ladislaus did not exercise his royal authority in Croatia, but considered Tvartko as his active agent. But when Tvartko subjected this country to his own authority, Ladislaus lost his confidence in Bosnia, and decided to regain his Croatian kingdom.

The Croatian nobility, itself disappointed in the Bosnian supremacy, gave him its full support. So already on June 15, 1391, Ladislaus exercised his royal power over Croatia, Dalmatia and Slavonia, by grant of lands and appointments to his administrative posts. The chief beneficiary of his dispositions was the Bosnian voyevode, duke Hervoye who was named vicar of the king, with the authority of the banus of Croatia and Dalmatia. Through numerous grants of estates to Bosnian and Croatian magnates Ladislaus wanted to create a political party against both Dabisha and Sigismund.

Seeing through Ladislaus' plans Dabisha at first attempted to retain Croatia and Dalmatia by force of arms, but since this violence aroused a fierce opposition of the Dalmatian cities and Croatian strongholds, Dabisha changed his policy, and offered his royal title over Croatian territory to king Sigismund, in exchange for the latter's recognition of his own right to the Bosnian throne. Negotiations ensued, and an interview of the two rulers was arranged in July, 1393 in the Slavonian town of Djakovo. This meeting resulted in a covenant by the terms of which Sigismund obtained the title to Croatia and Dalmatia, while Dabisha was recognized king of Bosnia, with the provision that after his death the crown of Bosnia will pass to Sigismund as legitimate monarch of that land.

In spite of the terms of this agreement, Sigismund realized that it would never become effective, unless he won over to his side the Bosnian magnates by generous grants and donations. As the most important among the Bosnian magnates, Hervoye Vukchich Hervatinich, who also was present in Djakovo, benefited most from Sigismund's policy, and his power reached a new climax. But the other Bosnian and Croatian magnates, including John Horvat, Vicar General of king Ladislaus' possessions under the crown of Hungary, repudiated the agreement and soon forced Dabisha himself to break the treaty.

Moreover, John (Ivanish) Horvat and his brother Paul, were given troops and the Bosnian stronghold of Dobor, as a nucleus for an invasion of Slavonia with a view to raising a rebellion south of the Danube.

Apprised of the new danger, Sigismund acted with speed and determination. Already in August, 1394 he himself, led a powerful Hungarian army in the Bosnian province of Usora against the stronghold of Dobor and the rebellious forces. At the news of the king's approach, the rebels became panicky while the two Horvat brothers deserted their own troops. The king surrounded the stronghold and after a brief siege, took it. Thereupon he pursued the fleeing rebels and captured the two Horvat brothers, with other ringleaders of the uprising. Upon the news of the rebels' rout king Dabisha rushed to see Sigismund and renewed the treaty of Djakovo.

Right after his victory at Dobor Sigismund sent the banus Nicholas Gara to Croatia and Dalmatia in order to wring out these lands from the hands of his Bosnian and Neapolitan opponents. Banus Gara attacked banus Vuk Vukchich, and in a decisive battle near Knin the forces of the Bosnian king were routed. In consequence, Dabisha definitely lost Croatia and Dalmatia. The rest of his short reign Dabisha spent on consolidating Bosnia in an attempt to keep it from falling apart. In this task death overtook him on the 7th of September, 1395.

According to the treaty of Djakovo, the Bosnian throne should now be occupied by Sigismund. But the Bosnian magnates wanted no foreign ruler in their country and appointed queen Helen to act as a regent until her son became of age. She ruled for three years modestly and without interest in foreign affairs. Three influential magnates acted as her advisors in Government: Duke Hervoye Vukchich Hervatinich, Prince Paul Radinovich, and Duke Sandal Hranich. These three were destined to direct the course of events in their country and abroad, for nearly a generation.

In 1398 Bosnia was invaded by a Turkish army, supported by the Serbian auxiliary troops. This invasion came as an aftermath of a great victory which sultan Bayazid, in 1396, had won over king Sigismund in a battle fought near Nicopolis in Bulgaria. Bosnia was devastated and much of its population dragged into slavery.

In the turmoil attending this invasion queen Helen was either killed or dethroned. For the last time she was heard of in March, 1399.

During the reign of Dabisha and Helen the first feud among the powerful oligarchs broke out, setting up the pattern for similar recurrences, which became fatal for the independence of Bosnia. The clan of Sankovichi ruled the province of Hum (Herzegovina) and owned part of the coastland between Dubrovnik (Ragusa) and Ston (Stagno). During the reign of Tvartko this family rose to high honors and was given by the king a part of the old duchy of Travunya (Trebonia), including the district of Konavlye (Canalese). In a certain deal with Ragusa they ceded this district to the merchant city, and gave it some trading privileges in their territory.

This unusual deal aroused the suspicion and jealousy of other magnates, including that of Prince Paul Radinovich and Duke Sandal Hranich who attacked the Sankovich brothers, took them prisoners, and divided their possessions. Paul Radinovich took the Konavlye district and made a new deal with the Ragusans in his own name. This case set the precedent for bloody feuds among the powerful barons until the very conquest of the country by the Turks.

RIVAL KINGS AND WARS OF SUCCESSION IN BOSNIA BETWEEN 1398 AND 1421

[Stephen Ostoya (1398-1404); Tvartko II (1404-1408); again Stephen Ostoya (1408-1418); Stephen Ostoyich (1418-1421); and again Tvartko II (1421-1443)].

The origin of Stephen Ostoya, successor of queen Helen on the throne, is obscure. Some believe that he was an illegitimate son of king Tvartko. Nonetheless, he had the support of his country's powerful barons, and especially that of Duke Hervoye, Prince Paul Radinovich and Duke Sandal Hranich, who actually dictated the king's policies.

The most powerful of the three was Hervoye, since July 17, 1391 vicar of the Croatian king Ladislaus in Croatia and Dalmatia. According to the report of the historian Lucio (Lucich), Hervoye ruled there more as a king than a vicar. During the reign of Dabisha and queen Helen, he was the first in authority at the Bosnian court.

Due to Hervoye's privileged position, king Sigismund wanted his presence at the conference in Djakovo, and his signature under the treaty. In spite of the provisions of the treaty it was Hervoye who prevented Sigismund from occupying the Bosnian throne, and clothed Stephen Ostoya with the royal purple. Furthermore, Hervoye became duke of Split, and ruler of the islands of Hvar (Lesina), Brach (Brazza) and Korchula (Curzola), along with extensive districts in Bosnia and Herzegovina. As a general he won all the battles, and as a shrewd statesman he could turn to his advantage the raging conflicts of his age, and when cornered by powerful opponents he could, by a daring thrust, break through the iron circle, and destroy his enemies. To top it all, Hervoye was a follower of the Bosnian Church.

Even as a puppet in the hands of Hervoye and other barons, king Ostoya could safely rule at home, and command, through the power and ingenuity of Hervoye, no small prestige abroad. He needed both for dark war clouds had gathered in the north. Incensed over the breach of the Djakovo treaty assuring him the Bosnian throne, Sigismund collected an army to break into Bosnia and enforce his rights. He broke into the Bosnian territory and advanced to the stronghold of Verbas in the north. Yet Hervoye not only defeated his troops, but invaded Sigismund's territory and attached the Dubitsa district to Bosnia. Thus, Hervoye saved Ostoya's throne, and spared the country the ravages of an invasion. Both these facts were gratefully acknowledged in the royal patent of 1400, in which the king favored duke Hervoye and his two brothers with the grant of new estates.

After Hervoye's victory Bosnia enjoyed a short period of peace and prosperity. Protected by the powerful arm of Hervoye, king Ostoya felt perfectly secure. But for all practical purposes Hervoye was the true ruler of the country. Whatever enhanced the power and prestige of the duke, the king did it. Thus, the foreign policy of Hervoye was the policy of Bosnia. In his foreign affairs Hervoye reverted to the policy of Tvartko I, John Palizhna, John Horvat and other rebellious Croatian barons, to keep the king of Hungary away from Croatia and Dalmatia. Having forced Sigismund out from Bosnia, Hervoye made up his mind to remove Croatia and Dalmatia as well from under his sovereignty.

The opportunity presented itself through the conflict of king Ladislaus of Naples and emperor Sigismund, rival pretenders to the throne of Croatia and Dalmatia. In this situation Hervoye wanted to gain foothold first in the coastal cities and especially in Zadar, a staunch supporter of Sigismund. In his capacity of "Vicar General of king Ladislaus and Ostoya" he summoned, in 1401, the Zadran commonwealth to join the banners of Ladislaus, in exchange for which he would give them protection against any outsiders. Having no other choice, the citizens of Zadar complied. Their example was followed by the cities of Knin, Shibenik (Sebenico) and Trogir (Trau). Hervoye promised that he would have the recognition of their ancient rights and privileges confirmed, both by Ostoya and Ladislaus. Ostoya promptly confirmed the agreement, while Ladislaus was still abroad.

Misled by the absence of Ladislaus from Croatia, king Ostoya supported his claim against Sigismund in the assumption that the king of Naples would not come to Croatia and assume the reins of Government. This would give him the opportunity to restore the authority of Tvartko I, both in Croatia and Dalmatia. But Ladislaus landed in June, 1403 in Dalmatia and on the 5th of August, 1403 he was crowned in Zadar amid pomp and festivities with the crown of Zvonimir, sacred legacy of the Croatian national dynasty. Furthermore, he was crowned by the Primate and arch-bishop of Hungary. Right after the coronation Ladislaus took legal possession of the territory of Croatia and Dalmatia, with their dependencies.

This turn of events changed the situation rapidly, and Ostoya with his supporters became an opponent of Ladislaus overnight. Furthermore, it was rumored that Hervoye, a heretic, made a deal with Ladislaus to become a Catholic as a price for the latter's support to make him the sole ruler of Bosnia. Also the power and fame of Hervoye caused him great anxiety. In execution of his plans Ostoya proceeded with bold strokes. By curbing or capturing Ragusa he planned to achieve such power that it would be easy for him to overthrow Ladislaus and crush Hervoye. The political situation for a war against Ragusa was propitious, since this Republic was an ally of Sigismund and consequently opposed to king Ladislaus.

Under a flimsy pretext Ostoya invaded in August, 1403, the Ragusan territory and beleaguered the city itself. The course of hostilities is not known, but it must have been disastrous for the Ragusans, since they promptly sued for aid in Zadar, Ladislaus' capital, and being denied there, sent envoys to the court of Sigismund.

In the meantime, king Sigismund crushed out the opposition in Hungary, and became a formidable foe for anyone who stood in his way. Sigismund's victory made Ostoya evaluate the new situation and reconsider his policy. He decided to effect at all cost a conciliation with Sigismund, for rumors had it that he was mustering up a huge army for a new campaign in the south. On the other hand, Sigismund himself wished to make up with the Bosnian king, and he sent John Maroth, banus of Machva, to the court of Ostoya. An agreement was reached by which Ostoya recognized the suzerainty of Sigismund, in exchange for his friendship and protection.

The sudden about-face of Ostoya's policy stupefied both his friends and enemies. In the first place it affected the decision of Ladislaus to remain in Zadar as an effective king of Croatia and Dalmatia. He realized that he could not withstand the combined attack of Sigismund and Ostoya, and already in October, 1403 he returned to his court in Naples. On the other hand Hervoye became infuriated against Ostoya and decided to destroy him at all cost. In an adroit move he concluded a military alliance with the besieged Ragusans who were the subjects of Sigismund while he was Vicar General of king Ladislaus. Ragusans were elated over this development for they were afraid that Sigismund would leave them to the tender mercies of Ostoya, while in his turn, Sigismund was pleased over the prospect to regain with the aid of Hervoye his sovereignty over Croatia and Dalmatia. On the other hand, Hervoye himself longed for a conciliation with Sigismund, and hoped that the Ragusans, trusted friends of Sigismund, would be instrumental in this achievement.

Confronted with the unexpected turn of events, king Ostoya again changed his position. For, indeed, of what use would be to him the friendship of the distant Sigismund, in a duel with the formidable power of Hervoye, which may break on him any day? So he made a frantic effort to make up with Hervoye, and later on with Ragusa. But neither Hervoye, nor the Ragusans were eager to make up, since they made a new plan how to depose Ostoya and put in the throne one of his enemies who took refuge in Ragusa. This new agreement took effect. While the Ragusans sent to the court of Sigismund envoys who were to convince the king that Ostoya was a worthless character and unworthy of his support, Hervoye and his barons put in the field large forces, with which they laid siege to the royal stronghold of Bobovats. In his desperate plight Ostoya sent his wife, queen Kuyeva to Sigismund's court in Budavar to sue for aid. Sigismund was moved by her entreaties and sent under the command of banus John Maroth a sizeable army to Bosnia with which he forced his way to the beleaguered Bobovats, dispersed the enemy forces and liberated king Ostoya.

After his restoration to the throne of Bosnia, king Ostoya strove to make up with all his enemies, and before all with the Republic of Ragusa. Yet there were some stumbling blocks in his dealings with Ragusa. Encouraged by Sigismund's support the Ragusans demanded the return of all their territory seized by the king of Bosnia, including the coastland north of Ragusa up to the height of Klek, a most valuable tract of the coast donated in 1399 to the Ragusans by king Ostoya himself. The return of this particular region was specifically excepted to in an agreement entered between Ostoya and Sigismund as a punishment to the Ragusans for their treachery in sheltering Ostoya's enemies and instigating rebellions against him. But by constantly applying pressure on Sigismund, the Ragusans finally obtained his consent to the restoration of the valuable coastland.

In order to counteract the intemperance of Ragusa, Ostoya made an effort to come to terms with Hervoye, through whose mediation he hoped to iron out his difficulties with the Republic. The move was partially successful and in March, 1404 the two were living again on good terms. Moreover, Hervoye made a serious attempt to restore peace and friendship between Bosnia and Ragusa. But the Ragusans were adamant in their stand on the question of the disputed coastland, and finally agreed to send envoys to the Bosnian National Assembly where they were to deliberate with the king and grandees of the country. Moreover, Hervoye tried to adjust the differences between Ragusa and those of the Bosnian magnates who fought on the side of Ostoya, and in the first place, duke Sandal Hranich and prince Paul Radinovich. Thus, Hervoye prepared the ground for general conciliation and peace.

The Assembly of the Nobility representing the political nation and power of Bosnia met in April, 1404 in Visoki, capital of the country. Besides the king present were all the grandees of the country, including duke Hervoye, duke Sankovich, duke Vukmir Yuryevich, etc., further the dyed (grandfather) of the Bosnian (Patarene) Church, with his suffragans. King Ostoya brought up before the Assembly the Ragusan demands, including that of cession of the coastland. The demands were in all probability rejected, for the envoys wrote to Ragusa for new instructions. The Council of the Republic instructed them to keep negotiating with the king, and should the results of their action prove unsatisfactory, let them break off the negotiations and return home.

The negotiations broke down on Ostoya's refusal to cede his maritime province. This time the Ragusans took the initiative in forming an alliance against Ostoya, with a view to depriving him of the throne. This alliance was joined promptly by the powerful trio: Hervoye, Sandal and Paul Radinovich, with their retinue of barons, while the Ragusans sent an embassy to the court of Sigismund to win him over to their side in the impending struggle with king Ostoya. In the meantime, Hervoye lined up the Bosnian magnates against Ostoya, with the purpose to dethrone him.

The magnates assembled for that purpose early in June, 1404, in Visoki, deposed Ostoya and selected Tvartko Tvartkovich, son of Tvartko I, king of Bosnia. Ostoya did not oppose the decision of the Assembly, but retired in his impregnable stronghold of Bobovats garrisoned by Hungarian troops, and waited for the propitious moment when he would come forward and occupy again his throne.

STEPHEN TVARTKO II TVARTKOVICH, KING OF BOSNIA (1404-1408)

Tvartko's accession to the throne brought for a short while peace to the country. The power of Hervoye was the chief factor throughout his reign, for Hervoye had him elected and kept him on the throne. Upon Hervoye's request Tvartko was appointed citizen of Venice. This was the zenith of Hervoye's power, and only Sandal Hranich could measure up with him. Hervoye was the actual ruler in two countries, and by 1404 he began to mint his own coins. In June, 1404 king Ladislaus of Naples, the titular king of Croatia and Dalmatia writes to Venice to treat duke Hervoye with the same trust as a king.

Intent on breaking up the party of the deposed Ostoya, Hervoye began to persecute his partisans and especially duke Radivoyevich of Herzegovina and his brother prince Vukich. At the same time the Ragusans negotiated a peace treaty with Bosnia, and were relying on the good will of Sandal Hranich and Hervoye for as favorable peace terms as they could obtain. In fact, king Tvartko II signed on the 24th of June, 1405 in the presence, and with the endorsement of numerous barons, including Hervoye and Sandal, a peace-treaty with Ragusa, accepting all the demands of the Republic and giving it indemnity for the damage caused by the Bosnian troops.

The eagerness of Tvartko to regain the friendship of the Ragusans, even at the price of heavy sacrifices for his country, was not inspired by unselfish motives, but was directed by the urgency of the moment. For new war-clouds appeared coming from the north. King Sigismund was organizing an overwhelming force in order to swoop down on Bosnia and restore Ostoya to power. He put into field three armies. One, under the command of the banus of Machva, was to break into the Usora province of Bosnia, the other, led on by the Croatian banus, was to advance through Una valley and capture the stronghold of Bihach, then under the authority of king Ladislaus and duke Hervoye. The third army was spread along the Slavonian-Bosnian frontier to secure the rear of the first two.

But Bosnia, too, made ready for a heroic defense. Duke Hervoye sought aid from Venice, Ragusa and the king of Naples. Venice, herself embroiled in a war in Lombardy, could not help him. Ragusa gave him indirect aid by supplying arms for the campaign. The king of Naples, on the contrary, sent him his fleet and troops, with which to strike at Sigismund's forces, should they attack the northern Adriatic coast and Croatia. But the main theater of war was in Bosnia. In the second half of 1405 banus Maroth broke into Usora, but was defeated by Bosnians and left the country except for the town of Srebrenik. The western group captured the stronghold Bihach, but could not hold it, and the royal troops soon retreated leaving the body of banus Paul on the battlefield. Thus Bosnia was saved.

However, the respite was of short duration. Both Tvartko and Hervoye became embroiled in quarrels and conflicts with duke George II Stratsimirovich, powerful ruler of Zeta (Montenegro) and northern Albania, and an ally of Venice. The conflict came over the possession of Cattaro, Dulcigno, Budua and Antivari, all important ports along the south Adriatic coast. This time Hervoye and Tvartko clashed with Venice, their former friend. Finally, on the 23rd of December 1407, they straightened out the dispute with a compromise, by the terms of which Sandal kept Budua, Hervoye Cattaro, and Venice the rest.

No sooner than the complications in the south were ended, new dangers threatened Bosnia from the north. King Sigismund could not forget the shameful defeat of his armies in 1405. He planned revenge and looked for allies. He found them in the person of Pope Gregory XII, and the king of Poland. Gregory XII proclaimed on the 9th of November, 1407, a crusade against the Turks and "the Arian and Manichean renegades," i.e., Bosnian heretics.

In the summer of 1408, at the head of a Hungarian-Polish army, 60,000 men strong, Sigismund broke into Bosnia advancing toward Srebrenik, the beleaguered city. In the face of a stubborn Bosnian defense Sigismund could proceed but cautiously and slowly. But in the decisive battle fought near the ill-omened stronghold of Dobor, the Bosnian troops suffered a crushing defeat. King Tvartko II and numerous barons were taken prisoner. Sigismund vented his wrath on the captured magnates, and had 126 of them beheaded, while their lifeless bodies were thrown into Bosna river. King Tvartko II himself, was taken to Budavar as prisoner of war.

STEPHEN OSTOYA, FOR THE SECOND TIME KING OF BOSNIA (1408-1418)

After his ringing victory at Dobor, Sigismund remained as the only power in sight to whom the Bosnian and Croatian barons, together with their over-lords, would look up with respect and awe. So they all hastened to declare their allegiance to the king and emperor Sigismund. Heading off the others, Hervoye and Sandal Hranich rushed to the court of Sigismund in Budavar. Both of them were received at the court with high honors. Sigismund was delighted to see them as his guests, for their visit and homage meant to him extension of sovereignty over a vast territory without striking a blow. Especially lavish in his blandishments and gifts toward Hervoye, Sigismund planned to consolidate his power in Bosnia, Croatia and Dalmatia through the good offices of this powerful lord. Moreover, Hervoye was accompanied by his father-in-law, prince Ivan Nelipich, the wealthiest and most powerful Croatian magnate of that time. So for the good will of these two men, Sigismund sacrificed his pride and confirmed both of them in their former offices and possessions. Moreover, he granted Hervoye extensive estates in Slavonia, including the important town of Pozhega. Further, he made himself his godfather (Hervoye was still a heretic) and appointed him member of the exclusive Dragon Order, which was founded shortly before this by the king and queen themselves.

Hervoye was very pleased with the turn of events, and so was Sigismund. But Ladislaus of Naples as the titular king of Croatia and Dalmatia, saw in Hervoye's move an act of treason. However, he could not do anything about it, nor could he hope to hold his power in these distant lands, in the face of such overwhelming odds. Therefore he decided to sell his possessions, reduced at this time to the city of Zadar, and his royal title over Croatia and Dalmatia, to the Republic of Venice. The Venetians accepted the offer and on the 9th of July, 1409, a treaty was signed in Venice, by virtue of which Venice purchased the city of Zadar and all his claims to Croatia and Dalmatia, for the sum of 100,000 ducats.

The deal between Hervoye and Sigismund concerning Croatia and Dalmatia, went through smoothly in spite of the fact that it was charged with grave consequences. But the deal between Hervoye, Sandal Hranich and Sigismund made at the expense of Bosnia, did not come through at all. Unmindful of the crushing power of the

three, the people of Bosnia repudiated every attempt to seat a foreigner on the throne of Bosnia, be he even emperor himself. They preferred to have the dethroned Stephen Ostoya for their king, to the exclusion of everybody else. An uprising broke out, in the course of which the over-lords of Herzegovina, duke George Radivoyevich and his brother prince Vuchich, raised in November, 1408, Stephen Ostoya again to the throne.

Ostoya renewed his former efforts to effect conciliation with his opponents. Indeed, he succeeded in establishing friendly relations with the Ragusans who declared that "they have forgotten all the quarrels which divided them in the past." They also consented to pay him the annual tribute, to which he as king of Bosnia and Serbia was entitled. On the 4th of December, 1409 Ostoya issued at his court in Visoki a charter confirming all the rights and privileges of the Ragusans granted them by his royal forebears. The charter was endorsed by numerous noblemen, but the signatures of Hervoye, Sandal and Paul Radinovich were absent.

Even though Ostoya was a weak ruler and thus perfectly harmless to Sigismund, the latter could not forgive his usurpation of the throne, which he should occupy himself. On the other hand, Hervoye could not bear that Ostoya, whom he once deposed, again became king of Bosnia. In his campaign, however, Hervoye proceeded with more vigor than tact, and aroused fear among the barons who even before were jealous of Hervoye's overwhelming power. Even the powerful Sandal Hranich, who also was irked by Hervoye's success at the court in Buda, joined the forces of Ostoya.

But this aroused king Sigismund and rather than to put up with disturbances of the past decade, he decided to conquer and dismember Bosnia. The new war was waged in 1410 and 1411. Aided by the forces of the Serbian despot, Stephen Lazarevich from the east and by Hervoye's troops from the west it was an easy task for the two armies of Sigismund to penetrate into the very heart of Bosnia. A whole series of strongholds and mining centers fell in the hands of the emperor. After breaking down all resistance Sigismund split up the Bosnian territory and gave the various administrative districts to his trusted magnates. So Hervoye obtained the

Lower Regions (Dolnji Kraji) while John Gara was given the duchy of Usora, and John Maroth the Soli district. In southern Bosnia the Serbian Stephen Lazarevich obtained the silver-mining district of Srebrenitsa, which ever after became a source of strife between Serbia and Bosnia.

In upper Bosnia proper, in Herzegovina, Travunya and along the upper reaches of the Drina river, Ostoya could successfully ward off all the attacks and retained his power to the end. In the meantime, order and security were at low ebb, and the country became prey to brigandage and anarchy.

After the war with Sigismund the power of Sandal Hranich rose to new heights. At that time he already had the support of the Turkish sultan, and with his troops he could defy even the powerful Venice, his ally and former protector. So when in May, 1411 the Venetians urged him to sell to them his claims to the port of Cattaro, they promptly withdrew their offer as soon as the Doge found out that Sandal was preparing to force Cattaro into submission, with the aid of 7,000 men of Turkish troops. Ragusans were also wooing the good will of Sandal and asked him to plead their cause at the Bosnian court.

Under these circumstances also king Sigismund strove to win Sandal over to his cause. He invited him several times as his guest to the court, and Sandal finally went in Spring 1412 to visit Sigismund in Budavar. Both he and Hervoye were the king's guests at the great festivities arranged in June, 1412, in honor of the Polish king Włodzisław Jagiello. Yet this time Sigismund's sympathy was on the side of Sandal, and he gave him the commission to join the forces of the Serbian despot, Stephen Lazarevich against Mussa Kesseji, a powerful Turkish free-booter who plundered and terrorized the Serbian territory. Sandal gladly undertook the task and in 1413 he annihilated the forces of Kesseji as he besieged the mining town of Novo Berdo.

On the other hand, Sigismund's friendship with Hervoye gradually cooled off. Even for him the power of Hervoye was too uncomfortable, especially in view of the fact that the duke entertained friendly relations with Venice, which not long ago confirmed his titles and possessions. Further, his popularity among the Bosnian and Croatian barons ebbed, while the Hungarian magnates were outright hostile to him. So his

neighbors and administrative chiefs of Bosnia and Serbia, John Gara, John Maroth and Paul Csupor worked against him at the court. Csupor went so far as to insult Hervoye in public. Deriding his hoarse voice Csupor accosted Hervoye, in the presence of others, in bellowing tones of a bull. Hervoye was extremely irritated over this offense, which he requited later with merciless cruelty. At home he clashed with Sandal Hranich over some family affair.

Hervoye realized that his star was tarnishing and that he had to use force in order to retain his power unchecked. So when Sandal Hranich took his troops to southern Serbia as an ally of despot Stephen Lazarevich in his campaign against Mussa Kesseji, Hervoye invaded his territory reducing its towns and devastating the countryside. Moreover, he invited the Turks to Bosnia as his allies. By this act Hervoye secured the undying enmity of his rivals while the other barons turned away from him. In the absence of Sigismund from the court, queen Barbara, influenced by John Gara and John Csupor, decided to overthrow Hervoye. She proclaimed him a renegade and traitor and declared all his possessions forfeited to the crown. So Gara and Csupor robbed and plundered his estates in Slavonia, and took away from him everything, with the exception of the city and stronghold of Pozhega. The citizens of Spalato, instigated by Hervoy's opponents, staged a rebellion, expelled his officers, and destroyed the fortress. Furthermore, he lost the three islands: Brach, Hvar (Lesina) and Korchula.

Confronted with hostile acts on all sides, Hervoye sent a message to queen Barbara, justifying his own actions, rejecting the charges of disloyalty, insisting on his own rights, stressing inviolability of his privileges as a member of the Order of the Dragon, reminding her of the king's pledges and obligations toward him, and forthright threatening to denounce the king for treachery before the whole Christian world, and to seek aid wherever he could find it in case he failed to obtain redress of his grievances. Yet the queen was adamant and, moreover, she persuaded the king also to declare Hervoye a renegade and traitor.

Realizing that a conflict with the powerful king and emperor Sigismund was inevitable, Hervoye looked around for aid. At first he urged

Venice to sell him a part of their fleet so that he might reconquer Spalato. Another time he offered to them a military alliance against Sigismund, and asked their mediation to iron out his differences with Sandal Hranich. With the exception of the latter service, the Venetians rejected all his demands, and Hervoye was never in a position to reconquer Spalato and the three islands. Another cause for worry was the attack of Sandal Hranich from the south.

In these circumstances Hervoye made up again with king Ostoya, a move that proved soon mutually beneficial. Sigismund, who was occupied at the Council of Constanza, where the alleged heresy of John Huss was on trial, had no time for Bosnian affairs, and sent there Tvartko II to stir up south of the Sava, as much trouble as he could. Tvartko's campaign at first was successful. The country was embroiled in civil war, which greatly enhanced Hervoye's prestige and doomed Tvartko's adventure to failure. As a winner in this test of strength Hervoye renewed his plan to conquer Spalato and seize the surrounding islands. So in April 1415 he sent envoys to Venice and Naples, soliciting aid for his impending venture. The Venetians again denied aid, yet opened their arsenal for sale of arms to the duke.

Apprised of Hervoye's preparations for a new campaign, his Hungarian enemies, Gara, Maroth and Csupor were mustering up a huge army for a final showdown with the Duke. Moreover, they were urging Ragusa to attack from the sea Hervoye's town of Omish (Almissa), situated at the mouth of Tsetina river. In such conditions it was a matter of survival for him to carry a crushing blow at his enemies and destroy them before they had time to cause him irreparable damage. So through mediation of king Ostoya who was on friendly terms with the Sultan, he sued for aid from Mohammed I. The Sultan was only too glad to assist Hervoye, for this gave him an unobstructed passage-way for a campaign against Slavonia and Hungary.

The decisive battle was fought south of the Sava in the province of Usora, and the Hungarian army suffered at the hands of Hervoye and his Turkish allies, a crushing defeat. A huge booty fell in the hands of the Turks. In hot pursuit of the fleeing Hungarians, the Turks over-ran Slavonia, Croatia and Styria, up into Carinthia. All

the leaders of the Hungarian army were taken prisoner, including the three overlords: Gara, Maroth and Csupor. In requital for the old insult, Hervoye had Csupor sewn in an ox-hide, and thrown in the river, with the words, "In human form you preferred to imitate the voice of a bull, so take now, in addition to the voice, also the shape of a bull!" After his momentous victory Hervoye spent some time at Ostoya's court. Here he entertained plans of conquering Ragusa for its disloyalty and seizure of his three islands. Because of Hervoye's death the next year, this plan had never been carried out.

In the meantime, grave complications took place in Bosnia itself. During an outing party, in which king Ostoya participated, Sandal Hranich had the equally powerful prince Paul Radinovich attacked by surprise and beheaded. After the bloody affair was over Sandal accused his victim of treason, which could not be left unpunished. Details of this gruesome affair are not known, but its consequences were fatal. A civil war broke out, in which prince Peter Pavlovich, with his partisans, took a bloody revenge for the murder of his father. He laid waste the possessions of both king Ostoya and duke Sandal, and made an open alliance with the Turks against both.

Throughout the winter of 1415 and good part of 1416 the Turks robbed and plundered the southern part of Bosnia and Herzegovina. They occupied the Upper Bosnia district with its capital Verhbosna. The commander of Turkish troops, serdar Isaac, was appointed by Mohammed I, governor (sanjak) of the occupied provinces. The sanjak had promptly introduced there the Turkish administration. Moreover, he subjected Sandal Hranich and the princely Pavlovich brothers to the authority of the Sultan. Hence, both opposing groups were treated as the subjects of Sultan and held their estates "by the grace of God and the great ruler Sultan Mohammed bey and his serdar (general) Isaac." Such was the deplorable result of the bloody strife between the Bosnian overlords.

Precisely at this time of turmoil and decomposition, when Bosnia needed him most, the great duke Hervoye passed away. For over a quarter of a century he deeply influenced the public life of Bosnia, Herzegovina, Ragusa, Dalmatia and Croatia. As a diplomat, general and politician, he had no equal east of the Adriatic. In the face of bitter opposition, hostility and treachery he could always assert his will to his own advantage. As a violent, cruel and obstinate character, he was merely a child of his age: the 14th and 15th centuries. As a proud and imperious oligarch of his time, he was probably the most colorful figure in Europe.

The huge possessions of Hervoye were inherited by his widow Helen, daughter of the wealthiest Croatian magnate, prince Ivan Nelipich. In order to restore his wealth and power, king Ostoya decided to woo the widow. So he divorced his wife, queen Kuyeva, and married Hervoye's widow. But even with huge resources at his disposal, Ostoya could not maintain himself long on the throne. The vindictive princes Pavlovichi who blamed him for the dastardly murder of their father, aroused their friends and other malcontents against the king. In a free-for-all fight the Bosnian barons were exterminating each other, and the entreaties of Ragusa and Croatian nobility to stop the carnage, were of no avail. In the meantime, the Turks plundered the country, and occupied district after district.

Even the Turks were horrified at the ghastly scenes of senseless bloodshed. Finally, sultan Mohammed sent envoys to the warring factions, urging conciliation between king Ostoya and the rebellious barons. The Turks persuaded them to hold a general Assembly. For lack of mutual trust the barons could not arrive at any agreement, except to proclaim the king the cause of all evil, and to imprison him, together with his advisors. Promptly informed by his men of the impending disgrace, Ostoya fled with his friends overnight, leaving the Assembly to do as it pleased. In the west of Bosnia he still had powerful friends, and the princes Pavlovichi who in the meantime, came to the conclusion that the Turks merely brought disaster upon their heads, and the rest of the country, effected a conciliation with Ostoya. So did many barons. Before he could reunite the country again, Ostoya passed away in 1418.

KING STEPHEN OSTOYICH (1418-1421)

After the death of his father, Stephen Ostoyich was elected king of Bosnia. The reign of Ostoyich was of short duration. His first year on the throne was uneventful. But in the second year of his reign Sandal Hranich plotted to destroy his arch-enemy, prince Peter Pavlovich. He prevailed on the Serdar Isaac to attack Prince Pavlovich as a traitor to the Sultan. Isaac promptly sent Turkish troops in the prince's dominion and ravaged the country. Prince Peter put up a valiant resistance to the Turks, but fell in battle. Sandal obtained from serdar Isaac the lands of the prince and so considerably expanded his own possessions. But the bloody acquisition inland was offset by the loss of the famous port of Cattaro, which was taken over on the 8th of March, 1420, by Venice. Sandal had to reconcile himself to the loss of Cattaro, and so did Ostoyich, as a sovereign of Bosnia and her dependencies.

But the loss of sovereignty over Cattaro was not the worst blow to Ostoyich. The exiled king Stephen Tvartko II, son of Tvartko I, reappeared early in 1420 on the scene. His success was rapid, for in August of the same year he issued decrees counter-signed by a number of magnates. In the meantime, things went from bad to worse for Ostoyich, and he is last heard of early in April, 1421, negotiating a treaty with Venice. After this event every vestige of his is lost.

KING STEPHEN TVARTKO II, TVARTKOVICH (1421-1443)

The long reign of Tvartko II is filled with the saddest episodes in the history of Bosnia. The civil war raged with unabated fury. This was no longer a struggle for principles, struggle for freedom of the "Bosnian (Patarene) Church," for defense of territorial integrity, for national sovereignty, or to enhance the power of the Bosnian king. It was a bloodshed instigated by the furies of hate, rapine and destruction of rival neighbours, all of them bent on the road of collective suicide. The authority of the king was disregarded altogether, and he could participate in the bloody melee only as one of the combatants, usually the least successful one.

It is a rare occurrence in history that a king of a once powerful country tried to give away his crown and country to a foreign power. Tvartko II was one of such exceptions. But still more unusual is the case where a foreign power, thus to be benefitted, declines the offer. Venice did it! Bosnia was no longer an asset, but a grave liability both for Tvartko II, and Venice. What the common people and the middle class, if any, went through all these years of bloody nightmare—can merely be conjectured.

The Turks were free to make their incursions unopposed, and frequently they made them at the invitation of the warring factions themselves. The once powerful Bosnia rolled headlong into the precipice, into which she "fell without a whisper." The unbridled oligarchy had its macabre feast unmindful of the destruction of the country, and its own downfall. Such scenes and episodes we are to review during the reign of the last three kings of Bosnia.

Right at the outset of his reign Tvartko II embarked on a policy of foreign adventure, which was far above his means, while gloomy prospects hovered over his throne. Probably stimulated by the exploits of his glorious father, Tvartkovich sought intervention in the affairs of Croatia, intent on destruction of its most powerful magnate, prince Ivanish Nelipich, brother-in-law of the late duke Hervoye. The plan seemed simple and alluring. In his fight with Ivanish he would be supported by the land and naval forces of the powerful Venice. The Venetians, on the other hand, had a grudge against prince Nelipich who thwarted their attempts at conquest of both Dalmatian and Croatian territory. So while the Venetians managed to occupy the islands and a few coastal towns, their advance on land was checked by the forces of Ivanish. This made the Venetian Senate look for an ally in the interior, and it found him in the person of King Tvartko II.

Negotiations were carried on for nearly two years, in the course of which all the details of strategy were fixed, including the arrangements for division of Ivanish's dominion. Even the date for the attack was fixed. Thus the war had to start on the 23rd of April, 1424. Yet, this campaign never came to pass. What happened then to avert this cloud from the troubled skies of Croatia?

Early in 1424 the Turks invaded Bosnia, and Stephen Tvartko went through some harassing experiences. As in the past, this time, too, the Turks had been invited by Bosnian magnates. On this occasion the sons of king Ostoya were the offenders, among them especially prince Radivoy who was embittered over the choice of

Tvartko II as the king, since he himself coveted the throne. He was supported by duke Radosav Pavlovich, but their combined forces were insufficient to overwhelm Tvartko II and his partisans. Hence Radivoy's pleading before sultan Murad II for aid! Murad II (1421-1451) welcomed the opportunity of meddling in the affairs of Bosnia, in order to restore the authority his father had exercised in that country. So Murad invaded Bosnia precisely at a time when Tvartko was making ready to carry the fatal blow against prince Ivanish Nelipich, the gallant defender of Croatia. At first Tvartko put up a fierce resistance to the invaders, but his forces waned and the king realized that neither prince Radivoy, nor sultan Murad II would rest before they destroyed his forces and occupied Bosnia.

So he looked around for aid. His cousin Herman, Count of Zell, and banus of Slavonia, was the first to hasten to his rescue. Moreover, he reconciled him with king Sigismund, with whom Tvartko II concluded an alliance in 1425. At the same time Venice, too, abandoned her plan of attacking prince Ivanish Nelipich. Even this move was ineffective since the Turks broke into Bosnia again in 1426. Through diplomatic means Tvartko sought to restore the security and peace of his kingdom. So he proclaimed his cousin Herman, the powerful Slavonian banus, his heir and successor to the throne of Bosnia. But neither could that help any, for the Turks established themselves in the southern districts of Bosnia, and kept ravaging the rest of the country. So the only way out of a hopeless situation was to make peace with the Sultan and submit to his terms. Apparently a number of towns were ceded to Murad, while others had to pay contribution, and remained under Turkish occupation, until the ransom money had been delivered. It seems that the contribution was in the neighborhood of 32,000 golden ducats.

No sooner than Tvartko II made peace with the sultan, he again returned to his old obsession of attacking and destroying prince Ivanish Nelipich of Croatia. In August, 1430 he declared war against Ivanish. But he soon abandoned this adventure, because a new menace appeared in the south-western part of his kingdom where duke Radosav Pavlovich, son of the murdered Paul Radinovich, engaged in a bloody struggle with the Republic of Ragusa.

The apparently innocuous quarrel between these two neighbors developed in no time into a spectacular drama. After the tragic death of his elder brother Peter, duke Radosav made up both with duke Sandal Hranich and the Ragusan Republic. Thereupon he concluded a treaty of friendship and alliance with the Ragusans, in which he confirmed all the rights and privileges in his part of the Konavlye district, which they enjoyed there during the life-time of his father Paul and brother Peter. In return for this the Ragusans promised to pay him an annual tribute of 600 perpers (Ragusan currency). Other provisions were inserted in the agreement, including the payment of a lump-sum of 13,000 ducats, which the Ragusans actually paid to duke Radosav. At that point it seemed that peace and friendship between the two contracting parties would last for a long time.

But soon Radosav figured out that he was defrauded by this deal, and under some pretext, he demanded the return of his property, the beautiful coast of the Konavlye district, from the Ragusans. In order to gain time while organizing their defense, and using their diplomatic channels, the Ragusans negotiated for awhile with the duke. Yet they sent envoys to king Sigismund, pleading that he promptly dispatch his troops stationed in Usora (north-east of Bosnia) against Radosav Pavlovich. They approached sultan Murad II, with the request to prohibit Radosav to ravage their territory. Nor did they pass up king Tvartko II and Sandal Hranich, offering them alliance against duke Radosav. However, to be sure that sultan Murad II would not prevent them from destroying duke Radosav, they offered the sultan 70,000 ducats to abstain from interfering in the impending struggle.

As he discovered the fatal plot that was threatening him with annihilation, duke Radosav turned in the first place to the Sultan as his sovereign, seeking protection and aid. Murad II was at that time in no mood to fight, so he applied pressure both upon Radosav and Ragusa to make up. In compliance with the wishes of his sovereign, Radosav made overtures to the Ragusans, but their terms were so unreasonable that the duke rejected them. At that point he decided to make up with the Bosnian king, in which he fully succeeded.

Detached from the alliance with Ragusa,

Tvartko II was promptly accused by Ragusa at the Court of Sigismund that he was threatening the Republic with war, for duke Radosav persuaded him that the Ragusans sought from the Sultan the permission to grab his lands, and thus detach them from Bosnia. Sigismund sent the Croatian vice-banus Vladikovich to Tvartko's court in order to persuade the king to renew his alliance with Ragusa. Tvartko II declined to follow this course, but promised to bring the Ragusans and duke Radosav together on amicable terms. Thus, Tvartko II mediated in the peace negotiations between the two warring factions. The peace between Ragusa and duke Radosav was actually signed on the 25th of October, 1432. Early in March of the next year this peace-treaty was confirmed also by Tvartko II at his court in Sutiska.

But no sooner than the peace was restored in the south-western portion of his kingdom, a new storm broke loose along the eastern border of Bosnia. This time the threat came from the Serbian despot George Brankovich, and the Turkish protege, prince Radivoy, son of the late king Ostoya. Despot Brankovich sought to extend his possessions in Bosnia beyond the silver-mining district of Srebrenitsa, which was given to despot Stephen Lazarevich by king Sigismund in his campaign of 1408 against Bosnia. While Bosnians were never reconciled to cession of such a valuable district to Serbia, the Serbian despots, on the contrary, sought to penetrate deeper into Bosnia. Seeing the weakness of Tvartko II and the desperate plight of Bosnia, George Brankovich planned to grab another slice or two from the richest part of Bosnia. Having no illusions about Brankovich's intentions, Tvartko rushed in April, 1433, with his troops, reinforced by those of Radosav Pavlovich, against the Serbians in the northeast of Bosnia. In an engagement near Zvornik, he repulsed the enemy. But before he could crush Brankovich's troops in a decisive battle, Tvartko II had to leave the Serbian theater of war, rushing south to defeat prince Radivoy who broke into the country supported by sizable Turkish forces.

As if that much misfortune were not enough for the distressed king, a deadly menace both for his throne and life appeared in the person of duke Sandal Hranich who joined hands with prince Radivoy and other enemies of the king.

Moreover, Sandal and the Serbian despot George, made a joint move to purchase all of Bosnia from the Sultan. So George Brankovich occupied the town of Zvornik and the duchy of Usora, while Sandal Hranich took the rest of the country.

Unable to defend his country any longer .Tvartko II fled to Hungary where he spent three years. In the meantime, violent fighting and bloody internecine war was carried on by the barons, while the Turks ravaged the country unimpeded. The most powerful opponent of Sandal was duke George Voyssalich, a nephew of the late duke Hervoye, who was also supported by some Croatian magnates. Voyssalich not only could protect the Lower Region, his patrimony, in northern Bosnia, but soon rolled back Sandal's troops, and chased them all the way into southern Bosnia, where in summer 1434 he established himself as the provisional ruler of the country. In the middle of this tragic struggle, the Grand Duke Sandal Hranich passed on, in 1435. His nephew Stephen Vukchich Kossacha (1435-1466) inherited the huge possessions of Sandal.

While in exile in Hungary, king Tvartko II vainly sued for aid. In the meantime his country fell into a pitiful condition. The Turks firmly established themselves in Upper Bosnia, and again made Verhbosna capital of the province. Serdar Isaac was appointed sanjak bey (governor) of the province. He actually controlled the possessions of Stephen Vukchich Kossacha, successor of Sandal, further those of Radosav Pavlovich and other barons, east and west. Devastation of the country was worse than ever, and every prospect of aid from outside was excluded.

Still believing that he could do some good for Bosnia, in her sad plight, king Tvartko II reached a momentous decision. He offered in 1437 to Murad II to become his vassal and pay him an annual tribute of 35,000 ducats, if he would leave him in possession of Bosnia. Murad agreed and Bosnia became from 1437 to 1439 a vassal state of the Ottoman empire. In summer, 1439, Tvartko II set up his court in the stronghold of Bobovats. But his power was merely a shadow of its former self. The towns lay in ruins, and Murad II dispatched the affairs of the State as actual sovereign. So in 1442 the Sultan confirmed the rights and trading privileges of the Ragusans for Bosnia, Serbia and Albania, and in exchange for protection of their trade, the Ragusans paid him the annual tribute, which they earlier paid to the kings of Bosnia.

It was bad enough for Tvartko II that the Serbian despot Brankovich seized Srebrenitsa, Zvornik and the Usora province, but it became much worse when Murad II, in 1440, attacked the Despot, over-ran all of Serbia and occupied all the Serbian territory including the annexed Bosnian districts. Naturally, Murad II retained his Bosnian acquisitions for himself, and Tvartko II looked helplessly at the dismemberment of his native land. He expected now any day that his country will become a voiceless vilayet (administrative district) of the Sultan. However, this precipitous fall of Bosnia was averted for another twenty years by favorable developments abroad.

Sigismund's successor Albert II died in 1439, and the Hungarian-Croatian Estates elected Włodzisław Varnenchik, king of Poland, as their king. His power and heroism was known abroad, and George Brankovich, together with Tvartko II, turned to him for aid impressing upon him that they are of same blood and speech as Poles.

Włodzisław took the task of liberation of southern Slavs to his heart, and after strengthening his position in Poland and Hungary, he prepared for a crusade against the Turks in 1443. He was supported by Yancu de Sibiu (Hunyadi-Corvinus), a heroic Roumanian leader (along with prince Markho, the greatest hero of the Slavic popular ballads, extolled under the name of Sibinyanin Yanko), who scored in 1442 two great victories over the invading Turks.

But neither Brankovich, nor Tvartko II were in a mood to rejoice over the long-drawn-out preparations. Tvartko II was expecting the disaster to break upon his head any day and gave much thought to his own personal safety, and that of his family. So in January, 1441, he asked for permission to send all his funds and valuables on deposit to Venice, and the right of refuge for himself and his family. He also offered the Republic to take his kingdom, openly or secretly, in her possession. Should the Serenissime Republic decline this offer, then he asked the Doge and the Senate to send him arms and munitions from their Dalmatian towns. The Republic declined to take over Bosnia, but permitted him to take arms and ammunition from Dalmatia as much as he needed.

This time he fought alone against Turkey, and scored signal success in defense of Bosnia. Yet, he did not feel sure about himself, and in April, 1442, he sent his valuables and a large amount of money for safe-keeping in Ragusa. At the same time he again sent envoys to Venice, pleading for aid. The Venetians politely, but firmly refused to offer any more succour to the distressed country.

In spite of the general agony, Tvartko II was spared the sight of the final calamity to which Bosnia was to succumb. In June, 1443 Włodzisław Varnenchik and Yancu de Sibiu set out on their campaign to liberate the Balkan Christians from the Turks. The Crusaders drove the Turks easily in the interior of Bulgaria occupying the capital Sofia and the town of Philippopolis. Furthermore, Włodzisław smashed Murad's forces in a great battle near the pass of Kunovitsa, and the Sultan was forced to sue for a peace of humiliating terms. Murad II had to evacuate both Serbia and Bosnia. The liberated territory was to revert to its lawful rulers: George Brankovich and King Tvartko II. However, Tvartko soon died and he never saw his country free again, even for a short period of time.

So ended the long, but inglorious reign of Tvartko II, who witnessed nothing but ruin, devastation, humiliation and unnecessary bloodshed, for which his own misguided policy was to no small degree responsible.

Reign of King Stephen Thomas Ostoyich (1444-1461)

Even though the Bosnian throne was bequeathed by Tvartko II to his cousin Hermann, count of Zell, the Bosnians elected to the throne Thomas Ostoyich, an illegitimate son of the late king Ostoya. Unlike his brother Radivoy who, in his struggle with Tvartko II, ravaged the country with the Turks, Thomas kept in hiding, denied his royal blood, and lived as a humble Bosnian faithful, with his wife Voyacha, in retirement.

When called to the throne, he placed himself in the hands of John Hunyadi (Yancu de Sibiu), the most powerful Christian leader in Central Europe, gave him all the privileges in Bosnia,

and promised to pay him an annual tribute of 3,000 ducats. Thus, he felt secure both from Turks and his domestic enemies, among whom the most important was the Grand Duke Stephen Vukchich Kossacha, since 1435 heir and successor to Sandal Hranich.

Although he came from a family attached to the Bosnian Church, and by this time nearly all of Bosnia turned to this sect, Thomas realized that the only way to save his country from the Turkish yoke was to seek protection from the powerful Catholic Church, and western Europe. Urged by Bishop Thomas of Lesina (Hvar), Apostolic delegate for Dalmatia, Croatia and Bosnia, to break loose from the heretics, and become a Catholic, the new king gave further thought to his plan. Furthermore, Pope Eugene IV offered to him the crown, as inducement to join the Catholic Church. King Thomas declined the crown for fear that his heretic subjects might turn against him, and invite the Turks, but he accepted the proposal to join the Western Church, and to give monastic orders wide concessions, which would advance the Catholic cause.

His political ambitions and desire to enhance his prestige before the barons, cost him a family tragedy. He had to divorce his wife Voyacha whom he dearly loved, and from whom he had a son Stephen, of whom he was equally fond.*

Separated through a papal absolution from Voyacha, Stephen Thomas looked around for a spouse who could proudly wear the crown of Bosnia. He found such in the person of Helena, daughter of Stephen Vukchich Kossacha, his powerful, but unruly subject. So, with this royal match the king thought that his reign would be safe and prosperous. Following the king's example many Bosnian magnates embraced Catholicism. Only Stephen Vukchich, the powerful Grand Duke, remained true to the faith of his ancestors and the Bosnian Church.

After 1446 intense religious activity commences throughout Bosnia. Some churches were built, and the wealthy magnates vied with each other in the erection of churches. On the other hand, the king resisted the pressure brought to bear on him to order persecution of the heretics.

---

* He had been married to her according to the custom of Bosnian Bogomiles, namely, under the condition that she be good and faithful to him, and as such a contract of the marriage did not involve insolubility, the Church considered such a marriage invalid.

On the contrary, he held the Church of Bosnia, and its chief, the "Grand-Father" (Djed) in high esteem. But even apart from this, it was a matter of political wisdom, not to arouse the powerful sect, for the experience of the past showed clearly how dangerous an uprising of the Bosnian Christians can be. So when accused by the impatient Franciscans in Rome of complicity with the sectarians, his arguments carried weight with Pope Nicholas V, and the conflict with Franciscans was ironed out.

After liberation of Serbia and Bosnia from the Turks, the old rivalry between these two countries was renewed. George Brankovich, who through Hunyadi's victory at Kunovitsa pass was reinstated in his possessions, aspired again at the Bosnian borderlands and especially at the silver-mine district of Srebrenitsa, which king Thomas decided to keep for Bosnia at all costs. After the fatal battle at Varna in 1444, which cost the life of king Włodzisław, Brankovich's raids became more persistent, and in 1445 he actually took Srebrenitsa. This resulted in an open break between Bosnia and Serbia and in the war that ensued, the Bosnian troops were defeated in the battle fought on September 6, 1448. But Stephen Thomas did not give up the struggle, and sought allies for his new campaign. In fact, developments outside of Bosnian frontiers brightened up his prospects.

John Hunyadi (Yancu de Sibiu), Governor of Hungary, in the name of Ladislaus, Posthumus, could not forget his defeat at Varna, but in 1448 made preparations for a new campaign against sultan Murad II. Among others he summoned George Brankovich, the Serbian despot, to join him, with the Serbian troops, in the campaign. Despot George not only refused to follow but also declared allegiance to the Sultan, hoping that as a Turkish vassal, he could more easily retain his grip on Serbia. Brankovich's treachery infuriated Hunyadi, and on his way to Albania, he devastated the Serbian towns and villages. But at Blackbird Field (Kossovo Polye), the Hungarian-Croatian army in a three-day battle suffered on the 17th of October, 1448, a crushing defeat, while Hunyadi, with the remnants of his forces, was intercepted by the Serbian troops at Belgrade, and incarcerated by despot Brankovich in the nearby stronghold of Smederevo. Only upon promise to pay a ransom of 100,000 ducats, and on leaving his son Ladislaus as hostage in custody of the despot, could Hunyadi cross the Danube to freedom.

Upon his return to Hungary Hunyadi met with the Estates General, where a new campaign against Turkey was decided, in the course of which fitting punishment would be meted out on George Brankovich and his associates. Terrified by the tidings of a new campaign, despot George hastened with prince Ladislaus, to Hunyadi himself, returning his son to him without any ransom, and offering his services to bring about peace between Hungary and Turkey. Hunyadi pardoned Brankovich's treachery and peace was actually concluded in May, 1449 in Smederevo for a period of seven years. According to the terms of the treaty Serbia was to pay to the Sultan only one-half of her former tribute, while Bosnia was to continue her payments in full and pay the major part of her arrears.

After conclusion of peace in Smederevo the Hungarian Estates General met in Budapest. King Stephen Thomas and Despot Brankovich sent also their representatives who should submit the Bosnian-Serbian strife to the Parliament for arbitration: The matter was delegated to a special tribunal, which decided the dispute in favor of the king of Bosnia. A number of charters issued by the king late in 1449 clearly show that he is once again in possession of the entire Bosnian territory.

By 1450 Stephen Thomas achieved a measure of security which he never enjoyed before. So he could turn now his attention to domestic affairs. In spite of his own passing in the fold of the Catholic Church and the fact that many magnates followed suit, the Bosnian sect was at that time stronger than ever. In the meantime, he had to make good on his promise to the Pope and John Hunyadi that he would take drastic steps toward extermination of the heretics. He was further goaded to this fatal policy by repeated demands of the Pope and Governor Hunyadi.

The news of new persecutions was answered by mass exodus of the population, part of which found refuge in Herzegovina, ruled by Stephen Vukchich. The rest of them fled to the Turkish territory, inviting the Turks to invade Bosnia and dethrone the oppressive king Thomas. On the other hand, the Pope issued on the 18th of

June a decree by which he extended to the king and his crusading army the privileges and indulgences for the duration of "the war they conduct in their self-defense against the Turks, and Manichaean heretics." So a new civil war and religious strife broke out in Bosnia, which shook Thomas' throne. Still worse, while he was in the midst of his struggle with the Turks and heretics, his old Serbian rival, despot George Brankovich invaded the country with the intention to seize the provinces which Hunyadi had him return to king Thomas.

Even though embroiled in the internal struggle, king Thomas made up his mind to have a final show-down with Brankovich, and made preparations abroad for a decisive campaign against Serbia. So in April, 1451 he sought in Venice either alliance against the Despot, or a status of neutrality in case of war with Serbia. Further, he asked the good services of the Republic at the Subline Porte, pleading with the Sultan that he should not interfere in the struggle between Serbia and Bosnia.

Through his successful arrangements abroad, king Thomas was making ready to start the war against the Despot. But before hostilities began, John Hunyadi appeared on the scene with recriminations and threats against Stephen Thomas. Governor Hunyadi accused the king of laxity in his actions against the sectarians, and threatened with invasion of Bosnia, should Thomas attack Serbia. In this hour of need king Thomas turned to Pope with bitter denunciations of Hunyadi, for breaking the treaty of peace and friendship he signed in the name of Hungary and Croatia. In his reply to the Holy See Hunyadi repeated the charge that king Thomas gave up his persecution of the heretics whom he should have exterminated. Thus, the strife between Serbia and Bosnia ended in a stalemate, each party keeping its own possessions.

Rise of Herzegovina under Stephen Vukchich Kossacha

In the meantime, king Thomas became drawn into another struggle which broke out at the southwestern borders of his kingdom. This time he became involved in war his father-in-law, Grand Duke Stephen Vuckchich waged against the Ragusan Republic. By the force of circumstances the king had to support Ragusa and the enemies of his father-in-law. To make the matters worse, Stephen Vukchich was, next to John Hunyadi and the Sultan, the most powerful person in the Balkans. Finally, the Grand Duke considered the king only the junior partner in the authority over Bosnia and her dependencies.

Stephen Vukchich was very proud of two things: 1) that his daughter Helena became the queen of Bosnia and 2) that he had obtained in 1448 the title of Grand Duke (Herzog) from the hands of the Roman emperor Frederic III. His lands became gradually identified by this title and to this day they are known under the name of Herzegovina, i.e. Grand Duchy.

Unusually successful throughout his career, the Grand Duke was a man of jovial nature and rather profligate. He liked the company of Italian merchants, and from them he heard of a beautiful Florentine lady of unusual charm and attractiveness. He ardently desired to see her, and at first sight he fell in love with her. Since the beautiful Cecilia did not object to his advances, the Grand Duke, at his mature age, took her in his court as his mistress. Naturally that provoked a storm of protests on the part of Helena, his legal wife, and his two grown-up sons: Vlatko and Vladislav.

As a result of the family-scandal Helena Vukchich, grand-daughter of Balsha III, famous ruler of Zeta (Montenegro), and her son Vladislav, took refuge in Ragusa. This act of Ragusan courtesy irritated the Grand Duke, and he summoned the Republic to expel the two refugees. Bound by their tradition of hospitality and right of refuge, the Ragusans refused to comply, and after some bickering the Grand Duke invaded the Ragusan territory, sowing death and destruction wherever his troops appeared.

This turn of events resulted in a diminutive Trojan war, with the most disastrous and shameful episodes in the history of Bosnia and Herzegovina. Since the Grand Duke was a follower of the Bosnian Church, the Ragusans sought aid at all the Christian courts against the heretic and friend of infidels. In the first place they sent envoys to Hungary with the complaint against Stephen Vukchich requesting the Parliament to inform the Grand Duke that his hostile actions against Ragusa, would be considered as an attack against Hungary. Vukchich disregarded the threat altogether and kept ravaging the Ragusan territory all the more vigorously.

The Ragusan Senate sent again envoys to Budapest asking the Parliament to have Governor Hunyadi, the Croatian banus Talovats and king of Bosnia jointly attack the Grand Duke, and dispossess him altogether. Other envoys were sent to Rome before the Holy See with a complaint against the Grand Duke and his numerous Italian allies who, as good Christians joined the troops of a heretic to fight against the Christian and Catholic Ragusa. And in June, 1451 Pope Nicholas issued a manifesto threatening with excommunication all those who in whatsoever way or manner supported the "unworthy Patarene Duke Stephen" against Ragusa.

While things moved slowly for the Ragusans, they placed their best hope in the aid of king Thomas of Bosnia. Thomas was for some time at odds with his father-in-law, because he sheltered in his land the Bosnian refugees and gave them protection. Further, repudiation of his legal wife Helena, mother of the queen of Bosnia, was an added affront to his own dignity. So he was ready to support Prince Vladislav, his brother-in-law, who rose against his own father, in order to deprive him of his possessions and proclaim himself ruler of Herzegovina. At first his campaign was successful, and in August, 1451 he seized a good part of his father's domain. That in itself was aggravating for the old Duke, but when king Thomas of Bosnia concluded in December, 1451, a treaty of alliance with Ragusa against him, the situation became hopeless.

In spite of this isolation the Grand Duke fought Ragusa throughout 1452 and in the first part of 1453. He was further distressed when in 1452 a number of his barons reneged their allegiance to him and joined the Ragusan side. The commander of the allied forces was no one else but prince Vladislav, his own son, who planned to ascend the throne after his father's downfall. Only the younger son Vlatko remained loyal to his aged father, refusing to sit in judgment over the acts of his sire.

After defection of his closest supporters the chances of the Grand Duke to crush his enemies were slim. Surrounded on all sides by powerful enemies Stephen Vukchich would have been defeated, if not for relief from unexpected quarters. The greatest threat came from Bosnia. But when Thomas announced the ban of his nobility, the barons in sympathy with the Bosnian faithful rebelled against the king, and a new civil war broke out in Bosnia. Thomas had to call off his aid to Ragusa, and managed only with difficulty to subdue the leaders of the rebellion: Duke Peter Voyssalich and Duke Vladislav Kleshich. At this point the papal Legate, bishop Thomas of Hvar, who was grieved over the sight of senseless bloodshed, intervened to reconcile the two rebel leaders and their friend to the king. Conciliation was effected on the 1st of July, 1452, a good omen for restoration of peace throughout the war-torn area.

Pope Nicholas V himself, attempted to bring about peace between Ragusa and the Grand Duke of Herzegovina. He studied the conflict between the two powers and it did not take him long to see through the intrigues of Ragusa, in which the Church was not interested at all. So he sent Bishop Pagaminus of Dulcigno to Stephen Vukchich to sound out his willingness to make up with Ragusa and his other enemies. Being in dire straits the Duke gladly accepted the proposal, and promised to join the Catholic Church, if an honorable peace was concluded. The Pope was delighted over the prospect of bringing Herzegovina into the fold of the Church and sent Pagaminus to Ragusa to prepare the ground for peace-negotiations.

In the meantime, the duke apparently obtained aid from the Sultan, broke off the peace negotiations, and threatened Ragusa again with invasion. The Senate of the Republic sent promptly envoys to the royal court in Budapest, imploring John Hunyadi to save them from the impending disaster.

In the meantime, the war between the aged Duke and his son prince Vladislav, continued with varying fortunes until in summer, 1453, Grand Duke Stephen won a decisive victory, which ended the war. Vladislav himself, returned to his father as a penitent seeking his pardon and grace. Late in July, 1453, the Grand Duke issued a manifesto, in which he proclaimed general amnesty and restored his virtuous wife Helen to her domestic rights. Finally, the Ragusans, left without allies and outside support, came to terms. On April 10, 1454, a peace-agreement was signed on a status quo basis, with that reservation, however, that the Grand Duke will not attack Ragusa, except under orders from the Sultan. So three years of bloody warfare served to nothing, but to establish the overlordship of the Sultan over all of them.

The policy of Stephen Thomas toward Croatia and Dalmatia followed the Bosnian tradition established by king Tvartko I. Right from his ascension to the throne, he assumed the title of "king of Croatia and Dalmatia" indicating that he was renewing the claim of his predecessors to these lands. His chances to wear the crown of Zvonimir, however, were better than those of Tvartko II who was confronted with the might of prince Ivanish Nelipich, and never got far enough even to test it. Now the banus of Croatia was Peter Talovats, a wealthy land-owner, but no match to the late Ivanish. Moreover, he was antagonized by the powerful count Frankapan, count of Zell, and the princes of Kerbava (Corbavia). The latter were, in addition, allies of king Stephen Thomas. The only point of strength of the banus was his friendship with Venice.

Pressed on all sides and in a moment of despair, banus Talovats offered all his possessions to Venice in exchange for security, privileges of a Venetian patrician and some amount of money. Venice declined the offer but sent to him arms and ammunition to defend his country. Gaining new force Talovats defeated Nicholas Ujlaki, a rival banus, and his other opponents. But he did not lose his contacts with the Bosnian king, to whom he also offered for sale some of his possessions. His negotiations with king Thomas were not propitious, for a conflict broke out between them as a result of which Talovats lost the cities of Ostrovitsa and Knin. However, in the peace-treaty of July 16, 1452, the differences were ironed out, and peace was restored.

A year later (1453) banus Peter Talovats died, leaving behind his widow and two sons. His death was the signal for the opponents of Talovats to grab as much Croatian territory as they could. Chief among the spoilsmen were Venice, Grand Duke Stephen Vukchich, Count of Zell, and king Thomas himself. This rivalry led to a civil war, in which the count of Zell defeated king Thomas and other rivals (1456). Grand Duke Vukchich, whose wife Helena died, wooed Hedwig, widow of Talovats, in the hope of adding the estates of the late banus to his own domain. At the end of his expansionist adven-

tures he actually added to Herzegovina the Maritime Province, with the strongholds of Omish and Klis controlling by far the largest territory Herzegovina ever possessed.

STEPHEN THOMAS ATTEMPTS CRUSADE AGAINST TURKEY (1458)

After the death of Murad II (early in 1451) the Ottoman throne was occupied by his youthful son, Mohammed II (1451-1481) who ruled for thirty years. In possession of huge power and fired with the ambition of further conquests, the 21 year old sultan decided to subject all of the Balkans to his authority. Two years after his ascension on the throne, Mohammed II captured Constantinople (1453), thereby opening, according to many historians, a new epoch in European history. The fall of Constantinople electrified all Europe and placed the Holy See in the forefront of the Struggle against Islam and its champions. Horrified by Mohammed's stunning victory Stephen Thomas sent his envoys to the Sultan, with expression of allegiance and pleading for his grace. At the same time he sent his representatives to Rome and other capitals describing the situation in the Balkans as disastrous, and Bosnia in need of financial and military aid.

In the meantime, Mohammed II sent, at the invitation of Grand Duke Stephen Vukchich, his troops to Bosnia, occupied its south-eastern area and established there a province (sanjak), with the town of Focha as its capital. In 1456 the Sultan demanded surrender of four strongholds, and a contribution in kind consisting of 20,000 bushels of cereals.

Nevertheless, a ray of hope came from the east, the land of George Brankovich. The victorious Sultan occupied, after the capture of Constantinople, in short order most provinces of Greece, Albania and Serbia. In 1454 Mohammed II summoned the despot George Brankovich to deliver to him all the Serbian lands which he inherited from despot Stephen Lazarevich. Apprised of the Sultan's decision despot George fled to Hungary seeking aid from Governor John Hunyadi. Assisted by the Hungarian troops George Brankovich expelled in 1455 the Turks from Serbia, but at the same time he offered to pay 32,000 ducats annual tribute to the Sultan. Incensed over the reverses of his troops, the ambitious Sultan collected forces for a new campaign, planning to invade Hungary through Serbia, at the head of an army, 150,000 men strong, and supported by 300 artillery pieces. Without any effort he over-ran in 1456, Serbia and laid siege to Belgrade, an out-post of Hungarian defenses. Upon the news of the siege John Hunyadi and John Capistrano, the papal legate rushed to the beleaguered city, and in a two-day battle (July 21/22) routed the Turkish forces.

The whole Christendom rejoiced over the brilliant victory of Hunyadi. At the same time there was another Christian leader of heroic proportions, who in the mountainous Albania held the Turks at bay for nearly twenty years. This was the famous George Castriota (Scanderbeg), who in his boyhood was forcibly converted to Islam and enlisted in the Janissary troops. Hence, his name Scanderbeg. Revolted over the atrocities committed by these troopers on defenseless Christians, Scanderbeg deserted the Turkish troops and joined the Christian fighters whom he led to victory until the end of his life.

Enthused over the example of his famous contemporary, king Stephen Thomas decided to undertake a crusade against the Turks. He was warmly supported by his brother Radivoy and a number of Bosnian magnates. But his greatest sponsor king Thomas found in the person of Pope Calixtus III. The Pope made a vibrant appeal to the Christian World for aid. Donations were solicited by the clergy everywhere. Out of the collected sum one-third was assigned to the king of Hungary, another to George Castriota of Albania, and a third to Stephen Thomas, king of Bosnia. In his own name king Thomas sent envoys to all courts in western Europe suing for military aid.

Unfortunately for Stephen Thomas, king Ladislas V of Hungary died in November, 1457, and in January, 1458 the youthful son of John Hunyadi, Mathias Corvinus was elected Hungarian king. Being a minor, king's uncle Michael Szilágyi (pronounced: *Ssilarji*) was made Governor. This period was attended by internal strife in Hungary, and all her forces became immobilized. Since the response of the rest of Europe to the Pope's passionate appeal for a crusade was negligible, king Thomas of Bosnia got into a predicament, for he engaged in struggle with Mohammed II, even before the crusade was

organized. It is true that the beginning of his campaigns was successful, for he recaptured a number of towns along the Bosnian-Serbian frontier, but Stephen Thomas realized that he could not fight a duel with the overwhelming forces of the Turkish Empire, and in April, 1458, he concluded peace with Mohammed, submitting to harsh terms and promising to pay the Sultan the annual tribute as fixed by the Treaty of Smederevo (May, 1449).

Conciliation of Serbia

For his loss of advantage toward the Sultan, king Thomas saw an opportunity for compensation at the expense of Serbia. The life-long opponent of Bosnia, despot George Brankovich died in December, 1456. His son Lazarus Georgevich inherited his possessions.

Under the threat of common danger king Thomas and despot Lazarus became friends and allies. Lazarus had a daughter, Helen, on her mother's side a direct descendant of the famous Byzantine dynasty of Paleologus. In a marriage tie between the Bosnian and Serbian rulers king Thomas saw a better future for both countries, and he arranged with Lazarus, marriage of his son Stephen and Lazarus' daughter Helena. But before the marriage was consummated, Lazarus died (January 20, 1458).

Since there were three claimants to the throne of Serbia besides Lazarus' daughter Helena, the marriage was delayed. But toward the end of 1458 king Thomas and his son Stephen visited with king Mathias Corvinus who called the Parliament in the city of Szeged (pronounced: *Sseggedd*). Here in the presence of the Estates and with the approval of Serbs, Mathias Corvinus appointed king Thomas' son Stephen, despot of Serbia, and also heir to all the lands the despots owned in Hungary. In April, 1459 Stephen married Helena and the two countries became for a short time united.

Turkish Conquest of Serbia

By achieving his cherished objective of extending his son's authority over Serbia, king Thomas gained no advantage. On the contrary, he shouldered a load far beyond his power to carry. The plight of Serbia at that time was tragic, indeed. It became the bridge-head of the Sultan's armies in their thrust toward Central

Europe. It would take the might of an Empire to contain the hosts of the Moslem zealots, in Serbia or elsewhere. The provincial despots or kings of the small Balkan lands could lead a shadowy existence only while the powerful arm of the Sultan did not reach out for them. But now the hour of decision was coming fast.

Mohammed II made, in 1459, large-scale preparations for the conquest of Serbia and to wreak vengeance on king Stephen Thomas of Bosnia. His attention centered on Smederevo, an impregnable stronghold at the confluence of the Morava with Danube. The new despot, Stephen Tomashevich established his residence there, with the rest of his wife's family. The city population was not in sympathy either with the new despot, nor with despot Lazarus' widow, Helen of the Paleolog family. They bore a grudge against her for having their governor-elect, Michael Zbogovich imprisoned and sent in chains to Hungary, while she placed herself under the protection of Mathias Corvinus, who in turn appointed Stephen Tomashevich despot of Serbia.

In such a frame of mind the Semendrians (Smederevo = Semendria) looked upon the new despot as upon a Hungarian agent and Catholic zealot aiming at conversion of Serbia to Catholicism. Consequently, they conspired against him, and as Mohammed II was approaching the city, its residents hastened to meet the Sultan and on June 20, 1459 they placed the keys to the gates of Smederevo in the hands of Mohammed II. In possession of the key citadel the Sultan reduced the Serbian towns, one after another, and conquered Serbia in a short time. The fall of Smederevo had a stunning effect upon Christian Europe. That a fortification rated second best to Constantinople could honorably fall without resistance, was taxing imagination. The spite-work of the Semendrians was not known and no one could believe that the stronghold could fall without treachery and treason.

Charges were levelled at king Stephen Thomas and his son Stephen Tomashevich that they sold out Serbia to the infidel. Mathias Corvinus was the loudest in his denunciations of the two innocent persons, accusing them of treason before the Holy See, and preparing a military invasion of Bosnia. The Pope, Pius II, himself believed at first the charges, supplemented by further complaints against king Thomas for interfering

in Croatian affairs, and selling the Croatian town of Zazvina to the Turks. Naturally, at the bottom of it all was no one else but Grand Duke Stephen Vukchich. The Pope took a serious view of the affair and decided to have the unfortunate episode investigated through ecclesiastic channels. Therefore, he instructed his Legate, bishop Thomas of Hvar, to investigate the whole affair and if king Thomas was found guilty, he should be excommunicated from the Church.

Apprised of the sordid intrigue being woven against him, king Thomas sent his envoys to the Pope to explain Smederevo's fall and the disputes connected with the ownership of some Croatian territory. Pius II at first refused to believe the story and reprimanded the envoys. But when bishop Thomas submitted his report, the aged king was vindicated and all accusations against him declared false. King Mathias Corvinus was not satisfied with the Pope's absolution of the Bosnian king, and protested the action of the Holy See. The Pope insisted on his rights, but promised Mathias that he would make no important decision in the Bosnian affairs before consulting first the king of Hungary. Being involved in a war with Frederic III, emperor of Germany, Mathias Corvinus abandoned his plan of invading Bosnia, and the aged Stephen Thomas gained some respite.

In spite of the temporary relief, the situation of Bosnia became worse every day. The country was exposed to Turkish attacks, and the pressure of Mohammed II grew in intensity. In May, 1460 Hassan Pasha demanded free passage through Bosnia, so that he might break with his forces into Syrmium. King Thomas was forced to accede. In fall of the same year Stephen Thomas sent his envoys to Venice portraying the danger to which Bosnia was exposed. He offered Bosnia to Venice, while he would keep up with the defense of the country. Should they even decline his offer, he asked them to support him with troops and ammunition. The Senate of Venice declined to take over Bosnia, but promised some aid, and urged conciliation between the king of Bosnia and Grand Duke of Herzegovina, Stephen Vukchich, whose dominion, too, was ravaged by the Turks.

In 1460 the issue of the Croatian territory seized from the heirs of banus Peter Talovats against became alive. Paul Speranchich, the new banus of Croatia, was bent on restoration of the

Croatian territory seized by the Venetians and their allies. He fought back on Venice on every occasion, and recaptured from them the Croatian stronghold of Klis (Clissa), and probably other districts. As a Venetian ally king Thomas fought on the side of Venice and against Croatia. Fierce fighting developed through 1461 and king Thomas fell in a battle fought on July 10, 1461. According to some, he was killed by his own brother Radivoy and his son Stephen Tomashevich.

THE LAST TWO YEARS OF THE BOSNIAN KINGDOM

Reign of Stephen Tomashevich (1461-1463)

Upon his accession to the throne Stephen found Bosnia in a desperate situation. He was already informed of Mohammed's preparation for war against Bosnia. Mathias Corvinus himself was an opponent, but engaged in war in Bohemia he could not have helped him, even if he had been on friendlier terms with him. Stephen Vukchich, Grand Duke of Herzegovina still was an enemy. Banus Speranchich, an opponent of Venice and her allies, was in a war-like mood. In the interior of Bosnia the situation was far from satisfactory. The Bosnian sectarians were on the defensive, but they sought aid from outside wherever they could get it. They laid great hopes in the Sultan, who encouraged their defection from the king. Moreover, the Sultan appeared as protector of the down-trodden, and the Bosnian peasantry deserted en masse to the Sultan. Some barons were left entirely without farmhands.

In his attempt to remedy on the situation, king Stephen moved in two directions. He needed financial and military aid from outside, so he sent his representatives to various courts of Europe describing the hopeless situation of his kingdom, and suing for prompt aid. Internally, he wished to effect conciliation with all his opponents, including his step-mother Catherine, and her father, Grand Duke Stephen Vukchich. He rallied also the other magnates, who were antagonistic to each other, around the throne. Conducive to both purposes was, in his estimation, the crown given to him by the highest spiritual authority, the Catholic Church.

Consequently, he sent envoys to Rome, with a message to the Pope. His argument centered around the immediate danger of Turkish invasion, and all the aid he needed to save his country. If the Turks conquer Bosnia they will turn it into a bridge-head and concentration area to fan out into Central and Western Europe. For they have designs upon Hungary and Italy as well. Preliminary to substantial military aid and material assistance he needs enhancement of his prestige and authority by obtaining a royal crown from the Head of the Church. The message of king Stephen carried weight with Pope Pius II, and he gladly complied with the wishes of Bosnia. The Pontiff sent his Legate to Bosnia who should support him in his action and place the crown on his head.

In the meantime, king Stephen transferred his court from the stronghold of Bobovats to Yaytse (literally "little egg," from the shape of the citadel) in the Lower Regions because the latter offered more safety in the face of Turkish attacks. Early in November, 1461, the Bosnian barons assembled at Yaytse and Stephen Tomashevich was crowned in the presence of the papal Legate and Bosnian nobility.

So Stephen Tomashevich was the first and last Bosnian king to receive his crown from the hands of the Pontiff. To this distinction soon another one was added. A few days after his coronation the envoys of the Ragusan Republic arrived at Yaytse to pay homage to the king, and ask him for the confirmation of their trading rights and privileges as granted to them by his royal ancestors. They promised to pay the king the annual tribute, whereupon a general settlement of the outstanding differences and war-damages was reached. At home peace was established among warring factions and internal harmony was in prospect. But all this came too late, for Bosnia's fate had already been sealed.

The hurricane that was to sweep off Bosnia's independence came from two opposite directions: north and south. In the north king Mathias Corvinus bore a long standing grudge against king Stephen because of the fall of Smederevo— so when he heard that a papal Legate placed the crown on Stephen's head he felt that by the Pontiff's action a great injury had been done to the crown of Hungary. He considered Bosnia a vassal-state of Hungary, while Pius II as the highest spiritual authority in Christendom, recognized by the fact of coronation both the sovereignty of Stephen Tomashevich and the independence of Bosnia.

Informed of Mathias' displeasure over the Bosnian developments, the Pontiff tried to change the king's attitude by clever diplomatic moves at his own court. At the same time he advised the Bosnian king to send envoys to Mathias' court, in an attempt to regain his friendship and win his support for the impending show-down with the Turks.

But the ire of Mathias could not be easily placated. Just by the Pope's letters and envoys' pleadings he could not be induced to make up with king Stephen whom he considered a disloyal vassal. In a long communication sent to Pius II, in answer to the latter's message of January 21, 1462, Mathias expressed himself fully on the issue and poured out his feelings. It was a sharp criticism of the Pontiff's actions in Bosnia and repetition of charges, long since declared unfounded, both against king Stephen and his father, king Thomas. The worst encroachment on his authority Mathias found in the fact of Stephen's coronation, and in the establishment of new bishoprics in Bosnia. He also took exception to Pontiff's remittance of funds for building of new strongholds in Bosnia.

Nevertheless, he hinted at his willingness to compromise, should the Pope urge a conciliation, however, under the condition that the king of Bosnia would be, in the future, more compliant with his wishes and make good on his past omissions through loyal obedience. To Venetian observers at Mathias' court the compromise meant a heavy ransom exacted from poor Stephen Tomashevich. And so it happened! For a huge amount of money Mathias let the by-gones be by-gones. The exact amount is not known, but it was large enough to redeem the crown of St. Stephen, a sacred symbol of Hungary, which Mathias pawned with Frederic III, emperor of Germany.

But this extortion of money from an impoverished country, was not the worst calamity that befell Bosnia. The peace-treaty between Bosnia and Hungary contained clauses far more ominous. So king Stephen had to cede four Bosnian fortifications, which were occupied by Hungarian troops. Further, he had to enter into alliance with Mathias for a common defense against the Turks. Stephen had to break off his relations with the Sultan, exposing himself to immediate retaliation by the all-powerful Mohammed II. Yet the fatal provision of the treaty, which became responsible for the immediate tragedy both of Bosnia and king Stephen Tomashevich, was the latter's pledge to refuse payment of the annual tribute to the Sultan. This insensate provision upset the hardly managed balance, and precipitated Bosnia's down-fall. On the whole, Mathias Corvinus, dubbed by the Hungarians "the just" (Meghalt Mátyás király, oda az igazság —"Ever since king Mathias passed on, the justice is dead"), displayed in the Bosnian affair a truly demoniac nature, which barely two generations later, cost the independence of Hungary herself.

With this we approach the moments of agony of the once powerful Bosnia, and martyrdom of her last king. When Mohammed learned about the Hungarian-Bosnian treaty, he was spurred into action. He sent a special envoy to Bosnia to collect the tribute which was overdue. Stephen Tomashevich, bound by the treaty with Hungary, refused to pay. The envoy reminded him of the dire consequences of this refusal, and left. Incensed over the challenge hurled at him by the Bosnian king, Mohammed II decided to retaliate, and prepared for a momentous campaign. This campaign had been scheduled for the spring, 1463.

Fully aware of Mohammed's plans, Stephen Tomashevich used the winter of 1462 for counter-preparations and sought military aid abroad. But as spring approached and he got from foreign courts nothing but vague promises, king Stephen realized his fatal errors of the preceding year, and made a heroic effort to correct them. He sent two envoys to the Sultan's court in Adrianople, begging the Padishah's pardon, promising prompt payment of the tribute, and asking a truce for fifteen years.

Stephen's move of despair only played into the hands of Mohammed II. It made it possible for the Sultan to play a double game. At his State Council Mohammed decided to grant the truce thus lulling the Bosnians into a sense of security, have them disarmed, and by a surprise blow to take over the country before any resistance could be organized or aid obtained from abroad. Furthermore, it was fixed that the Ottoman army would move five days after the Bosnian envoys left Adrianople. The destination of the army's advance was a guarded secret.

Overjoyed at the success of their mission, the two envoys were preparing for their return trip. But before they left the capital, they were warned by a good-hearted Serbian renegade, Michael of Ostrovitsa, who occupied a high position at Sultan's court, of the stratagem. However, they were in no mood to listen to private informers, and ignored the warning.

A few days after their departure the huge Ottoman force was set in motion. It consisted of 150,000 horsemen, many more foot-soldiers, baggage-trains and auxiliary troops. The destination of the advance remained undisclosed. For better dissimulation of his plans he sent a part of his troops to Serbia threatening an invasion of Hungary. The stratagem was successful, and the huge army appeared in Bosnia, before any resistance could be put up.

The Ottoman troops invaded the upper reaches of the Drina owned by duke Tvartko Kovachevich, who was caught by surprise. The duke himself was captured and beheaded. Through the Drina valley the Turkish forces broke into Upper Bosnia, and laid siege to Bobovats, impregnable stronghold, with royal residence. The commander of the citadel was prince Radak, a former sectarian and unwilling convert to Catholic faith. For bribe or out of spite Radak surrendered the city, which could have endured a year's siege, in three days. But instead of giving him the expected reward, the Sultan had him beheaded.*

The fall of Bobovats, the pride and hope of Bosnia, created wide-spread confusion and panic throughout the land. King Stephen, who retired with his family into the strongly fortified Yaytse, hoped to gather an army in the north, and to hold out until aid came from abroad. But at the news of Bobovats' fall, the resistance collapsed, and part of the population bowed before the Sultan, while others fled to Croatia and Dalmatia.

When the king saw that resistance was impossible, he also thought of his own personal safety and welfare of his family. But he came upon this idea too late. After the capture of Bobovats the Sultan sent Mohamet Pasha with his light cavalry to encircle Yaytse, Bosnia's capital. As Mohamet arrived at Yaytse, the king was on his way to Croatia. Mohamet rushed after him, giving the unfortunate fugitive no breathing spell. In the meantime, king Stephen arrived at the stronghold of Klyooch (Kljuc), where he took some rest. But Mohamet's cavalrymen were right on his heels, without even knowing that the king was in the citadel. However, a wretch sold the precious secret to the enemy, and Mohamet promptly surrounded the city with strong cavalry detachments.

From that moment on no escape was possible. On the other hand, Klyooch was a fortified stronghold, and Mohamet feared that months would pass before his forces could take the city by storm. For this reason Mohamet pasha began to negotiate with the king about surrender. The general promised the king on oath that his life and freedom would be safe. Moreover, he issued a charter guaranteeing the king's safety and freedom. Having no other choice king Stephen surrendered, together with the garrison, to the Turks, hoping to win the Sultan's grace.

Mohamet pasha reported to the Sultan with his august captive. This was a moment of triumph for both. Yet it brought a great deal of worry to Mohammed el Fatih. It was his practice to behead all the captive sovereigns of the countries he conquered. This was, in his opinion, the easiest way to retain his sovereignty over the conquered lands. Stephen Tomashevich was an exception. Mohamet pasha not only swore to the king's security, but also issued in the Sultan's name a safe-conduct guaranteeing the life and freedom of the Bosnian king. So he sought the legal opinion of a learned Persian jurist, the aged Sheik Ali Bestami, who was in his camp. Before leaving Bosnia Mohammed summoned the prisoner to his tent. Stephen Tomashevich took along the safe-conduct issued by Mohamet pasha and submitted it to the Sultan. But Ali Bestami declared the document null and void, because it was issued by a servant of the Sultan, without the permission of his master. At the same time the Persian condemned the king to death. Upon making this statement Ali Bestami drew out his sword and lopped off the king's head on the spot. After Stephen, his uncle Radivoy and a cousin of his, met the same fate.

In less than two months all of Bosnia was

---

* According to tradition, Radak was thrown from a steep precipice. Today still stands a rock near Bobovac under the name of "Radakovica" (Radak's Rock).

conquered. In June, 1463 the Sultan took 70 Bosnian cities and strongholds; 100,000 persons of both sexes were driven into slavery, and 30,000 boys were converted to Islam and enlisted into janissary troops.

Contrasting with the collapse of Bosnia was the heroic resistance of Herzegovina under the leadership of prince Vladislav and his father, the Grand Duke. While Mohammed II tarried in Bosnia, the two leaders organized the defense of the country and blocked the passage of Turkish troops. The rugged highlands of Herzegovina, with deep gorges and narrow passes, were suitable for successful resistance by small groups to overwhelming forces of the enemy. This made it especially difficult for the Turkish cavalry. All it could do was to over-run some fields and valleys, but it could not get further inland. Confronted with unexpected difficulties, Mohammed attempted to take the stronghold of Blagay, capital of Herzegovina. But after a few days he raised the useless siege, and retired with his army to Adrianople. On his way back Mohammed II occupied several districts and put their rulers to death. However, nineteen years later the heroic Herzegovina, too, submitted to the irresistible power of Sultan.

No less tragic was the lot of king Stephen's family. His wife, queen Maria, fled to Croatia but was seized by banus Paul Speranchich, a bitter enemy of her husband. Upon her release she went with a group of courtiers to Split which was under the Venetian authority, and spent there three years. In 1466 she went to Hungary where she died. Queen Helen, widow of king Thomas and daughter of Stephen Vukchich, went through a personal tragedy of her own. Her children, son Sigismund and daughter Catherine, became Mohammedan converts, and that broke her heart. She fled first to Ragusa, where the Senate honored her with a regal pension. But she left Ragusa and went, together with her court retinue, to Rome where she was honored as a titular queen of Bosnia. She lived there in peace and comfort. On her death-bed she bequeathed the kingdom of Bosnia to the Holy See. She died on October 25, 1478, and was buried in "Ara Coeli" Church in Rome, near the old Roman Capitol, where her tomb is marked by an inscription in Croatian and Latin.

Thus ended the glorious Kingdom of Bosnia.

PARTIAL RECONQUEST OF BOSNIA AND EXTINCTION OF CHRISTIAN POWER IN BOSNIA AND HERZEGOVINA

Struggle of the Ottomans with the Hungarian-Croatian kings for possession of Bosnia continues for another sixty-five years. With the successful campaign of Sultan Mehmed II in 1463, all of Bosnia was not definitely conquered. For the remainder of Bosnia, long and fierce fighting continued until the fall of Yaytse in 1528.

Realizing the magnitude of disaster, of which his own selfish policy was the immediate cause, king Mathias Corvinus, who at that time was fully absorbed by his campaigns in Bohemia, organized in summer, 1463 a large army for the invasion of Bosnia. In the meantime, Mathias' generals fought the Turks in Serbia where they defeated the troops of Sultan Mehmed's general Ali beg, and liberated 15,000 Christian prisoners.

Upon concluding an alliance with Venice, which also joined the struggle against the Turks, king Mathias invaded in October of the same year (1463) with his troops, northern Bosnia, and within three months he re-captured a large part of the country, including many strongholds and the fortified city of Yaytse (Jajce). Irritated by his failure to hold the conquered territory the Sultan came next year (1464) at the head of a large army to Bosnia and laid siege to Yaytse. But his troops were again defeated, and he returned to Constantinople.

Thus, with the armed success of king Mathias, two Bosnian banates were rescued from the Turkish conquest: Banates of Srebrenitsa and Yaytse. Satisfied with this result, Mathias established a new "Kingdom of Bosnia," appointing one of his magnates: Nicholas of Ilok (Ujlaki), king of Bosnia.

In the meantime, the Turks, under the command of Mahmud Pasha campaigned in Herzegovina and after a long and bitter struggle, occupied that country in 1482. Established in Bosnia, the Turks made many inroads into the neighboring countries, notably into Dalmatia, Croatia, Carniola (Slovenia), and Styria. Attempting to check the return of the Bosnian Yakub Pasha the Croatian Banus Derenchin engaged him in a battle near the town of Udbine, on the Kerbava highlands. In this fateful battle fought in 1493, compared by many with the

Serbian disaster on the Blackbird Field in 1389, the Croatian forces were utterly defeated, which encouraged further Turkish inroads from Bosnia. After the fatal battle of Mohách in Hungary (1526), Husref-beg, the famous Bosnian general and sponsor of Islamic culture in his native land, conquered the remaining parts of Bosnia and took the Christian capital of Yaytse in 1528.

With the fall of Yaytse, the last vestige of Christian power in Bosnia vanished. Thus Bosnia and Herzegovina became an organic part of the Ottoman Empire, in which they were destined to play an outstanding role. Even before the fall of the Bosnian Kingdom, both as the bridgehead of Turkish expansion west and north, and for centuries as the impregnable bastion of Mohammedan Power in the very heart of Europe, in 1463, the Turkish power was gradually extended north of the Serbian areas, most of which were conquered and held in suzerainty shortly after the battle on the Blackbird Field in 1389. Later also kings of Bosnia paid yearly tribute to the Sultan, while some powerful overlords of Bosnia submitted of their own will to the Sultan seeking his armed support in their internecine struggle. So Mehmed II et Fatih found in Bosnia a ground well prepared for perpetuation of his rule.

A dynasty of local Mohammedan converts known under the name of Hranushichi tended to the interests of the Sultans in Serbia and southeastern Bosnia, since 1414. They ruled in their duchies or sanjaks, watching the developments in Bosnia. The most illustrious member of this family is Isabeg Isakovich Hranushich who from 1440 to 1463 ruled as "the Duke of the Western Parts," and from 1464 to 1470 as Governor of Sanjak. He founded the city of Sarayevo and can be regarded as the forerunner of Husrev beg, who was one of the most brilliant generals of Sultan Suleiman, the Magnificent, and at the same time, a sponsor of monumental architecture, patron of arts and a grand pioneer of Moslem culture in Bosnia.

Even during the governorship of Isabeg Hranushich (1464-1470), the Turks frequently raided the neighboring provinces such as Herzegovina, Dalmatia, Croatia and Carniola (Slovenia). A more vigorous campaign was undertaken during the governorship of Ayaz-beg (1470-1475), who in 1472 invaded the northern provinces, broke

into Istria and Friulia, and marched up to the city of Udine on the Italian frontier.

In the course of the sixteenth century the Turkish and Bosnian invasions crushed the resistance of the Central European peoples, and Vienna itself was besieged (1529)—but not taken —by the armies of Suleiman and Husrevbeg, leader of Bosnia. In part through religious fanaticism and in part through vindictiveness and lust for destruction—so plainly evident in our own days—in short, through degradation of human nature, the Sultan's conquests were usually attended by senseless bloodshed, plunder and devastation, and punctuated by driving into slavery of large sections of population of whole districts, nothing to say of the forcible separation of teen-age boys from their Christian parents for enlistment into Janissary troops. However, the worst excesses were usually committed by the native converts to Mohammedanism. Such were, among others, Murad beg, Malkoch beg Dugalich and Ulama beg, successors of Husrevbeg.

As governor of Bosnia Malkoch beg was succeeded by the famous family of Sokolovichi. The founder of this clan was Mehmed pasha Sokolovich (in Turkish: Sokolli), Grand Vezir of the Ottoman Empire, also a Bosnian convert to Mohammedanism. In 1565 Mustafa beg Sokolovich became Governor of Bosnia and he prosecuted with vigor the policy of conquest he inherited from his predecessor, Malkoch beg. Together with Malkoch beg he was the worst foe of Croatia who practically conquered or devastated the whole country. His uncle, Mehmed pasha Sokolovich, the Grand Vezir of the Empire, came into conflict with the Hapsburgs and declared war against emperor Maximilian. During this campaign the siege and capture of the stronghold of Sziget took place. This episode, with its heroic defense by Nicholas Shubich Zrinski became glorified, both in tradition and epic poetry as one of the most dramatic moments in Croatian history. Suleiman himself died under the walls of Sziget. Finally, the stronghold was taken and demolished by the two Bosnians: Grand Vezir Mehmed Sokolovich, at the head of Sultan's army, and Mustafa beg Sokolovich, in command of his Bosnian troops.

The stronghold's captain Zrinski died a heroic death. The Grand Vezir had the head of his opponent severed from his lifeless body and sent it to Constantinople, adorned with a silver helmet. But during the siege the two leaders carried on correspondence in Croatian, which is replete with feelings of friendship and mutual admiration sobered up with the bitter irony of their fate that as members of the Croatian people they have to shed each other's blood.

During the Venetian-Turkish war for the possession of Cyprus (1570-1576), struggle along the Bosnian frontiers was renewed, under the leadership of Mehmed beg and Ferhad-beg Sokolovichi, in the course of which much Dalmatian and Venetian territory was conquered by Bosnians. Only in the year 1576, 50 to 60 Bosnian incursions are recorded.

In 1591 the belligerent and bloodthirsty Gazi Deli Hasan Pasha Predoyevich was appointed Governor of Bosnia. His campaigns against Croatia and Alpic region are the classics in the struggle between Mohammedanism and Christianity. He was opposed by famous Croatian and Austrian generals, who by their fierce and stubborn resistance, bled white the fighting armies of Sultan. After thirteen years of continuous fighting, the great war ended in 1606 with the peace-treaty of Zsitva for the first time in history, on the terms of a Christian ruler.

Conversion to Islam

After the fall of Bosnia the most important event is the social and religious reorganization of the country. Before 1463 there is not one Mohammedan in the country. By 1526 Bosnian legions fight under the banners of the Sultan, and on the field of Mohách carry a death-blow to Hungary, the age-old enemy and conqueror of Bosnia. Within two generations social and cultural changes take place in Bosnia, which transform a Christian State into an advance-post of Mohammedan expansion in Central Europe.

The question is how did the Bosnians of various Christian denominations turn so quickly Mohammedan and become crusaders for the cause of Islam. Undoubtedly this is a riddle, which has not been solved fully to this day. From the testament of queen Katherine, wife of Styepan Tomash and daughter of Grand Duke Stephen Vukchich Kossacha, we know that both her son Sigismund and daughter Katherine abandoned Catholicism for Islam. Queen Katherine's

youngest brother Stephen, likewise, changed his allegiance to the Bosnian Church for that to Islam, assuming the name of Akhmed beg. Furthermore, he was raised to the dignity of Grand Vezir, and became Sultan Bayazid's son-in-law. And this was the case of many other Catholics and of all of "Patarenes," both noblemen and peasants. The Catholic population was further reduced by flight to neighbouring Christian countries, namely Dalmatia, Croatia and Slavonia. Depopulation of the conquered land assumed such proportions that Angelus Zyvezdovich, a courageous Franciscan monk, went to see the Sultan, Mehmed II, and explained to him that Bosnia would lose her population if persecution of Catholics was not discontinued. Mehmed was impressed by the monk's pleading and issued a patent (Ahd-Name) to the Franciscans by which he confirmed free exercise of worship to Christians. Since that time Franciscans in Bosnia and Herzegovina were the only protection and refuge to Christians in that country.

Turkish Land Policy

The case of the Bosnian heretics was of a different nature. We have already mentioned that the Sultans promised freedom and land to those Bosnian peasants and serfs who would flee from Bosnia and adopt Islam. In their messages to the Holy See both king Stephen Tomash and his son Stephen Tomashevich complain of this propaganda, which they deemed dangerous because the peasants believe in it and are easily duped. However, this was not a mere stratagem, but a clever political move, and we know it from the history of Serbia and Bulgaria under the Turkish rule, where the Ottomans freed all the serfs on the estates of the native nobility, in order to break their power and seize their land possessions. Similar was the case in Slavonia where Suleiman the Magnificent, proclaimed in 1536 the freedom of serfs from their landlords. Thus, the peasants did not look at the Turks with the same eyes as their masters.

Protective Hand of the Sultans

Still more tempting was the change for the heretic nobility in Bosnia. As age-old opponents of both Catholic and Orthodox Churches, they frequently applied for aid to Turks, be it against the foreign powers, or in their domestic feuds.

We recall the pertinent instances in our story of Duke Hervoye, Duke Sandal Hranich, Grand Duke Stephen Vukchich Kossacha, sons of prince Paul Radinovich avenging the murder of their father, sons of king Ostoya, and many others. Further, the powerful Turkish barrier secured them from fearful Hungarian invasions which for three centuries disturbed the peace of the country. This security also conveyed undisturbed exploitation of precious Bosnian mines, an important source of the country's wealth, coveted by the kings of Hungary. On the whole, the Bosnian nobility did not mind much the change of masters, especially if it could retain its landed estates and social privileges, or in some way still further improve its position. All these expectations were fully gratified by the power and dispositions of the Sultans.

Redistribution of Land

When a country was taken over by the armed forces of the Khalifs, all its previous laws and obligations were abrogated. By the Ottoman constitutional law the conquered land became the property of the Sovereign: *erazi-i-emirie*, i.e., the land of Emir. Thus the Sultan in his capacity of Khalif, or religious head of Islam, could not grant the use of land to the Infidels. Any other procedure would be not only in violation of the Mohammedan Law, but also in defiance of the Ottoman Constitution. Thus, the only way for the landlords, whether belonging to the Bosnian Church, or converted to Catholicism, to retain their old possessions and gain new property, was conversion to Islam. It is assumed that the conversion was gradual and took probably the life-time of a generation.

Another incentive for conversion was the power and glamor of the Ottoman Empire, which became a world-power of unprecedented expansion and wealth in which ambitious individuals could attain high rank in Government and services of the Empire. Thus, Constantinople and the court of the Sultans became centers of attraction for military adventurers, and other enterprising Bosnian converts.

Brilliant Careers for Converts

Even among Dalmatian Catholics cases were frequent where a young adventurer went to Constantinople and rose high in the Ottoman hierarchy. Among such Dalmatian career-men we find Ahmed Pasha in the reign of Suleiman who conquered Rhodes Island, and schemed to become Sultan of Egypt. He was defeated and killed by another Dalmatian, native of Shibenik, Ferhat pasha who married a sister of Suleiman. A peasant boy from the vicinity of Vrana, by his native name Joseph Matashkovich, was promoted under the name of Jusuf Pasha to the rank of admiral and elder Statesman, who took during the Cretan war the stronghold of Kanea from Venetians. Equally interesting is the case of Murat beg, a native of Shibenik, whose brother Don Yurye, was a canon in Shibenik. The two brothers lived in amity, and the mayor of the city arranged a brilliant reception in honor of the Ottoman dignitary when he visited his native city.

Glamor of Orient and Sultan's Court

Since the glamor of the Orient and the fame of the Sultan's court were such a powerful attraction for even Catholics in a country not under Turkish control, we can easily fancy how potent the urge was in Bosnia to take advantage of the new opportunities. Thousands and thousands of Bosnians achieved fame and wealth in the first two or three generations of the Ottoman rule in Bosnia. Some writers claim that Suleiman, the Magnificent, from his mother's side, was also a Bosnian. The greatest Turkish poet of the 15th century, Adni, was called "Mahmud, the Croatian." He came as a young captive to the Turkish court, obtained his education together with the later Mehmed II, who made him his Grand Vezir, during the occupation of Bosnia. In the gruesome incident at Yaytse, Adni insisted on sparing the life of king Styepan Tomashevich, which brought him into conflict with Sultan. Later on Adni, too, was beheaded. Ominous is the figure of another Bosnian, Hadum Jakub, a brilliant but brutal general, who defeated the Croatian forces on the Kerbava field (1493) and took prisoner banus Derenchin. However, the most brilliant of them all was Husrefbeg, Suleiman's victorious general who was also a generous patron of arts and promoter of general welfare. In the book of Safvet beg Basagić "Znameniti Hrvati u Turskoj Carevini" (Famous Croats in the Turkish Empire) hundreds of such names are listed.

"Imponderables" of Conversion

Even without going into further details, the above listed social, economic and political motives would appear sufficient, as the incentives to so thorough an Islamization of Bosnia and Herzegovina. However, some writers cling also to certain "imponderables" of this conversion, while others hotly contest the theory. This is namely the alleged ideological affinity between Bogomil and Mohammedan doctrines as monotheistic sects. Others will refer to the existence of a dualistic Manichaen sect among the Mohammedans which was in close contact with the Christian Manichaens and Paulicians. Should even all this be true, it is highly dubious that any such link existed between "the Bosnian Christians" or "good men" and the Mohammedans. We could not subscribe to such theory for the simple reason that up to this time no reliable conclusion has been drawn on the religious beliefs and practices of the heterodox Bosnians.

This problem we shall discuss in the next Chapter.

Prosperity and Culture under Mohammedans

Even the dark clouds of Turkish invasion were not without their silver lining. After the bloody and painful process of occupation was over, a new social order was established under the aegis of Islam. The Turkish Sultans considered themselves Kaliphs (successors) of the Prophet and devoted all their energies to expansion of Islam. Being a universal religion, Islam made its appeal to the whole humanity, without distinction of race or nationality. Therefore, its message was to spread throughout the world as that of Christianity itself. However, in distinction from the Gospels, which were to be taught by kindly words and good deeds, al Kuran could be spread also by sword and fire. In reality the tactics of Moslem conversions were twofold:

1) that monotheists were to be subjugated and made to pay for their restricted liberty and privilege of keeping and practicing their religion and

2) that pagans or polytheists were to be forced to accept Islam or accept the Koranic definition of slavery.

Following the example of the Prophet who imposed his teachings on his own native city and various tribes by force of arms, the Moslem warriors conquered countries in order to convert them to Islam, or enslave their populations as "infidels." The "infidel" should be either blotted out, or degraded to toil for the "believer" as a slave. The Moslems who faithfully carried out the tenets and prescriptions of Kuran, were entitled to enjoyment of worldly goods in this life, and to bliss, based on sensuous desires, in the great beyond.

Thus, of necessity, a great social division takes place in the Balkans after the Turkish conquests. To present a balanced picture of the new situation in Bosnia, let us first present the dark side of the new regime that weighed so painfully upon the Christian remnants of the Croatian population in Bosnia and Herzegovina. Then we shall proceed with the exposition of the prosperity and cultural achievements of the new ruling class.

Oppression of Christians

In the opening pages of his book Komlossy (op. cit pp. 2ff) presents a dismal picture of the life of rayah (Christian peasantry) throughout the Turkish rule in Bosnia.

"While the Moslems were the true masters of the land—says Komlossy—and enjoyed all manner of personal liberties, the Christians had no political or civil rights. A rayah could never appear in court as a witness, and his very life was never secure in the face of the arrogance and mischief of the oppressor. As I was told by reliable eye-witnesses such conditions prevailed until the very entrance of the Austro-Hungarian occupation troops (1878) into Bosnia. Under the Kanuni-rayah regulations of Khalif Omar, a Christian had, under heavy penalties, to get out of the way of a Moslem coming in his direction. If riding on horse-back he had to dismount and wait until the Mohammedan passer-by was behind him. The exercise of the Christian worship was beset by numerous obstacles. The use of church bells was strictly forbidden."

There were other abuses, which would now-a-days be classed as "crimes against humanity." Such was, for instance, rape of Christian maidens and women, the so-called "ius primae noctis," which was a privilege of a Mohammedan landowner over his Christian serfs. We mentioned already the ghastly practice of forcible abduction of Christian teen-age boys to be converted into Mohammedans and trained as dreaded "yeni-cheri." Over and over, pregnant Christian women were taxed on the theory that they may give birth to a male child.

But the real horror of the Christian life was in the economic field. In the first place the rayah had to pay a tithe to the State. The taxes being auctioned off to tax-farmers, the latter did not stop before extortionist practices supported by the police-organs. To the tithe the head-tax was added, levied in the amount of one ducat from each inhabitant from his seventh year on.

Still worse was the haratch or income tax, collected by the land-owners (agas and begs) from their serfs to the extent of one-third of their income. Another third was taken from their field produce, while the landowner had the first choice of the crop. In addition, the serf, with his wife and children, had to perform one hundred days a year manual labor on the fields of his landowner. Finally, another tithe went to the Greek-Orthodox clergy, while the bishop was entitled to a gift from every Christian household.

So night-marish was the life of the Christian rayah in Bosnia and Herzegovina for centuries.*

Moslem Privileges

In contrast with this, the reverse side of the medal was bright and shining. It was the life of privilege, wealth, political power and military exploits. Such was the existence carried on by Mohammedans of both high and low station in life. On the whole, the nobility and town-residents became Mohammedans. The native nobility of agas was strengthened by the incoming Turkish military nobility of begs. These two elements ruled the country and formed the backbone of the Ottoman power in the north-western Balkans and Central Europe.**

They were both the striking arm and battering ram of the Sultan in his effort to break through the Alpine barrier and the bastions of Central Europe into the western world. The Bosnian

nobility took great pride in its well-deserved title of "bulwark of Islam."

With this we have brought out a sharp contrast in the life of Bosnia before and after the Turkish occupation. In the 14th and 15th century the Bosnian nobility engaged in internecine struggle and continuous dispute with the sovereign. With the Turkish occupation all this vanished overnight for the absolutist authority of Sultans did not brook any opposition, while the practices of Islam claimed full devotion and undivided attention of the converts. Thus the internal friction and strife that blighted the life of the pre-Ottoman Bosnia vanished as if by the touch of the magic wand.

Further, the former dread of Hungarian invasions was replaced by a sense of security and no energies were wasted for the defense of the country. In addition, Bosnian military campaigns were now conducted on foreign soil, with an opportunity of unlimited plunder and booty. The wealth and prosperity of Bosnia gradually assumed unheard-of proportions. Through their military prowess and growing wealth the Bosnians asserted their influence also in Constantinople and in the court of the Sultans. Bosnia achieved through her nobility a privileged position in the empire.

Another important development exalted the position of Bosnian Mohammedans. The Sultans were not interested in a forcible conversion of their subjects into the Turkish or any other particular nationality. They respected the local traditions, and language, so that the Croatian characteristics of the country did not deteriorate much during the Turkish occupation. Both the writing and language remained the same, and were expanded into the other parts of the Turkish empire, including Constantinople. According to M. A. Pigafetti, an Italian traveller of the middle of the 16th century, "Istambul is governed chiefly by the Christian renegades. In diplomatic negotiations in Constantinople only official decrees and replies are communicated through interpreters in Turkish, in Croatian, with which most Turks were familiar, and especially men of military profession."*

---

* All these things varied greatly in different times, and sometimes according to different landlords in the same times. Some of these practices were carried on even by Christian feudal magnates in Europe.

** The begs were native nobility converted to Islam while some of the agas were Turks rewarded for their military exploits.

* ("nei ragionamenti piu particolari e di meno importanza, ove in qualche digressione, che allhora senza dragomani in crovata lingua parlavano, quale e familiare a tutti quasi i Turchi e specialmente gli huomini di guerra.") /J. Horvat, op. cit. p. 254/.

The preservation of the Croatian and Serbian languages in Bosnia saved her Slavic characteristics through four centuries of Ottoman rule, and moreover helped to Slavicize also the Oriental and Romanic (Wallachian and Tsintsar) elements, which settled down in the country. It is true that the Bosnian speech is permeated with Turkish, Arabic and Persian words reflecting the religious, artistic, industrial, political, economic and cultural life of the Orient, together with its judiciary system and military affairs, yet the phonetic, morphological and grammatical features of the language remained Croatian and Serbian. Precisely through these influences the old Croatian nobility of Bosnia and Herzegovina gradually lost its national consciousness, giving up mostly its nationalism for religious universalism.

Mohammedan Architecture and Plastic Arts

An immediate effect of the Mohammedan prosperity was the ambition to dot the country with gems of oriental architecture. Religion and scholarship were the prime-motives of this activity, but economic pursuits and social welfare also benefitted. Both monumental and practical buildings were erected through philanthropy of wealthy Moslems, for the most part statesmen and generals. Through disposal of booty and unchecked plunder in the countries of "infidels," the military leaders amassed huge wealth, and invested part of it into erection of public buildings, bridges, aqueducts, gorgeous fountains, public baths, bazaars, schools and libraries, Moslem monasteries (hanikah, tekiye), free public kitchens (imaret) and dormitories (musafir han), clock-towers (sahat kule) and observatories, and, foremost of all, places of worship in the form of modest or magnificent mosques. Moreover, since care-taking of these buildings required proper personnel and expendable materials, all these buildings were supported by an impressive trust-fund or income-property, called *vakuf*. At least until the last war such estates were still in existence, and some of them were quite prosperous, even though they had been established early in the 16th century.

Early Mosques and Their Builders

Because of their claim of survival through centuries and sometimes gorgeous artistic execution of details, our attention is arrested first on the stately mosques and their graceful minarets, reminding us frequently of the lofty spires of Gothic Cathedrals. By the trail of mosques in their chronological order and progress toward central Europe we may measure the crusading zeal of Islam, and its self-assurance in the final victory. So even during the first Turkish raids in Upper Bosnia mosques were erected. The Hranushich family of Bosnian converts was their first and most generous patron. Then came Ferhad pasha, Jakub pasha, Husref beg and others in a long line of builders ending with the graceful structures of the family of Hussein Gradashchevich, the Dragon of Bosnia, put up in the 19th century.

However, we shall restrict our survey to mosques and their auxiliary structures that were erected in the 15th and 16th centuries.[*]

According to Bashagich (op. cit. p. 34 f) and Truhelka (op. cit. p. 59) Gazi Isa Beg Hranushich (1436-1470), founded the proud city of Serayevo (originally: *Sheher Seray*, "City of Palaces"). Even though some other sources claim that Serayevo was founded under the name of *Vrh-Bosna* (Upper Bosnia) by banus Styepan Kotroman, father of Styepan Kotromanich, there is no real contradiction in the two claims, for Isa beg could have lent to the captured city its "palatial aspect," after proper appraisal of its economic importance and geographic location. "Alongside the Kyarubani-seray (Karavan-hostelry) by which later on the whole city was named, he (i.e., Isa beg Hranushich) built two public baths (for men and women), the mussafirhan (the great Kolobara hotel) and mosque which he later donated to Sultan Mehmed Fatih when the latter conquered Bosnia (this is the 'Emperor's Mosque or *Tsareva Djamiya*'), and on the opposite bank of Milyatska creek he erected a hotel for the caravans. Besides this he built in the Bendbasha district a mill with nine

---

[*] In this effort we shall rely on testimony of Dr. Chiro Truhelka's "Gazi Husrefbeg, his Life and Time" (Gazi Husrefbeg, njegov zivot i njegovo doba. Sarajevo, 1912); further, Dr. Ivan Esih's "Dictionary of Turkish, Arabic and Persian words in the Croatian Literary Language and Popular Speech" (Turcizmi, Rjecnik Turskih, Arapskih i perzijskih rijeci u Hrvatskom Knjizevnom Jeziku i Puckom Govoru. Zagreb, 1942); and the biographic dictionary of Safvet beg Bashagich entitled: "Famous Croats of Bosnia and Herzegovina in the Turkish Empire" (Znameniti Hrvati, Bosnjaci i Hercegovci, u Turskoj Carevini. Zagreb, 1931).

wings and a number of other buildings, which formed the foundation of the later Serayevo." (Bashagich, op. cit. p. 34 f.) According to Truhelka (op. cit. p. 59), Isa beg built also the bridge spanning Milyatska creek, a dervish monastery (tekiye), and other small buildings.

But even before the monumental structures of Husref beg, Serayevo was dotted with a number of small mosques (mesdjid) built by other men of prominence. So, according to Truhelka (op. cit. pp. 89, 44), the oldest mosque in Serayevo, the Have-hatun mosque was built in 1436, that of Nesuh beg in 1452, Emperor's mosque in 1459; mesdjid (small mosque) of Bagdadi in 1463; mesdjid of Hadji-Hussein in 1473; the mosque of Ayaz beg in 1474; mesdjid of Jakub pasha in 1491, mosque of Jahya pasha in 1494; mesdjid of Mimar Sinan in 1496; mosque of Sheyhi Ferah in 1499; mesdjid of Hubyar aga in 1502; mosque of Gazi Bali beg in 1506; monumental mosque of Mustapha beg in 1517; mosque of Mehmed beg Hranushich in 1519; mesdjid of Hassan Pehlavan and mosque of Smail Saracha in 1521; mosque of Hadji Mustapha Chekarji in 1523; and mesdjid of Hadji Ali terzi-bash, in 1524.

Naturally, they all were exceeded in grandeur and magnificence by the majestic mosque of Husref beg, built in 1530. Before we devote our attention to Begova Djamiya or Husref beg's mosque, let us make a survey of the mosques erected in various parts of Bosnia in the course of the 16th century.

According to Dr. Ivan Esih (op. cit. pp. 44 ff), whose statements are based on the work of Hamdi Kreshevlyakovich, a prominent Croatian Moslem scholar, the following is the chronology of the more conspicuous 16th century mosques in Bosnia and Herzegovina.

No.	Name of Builder	City	Year Built
1	Sinan Chaush	Livno	1529
2	Lala Pasha	Livno	1567/8
3	Hadji Ahmet	Livno	1588
4	Hassan Nazir	Focha	1550
5	Hassan Aga	Travnik	1549
6	Karadjoz beg	Mostar	1557
7	Mesuhh aga	Mostar	1564
8	Hadji Ali	Pochitel	1562/3
9	Sinan beg	Chayniche	1570
10	Mehmed chaush	Konyits	1579
11	Ferhad pasha	Banya Luka	1583
12	Tefterdare	Banya Luka	1594/5
13	Kizlar aga	Vartsar-Vakuf	1595
14	Sultan Suleiman	Blagay	about 1550
15	Lala pasha	Tomislavgrad	1550
16	Yussuf pasha	Maglay	1550
17	Buzadji hadji	Serayevo	1555
18	Gazi Ali pasha	Serayevo	1561
19	Ferhat beg	Serayevo	1562
20	Hodja Durak	Serayevo	before 1600

Among these we shall keep in mind as the outstanding specimens of the oriental art, especially the Aladja mosque in Focha and the Kurshumli mosque of Maglay, still admired as the most beautiful oriental buildings of Bosnia.

Begova Djamiya (Beg's Mosque) and Other Architectural Legacy of Husref Beg (Died in 1541)

The gigantic figure of Husref beg in the history of Bosnia can best be compared with that of Maecenas in Rome during the reign of Julius Augustus. As a brilliant general, right hand and friend of Suleiman the Magnificent, conqueror in many battles, a successful administrator, man of huge wealth, patron of arts, religious leader, and before all, a grateful son of Bosnia, he was fired with the ambition of making Serayevo one of the leading centers of religion, arts, science, trade and commerce in the Ottoman Empire.

Besides his mosque Husref built in Serayevo a college and seminary (medress), dervish monastery, two commercial arcades, two monumental public baths, public kitchen and hostelry for the poor, entire rows of stores, attaching all his chattel and estates throughout Bosnia and Thrace for the upkeep of his religious, educational and other establishments in Serayevo. He also built the city aqueduct distributing the water through 21 fountains.

The glory of his name is attached chiefly to his mosque, a sort of Taj Mahal of Bosnia. In a busy commercial center the minaret of the mosque rises gracefully 150 feet, while the body of the building is topped with a dome covered with a lead roof. The interior of the building forms a square about 43 by 43 feet large, with the ceiling about 65 feet above the floor, and 86 feet to the top of its dome. Thus the full height of the building is exactly the double of the width or length of the main hall. The walls are about 7 feet thick. The interior is simple, lacking any sumptuous columns (such as we saw in the Temple of Jupiter or St. Domnius' Cathedral of Split), but the side walls and superstructures are adorned with lace-work carvings of lovely oriental designs. The auxiliary structures such as the pulpit (Mimber), preachers' platform (kyurs), muyezzin's octagonal gallery supported by 8 marble columns, etc., are richly decorated with ornate oriental carvings. The floors are covered with sumptuous Persian carpets. The light problem is solved by spacious and stylish arched windows. Although the main hall (nave) can house a large crowd of worshippers, two wings (gyinah) are added to the main premise in order to take care of the over-flow crowd.

The two lateral halls also form squares, about 23 ft. in length and width, while the ceiling rises about 46 feet above the floor. In front of the main hall there is an arcade with 5 vaults supported by four marble columns about 17 feet high and over 2 feet in diameter. The two end-vaults are carried by side-walls. The main entrance is reached through a shallow marble arcade topped by rows of stalactites recessed in the ceiling. The entrance door itself is made of wood, with elaborate carvings and above it a marble plate is fixed in the wall, carrying in decorative style a laudatory verse (tarih) in Arabic, which explains the motives which inspired Husref beg to erect the magnificent temple.

Connected with the mosque is the library with 1800 sacred books, 1000 of which are in handwriting. Some of them are illuminated with beautiful colored arabesques. Adjacent to the mosque are two mausolea, one of which houses the sarcophagus (turbet) of Gazi Husref beg himself, and the other that of his first estate manager (muteveli) and friend Murat beg. Both places became shrines highly venerated by the local Moslem population.

We have already listed numerous other buildings of the Husref vakuf, dedicated to their high religious, social or educational purpose. Even though their artistic value is but moderate, their economic and social function in Mohammedan Bosnia, bears witness to Husref's keen sense of practical philanthropy exceeded only by his lofty idealism in the domain of religion, art and science.

THE BOSNIAN STATE

Conditions in Croatia in the 11th Century

Even in older historical literature it has been observed that there is some connection, although not clearly perceived, between the fall of the Croatian national dynasty, i.e., Croatia's union with Hungary, and the rise of Bosnia, as an impressive national State, with every attribute of national sovereignty. In this connection we should recall a few other significant details. After Koloman became king of Croatia—through right of conquest as the Hungarian historians claim, or through pacta conventa as the Croatian historians know—nothing is heard of the national party which, under the leadership of Peter Svatchich, lost the battle of Gvozd, in its struggle against both the Hungarians and their Croatian allies.

The question arises now what happened to these warriors and their numerous supporters? Have they all been killed or did they suddenly become converts to the cause of Hungary? Naturally, neither could be the case! What is the answer? The answer is: emigration to Bosnia, similarly to the exodus of the nationally-minded Croats and Serbs from under the contemporary Tito-regime to scatter throughout the world. But even before the Gvozd-disaster the national party was fighting also the Latin element. Both the Dalmatian cities and their Croatian allies were combatting the national party on the issue of a free and independent Croatian Church, the chief characteristics of which were the use of the Croatian liturgy, marriage of the clergy and some traditions left behind by Methodius and his disciples, propounders of the Moravian cult.

All this coincided with a social movement gaining momentum through its conflict with the Croatian cause. This was the return of the romanized Illyrian highlanders from their centuries-long mountain retreat to the sea-coast and river-valleys inhabited by the Croats. At the same time the Latin element of the coastal cities, protected and favored by the Croatian dynasts, also expanded to the detriment of the ethnic Croatian element, which was to be disrupted, ground up and absorbed by the pincers' movement of the Romanic populations. This caused a reaction among the Croats which provoked the civil strife in the Croatian kingdom, the Latin party supporting the king, the Latin liturgy and hierarchy, the Cluniac reform, and the maritime cities, while the national party opposed the king and the Latin Church staunchly defending the Croatian liturgy, family life of the clergy, independent church administration and greater influence in national government.

When the power of the national party outgrew that of the king to such an extent that it could remove from the throne or destroy such a powerful dynast as king Zvonimir, the Latin party turned to the Hungarian Árpád dynasty, queen Helena's nearest king, for aid. This movement resulted in the Hungarian intervention and downfall of the national dynasty. Finally, in order to appraise fully the importance of the pincers' movement of the Romanic population in Dalmatia, let us keep in mind that similar phenomenon contributed in Dacia, Wallachia and Moldavia to romanization of the Slavic and Kumanian population, as well as to annihilation of the native landed nobility in Bulgaria and Serbia after their conquest by the Turks. To what purpose the Turks used the same element in Bosnia and Herzegovina, we shall see in another chapter.

Thus, we have all the elements needed for comprehension of the events that took place in the 12th century in the Croatian banate of Rama or Bosnia, both names being used to designate the same territory. The first scholar to establish connection between the events unfolding in Croatia and Dalmatia, and the rise of Bosnia as a strong national State was Dr. F. Milobar (Petriniensis) in his work: "Bosnia and Croatian Constitutional Law." (Bosnien und das kroatische Staatsrecht, Zagreb, 1898), and in his doctoral dissertation entitled "The Historical Relationship of Bosnia to Croatia and Hungary" (Das geschichtliche Verhaltnis Bosniens zu Kroatien und Ungarn), Zürich University. This subject was further developed by L. V. Südland (Ivo Pilar) in his treatise on the "Southern Slavic Problem and the World War" (Die Süd-

slavische Frage und der Weltkrieg, Wien, 1917) and confirmed by Dr. Josip Horvat in his "Millenium of Croatian Culture" (1000 godina kulture Hrvata, Zagreb).

Early Relations Between Bosnia and Croatia

Based on a comprehensive study of the Byzantine writers, Dr. Milobar arrives at the conclusion that Bosnia right from the beginning of the Slavic settlement in Illyricum and Pannonia was a Croatian country. His two main authorities are the oft-mentioned Constantinus Porphyrogenitus, and Cinnamus, a high official at the court of Manuel Komnenos. His chief source is Chapter III of Constantine's "De Administrando Imperio" in which the imperial writer relates of the coming of Croats from their Trans-Carpathian "White Croatia" into the Dalmatian thema, upon the invitation of emperor Heraclius (610-641). The emperor's plea was to clear this province and the rest of Illyricum of the troublesome Avars who had designs upon Constantinople while the emperor concentrated all his forces upon war against Chosroes, emperor of Persia. Indicating the power of the Croats, according to Milobar, is the fact that after years of bloody struggle, the Croats not only cleared Dalmatia of the Avars, but also expelled them from Bosnia and southern Pannonia, pressing them into the great Hungarian steppe-land where they were routed by Charlemagne. Thus, the Croats took over a vast territory by right of conquest and imperial franchise, settling down with their tribes in seven different districts called banates. One of these banates was the territory of Bosnia expanding southwest into the tetrarchy or "Red Croatia," and east up to Morava river, in the present-day Serbia. On the authority of Cedrenus, Theophanes, Nicephor Bryennias, and some domestic sources, Milobar argues that the Croats had common frontiers with the Bulgars along the Danube and Morava river, south to Nish (Naissa), while the Serbs occupied the area further south: in Macedonia up to Salonica, and up to the head-waters of the Tara, Piva and Drina rivers in the west. During the reign of Peter Kreshimir the eastern Croatian frontier should have reached the Bulgarian town of Viddin, and in the lifetime of Zvonimir the eastern frontier followed the course of Morava river, east of Belgrade.

Even though Constantinus assigns a part of Bosnia to Serbs, Milobar places full stress—in addition to other points of argument—upon the chronicle of Cinnamus (about 1160) who asserts that "Bosnia is not subjected to the Grand Zhupan of Serbia, for an independent people lives there and has its own Government." This is confirmed by Südland-Pilar, who declares on the authority of the Byzantine historian Gfrörer, and also Rachki, that Porphyrogenitus was in part ignorant of the situation, and in part partial to the Serbs for political reasons. On the other hand, Milobar explains this discrepancy through difference in chronology which could have misled Constantine, for he describes the conditions as of 949, when Croatia was torn by internal strife, and Serbia gained ascendancy.

However, the testimony of the Dioclean Priest also favors the Serbian cause in the case of Bosnia, while the Hungarian Komlóssy takes the Dioclean chronicle at its face value, even though it contains many names and stories with no connection whatsoever, either with the Croatian or Serbian history, and most of its assertions are taken only as legends, with little, or no historical value.

Thus, according to Milobar and Croatian historians, the banate of Bosnia was from the beginning a member of the Croatian tribal confederation, and only second in importance to the banus of White Croatia. Moreover, as elector of the Croatian Kingdom, the Bosnian banus was eligible to the Croatian throne. In the reign of Zvonomir the Bosnian banus was an opponent of the king who in exalting his own power, tried to curtail that of the bani. After the disaster of Peter Svachich, the banus of Bosnia remained the only champion of Croatian independence waiting for the occasion to cross his sword with that of king Koloman. The power and prestige of the Bosnian banus was enhanced through retreat of the Croatian national party in the mountains of Bosnia, and continued political immigration for nearly a generation. There the Croatian nobility, with its national traditions, equally adverse to Latins and Hungarians, established itself in another part of the national territory, and contributed its skill and energies to the aggrandizement of Bosnia. By the end of Manuel Komnenos' war a great figure emerges on the Bosnian throne who announces himself in the style of a true sovereign, with "I, Kulin, banus of Bosnia."

The National Party Finds a New Home in Bosnia

Thus, what Croatia loses in the coastal area and along the Drava river, gains in the mountain ranges of Bosnia where a strong political power and national church organization cause much worry both to the Roman Church, still adverse to Croatian liturgy, and to the kings of Hungary who need Bosnia for territorial continuity of their dominion between Hungary and Dalmatia.

On the 15th of June, 1103, king Koloman, in a patent issued to the city of Split, assumes for the first time the title of king of Bosnia (. . . rex Ramae), along-side his titles: king of Hungary, Dalmatia and Croatia. Milobar explains this move as a threat to the recalcitrant banus of Bosnia who refused to recognize him as his sovereign. The Hungarian, Komlóssy sees in this act an armed conquest of Bosnia, an assumption rejected by Südland-Pilar, for lack of historical proof to substantiate such a momentous undertaking. According to Milobar, the banus, whose name has not been recorded, collected forces and bided for the opportunity to strike at the Hungarians in the same way as Peter Svachich did. The banus and the national party were watching the moves of Koloman and his struggle with Venice, which was in the offing. Any thrust against the Latins, both on the coastland and across the sea was welcome to the Bosnians and the Croatian national party, so that the original zeal for a war against Koloman waned. Moreover, the pacta conventa appeared to them less reprehensible since they provided for the election and crowning of the Croatian king who not only defended them against Venice, but also against Hungarians, for Koloman specifically prohibited admission of Hungarians to the Croatian territory, except by invitation or consent of the local authorities. Furthermore, throughout his reign Koloman was loyal to his obligations as king of Croatia, and was under constant threat by his brother Álmos, who claimed the Croatian throne on the principle of secundogeniture established by their uncle king Ladislaus who designated Álmos as his successor on the Croatian throne. All these circumstances brought about a political equilibrium and the Bosnians recognized the pacta conventa, thus becoming the foremost Croatian power which guarded the inviolability of the covenant and opposed the Hungarians whenever they were tempted to breach it.

The Bosnian bani, due to their exalted position, became the leaders of Croatia and by defending their own rights emanating from pacta conventa, they defended the rights of Croatia stemming from the same source. Thus, in union with Hungary the constitutional relationship between Croatia and Bosnia was tightened and the two went together either as allies or opponents of Hungary. So under banus Borich Bosnia and Croatia are supporting the king of Hungary in his struggle with emperors of Byzantium, but in the throne succession strife Borich and Croats sided with Stephen IV. Yet Stephen IV was defeated by his nephew Stephen III, who waged war against Borich and probably killed him in battle.

Renewal of Pacta Conventa

After the death of Manuel Komnenos, both Croatia and Bosnia rid themselves of the Byzantine governors. In 1180 they both returned under the sovereignty of Béla III, yet with the provision of secundo-geniture, or permanent establishment on the Croatian throne of a lateral branch of the Árpád dynasty. This promise was never kept, for the elder members of the family were steadily after both crowns: that of Hungary and Croatia. In the meantime, the Bosnian State achieves political and economic ascendancy, which it does not relinquish in spite of temporary setbacks, until its fall in 1463. The first great Bosnian ruler was banus Kulin (1180-1204), whose memory is still alive among the common people of all Croatian lands. The popular legends all recall the prosperity and prestige Bosnia enjoyed during Kulin's reign. A banner-crop still today is called "Kulin's crop," etc. The ruggedness of the Bosnian people and devotion to their country produced a wealth of farm-products and manufactured goods. Mining flourished and export was taken care of by Ragusans whom Kulin endowed with grants and trading privileges. His dynastic ties with the Serbian Nemanides were established by his marriage to a sister of Stephen Nemanya. Before his conversion to Catholicism, he was a member of the Bosnian Church, and its protector. But even when this membership

is abjured in Bolinopolye, together with that of some other heads of the Bosnian Church, no dogmatic changes are provided in their creed, but rather administrative and liturgical accommodations to the prevalent Catholic practices, are stipulated in the conversion. In connection with ecclesiastic disputes, a Hungarian invasion was averted through the skillful diplomacy of Kulin.

A gigantic struggle between Bosnia and Hungary develops under banus Ninoslav (1232-1250) when the kings of Hungary decide to turn the sovereign Bosnia into a Hungarian province. Duke Koloman, son of Andrew II and brother of Béla IV, conquered Herzegovina and invaded Bosnia. Almost providentially, Bosnia gains respite from Hungarian attacks through the Tartar invasion of Hungary and parts of Croatia. After withdrawal of the Tartars Béla IV undertakes in person, successful campaigns against Bosnia, but Ninoslav's stout defense of his country nullified Béla's successes, and a status quo peace was the national tradition and the Croatian State policy laid down in the pacta conventa.

Out of the above description we can safely conclude that all the Bosnian bani, from Borich to Tvartko did recognize the sovereignty of the Hungarian-Croatian king. This relationship arose from the Croatian Constitutional Law by which Bosnia was a part of the Croatian kingdom.

Further, the Bosnian bani resisted the power of kings when the latter, under the guise of "anti-heretic" campaigns, invaded Bosnia to curtail the near-sovereign power of the bani, i.e., when they tried to enforce their unjust claims to the rights of Bosnia established by ancient tradition and guaranteed by pacta conventa.

Bosnia, a Champion of Croatian Freedom

As a true Croatian country, Bosnia remains throughout the reign of the Árpád kings, in the forefront of a fight for national independence, and therefore the Bosnian banus rises in power and prestige above the other Croatian bani. The constitutional relationship to Croatia does not change thereby, but, on the contrary, is tightened. The struggle of Ninoslav is significant because in his reign the Hungarian State-idea comes for the first time into conflict with rights arranged for in pacta conventa. Hence, Bosnia's relationship to Hungary remained the same as that to the rest of the Croatian lands, which is not denied by Bosnians, but on every occasion confirmed and stressed.

Even though the legal relations remained the same among the three countries, factually the situation underwent a significant change. Viewed from this angle, the situation of Bosnia was much better than that of the Croatian mother-country. For the personal union between Croatia and Hungary had the tendency to degenerate into Croatia's subordination to Hungary as a protecting power. On the other hand, Bosnia rose to the position of a semi-sovereign power under the Árpád kings. So while Bosnia was on her way to become an internationally sovereign power, Croatia took a dip into a status which would have gradually turned that country into a Hungarian province. However, the stormy events of 1299 (rebellion against Andrew III), reversed the trend and Croatia shook off the Hungarian protectorate, while Bosnia once more tightened her traditional ties with Croatia.

With the coming of the Angevine dynasty a new period begins in the relations of Hungary and Bosnia. While the Angevines are enthroned in Hungary, the members of the Kotroman dynasty arise in Bosnia lending the country power and prestige never attained during the reign of former bani. Moreover, both houses enter into a blood-relationship which exerted a considerable influence upon the shaping of Bosnian history.

Hungarian Claims

In spite of the well-known course of relations between Croatia, Bosnia and Hungary, the Hungarian historians do not yield in their assertions that the sovereignty of their kings over Bosnia was acquired by force of arms, and so maintained. For F. Komlóssy, Koloman conquered the land of Hum (Herzegovina) and Rama (Bosnia) during his campaigns in Dalmatia, on which he issued his famous patent to the city of Split "pleno jure" as "Dei gratia Hungariae, Dalmatiae, Croatiae, Ramaeque rex." Curiously enough this "conquest" is forgotten for over thirty years, for the next instance of Bosnia's insertion in the set of royal titles takes place in 1135 in the reign of the blind and sickly king Béla II. Disregarding the Croatian side of the story Komlóssy lists all the instances of administrative dispositions, which were taken hundreds of miles from Bosnia's frontiers, in execution of some nominal rights (de jure, de nomine), but not through exercise of factual power in the land itself. A number of incursions in Bosnia are for Komlóssy new conquests, followed regularly by still newer ones, until the very fall of Hungary.

Equally interesting is his survey (pp. 37 ff) of the "legal relationship existing between the kingdom of Hungary, and her Bosnian province" during the Angevins when one member of the Croatian Brebir clan was strong enough to "dispute his (Charles Robert) royal rights" in Bosnia. Still more original is Komlóssy's claim that Louis I, king of Hungary, permitted banus Tvartko to take the title of "king of Serbia and Bosnia" and have himself crowned at Mileshevo. Hence "if the same ruler (Louis I) was moved to bestow upon one of his subordinated bani the royal title, he must have had very good reasons for such a benevolent gesture." Reasons? According to Pray and Katona the title was given "as an incentive for a more efficient resistance to the Turks." Unfortunately, Tvartko and Lazarus Greblyanovich were interested more in fighting princes Balsha and Altomanovich than the armies of Sultan Murad. But according to Horváth Mihály (Magyarok története II, 152), by the grant of royal title, Louis I wanted to attach Tvartko "by bonds of gratitude to the Hungarian crown," etc. However, it is not known that Tvartko asked any permission from Louis I, but merely informed him, as he did other courts, of the fait accompli. Among other claims of the Hungarian thesis equally fictitious is the one that the Hungarians looked in Bosnia for nothing but "honor and glory," and that they magnanimously protected the Bosnians "from the oppression of their own native princes."

Hungarian Sovereignty Reviewed by an Austrian Statesman

In his monograph entitled "Bosnia and Herzegovina in the Pre-Turkish Period" (Bosnien und Herzegowina in der vorottomanischen Zeit, Wien, 1918), Dr. Joseph Maria Baernreither, a former Austrian minister and life-long student of Bosnian affairs, discounts fully the Hungarian claims by saying: "the prevailing opinion in Austria is that from the political connection of Hungary with those countries in the pre-Turkish period, a constitutional sequence to our own days cannot be derived, and that from the title: 'rex Ramae' carried by the Hungarian king, no conclusions can be made." (P. 7.) And further: ... "it is immaterial to which constitutional personality these (i.e., sovereign) rights belonged, but what matters is what were the historical characteristics of these rights, and whether or not they can be regarded at all as an expression of sovereignty." (P. 8.) After these introductory remarks Dr. Baernreither passes in review through 7 chapters, the full complex of pre-Turkish Bosnia's political history and summarizes in the 8th chapter his observations and deductions.

So from the survey of the historical facts which he attempted to establish it appears to him that the old relations between Hungary and the countries south of the Sava, are "by the political motives laid down at their foundation, by their content and territorial expansion, exceptionally fluid (changing)." So for a certain period when Hungary acts as a striking arm of the Roman Curia, the intervention in Bosnia was inspired chiefly by religious motives. This is followed by the Angevin period when dynastic ties are established between forceful ruling personalities, and Hungary finds in Bosnia an ally and military base for expanding her influence in the Balkans. Soon after her rise to kingdom, Bosnia falls into the vortex of internal troubles so that Sigismund is forced to police the country and keep it away from a Turkish alliance, toward which it was drifting.

But even armed interventions in Bosnia assumed varying forms. At first these were crusades without territorial objectives and designs, then manifestations of the lust to conquer aimed at single portions of the realm, more so at Bosnia than at Herzegovina. The intensity of these actions also varies, from mere inroads to attempts to create order in the war-torn land. Only Mathias Corvinus seizes with strong hand the sovereignty—not merely by theoretical protestations—but rather posthumously, when Bosnian independence was dead, and the greater part of the country in the Sultan's hands. In the northern part of the country the Hungarian sovereignty is now actually established, but only for a few decades when Hungary herself shares the fate of Bosnia.

Then really, what were these much-claimed "sovereign" rights of Hungary? In the modern acceptance of the term "Sovereignty," they did not exist. The kaleidoscopic panorama of continuous changes cannot provide any foundation for stability, and eo ipso for exercise of sovereignty.

In Baernreither's findings Bosnia was not modeled after Roman provinces in which the barbarian states of the Middle Ages were founded. Bosnia was an amorphic political structure, in which it was difficult to establish the sovereignty of the native rulers themselves. The banus of Bosnia was not a generally accepted autocrat or dictator. He was merely primus inter pares, a peer among the powerful magnates. As soon as a king gained effective power, it was immediately contested by his peers. Thus, if the sovereignty of the native princes was so wobbly, how much less meaning and effect the Hungarian sovereignty must have had. The kings of Hungary placed Bosnia constantly into a position of subordination and subserviency, but could never exercise direct and effective power in that country. "They had no share—says Baernreither—in the tolls and custom duties in Bosnia as they had in Dalmatia; they did not perform any supreme judicial functions in the judiciary system of the country; no chronicle-writer informs us of administrative measures, which they should have taken in the interior of the country, and of no laws they enacted."

Thus one should not lose sight of the fact that "Hungary was never exerting her conditional and unstable influence upon the country itself, but only upon its bani and kings in an attempt to make them her political tools." But even this was inefficient for the rulers of Bosnia were not appointed by the kings of Hungary, but selected by the native barons, and by far not unanimously. The Hungarian kings assumed merely the right to confirm such election. In this respect the Hungarian influence was felt in the support of one banus against another, or against the rebellious magnates, and in restoration to power of an expelled banus or king. But such influence Hungary exercised also in Serbia and other countries, which came from time to time, within the orbit of the expansionist Hungarian policy in the Balkans. However, these were all temporary affairs promptly forgotten as soon as the force of the moment was spent.

Fallacy of the Hungarian Sovereignty

Since the positive content of a supremacy for a well-defined period in a definite country must be determined by historical facts, we are to conclude, from the full body of facts presented in the foregoing pages, that the social order, economic situation, status of the peasantry, internal peace, and security of both life and property from time to time, had been in a most deplorable condition, and that Hungary, in spite of her political ambitions, did not do, or could not do anything whatsoever toward their improvement. "That Hungary undertook anything," says Baernreither, "for the benefit of Bosnia's destiny, by enacting efficient laws for the improvement of the lot of the Bosnian people, is not known to history. But that Hungary tried to connect these countries, if only loosely, with the western world; to defend the Catholic faith, or even save it from extinction, and to introduce at least temporarily some semblance of order at a time of worst disorders, should be recognized as the full volume of Hungary's historic mission, which reaches its climax during the reign of the Angevins and Mathias Corvinus. Hungary was unable to do anything more in these countries. The positive content of Hungary's relations to Bosnia and Herzegovina consisted by no means in a systematic and stable rule over the country, but in the exercise of a mutable and unstable—at times expanded or again restricted—political influence upon its bani and kings. A supremacy of this kind, the pursuit of political objectives and pressure upon the rulers, should never be confused with the exercise of sovereignty in a country. Property rights upon these countries in the sense of a state-union with the Crown of Hungary, as was the case with Croatia, or the exercise of Government power as it took place in Dalmatia, from the course of historical events cannot be concluded also in relation to Bosnia and Herzegovina."

Annotation No. 5

J. M. Baernreither and Ivo Pilar

The importance of Geheimrath Dr. J. M. Baernreither, minister of commerce and social welfare in various cabinets of the Austrian Monarchy, his influential work as a member of the "Austrian-Hungarian Delegations" in the imperial Parliament of the Dual Monarchy, his lifelong specialization in the problems of Bosnia-Herzegovina and Southern Slavic aspirations, along with his literary activity in this field, is well presented in Ante Malbasha's: "Bosnian Problems and Austria-Hungary in the light of the political diary of J. M. Baernreither" (Bosansko pitanje i Austro-Ugarska u svijetlu politickog dnevnika J. M. Baernreithera, Sarajevo, 1933). The most interesting point in Malbasha's book bearing on the subject matter of this and preceding chapter, is his report on an interview between Baernreither and Dr. Ivo Pilar (L. von Südland) which took place on February 3, 1913, in Vienna. They had a thorough discussion of the Bosnian situation, Southern-Slavic problems, and of the "Bogomil" Church which Dr. Pilar wished to revive as a synthesis of the Western and Eastern Church with Mohammedanism in Bosnia. In this connection Malbasha presents in the same chapter (pp. 62f) the interesting biography of Dr. Ivo Pilar (1874-1933), whose scientific and cultural work, in Malbasha's estimation, obtained the best interpretation in the article of Dr. Ivan Esih, a well-known literary and art-critic, published on September 4, 1933, in the Zagreb daily "Jutarnji List" (Morning News).

This little excursus was deemed necessary in this place for a better appraisal of Dr. Baernreither's "Bogomil" theory, in view of his final note attached to the bibliography of his volume reading as follows:

"During the printing of the instant historical sketch I obtained the preliminary manuscript of a grand and interesting book: 'The Southern Slavic Problems and the World-War' by L. v. Südland (800 pages). This work comprehends the national-political development of Serbs and Croats in an entirely new illumination and arrives in the Bogomil question at results which, in many respects, coincide with my own conclusions, and especially with reference to the decisive role this sect played in the historical fortunes of Bosnia and Herzegovina."

Vitality of the Bosnian State

With all our respect and admiration for these two eminent writers, which yield in nothing to our delight in Rachki's "Bogomils and Pata-renes," to the esteem for Klaich's History of Bosnia, Jirechek's History of Bulgaria and History of Serbia, to Milobar's fine work on Constitutional History of Croatia and Bosnia, we must insist on the supreme evidence of archeology as unfolded in the preceding chapter, and declare all their views bearing on the vital "Bogomil" question as utterly erroneous, or at least open to serious doubt. The facts brought out in the preamble of this chapter vindicate, in our estimation, fully the vitality of the Bosnian State, exposed for centuries on all sides to the attacks of overwhelming powers, and beset by internal strife due to evolutionary process of the feudal society and the balance between the centripetal tendencies of the monarchy and centrifugal forces of the high nobility, to say nothing of the demographic flux and reflux which changed the ethnic picture of both Bosnia and Herzegovina. In our estimation the "Bogomil" Bosnian State did twice as well as the "orthodox" Serbian empire, much better than Croatia, and positively better than the mighty Hungary which collapsed under the crushing blows of Mohammedan Bosnia and her allies in the world of Islam.

In conclusion of this chapter let us sum up the results at which we arrived. On the evidence of Milobar's materials and conclusions, we were informed that Bosnia was from the beginning a Croatian country, one of the seven federated banates. During the reign of the Croatian dynasts, the Bosnian banus was a powerful elector, himself being eligible to the Croatian throne. With the fall of Peter Svachich and his national party, Bosnia remains the only center of Croatian resistance, both in the planned counter-attack against the Hungarian Koloman, and later as a staunch defender of pacta conventa.

Croatia and Bosnia in Opposition to Hungary

Dr. Baernreither dissipated all Hungarian claims to effective Hungarian sovereignty in Bosnia, whether during the Árpád, Angevin or later dynasties. The question is whether he did similar damage also to the Croatian claims of a political and constitutional unity with Bosnia. Far from doing that, in our estimation, he confirmed them and strengthened them. Since Hungary did not effectively rule in Bosnia and Herzegovina, the Bosnian power in times of its

growth and efflorescence was directed against Hungary and thus electrified the Croatian nobility to a more forceful resistance to the kings of the Árpád dynasty. The Croatian oligarchy shook the national life out of its somnolence and established a barrier against the Hungarian penetration. The Bosnian magnates of the frontier area joined in the movement.

On the true situation in Croatia and Dalmatia during the Árpád kings, the following lines of Gergo Novak, author of "Paul of Brebir, banus of Croatia and Sovereign of Bosnia" ("Pavao Bribirski, Ban Hrvata i Gospodar Bosne," Split, 1932) will throw ample light. "Since, through concatenation of circumstances, the Croats received at the beginning of the 12th Century as their kings, rulers of alien blood, members of the Hungarian Árpád dynasty, aliens became bani of Croatia. At that time political life in Croatia became nearly extinct, as if, with the elimination of the Croatian rulers, also the will for political life vanishes. It is true, the old Croatian nobility, until then strong and active, remained in its estates inter-connected with blood-ties. . . . But the Croatian magnates could not reach any higher position of power in the first place because the king's entourage was wholly Hungarian. The Hungarian nobility controlled all the highest political offices, including the Office of the Banus. . . . The Office of the Banus was, regularly in the hands of prominent Hungarian magnates, who directed the policy of the State."

This fully agrees with the statement of Milobar, who in the concluding paragraphs of his book reminds us that while Croatia was drifting into Hungarian servitude, Bosnia was rising into a position of sovereign power. The national nobility of Croatia, after its withdrawal into the Bosnian highlands, not only prepared the ground for resistance, but through building up the power of Bosnia herself, kept the slumbering national consciousness of Croatia awake in its opposition to the expansionist policy of Hungary. The first symptom of this awakening came with the introduction of the Angevin rulers into Croatia and Hungary, followed up later by the invitation of Neapolitan Ladislaus as king of Croatia, and his support by Duke Hervoye Hervatinich in the face of the Hungarian opposition.

As a grateful daughter, Bosnia came to the

aid of her Croatian motherland whenever the need was greatest.

Religious Life in Medieval Bosnia and Herzegovina

Unlike the neighboring states of Serbia, Bulgaria and Croatia, there was no State religion in Bosnia from the days of banus Kulin up to the conquest of the country by the Turks. Through all these centuries three religious groups and rites vied for supremacy: the Catholic Church, the Greek Orthodox Church and the Bosnian Church. For this reason neither of them could establish a permanent status, but everything was unstable, passing and insecure.

The Catholic Church. Already in the most remote past a diocese is mentioned in Upper Bosnia, as one dependent upon Rome. The seat of this diocese (ecclesia Bestoensis) was in all probability in the present towns of Foynitsa or Kreshevo, located in the center of Upper Bosnia. At first this diocese was subordinated to the Archbishopric of Salona (Split), but in 1067 it was attached to the arch-diocese of Antivari-Doclea, later to that of Dubrovnik, and in 1247 to Kalocha in South Hungary.

In the 12th or 13th century the seat of this diocese was transferred to the town of Berdo in the county of Upper Bosnia (Verhbosna). The cathedral of St. Peter was erected there, together with the chapter. About 1238 not only Upper Bosnia, but also Usora, Soli and a part of the lower regions became subordinated to it. The Croatian duke Koloman donated to the bishop of Bosnia also the town of Djakovo in Slavonia.

As the Bosnian State began to expand toward Croatia, further ecclesiastic districts were attached to the original diocese, so that by 1344 there were three Catholic bishoprics in Bosnia; the Bosnian proper, Dumno and Makarska dioceses.

After 1395, amid struggles of overlords for the throne and Turkish inroads, the heretic Bosnian (Patarene) Church gained momentum and became almost an overwhelming power in the whole country. The Catholic churches became neglected and destroyed; the bishops of Bosnia who transferred the seat of their organization to Djakovo in Slavonia, lost nearly all power south of Sava river. The administrative activities of the Church became nearly extinct. The only teachers and defenders of Catholicism throughout the 15th century were the Franciscan friars.

The Franciscan order in Bosnia was established around 1235 and its members were called to assist the local bishop in combatting the heresy. In 1327 they were vested with the power of inquisition and soon branched out over the whole country. They put up numerous monasteries, which further increased their strength.

The Eastern (Greek-Orthodox) Church. Monasteries of the Greek-Orthodox rites were mentioned already in the 11th century indicating that adherents of the Eastern Church lived in Bosnia. However, there was no orthodox bishop in the land until 1376 when Lim and Drina valleys became attached to Bosnia. In the 15th century the Dabro-Bosnian bishop moved to Mileshevo monastery, and after the Turkish conquest he established his residence in Sarayevo.

In Herzegovina the orthodox bishopric was established by St. Sabbas (Sveti Sava) in the town of Ston (Stagno). Later the seat of the bishopric was moved in the interior of the country, while in 1777 it was transferred to Mostar.

The Bosnian (Patarene) Church appeared in Bosnia in the second half of the 12th century and at first it was violently persecuted and nearly exterminated. But later it gained momentum and in the 15th century it became a powerful organization, to which the notables and overlords of the country belonged. The new Church became so popular that people gave it the name of "Bosnian Church."

The followers of this sect did not identify themselves by any special name, but referred to themselves as "Christians," "good Christians," or "good people" (christiani, boni christiani, boni homines), considering their faith to be the true faith of Christ. They spread by the middle of the 12th century throughout southern Europe, southern France, north of Italy, Greece, Bosnia and Bulgaria. By church members of other denominations, they were called different names, according to each country. So in Bulgaria they were known as Bogomils, in Bosnia as Patarenes, in Italy as Patrini or Patariste, in France as Albingensi, and further as Baboni, Manicheans, Paulicians, Massalians, etc.

In all these countries these deviates from Christian teachings of the Nicean creed had a more or less similar ideology marked by aversions to the elaborate rites, administrative apparatus and artistic creations of the established churches, whether eastern or western, and stressed very simple rules of life both in dress, food, shelter and social contacts.

Their cosmogony was simple, too. They believed in one God and Trinity, but claimed that God had created merely the spirit and invisible world, while the Satan or devil created the matter and visible world. Even man is the creation of these two creative forces; his soul being created by God and his body coming from the devil.

Their whole system of ethics and philosophy of life is based, in all its details on this two-fold division of existence, one part of it coming from God, the other from devil. Accordingly, since the body is the prison of the soul, the latter will be freed upon the death of the man. If he led a clean and virtuous life, his soul will go straight to heaven, and if not, the soul will have to join another body in an attempt to gain its salvation. There is no need to pray for the dead, because the souls, if they went through penitence, come to heaven, and if not, they will have to pass from body to body, until they become clean. There is no resurrection of the body, because the substance of the body is created by Satan.

Since Jesus—also merely an angel—left only his teachings to mankind, so all the sacraments of the Church have to be rejected and condemned in line with the belief that these material symbols can not come from God. They rejected the baptism, especially that of infants who cannot believe, and thus be saved before they come to reason. Confirmation, confession, extreme unction and sacrament of marriage are rejected, together with the belief in trans-substantiation of bread and wine in the body and blood of the Lord.

Reception into a "Christian" (Patarene) community was accomplished by a solemn rite. The novice was assigned a period of time for confession, fast and continuous prayer. Then they placed on his head the Gospel of St. John, invoked the Holy Ghost and chanted the Lord's prayer. After this ceremony, they assigned to him a time for more thorough education, stricter living and cleaner prayer. Then they demanded proof of performance of these tasks. If the proof was satisfactory, the novice was passed through

final rites. He is made to face the sunrise, again the gospel book is placed on his head, both men and women place their hands on him and sing a hymn of praise for his observance of the rules. During the ceremony the novice was dressed in a long black robe as a monk, and after the due prayers, he was breathed at and anointed from head to toes.

The members of the Bosnian Church were divided into two classes; that of the perfect or perfectible members (perfecti, Electi) and the ordinary faithful (credentes). The perfect members have been ordained by two rites, while the ordinary members have been received in a simpler way. In addition, the perfect members were eligible to become the heads of various church communities. The Bosnian "Good Christians" discarded and condemned the church orders, and denied that Jesus had set up bishops, archbishops and prelates; however, they had to have some church organization. Yet such a church community was independent from any other; they did not have a common head, but the various church communities communicated with each other whenever it was necessary. At the head of each church was a grandfather (senior, ancianus). To him a class of teachers was subordinated while the most important of them, were the guests and the elders. The guest was considered usually a replacement and successor to the grandfather. Clergy proper was not available since every perfect member could teach and propagate his faith.

Likewise, the divine services of this church were simple. They rejected the church buildings, asserting that God cannot be worshipped by a human hand. There is no need for buildings to worship God, who can be praised everywhere. Further, they have rejected the Cross, calling it a "gallows"; they couldn't figure out how a Christian can worship the tree of the Cross, on which the Son of God had been crucified. If somebody killed the son of a king with a club, would that club please the king? So should the murderer of the Saviour be worshipped? They further rejected all the statues and scoffed at the Christians for worshipping those; they likewise condemned the decorations in the churches, bright raiment, and church vessels. They rejected holy water. Therefore their temples were ordinary houses without campaniles and bells, which they considered as the devil's trumpets; furthermore, they had no pictures or statues or artificial pulpits. Their only furnishings were the benches, a table covered with white linen, being used in place of the altar on which the Gospel book was opened; this was all the decoration of the temple. One should mention that such temples were put up only in larger communities.

Service in their temples was very simple, and consisted of the Lord's Prayer, which was their only prayer, of the reading of the portion of the Gospel, of a sermon and benediction.

The morals of these church-goers were also peculiar, for many features of their living were antagonistic not only to the church regulations but also to the laws of the State. In the first place they did not recognize the so-called "venial sins" but they considered all the sins as "grave." Before all, they demanded from the true Christians to hate the world as the creation of the Devil, and to give up riches, since they were "corrosion of the soul." A true Christian will become satisfied with the basic necessities of life; all the rest he should contribute to the community chest for the upkeep of the church, for the sick people and for those members who are preaching the new faith. Therefore the members of the other religious denominations considered these church members too stingy and excessively parsimonious, and they upbraided them for doing manual work on Easter itself. Further these sectarians considered every flesh diabolic, carnal intercourse they rated as unclean and the birth sinful. For this reason they condemned not only carnal intercourse in general, but marriage itself. The followers of this faith considered the marriage of the Catholics as adultery, stressing that true marriage is only between Jesus Christ and the Church. Whoever wanted to join their faith, had to give up his wife. However, even among them there were different views on marriage. One section of them admitted that the marriage is permissible and good, if the man and wife decide to have a clean life, and only the carnal intercourse of the husband and wife was condemned.

Having a contempt for anything that reflects flesh, they disapproved also of certain food items deriving from animals, for every meat is the work of evil and was originated by carnal intercourse. These sectarians condemned also the assassination of another human being because

assassination was shortening the time of penitence of the soul in the body. Accordingly, the soul was forced out from its prison without properly preparing itself for the better mode of existence. Every assassination of a person, whether in punishment, or in self defense, was considered a mortal sin. With this reason they stressed that the rulers are committing grave sin by punishing the criminals and members of another faith, that the Roman Church is creating evil when she persecutes them, while, on the contrary she herself should go through persecutions. They further hated war saying that it is not permissible to defend, by resort to war, either oneself or somebody else, and it was not proper to take revenge, especially in blood feud. Their followers were forbidden to communicate with members of another faith, "with people of the world," except under the condition that they will try to convert these men of the world to the true Christian religion. Finally, they considered every hiding of the truth as a grave sin; therefore, they prohibited not only the lie, but also the oath, whether it was just or unjust. Therefore, the perfect believers would rather brave death than take oath, and they held in worse contempt than a murderer the one who would force another person to take oath. Therefore, they hated also all the judges who demanded from them to take oath.

Whatever so far has been said about the duties in the life of the Bosnian Church members, applies for the most part to the perfect or select members of the sect (especially in regard to marriage, abstinence from meat and abstinence from warfare). Thus we can easily see the picture of a true and perfect Bosnian heretic. He gave up the world, his wealth and delights, to live in poverty, and became satisfied with the daily necessities. He set himself loose from all family obligations, and even his former connections with persons of another faith; he retired from public life, from the court of law and the theatre of war.

His vital needs were small, his food was restricted to vegetarian dishes, and from the animals he could eat only fish. For the seasoning of his food he could only use olive oil, since grease and butter were forbidden. The true Bosnian Church member used for his food usually bread and lentils, and drank water, even though he was permitted to drink wine. In is personal appearance he did not show any sign of haughtiness: he wore garments which were neither expensive nor excessively simple, but usually long black garments. Personal conduct of these church members was modest and unpretentious.

They did not engage in commerce, only in order to avoid lie, fraud and oath, but made their living usually as artisans, and among their teachers there were such who engaged in tailoring. They did not accumulate wealth, but were contented with the necessities. They were also pure and innocent, moderate in food and drinks, they did not visit inns, nor dances, nor any other kind of entertainment. They were abstaining from anger, they were always working, teaching and being taught, but offered only a few prayers. They abstained from slander, light-mindedness, lie and oath. To the questions asked from them they would reply directly only on few occasions for they were permitted only to say: "Yes, yes" and "No, no."

Even though it appears by this description at first glance that the true Bosnian Church members were kindly persons, not dangerous, yet in many respects they were the opponents of the existing social order. Their enemies were accusing them that they refused to submit to authority, that they are destroying the authority by teaching that no one should submit to the chiefs, only to God, to denounce the rich man, to scoff at the superiors, to chide the nobleman and to class as odious to God all those who served the king; that they incited the slaves not to work for their owners, etc. If we further consider that these heretics have rejected marriage and thereby the family, communication with members of other faith and religion and that they were condemning war and forbade the oath, by this very fact alone they have declared war not only on the Christian Church but also on the society and the state.

With so stringent moral principles teaching the new faith, this heresy would hardly have gained a considerable foothold, especially in Bosnia of landed nobility, if the teachers of this religion had not been especially careful. One should keep in mind that the above described sacrificial life was obligatory for the perfect or selected members who were relatively few; a much greater number of these sectarians, that

is the common faithful, were living a much more acceptable life. Only in this way the heretic teachers could win over to their faith a large number of Bosnian noblemen, magnates, princes and dukes. The usual run of the heretics, that is the simple believers, could have a wife and family; on the other hand they did not contract a true marriage, but were taking wives under the condition that "they should be faithful to them and that they could send them away as they wish." Furthermore, the common believers could also own and accumulate wealth, were permitted to carry on war and enjoy all kinds of food. But for this reason each believer, because of his great sins, had to make once a month a public confession, and besides this he had to promise, that if not sooner, at least by the end of his life he would join the order of perfect Christians. Due to these alleviations the Bosnian faith found adherents and followers even among the most respectable and wealthiest families.

Propaganda Methods

The perfect or selected Christians were untiring in their efforts to win over as many followers to their faith as possible. The way of their getting in the midst of the princely families is described by some writers in this way: "The heretics are cunning in their effort to penetrate into the household of the noblemen and magnates, trying to win their friendship. They would offer to the people of higher classes and especially to the ladies, some kind of goods which they favor such as rings and veils. When they saw this and asked for other things, they replied, they have still more precious goods which they would pass in their possession if they will promise not to deliver them to a Latin priest. Upon getting that assurance the heretic would say, "I have a pearl so bright that through it a person can see God; and another one so shining that it will arouse love for God in the one which possesses it." Then he would resort to imagery and with quotations from the Holy Scriptures he began to denounce the Catholic Priests and Friars. As soon as he noticed that the listener favored his talk he would compare his own faith with the Roman or Greek faith in this way: "The and want to be called by their fellowmen rabbis; teachers of the Roman Church are haughty in their behaviour, they like the front row seats we, on the other hand, do not require that. They are too rich and stingy, for of them it is said: 'Woe to you rich men, for in your wealth is your consolation'; we, on the contrary are satisfied to have food and clothing, with which to cover ourselves. They, further, are carrying on wars and condemn poor people to death and to the stake: it is said about them: 'Whoever draws the sword, will die from the sword'; we, on the other hand suffer their persecution because of justice. They eat without doing any work; we, on the contrary, work with our hands."

"There are hardly any among their teachers who know three continuous chapters of the New Testament, while in our ranks there is hardly any man or woman who would not know all of the Holy Scriptures by heart in the native language. Besides, they merely talk and do nothing about it. Thus they place a heavy load on a man's shoulders, but they would not move it even with their finger; we, on the contrary, do what we teach. They further impose on the penitents the most difficult exactions without giving them any assistance or consolation; we, on the contrary, by following the example of Jesus Christ, tell the sinner, 'Now depart and do not sin anymore' and by placing our hands on him we forgive all his sins and we send his soul after his death in heaven, while they send nearly all the souls descending into hell." After the heretic had explained this and similar things to his listener, he would say: " 'Now think it over, which condition and which religion is more perfect. Is it our own or the teachings of the Roman Church? Pick out the more perfect one.' In this wise so many people, influenced by their propaganda, are detached from the Roman Church, and become the followers and protectors of the heretics. They keep them hiding in their own homes for several months and during that time they are being coached in their faith."

It has been already stated that the perfect Bosnian church members displayed in the external life a certain attractive seriousness, and even sanctity, and this could not remain without effect on the mass of the common people. That is why the contemporary members of other faiths disclose that the Bosnian Church members with their serious and sober conduct powerfully attracted the Christians who came to them and were asking them about the salvation of the soul and about many other things. And when these sectarians were persecuted, people thought that they were suffering for just cause and that for being thrown into prisons in this world, they will receive fit rewards in heaven.

But besides the impressive appearance of the members of the sect, there was another force in the Bosnian Church. By the very fact that they had discarded all hierarchy in the proper sense of the word, they were favored and supported by the ancient Slavic patriarchal democracy, an age old organization of the Slavic family and community. In addition, they were, to a certain extent the torch bearers of the social reform in the Middle Ages, and for this reason their teachings found a powerful echo in the popular masses, and were able even to attract the nobility, especially in Bosnia, where the majority of the dukes and princes followed their principles and faith.

The Bosnian Church made a powerful impression upon the southern Slavs for it was in agreement with their nature, institutions, and mode of life. But what is the most important is that this sect was at the same time an important cultural phenomenon. It is well known that these sectarians had, in general, been praying less, but spent more time on reading the Gospels and the Apostolic writings; but what is still more significant, they laid stress, as it was done later by the Protestants, on the principle of public reading and interpretation of the Holy Scriptures. The natural consequence of this was that the Bosnian heretics in spite of their great errors in the field of religion and prejudices in the same field, were in the cultural respect somewhat more progressive than the other Christians of Bosnia and neighboring lands. This very phenomenon started a literature which in comparison with the books read by the followers of both the Western and Eastern Church, was written in a more popular style, and thus became a powerful medium of popular education and intellectual uplift of the masses.

The books and writings of the Bosnian Church members were of two kinds: holy books and legends. From among the holy scriptures the most widespread was the Gospel and that in the popular language, so that everybody could read it and interpret it, thus creating, quite naturally, a huge field of popular exegesis. In this stream of popular philosophy also Apocryphic books have been used by the Bosnian sectarians, among which the better known are: "The Tree of Cross," allegedly written by the Bulgarian preacher Bogomil, then "The Vision of Isaia" (Visio Isaiae) and "The Book of St. John, the Apostle." Alongside these holy books, whether orthodox or apocryphal, with diverse legendary stories concentrating on the issues and scenes from the Holy Bible, their literature had also a wealth of popular stories, about some mean shaking witches (Tresavitsa), and likewise about some vicious characters of supernatural powers (nezhitie) but all these popular fables are mixed with stories from the Bible. Especially the stories and legends issuing from among the members of the Bosnian Church, set up for the enlightening of the common people, made such a deep impression on the popular mind, that many of them became their source of enjoyment, their popular treasure. Thus it happened that even nowadays among the Croatian people there are many legends and poems which are of Bosnian origin. Many poems of diverse collection such as for example: The Flaming Mary in the Hell, The Sinful Widow in the Hell, The Sisters of St. Peter, are either directly or indirectly of the Bosnian origin. Probably also the numerous legends about Solomon, come from the same source.

The seat of the grandfather of the Bosnian Church was in the town of Yanyichi. By their names the following chiefs are known: Grandfather Miroslav (1303), Radomyer (1404), Miloye (1446). Guests were Radin (1453-1466) and Radosav Bradievich (1454); and elders; Dmitar (1403), Mishlyen and Lyelko (1404). In the year 1446 the membership of the Bosnian Church was so powerful that King Stephen Thomas himself had to recognize them and turn over the estates of Dragishich family to their protection.

The Church of Bosnia

The enigma of the Bosnian Church has intensely preoccupied the minds of historians, theologians and archeologists for the the last hundred years. Consequently, the literature on the subject has grown in volume, and many brilliant pages have been contributed to our store of knowledge. Yet, in spite of all the effort, the enlightening truth is coming out of the mass of artifacts, documents and collateral evidence, only in small parcels, and most of it still has to come.

In accordance with the type of research employed in the solving of the "Bogomil" riddle, conclusions also went far apart. On the whole, we can place here, side by side, the diplomatic and archeological evidence, the former admitting a wide range of conclusions, yet on shaky grounds, and the latter providing firm and positive evidence, but on a narrow stretch of ground. Rather than to engage in an elaborate discussion of medieval sects and heresies first, in order to make later such admissions as will nullify the premises, we shall set out here with the restricted scope of evidence furnished, as in our previous discussions, by tombstones and funerary furnishings. Despite the refutation of the Bogomil theory in its application to the Bosnian Church, the term Bogomil is still used, and will continue so, due to the pleasant connotation of its meaning. The name stands for liberal translation of the Greek *Theophilos*, which gives in Latin *Deo carus*, in German and English *dear to God*. After centuries rolled by, memory of persecutions and struggle was effaced in the popular mind, while the term preserved its popularity through its exalted meaning.

" 'Bogomil' Tombstones"

In examining archeological data we shall present on one hand the findings of the closing years of the 19th century as analyzed in the familiar work of Robert Munro, and archeological results forty years later as distilled in the work of Prof. Josip Horvat entitled "A Millennium of Croatian Culture" (Zagreb, 1939). Prof. Munro visited in person the "Bogomil" necropoles and studied the disposition of the tombstones in various localities. At present these sarcophagus-like monoliths are called *mramorovi*, "marbles," *stechak*, "sarcophagus," *masheta*, "hero memorial." But the inscriptions themselves call them *bilig*, "marker."

Shape and Location of Megaliths

After the study of these stones in situ (i.e., on the spot), Prof. Munro writes as follows: (Op. cit. p. 365.) "They are met with singly or in groups, comprising in some instances several hundred, not only in the vicinity of the present villages and highways, but also in the more unfrequented places—lonely hill-tops, secluded valleys, and even in the impenetrable depths of primeval forests. Some, rolled off their pedestals or broken by rude hands, are partly or entirely sunk in the earth; others are closely set in rows in confined areas, or irregularly scattered over the bleak moor. Unlike the dolmens and rude stone monuments of Western Europe, they are hewn into rectangular blocks, varying in size from about 6 feet in length by 3 or 4 feet in breadth and height, to huge masses so heavy as to make it a puzzle how they have ever been transported from the quarry in which they were hewn. Some of the larger examples are like tall cubes, with the peculiarity of being narrower at the base than at the top, a feature which gives them a very original and striking appearance. Others have the aspect of roof-shaped sarcophagi, a form probably borrowed from the Romans; but if so, the resemblance has not been carried beyond the external configuration, as none of the Bogomil stones are hollow, and the interment is always in the earth beneath. In a few instances the top takes the shape of a double roof, indicating thereby a twin-burial. Generally these *megaliths* are supported on large flag stones which actually cover the graves, and in which there is usually a shallow bed chiselled out to receive the upper stone. Not infrequently the monument resembles two stones so placed but hewn in one solid block."

Territorial Expansion of the Burial Custom

From this graphic description we gain a fairly good impression of the appearance and location of these monuments. Another important moment is the territorial expansion of these tombstones and their numbers. Again we turn for information to Dr. Munro (Op. cit. pp. 372/373):

"The area of their geographical distribution," says Dr. Munro, "extends but slightly beyond the present limits of Bosnia and Herzegovina. Examples have been found as far south as the borders of Albania, and as far east as the right bank of the Drina. They are not, however, equally distributed within this area, being less numerous in the northern parts of Bosnia, and most numerous in the district of Vlasenica, where not less than 6,325 have been counted. In Herze-

govina their number amounts to 22,000, and their total number in both provinces is estimated at 60,000. On the other hand, they are most sparsely met with in the northwestern part of Bosnia bordering on Croatian lands, as in the fourteen departments belonging to Banyaluka and Bihach only 706 are known."

In his monumental work "Millennium of Croatian Culture," p. 208, Prof. Josip Horvat confirms these figures, adding a point of explanation. His statement reads as follows:

"Even in these days one can see on hill-tops and mountain slopes, far from inhabited localities, or any trace of them, lonely tombstones, or disposed in groups of a hundred, forming some strange, mysterious necropoles, as enigmatic witnesses of the Middle Ages still obscure and unexplained. In Herzegovina alone roughly 22,000 of them have been counted, while in the district of Chaynich 6,325 of them have been discovered. They are located everywhere in the highlands of central Bosnia, but their number diminishes toward the north. *The north was the first to take the blows of the anti-heretical campaigns.*"

This seems to us a very important conclusion.

Still more important is the finding of Dr. Lyubo Karaman, the learned archeologist and art-critic who succeeded Dr. Fran Bulich as curator of the all-important Split museum. In his book "Dalmacija kroz vjekove" (Dalmatia Through Ages), Split, 1934, under the caption: "Bogomil" tombs, the author (pp. 73 ff) makes the following statement:

"The interior of Dalmatia conserves a series of interesting monuments, which owe their origins and characteristics to the conditions of life such as developed in the interior of medieval Dalmatia. These are the tombstones in the form of a large rhomboid stone-plate which was roughly hewn and placed over the grave, or was installed over the resting place of the deceased in the form of a massive, i.e., non-hollowed sarcophagus. In Dalmatia, and still more in Bosnia, Montenegro and some parts of Serbia, there are a number of cemeteries counting several hundred of such monuments, which we usually call 'stechaks' or 'mashetas'" (i.e., tombstones, as previously explained).

This is a most important statement especially in view of the archeological authority making it. Its testimony impresses us with two things at once: (1) this was the territory where Croatian influence, free from either Latin or Hungarian interference, was the greatest, therefore the area where the Croatian Church, so stoutly defended by Bishop Gregory of Nona, and the "grandfather" (djed) Vuk of Kerk (Veglia), reigned supreme, (2) with the exception of Split and Trogir, which were the battle-ground of the Croatian and Latin Churches, no "bogomil" tombstones were found in any of the early Latin cities, which were all antagonistic to the Croatian Church.

Absence of "Stechaks" in Bulgaria and Byzantium

With these clues in mind let us follow up the solid and substantial argumentation of our archeologist. "In the scientific literature," proceeds Dr. Karaman, "these monuments are frequently connected with the religious sect of Bogomils, and by that token are called 'Bogomil tombs.' To be sure, these tombs appear at a time and in places where Bogomils existed. But no proof has been adduced so far, that the appearance of 'stechaks' had been in any casual connection with the spreading of the Bogomil heresy in our parts. Nor should all the 'stechaks,' wherever and whenever they make appearance, be considered as tombs of the followers of the Bogomil faith. *In Bulgaria, the country of birth of the Bogomil sect, there are no such things as 'stechaks.'* On the other hand, in Dalmatia the stechaks are a common phenomenon in the cemeteries of medieval churches not only on Pelyeshats (Sabioncello) peninsula, or in the interior of Dalmatia, along the Bosnian border, but also in the immediate vicinity of such diocese centers as Split (Spalato) and Trogir (Trau), where public Bogomil cemeteries certainly would not have been tolerated for any length of time."

Out of the above disquisition of archeological relics, the existence of which cannot be either denied or disputed away, nor the geographical location of which, for the sake of argument, can be shifted, we gained one broad impression, that the location of these grave monuments coincides exactly with the range of influence of the Croatian Church, unhampered either by Latin or Hungarian antagonism. When it comes to such discovery in Montenegro, now admittedly

a Serbian country, we should not forget its Croatian past as a part of the early Red Croatia. Finally, the most potent argument of Dr. Karaman that no "stechaks" have been found in Bulgaria, birth-place of the Bogomil sect, should be given its full weight. Here we could add that neither in Constantinople, nor in Thrace, Chalcidice or Morea, all of which were places of violent persecutions of Bogomils and Messalians, under their different names, any "stechaks" are on record. Correlation of these facts compels a distinct separation of the "Church of Bosnia" from the Bogomil sect and Manichean doctrine in spite of the earlier opinions based on diplomatic evidence, to the contrary.

The Bogomil Legend

The above conclusion will set us in opposition to a well-organized camp of historians, who will not hesitate to declare anyone a heretic who does not subscribe to the Bogomil heresy of the pre-Turkish Bosnia. The most solid foundation for Bogomil or Patarene characterization of the Bosnian Church was provided by the fascinating work of the eminent Croatian historian Monsignor Dr. Francis Rachki, the first president of the Yugoslav Academy of Science. The work in question is "Bogomili i Patareni" (Bogomils and Patarenes), a work of stupendous scholarship in comparative religion, published in 1870 by the Yugoslav Academy of Science in Zagreb, and re-published in 1937 by the "Serbian Royal Academy of Science in Belgrade." As a specialist in history of religion, Dr. Rachki did marvelous work in presenting the history of the Bulgarian Bogomils, Greek Messalians, Italian Patarenes, French Albigensi and Valdenses, Belgian and German Cathari, Bohemian "Moravian Brothers," fore-runners of Hussite and German Reformation, etc. Furthermore, Dr. Rachki dives with sure orientation into the problems of the early Christianity including various branches of gnostics, Judaic-Christian sects, Manichaeans, Paulicians and others. The effect of Rachki's work was immense, and he attracted to his views such historians as Klaich, Jirechek, Jagich, Aleksandr Aleksandrovich Gilferding, etc. The archeologist Truhelka, and even the later writers such as the learned Austrian statesman Joseph M. Baernreither, and finally L. Von Südland (Dr. Ivo Pilar) in his monumental "Die Sudslawische

Frage und der Weltkrieg," 2nd ed. Zagreb, 1944 (The South-Slavic Problem and the World-War), were swayed by Rachki's conclusions. The impact of Rachki's work was so great, and its effect so deeply rooted, that even such modern scholars as Dr. Josip Horvat and Dr. Lyubo Karaman, are not inclined to reject *in toto* the old, but not fully discredited theory of Bogomilism of Bosnia.

Sculptured Scenes of Bosnian Life

With this incursion into the "diplomatic" history of the Bosnian Church, let us proceed with our study of archeological evidence, which, we believe, will outweigh the subjective, and therefore debatable "diplomatic" evidence, produced by human interests and passions of a turbulent age. Dr. Josip Horvat probably, after a thorough study of evidence, unfortunately not at the disposal of this writer, arrived at the conclusion that the Bosnian barons, i.e., Hervoye, Sandal Hranich, Stephen Vukchich, Stephen Kotromanich, his nephew king Tvartko, Paul Radinovich, Vlatko Voysalich, etc., were the followers of the Croatian Church, so eloquently defended by Gregory Nin at the Church Council of Split, and represented by dyed (grandfather) Vuk before the Roman Curia. Let us now see what archeological proof our learned writer has for his remarkable thesis. Let us weigh his own words: (Op. Cit. p. 208.)

"The most eloquent testimony of the spirit of the Bosnian nobility, about their daily life which is in extreme contrast to any asceticism, are those monuments of the early Bosnian art—known under the name of 'stechaks' and scattered all over the Bosnian lands—which we find in all those regions where the might of the Bosnian grandees asserted itself, and which, quite erroneously, are considered monuments of Bogomilism. The motives, carved in these 'stechaks,' provide the most decisive rebuttal of any such allegation."

Similar is the conclusion of Dr. Munro, who says: (Op. cit. p. 372.)

"It has been observed that the sepulchral representations on these monuments have no tendency of sadness, but, on the contrary, are selected from the gayest scenes of life, such as hunting tournaments, dancing, etc."

Both Dr. Horvat and Dr. Munro devote much space to describing both ornamentation and inscriptions appearing on "stechaks." Let us follow up the impressions of Dr. Munro, keeping in mind as psychological evidence, two things: (1) Realization of the fact that the love for flowers, delight in geometrical delineation of the material world, sportsmanship in hunting edible animals, social entertainment by group dancing, unavoidably attended by rhythm and tunes of musical instruments, manufacturing of which presupposes professional skill of craftsmen, etc., etc., that all this does not fit in to a morose and morbid psychology assuming mass proportions, according to which all the beauties of nature, the palatable morsels of a stag's steak, dashing thrills of a mount, the refining contacts of a social group gracefully sliding and whirling under the strain of music, the minstrel song that in its infinite variations reverberates the natural desire for carnal intercourse, *are the works of Satan*, i.e., the devil's devil, *who can be defeated by vegetarian diet*, endless repetition of some conventional words, and insistence on a cosmogony that was twisted and distorted from place to place through ignorance or misunderstanding of foreign languages. This particular moment we shall invoke frequently in refutation of the learned and authoritative work of Dr. F. Rachki, who, in our opinion, with his formidable panoply of diplomatic evidence, missed his Bosnian target through disregard of the archeological and linguistic evidence. It is quite beside the point that Bosnian archeology did not exist at his time.

2) While stag-hunting with falcons and baying hounds, was distinctly a pastime of barons; while knights' jousts and heroic exploits were the privilege of feudal lords, the kolo-dance (a spiralling group-dance), which always is supported by the popular bag pipe (guyda) or appropriate instrument, was a popular dance, and still it is. It is also attended by singing in the vein of light melody, and by versified challenge of the participants, with the inevitable repartee.

In addition to the Kolo-scenes of "stechaks," we shall invoke the universally known truth that the common people follow the manners and imitate the ways of their privileged class whether in dress, architecture, linguistic expressions, social ways or economic pursuits, etc. This moment is of importance in questioning the validity or merit of those theories which claim that the Bosnian nobility was of a faith entirely different from that of the common people.

The "Stechak" Reliefs

After this analysis of facts of life let us examine the testimony of two distinguished scholars: Dr. Munro and Dr. Horvat. With reference to the carvings on "stechaks" Dr. Munro has to report the following (op. cit. p. 366 ff): "This ornamentation may be architectural only, or it may be combined with floral decorations and figure designs. The architectural elements most commonly met with are the arch and columns, rope-pattern borders, spirals, zigzag and wavy lines. Floral decorations appear as borders of running trefoils, tendrils, sexfoil-stars, the lily and other foliage. The cross, plain or ornamental stars and half-moons, are occasionally represented. The frequency of the half-moon or crescent on these stones has given rise, in the minds of some people, to the idea that they owe their origin to the Mohammedans. But it must be remembered —a fact which may not be generally known—that the crescent is a pre-Turkish symbol, prevalent among the southern Slavs long before taking of Constantinople, when it was adopted by the Moslem-Turks. Shields and swords, especially the double-headed weapon so characteristic of the fourteenth century throughout a large part of Europe, may occasionally be seen sculptured in relief on all the varieties of these monuments."

"But of special interest is the figure—ornamentation, consisting of men and animals, generally depicted in low-relief, and representing a variety of social events, such as incidents from the chase and the battlefield, the dance and other idyllic scenes. In these the huntsman is seen often on horseback, armed with sword, lance, or bow, pursuing the deer, bear or wild boar. The 'Kolo' dance is usually represented by rows of men and women, or the members of the same family, with hands joined and dressed in fitting costumes, the men in tight trousers and short kilts, and the women in long flowing garments. The figures in these national dances are sometimes reduced to the simplest conventionality. Human beings, male and female, are also depicted singly, possibly an attempt at portraiture. Mythical subjects are represented by the winged horse, flying dragon, and other fanciful animals; also by geometrical designs of a bizarre character."

"The artistic skill displayed in these decorations is not of a high order—with, however, some exceptions—and in this respect there is a marked difference between those of the north and the south, the latter being architecturally superior to the former."

The Grand Monument

Both Dr. Horvat and Dr. Munro devote a great deal of space to the description of the huge "stechak" of Dolnye Zagoshche, about sixty kilometers north of Sarayevo, in the burial ground of "Gjaursko Polye" (The Field of the Unbelievers). In the time of Dr. Munro's visit it was still in situ and split along a diagonal into two unequal parts. Now this monument is in the Bosnian Museum of Sarayevo, restored in one piece. Dr. Horvat focuses his attention on the transversal front-side of the sarcophagus which is divided into four galleries, the top-most of which is filled with carvings of four bastions, with a large vaulted gate in their midst. The gate is topped with three star-like multi-foil ornaments having probably some religious or mystic significance. In the gallery below, three human figures are carved surrounded by a board fence on each side, with the figure of a plant in each corner, resembling the tree of life. The human figure in the center appears seated on a throne, with his right hand raised in the manner of Croatian rulers. According to Dr. Horvat the central figure would be that of a banus assisted by two courtiers. The gallery below represents a wide band filled in with carvings of geometrical figures, interlaced with elements of foliage. In the bottom gallery figures of two prancing steeds are carved in, with their attendants.

Dr. Munro is more interested in the longitudinal surfaces of the sarcophagus. Here is what he sees:

"The other side is divided lengthwise into two panels by a pretty decoration of lilies. The upper contains five mailed knights on horseback, carrying spears in their hands. The lower represents a hunting scene, in which two huntsmen are seen in the act of attacking a deer and a wild boar followed by hounds; also three conventional trees, to one of which a hunting tiger is chained, and above this is a winged dragon. The end view in the illustration is ornamented. The back side of the sarcophagus is ornamented with twelve panels bordered with lilies and each is filled with a circle circumscribing sexfoils and rosettes."

Equally interesting is the opposite longitudinal side also divided into two panels by a narrow band of lilies, the upper side being about twice the size of the lower panel. The upper panel is divided into five columns, the first four containing a pair of super-imposed circles, three of them including sexfoils, while the first pair contains seven multifoil starlets, or rosettes, each. The full length of the fifth column is filled with carvings of a large plant, probably the tree of life. Beneath the narrow richly decorated band, the panel is again divided into five sections, each one filled in with the figure of a mounted warrior holding a spear in his raised right hand. The edges of the side are richly decorated with carvings combining geometrical figures, lilies and lichens.

If there is anything to reproduce the symbolism and reality of the Bosnian life in the Middle Ages, that is the set of carvings on this "stechak" from the cemetery of the "Infidel!". For they placed into prominence the surge of vitality, feats of chivalry and daring exploits of a warrior race, established in its castles, and supported by common people. The commoners lead also a happy existence, with outbursts of joy taking the shape of dance, song, music and enjoyment of choice viands. And inversely, this profusion of joyous vitality would change promptly into a furious resistance and fighting pitch whenever the Bosnian way of life was disturbed from outside by intrusion of foreign invaders. And this is precisely the picture of the pre-Ottoman Bosnia and Herzegovina, before a single Moslem settled down south of the Sava, west of Drina and north of Neretva rivers. We shall vainly seek this pattern of life in the pages of Dr. Rachki's "Bogomils and Patarenes." On the contrary, whatever exaltation we find in their weird practices stemming from a peculiar cosmogony and dualistic theological concepts, is entirely lacking in the stone-carvings of "stechaks."

Testimony of Tomb Inscriptions

One more point of testimony on the part of stechaks and we shall close the circle of our archeological evidence. Out of the mass of 60,000 tombstones discovered so far, 2,000 of them bear ornamentation, with over 200 pieces provided with short epitaphs. These epitaphs follow about the same pattern. The important feature of the message is that the deceased is interred in "his own *noble soil*," or, in "his own patrimony"; if he fell in battle abroad, the inscription records it with words "he rests in alien soil." Some Epitaphs begin with "In the name of the Father and Son and Holy Ghost, amen!" which brings the deceased within the fold of the western or eastern Church. The sanctity of the grave should not be violated, hence the admonition "And I beseech you not to step on me; for I used to be what you are now, and you will be later what I am now." Similar is the enjoinment on another epitaph: "Please, brothers, aunts and sisters-in-law, come and bewail me, but do not step on me with your feet. For you will be what I am now, but I can no longer be what you are!"

Entirely in harmony with the carvings of figures, the tenor of epitaphs repeats over and over the love of the *native soil* and veneration of one's patrimony: *the noble soil;* the pride of serving the banus and king, and grateful recollection of those who fell on alien soil. Belief in Holy Trinity alone repudiates the assignment to "good Christians" or the "Bosnian Christians," of the monotheistic sectarianism. In the Manichaean dualism decomposition of body as prison of the soul, is welcomed, and no provision is made for its undisturbed resting. Thus the spirit of the epitaphs, in consonance with the scenes of life carved out on the sides of "stechaks" are in a headlong clash with the life and religious practices of either Bogomils or Patarenes as we find them described in Dr. Rachki's treatise.

Bogomil Legend and Croatian Church

Therefore, we fully subscribe to Dr. Horvat's conclusion:

"Popular masses as well as the nobility are adherents of the Bosnian Church, successor and branch of the Croatian Church, from the days of the Croatian national dynasty. They grew up with it and defend it as their own achievement, precisely as the glagolitic congregations did during Kreshimir's reign, with even greater determination, since they came to realize that its enemies do not pursue religious aims, but political and military ambitions. With renewed passion and in a new form the old conflict between the Slavic conservatism and western influences is renewed on the cultural and social ground.... The conflict will be more and more exacerbated, will draw in its vortex even larger masses of people, and reach its historical climax with the fall of the Bosnian independence and victory of Islam."...

With this, however, the controversy over "Bogomils" in Bosnia is not settled. Dr. Horvat himself admits infiltration of these sectarians from the Balkans, who in the general turmoil of the struggle make inroads on the pastorate of the Bosnian Church. Through fanatical "agitation of the extremist irreconcilable Bogomils, which gains an even wider acceptance among the prestige and authority of the sect is on the increase."...

The latest echo in this debate comes in the form of an annotation to a similar disquisition by L. Südland-I. Pilar in his book on the "South Slavonic Problem and World-War" (pp. 189/192), which reverberates a resounding refutation of any "bogomilism" in Bosnia and Herzegovina. Pilar's book appeared in 1917 and second edition of it was published in 1944 under the auspices of Dr. Mile Starchevich. The annotation seems written by Mr. Joseph Horvat, a noted historian. Because of its uncommon interest and trenchant argument, we reproduce of it here as much as possible.

Annotation No. 2

"After the union," says the annotation, "between the Croatian and Hungarian kingdoms was established, Bosnia gradually seceded, forming her own State. The formation of an independent political and cultural entity was enhanced by the configuration of the Bosnian terrain, with its clear-cut or towering borders: in the east the Drina, in the west the Dinaric mountain ranges, and in the north the Sava valley. This preponderantly mountainous country, protected by impassable frontiers, is in fact, a stronghold of political and cultural conservatism. Here the old social organization, the old political system and the old religious organization will maintain themselves unchanged. Without any doubt all those who were dissatisfied with the policies of the Croatian-Hungarian union took refuge in Bosnia. In the first two centuries of the Croatian-Hungarian political unity, Bosnia maintained its adverse position toward this commonwealth, even though she was attached to it for a long time by the ties of vassaldom, which, as a matter of fact, was a more 'de jure' than a 'de facto' affair. On the other hand, Croatian-Hungarian kings were steadily contriving at the conquest of Bosnia, since this country provided the only guarantee for a secure connection with the sea. Because of its wealth of minerals, Bosnia was always a magnetic attraction for every conqueror. The plans of conquest of the Croatian-Hungarian sovereigns were based on the slogan of being under obligation to conduct crusades against the 'heretical Bosnia,' which was accused of bogomilism.

"Through the latest research of the Croatian historians it has been established that this accusation of heresy was intentionally or even maliciously invented. There was no 'bogomilism' in Bosnia! The ecclesiastic life was organized in the form of the 'Bosnian Church.' Due to the difficulties of the terrain continued missionary work of the Roman Church was prevented, and thereby primitive Christianity was preserved, which blended fully with the oppositional aspirations of the country. The chief characteristic of this primitive Christianity was divine service in Croatian and absence of a church organization firmly cemented. The same situation applied also to the coastal areas of Croatia, and even now this is the case in some parishes.

"The attempt to build a church-organization with the aid of a higher clergy of alien extraction never succeeded, since foreign priests did not wish to establish themselves permanently in a country with tough climate, poor communications and a simple way of life. The last foreign bishop left Bosnia at the beginning of the 13th century and settled down in the town of Djakovo (Slavonia) where he established the seat of the 'Bosnian Diocese.' Thus, the ecclesiastic center was outside of the country while Christianity lived on in Bosnia, but within the frame-work of a free organization, the so-called 'Bosnian Church.' Within its jurisdiction the higher clergy was freely elected, a fact in full agreement with the prevailing electoral system, which was equally applied to all the other branches of political and social life.

"The view of the Roman Church in the Bosnian question politically was quite clear, but dogmatically sorely inconsistent. 'The Bosnian Church' was a state Church, and as such it resisted every attempt to subordinate it to a metropolis outside of the country. From time to time the 'Bosnian Church' was subordinated directly to the Holy See. However, resistance came whenever attempt was made to subordinate it indirectly, and that at the expense of Bosnia's political independence. Even the Holy See itself seems to have been in the dark about the character of the 'Bosnian Church.' This was at the time of the great ecclesiastic dogmatic upheavals which climaxed in the Albigensian movement.

"At the same time in the eastern part of the Balkans, notably in Bulgaria, a heretical sect was thriving under the name of 'Bogomils.' They formed an ascetic group of dualistic Manichaeans, with a strong dose of primitive socialism, as a reaction to the attempts to introduce feudalism. The Bogomils have been persecuted with equal determination by the Serbian, Bulgarian and Byzantine rulers. From the Roman perspective these ascetic-anarchistic Bogomils, appeared, even without stretching one's imagination, identical with the 'Bosnian Church,' that is, the ecclesiastic organization of a national State of a peculiar feudal type.

"In the sharpest contrast to the 'Bogomil' faith stand out the so-called bogomil tombs. These tombstones are a proud example of the native Croatian sculpture which had nothing to do with asceticism. Apart from those of the Egyptian funeral art, these are the gayest sepulchral monuments. They all interpret or symbolize the joy of life, portray jousts of noblemen, relate of hunting parties, dances and parting of knights from their dames. These monuments are from a technical point of view truly marvellous achievements, and no anarchistically inclined people could have set them up. They could be the creations only of feudal lords, rich members of a socially and politically powerful organization.

"Also hand-written church-books of the Bosnian church have been preserved, missals adorned with attractive miniatures, whose text provides the most cogent refutation of the heretic nature of the Bosnian Church. 'The Bosnian Church'

was the expression of the political and social aspirations of the country. It could be taken sooner for a precursor of protestantism, but never for a heretic organization. It is quite certain that to a still lesser degree this organization could be the expression of an anarchistic frame of mind on the part of the Bosnians, or even the cause of dilapidation of the Bosnian State. Cooperation of Bosnia with the Ottomans should be explained by political and economic causes, but in no way by the religious affinity with Islam."

In recapitulation of the subject it seemed necessary to reproduce these illuminating lines: first because of their recent publication, and second, because they focus all the results of the latest research exclusively on the Bosnian conditions, and restrict the argument to the Bosnian terrain and realities alone. Even though this seems to be the most satisfactory disposal of "Bogomil" controversy, we do not ascribe it the certainty of truth, for it also has points of detail unexplained. The chief of them is the mystery of the sepulchral monuments (stechaks) which still defy the question why did they become the symbols of the Croatian and Bosnian Church organizations, and where do they come from, since nothing of that kind is known in the rest of Europe, and still less among the other Slavs. With the solution of this problem, perhaps some other questions will be answered as well.

Dr. Vego's Theory on "Bogomils"

Partly coinciding with the views expressed in the annotation is the theory of Dr. Mark Vego, author of the "History of the Hum Country (Herzegovina)." Part I, Samobor, 1937. Dr. Vego passes in review (pp. 123/157) all the known theories on the Bosnian "Bogomils," including that of Dr. Petranovich and Glushats who argue that the Bogomils of Bosnia were a branch of the Serbian Orthodox Church; further, those of Dr. Rachki, Dr. Peisker and Südland-Pilar who stress their Manichaean dualism, although he omits comment on Dr. Baernreither's views, similar to those of Südland-Pilar.

Dr. Vego analyzes the materials used by Dr. Rachki, and gives them a different interpretation altogether. He proceeds with a great apparatus of modern scholarship and versatility in the literature of the subject. Although he seems well-posted on the Bosnian archeology, he uses the testimony of the stechak epitaphs only to establish the belief of the Bosnians in the Holy Trinity as the chief argument in refutation of their alleged Manichaeism. After a learned discussion of the problem the author arrives at the following conclusion:

"From this we judge that every member of the so-called Bosnian Bogomils believed in the Blessed Virgin and the Saints. This is a clear proof, which is in a head-on clash with the teachings of the Bulgarian Bogomils, such as we learn from Kosma, the Presbyter. For these reasons we conclude that the alleged Bosnian-Herzegovinan Bogomilism—erroneously so-called—is not an alien importation, but a pure popular Catholic faith, which neither had a fully perfected system, nor all the institutions which had developed within the fold of the western peoples."

Bosnian Church a Precursor of Protestantism

Interesting in the annotation is the conclusion that the Bosnian Church should be considered a "precursor of Protestantism," which view is shared also by Sir Arthur Evans (Bosnia and Herzegovina. Introd. pp. 42, 43) and Dr. Munro (pp. 387/8/9). In accordance with the older views, they believe in "bogomilism" of Bosnia, but this does not affect their conclusions. Sir Evans says:

"During the troublous times of the Bosnian kingdom the Bogomils increased in strength, and, what is extremely significant, the heretics of Bosnia begin to play a part in the revival of the Protestant movement throughout Europe." (p. 40.) Further: "From the twelfth century to the ... sixteenth ... Bosnia presents the unique phenomenon of a Protestant State existing within the limits of the Holy Roman Empire, etc." (p. 42.) Finally: "But those who perceive in Protestantism itself nothing more than a stepping stone to still greater freedom of human mind, ... will be slow to deny that England herself and the most enlightened countries of the modern world may owe a debt, which is hard to estimate, to the Bogomils of Bosnia" (p. 43).

Dr. Munro (p. 387) makes the following observations:

"One thing, however, is evident, that the chief element of their creed was a strong objection to the growing ritualism of the Church, and a desire to go back to the simpler and purer forms of worship, such as were practised by the early founders of Christianity. If so, the despised Bogomils may be regarded as the precursors of the Reformation in Europe."

"A searching investigation of the social and religious principles held by this almost forgotten sect is therefore greatly to be desired, not only because of the part it played in the history of the country, but on account of its relationship to Protestantism." Finally ... "out of several hundreds of inscriptions of the period now brought to light, not one betrays the slightest taint of devil-worship, or of any doctrine that would not be tolerated in Calvinistic Scotland." ...

From here on the latest bibliography and discussions are presented.

Abstracts from World Literature on the Subject The School of Dr. F. Rachki on Bogomils in Bosnia

Since the publication in 1870 by the Yugoslav Academy of Science in Zagreb, of Rachki's impressive treatise on "Bogomils and Patarenes," it was taken for granted that the Bosnians were Manichaean heretics known under the name of Bogomils or Patarenes, according to their inclinations to the sect flourishing in Bulgaria, or that in the Alpic regions of Italy. The views of Rachki were adopted by the eminent historians V. Klaić and K. Jirecek, and with some modifications also the later historians and writers, including L. Thallóczy, J. M. Baernreither, L. V. Südland-Ivo Pilar, etc. In order to go along with the tradition, and to avoid the appearance of iconoclasm, this writers, too, has used the conventional names of "Bogomil" and "Patarene"; however, in the sense of corrections made in the preceding pages of this chapter. This is a process of using the old label for a new substance.

Based on the study of medieval sects by P. Schmidt: Histoire et doctrine de la secte de Cathares (Paris, 1849), and in refutation of B. Petranovich's: "Bogomils, Bosnian Church and Christians" (Zadar, 1867), the work of Dr. Rachki was a novelty impressive by its erudition and comprehensive treatment of the subject. However, he has not adduced a shred of archeological evidence in support of his statements and conclusions, and, what is still worse, no direct statements from the sectarians themselves. All his evidence is based on depositions and cross-examinations of witnesses and defendants in trials of capital cases, during a period of religious persecutions and upheavals. With reference to Bosnia proper, Rachki makes a thorough study of the Papal and royal decrees, correspondence, etc., that are published in the familiar collections of documents (A. Theiner, Rachki, Farlati, Fejér, Kukuljević, Mokloshich, Katona, etc.) on the history of Hungary and Southern Slavs.

Not unlike the reports emanating from heretic trials, these documents, too, are one-sided and reflect the bias of a heated debate or armed struggle. In fact, some of these decrees are tantamount to declaration of war against the insubordinate Bosnians, others are discussing "casus belli" or a situation known to the interested sovereigns only through one-sided reports, etc. From the mass of episodes reported in these documents we know with certainty only that much that the Bosnians have been often in conflict with Hungary, but that their opposition to the Roman Church was tempered with frequent compromise, and that Popes themselves tried, from time to time, to effect compromise between Bosnia and Hungary.

With remarkable erudition and assiduity Dr. Rachki tried to shell out grains of truth from the controversial materials, and precisely this method involved him in grave errors. In his time, prior to 1878, Bosnia and Herzegovina were still a part of the Turkish empire, and beset by grave internal troubles. There was not the slightest hint at the Bosnian archeology and the treasure-house of knowledge deriving therefrom. A victim of circumstances, Dr. Rachki amplified his materials with collateral evidence by diving deep into the teachings, liturgy and political fortunes of various heterodox sects throughout medieval Europe. Thus, operating by broad analogy, he thought that he was shedding light on the Bosnian conditions proper, just because Bosnians were called ugly names in order to justify subjugation or subordination of Bosnia to alien authority. Naturally, they were called: Manichaeans, Massalians, Patarenes, Cathari, Bogomils, Arians, etc., according to the time and occasion. It is astonishing, indeed, that Dr. Rachki overlooked the epithet "Arians", which was also hurled at them, and failed to draw a similar conclusion.

On the whole, Rachki's monograph is a magnificent work and an illuminating contribution to comparative religion. It is unfortunate that it could not be translated into German or English for the benefit of universal scholarship.

Regardless of clashes of views and contradictions apearing in the sources of great authority, we present here the theses brought to light both by foreign scholars and the native investigators of this problem.

The following text is based on the article of Frederick G. Powicke, A Brief Survey of Historical Literature on the Bosnia published in the volume 2 pages 784 and 785 in the Hastings Encyclopaedia of Religion and Ethics. We shall go briefly over the main items of information presented in this article. Powicke says: "The Bogomils were a sect of dualistic heretics whose doctrines clearly declare their kinship with the Paulicians and Euchites or Messalians. Mainly to the former may be ascribed their peculiar form of dualism and to the latter their specifically ascetic element. Both these earlier movements took root in Thrace during the 8th, 9th, and 10th centuries-exotics from their native soil in the Eastern Byzantine provinces (Armenia, Mesoptamia and Northern Syria). They flourished most amongst the people of Slavic race, particularly the Bulgarians. Here they passed through a process of inter-mingling and local modification which issued in a system relatively new and strange, whose adherence increased rapidly though secretly, and are known to have been called Bogomils in the beginning of the 12th century, if not from the middle of the 10th.

The origin of the name has been usually found in the frequent use by them of the two Slavic words (Bog) (Milui) meaning "Lord, have mercy", as if it were the Slavic translation of the Greek Kyrie Eleison. A more likely explanation derives it from Bogomil (Beloved of God) in which case it may be taken to denote the idea of a pious community analagous to the later "Friends of God" "Freundes Gottes". Two early Bulgarian manuscripts have been discovered which are confirmatory of each other in the common coin that a "priest" Bogomile was the first to promulgate the "Heresy" in the vulgar tongue under the Bulgarian Tsar Peter who ruled from 927 to 968. This would seem to afford a surer clue to the name and put back the active emergence of the movement to the middle of the 10th century.

Euthymius Zigabenus (died after 1118) is the main source of what is known about the Bogomils. His account is given in Titulus or Chapter 27, of the work Panoplia dogmatica which he devoted to the refutation of 24 different heresies. He was a favorite of the reigning Emperor Alexius Commenus; and the story told by Anna, the daughter of the latter shows us how he came by his information. Alexius having invited the physician Basilius, chief apostle of the sect, to Constantinople, induced him, under an affectation of sympathetic interest to make a free statement of his doctrines; meanwhile his stenographer, hidden behind the curtain in the room took down a verbatim report of the conversation and at the end of the interview the curtain was raised. In this way Basilius found himself ensnared and self-accused. His doctrine thus craftily obtained is set out by Euthymius under 52 heads of which the main are following:

(1) The Bogomils rejected all the Mosaic books of the Old Testament, but accepted as canonical the Psalms and the Prophets. In addition they accepted the four Gospels, the Acts of the Apostles, the Epistles, and the Apocalypse, assigning a peculiar sacredness and authority to the Gospel of John. So far as Moses was used, it was an allegory to support their own views. A favorite book was the portrayal "Visio or Ascensio Isiae".

The most interesting part of this doctrine is its cosmogony. It runs as follows:

"God's first born son was Satan (the Satan of the New Testament), the highest of the spiritual beings, his Father's universal viceregent. Tempted by his pride, however, he sought to set up an empire of his own, and drew after him a great company of the angels. Cast down from heaven on this account, but not yet deprived of creative power, he made a new heaven and a new earth. They held Satanel also made man, but could do no more than fashion his body. For life or spirit he had to fall back upon God, whose help he besought and obtained on condition that from the human race the places of the fallen angels in heaven should be refilled. So God breathed into man's body the breath of life."

But Satanel, ruled by envy of man's glorious destiny, repented of his promise. He seduced Eve; and Cain, their offspring, became the principle of evil in humanity. This principle prevailed over the good principle represented by Abel, the child of Adam and Eve. By its aid he imposed himself upon the Jews as the Supreme God. Moses unwittingly acted as his instrument and the Law—which begat sin—was his fatal gift. Thus all men, save a few, were led astray. Then the good God intervened. In the 5500th year after the creation of the world, a spirit called the Son of God,—the Logos, the Archangel Michael, the angel of the Great Council came forth from him, entered the world in an ethereal body by the channel of Mary, (through the right ear of the Virgin) and proceeded to overturn his evil brother's kingdom. Satanel plotted and brought to pass his death—unaware that, being bodily in appearance merely, he could not be affected by any physical pain. When, therefore, Jesus showed himself after the resurrection in his true heavenly form, Satanel had to acknowledge defeat. His divine powers departed from him. He lost the angelic syllable (EL) in his name and became Satan only. Christ then ascended into heaven and took the seat of power once held by Satan. His own place among men was hereupon taken by the Holy Spirit—produced by the Son as the Son of the Father.

The 12 apostles were in a spiritual sense the first creation of the Spirit; and the true successors of these, in whom alone he continued to dwell, are the Bogomils and their converts. As habitations of the spirit they spoke of themselves as relations of God.

People of true faith can not die, but maybe said "tamquam in somno transmutari" (They are changed as in sleep.)

The monk and physician Basilius seems to have been the first martyr of the sect. He did not recant the confession obtained from him in the manner already described, and was led away into prison. That was about 1111 at which time he had governed the community of the Bogomils for forty years. In 1119 he died at the stake.

At the end of the article there is a copious bibliography among which was the article of Louis Léger "L'hérésie des Bogomils en Bosnie et Bulgaire au Moyen Age."

The next source comes from the Encyclopedia Britannica, Volume 2 pages 779 and 780.

Let us take a few references from this book on our subject:

"Thus Slavonic sources are unanimous on the point that this teaching was Manichaean. Zealous missionaries clad like Mendicant Friars, carried these doctrines far and wide. In 1004, scarcely 15 years after the introduction of Christianity into Russia, we hear of a priest Adrian teaching the same doctrines as the Bogomils. In 1125 the church in the south of Russia had to combat another heresiarch named Dimitri. The church in Bulgaria also tried to extirpate the Bogomil sect but it survived for several centuries. The Popes in Rome who were leading the crusade against the Albigenses, did not forget their counterpart in the Balkans and recommended the annihilation of the heretics.

"The Bogomils first spread westward, and settled in Serbia; but by the end of the 12th century Stephan Nemanya, King of Serbia, persecuted them and expelled them from the country. Large numbers took refuge in Bosnia where they were known under the name of Patarenes. From Bosnia this influence extended into Italy (Piedmont). The Hungarians undertook many crusades against the heretics in Bosnia, but toward the close of the 15th century the conquest of this country by the Turks put an end to their persecution."

This is followed by a bibliography chiefly based on Euthymius Zygadenus in his work on 24 heresies (Migne, Patrologia, Graeca, Volume 130; Narratio de Bogomilis, edited by Gieseler).

The next source which we shall use in portion is the article of Arturo Cronia, published in the second volume of the Encyclopedia Italiana (Italian Encyclopedia), page 277.

"The doctrine of the Bogomils can be summarized as dualism according to which God had created only that which is spiritual, and therefore eternal and outside of the contingent and casual; in the meantime that which is material, temporal, casual—therefore; the world and the human body—is the work of the demon, who was in conflict with God. Thus the entire community became the spoils of the devil, until the coming of Christ, who could not put on a mortal body (Docetism); also the Old Testament is false, with its Laws and its prophets. It is apparent that these beliefs and practices have been inherited from the older dualistic-gnostic sects (Manichaeans, Paulicians, Messalians) but there is also some trace of the primitive religion of the Slavs, borrowed from a natural dualism.

"By the terms of such doctrine, the orthodox Christianity is not the true religion of Christ, being profaned by false ceremonies and still further distorted by the teachings contrary to the Gospels. The true Christians, 'The Good Christians' are only the Bogomils who avoid everything which is material and have a trend toward the pure ascetism. They rejected a great deal of Sacraments, since it is presumed to attract through them the Divine Presence which is in conflict with the sermons of Christ, or by resort to profane and perishable matter. They are naturally adverse to the matrimony and to the birth by which the imprisonment of the spirit in the body is perpetuated. With a special vehemence they have been combatting the cult of the cross, which is made of perishable material and recalls the crucifixion of Christ, who indeed, is a pure spirit. For similar motives they abhor the sacred pictures and ornaments; the churches are demolished and abandoned because God being present everywhere, cannot be worshipped in closed places. Therefore, the assemblies of the community are arranged preferably in the open; however, when it becomes necessary to hold these meetings in closed places, it is sufficient to gather in a simple room of a private house, where there are no pictures nor ornaments, nor parchments, nor belfries ("the trumpets of the devil").

"The most solemn ceremony is held when a convert joins the community after a long period of penitence and purification. The solemnity of the occasion consists in lighting of small candles placed on the walls of the room and in celebration of their acustomed rites. Besides, the rites and ceremonies are very simple; prayers, sermons, reading of the New Testament, benediction. The Eucharist is not rejected, and appears on the fraternal table, where the oldest member of the community performs the rite of the breaking or benediction of the bread, recalling the last supper of Jesus. The prayer for the most part is the Lord's Prayer, being quite frequently recited, seven times during the day and five times at night; for the deceased no prayer is offered because the purgatory simply does not exist.

"In accordance with their religious ideas, the Bogomils do not recognize the earthly authorities, they hate the powerful ones, they stay poor by working only as much as is necessary to help the sick ones and the elderly ones in the community. All that is related to matter, which imprisons the spirit, is rejected by them; therefore, they abstain from animal food. In homicide it is not possible to perform penitence; war, which is provoked by earthly desires and which forces to kill, is repudiated by them. They are affectionate to each other, and cooperative. Toward outsiders they were cool, distrustful and contemptuous to the point that they had been taken for dangerous conspirators; hence the persecution.

"There were Bogomils in Dalmatia so to say to the very gates of certain cities, and especially in Ragusa.

"It has been ascertained that the popular and anonymous literature of the southern and oriental Slavs contains obvious traces of their doctrine."

Another source of information on Bogomils and Bosnian problem is the article of Prof. F. Vernet, professor of ecclesiastic history of the University of Lyons. This article is published in Vol. 2 of the "Dictionnaire de Théologie Catholique," Paris 1923; p. 925.

"The Bogomils are one of the dualistic sects, which from gnosticism to albigensism, have succeeded themselves throughout the history of the Church. The questions have been posed whether among these sects, and especially between the Bogomils and Cathars of the West, there was a link of real connection. The opinions have varied on this point. It appears that the Bogomils have been at least a branch of Catharism, but that the origins of both the western and eastern Catharism as well as those of bogomilism, should be sought in Bulgaria."

Passing up the paragraphs of the text which have been amply discussed also in the treatment of other sources, here we summarize its effects on the imperial city of Constantinople. We have already reported on the known incident between emperor Alexis Komnenos and Basile, the chief preacher of the new doctrine, which ended with the martyr death of the latter. In spite of violent and brutal persecutions of the authorities, the Bogomil doctrine did not die out in the imperial city, but kept on its apostolic course. So in 1140

the Synods of Constantinople ordered to burn all the writings of Constantine Chyrsomale which were saturated with the ideas of the heretic sect, but were avidly read in the monasteries. Three years later two Cappadocian bishops have been deposed for their attachment to this heresy. Also Cosmo, the patriarch of Constantinople was deposed for his support of the Bogomil monk Niphon (1147).

During this period Bogomilism was in ascendancy in Bulgaria. By the end of the 12th century, it penetrated into Serbia, from where it was eliminated through severe reprisals. In the beginning of the 13th century it established itself in Bosnia, and from there passed over to Slavonia. After the capture of Constantinople by the crusaders, the capital of the Greek empire, and seat of the Patriarch of Constantinople was transferred to Nicea, the Bogomils appeared in Asia Minor and engaged in an ardent proselyting. The Patriarch Germanios fought them (1226) by word of mouth and through writings. In spite of persecutions the Bogomil communities maintained themselves throughout Hellas. Condemnations were issued against them by the synods of 1316 and 1325, which were held in Constantinople. Yet they did not prevent the new doctrine to reach the mount of Athos with its numerous monasteries where Massalians, Bogomils and Hesychasts compared and developed their teachings.

In Greece, Bulgaria and Bosnia the Bogomils survived until the conquests of these countries by the Turks. The Holy Seat identified them with the Catharians of the west, and designated them by the same name, or still more frequently by the name of Patarenes. The sectarians themselves took the name of "Christians", while the Slavic texts call them Bogomils. It is probable that the Bosnian and Bulgarian Bogomils embraced the faith of the victorious Moslems.

In a set of enlightening statements Prof. F. Vernet explains the Bogomil cosmogony in its relation to the creation of man from clay, issuance of the snake from the muddy substance of his right foot, creation of Eve, and her seduction by Satan, from which union two children are born; son Cain and daughter Calomena. However from Adam she had the son Abel.

Prof. Vernet's article is of remarkable precision, and is attended by a copious bibliography especially of medieval origin.

The new source is that of Dr. Alexander Solovyev entitled "The Religious Teachings of the Bosnian Church". Published in Zagreb in 1948 by the Yugoslav Academy of Science.

This writer engages in a deep analytical study of the writings on the Bosnian Church, preserved mostly in fragments, and derives his own conclusions on the basis of the texts reflecting certain doctrines of the Bosnian Church. Before attempting this task, Solovyev surveys the existing Croatian and Serbian literature on the subject and shows up certain merits and errors of each particular theory.

Thus in the first place he quotes the statement of an important Bosnian Historian (Gregory Chremoshnik) who stresses the difficulties of the subject, as well as the failure to provide a satisfactory solution to the great historical phenomenon, by some called Bogomils, by others Patarenes, etc.

Chremoshnik writes as follows: "For sure, no history of any nation is filled with so many riddles, unsolved and unsoluble problems as the history of medieval Bosnia. But by far the greatest mystery of the Bosnian history is the Bogomil issue. What has not been written and guessed in this matter! Even the serious historians have invested their best talents in order to solve this problem, while some reckless amateurs have given free reign to their imagination to still worse entangle the issue and provide the most incredible solution.

"However, all their efforts remained fruitless, and no serious historian would take it upon himself nowadays to assert, that he had solved this matter accurately, without a trace of doubt."

Indeed already 80 years the Bogomil question has been thrashed out in our literature, while for centuries its has been an object of study in the world literature. In the last quarter century many new works have been published with quite daring and entirely conflicting assertions, yet they were not able to solve "the riddle of the Bosnian Church." On the contrary they have still worse entangled it and introduced confusion in the ranks of the scholars as well as in the wide circles of readers.

As it is well known, the Roman Curia has been accusing for a full three centuries the "Bosnian Church" for its alleged Patarene and Manichaean heresies. It had been summoning the kings of Hungary to undertake crusades against this heresy; then it had been sending to Bosnia at first, the Dominicans, and then the Franciscans, to preach "the true religion" and to eradicate the heresy.

Already the Alsatian professor, Charles Schmidt, considered the Bosnian Church as the Bogomil organization and connected it with the movement of the Bogomils in Bulgaria and Byzantium and with the movement of Cathars in Provence and Lombardy.

During the reign of Prince Michael, when in Belgrade interest was aroused in Bosnia, the learned Serbian Society announced in 1864 a prize of 50 imperial ducats for work on the history of the Bosnian Church. This prize was given to the well known Serbian patriot from Dalmatia, Dr. Bozhidar Petranovich, who in 1867 published in Zadar his monograph on the Bogomils and the Bosnian Church. Petranovich has portrayed, in the footsteps of Charles Schmidt, the general development of the Bogomil heresy but he aded to this portrayal the recently published "Sermon of Presbiter Kosma", which was not known to Schmidt. Upon studying the Bosnian decree published by Medo Putsich and Mikloshich, in which the Orthodox sanctions are brought to light, Petranovich expresses a new theory. In accordance therewith "Bosnia had been right from the beginning Greek Orthodox but in the 11th century began to infiltrate, probably from Serbia and Macedonia, Slavic heretics, which are known to be especially interested in Slavic education, and have, precisely for this, hated the Latin Clergy".

They "began to exert influence upon the Church and religious education of the people in the spirit and by the principles, of the popular Bogomil type, and in this effort they became successful to the point that they had replaced the unstable church organization which existed up to that time with a purely national organization, but after the model and shape of the heresy". The heretics succeeded "in establishing themselves in the Bosnian Church to such a degree that they constituted its most important factor—the monastic order". The external form and the hierarchy of the church was heretic. But the dogmatic damage was small. The heresy was restricted to a small number of "Christians," but their number was ebbing every day, while people remained loyal to the Orthodox Church.

At the same time the first president of the Yugoslav Academy of Science, Francis Rachki, completed his great work on the Bogomils and Patarenes on which he worked for 15 years. It was based on his excellent knowledge of theological literature and on numerous published and unpublished sources. This work provided an extensive background concerning the development of the Bogomil heresy in many counries of Europe. Rachki has minutely and critically presented the history of the Bosnian Church, and argued that it was a heretic organization after the fashion of the Catharian church in Provence.

The view of Francis Rachki remained unassailed a long period of time. This view and opinion have been accepted by the best Slavic historians: Vyekoslav Klaich, Ferdo Shishich, Constantine Yirechek, Stanoye Stanoyevich, Vladimir Chorovich, Truhelka and others.

Yet, Rachki's inability to find in the Bosnian monuments positive traces of the Bogomil doctrine, was a weak point in his argument. On the contrary, the code of Christian Hval, published by Danichich, in 1871, contained many pictures of saints, which is in sharp conflict with the Patarene teachings. Therefore, in the local literature discussions continued which, in the spirit of the thesis of Petranovich, have been proving the overwhelming orthodox characteristic of the Bosnian Church.

Thus the monk Gennadius asserted in 1891 that "the Bosnian Church was in the time of the kings neither heretic nor Roman, but purely Greek Orthodox." He admits that the "Bogomil heresy had penetrated only in the second half of the 12th century into Bosnia, but up to that time the national independent Bosnian Church and Bosnian religion existed on a solid foundation, but this church had been called by the aliens 'Bogomil Church'." However, he cautiously adds, saying: *"I have not the slightest intention to assert that there were no Bogomils in Bosnia, but I wish merely to clarify this matter and prove: that the Bosnian Church and Bosnian religion was not a Bogomil religion and church."* There were Bogomils, but they were "submerged

in Orthodoxy", and "Bosnia again became Serbian".

After the monk Gennadius, Atom (Sima Tomich) published in the periodical "Bosanska Vila" an extensive dissertation, in which he again repeated the argument of Petranovich and drew similar conclusions. He begins with the Serbian literature reflecting two different views: one claiming that the Bosnian Church was heretic, and the other that it was Serbian Orthodox. And he also admitted: *"That in Bosnia in the middle ages (12-15th century) there were heretics, which cannot be disputed."* "The Bosnian heresy is identical with that of the Bogomils who were carrying on in the old Serbian and Bulgarian state." But he is set against the allegation *"That almost the whole people in Bosnia of that time lived in the shadow of the institutions of the same religious apostasy."* After having analyzed, once again, the Serbian, Ragusan and Bosnian documents he draws the following conclusions: *"In Bosnia there were Bogomil heretics, but their number was insignificant. The Bogomil faith was not a state religion: The mass of Bosnia's population consisted of the orthodox faithful."*

"The Bosnian heresy did not submerge in the Islamic religion, but because of its impotence it has gradually, even before the Turkish invasion, returned to the faith from which it had defected."

Still a further step was made by the sympathetic amateur Vid Vuletich Vukasovich, who on the basis of an inscription of Duke Stephen in the church in Gorazhd, made the assertion that "in Hum (Herzegovina) and Bosnia there were no true Bogomils or Patarenes, but they had been only adherents of the popular Bosnian Church, and have applied to each other the term "Brothers" and "Christians" but have acknowledged the church and practiced in some way the sacraments of the faith". He was the first to assert in public the claim of the Serbian "National Bosnian Church" which was adopted then by Vaso Glushats. *"This church had issued from the orthodoxy and returned to the same".*

On the other hand, on the Croatian side there is an increasing belief that the Bosnian Church issued from the Catholic religion and returned to the same. Thus in 1901 the learned Jesuit, Alexander Hoffer, had argued that Bosnia from the most ancient period belonged to the jurisdiction of the Roman Church, but that it had "A Greek ritual in the Slavic language with the Cyrillic script." According to him, Bosnia was "in the latest period (in the 11th and 12th centuries) separated from Serbia and spiritually associated with the western and southern Catholic countries". He admits that thereafter there were Patarenes, but claims that banus Kulin was not of Patarene faith, since he was a Catholic. The same applies also to his successors, and especially to King Tvartko.

We shall not waste time in reproducing numerous subsequent, frequently amateurish discussions, in which the Bosnian Bogomil sect had been identified with the continuation of the primitive Slavic dualism or as an expression of the Slavic trend towards social democracy or communism. This has been properly clarified by Dr. Yaroslav Shidak in his great bibliographic study, in which, however there are many lacunae.

In 1924 the monograph of Dr. Vaso Glushats had been published in Belgrade, in which he returns to the view of the writers in "Bosanska Vila" and "Bosansko-Hersegovachki Istochnik" from 1890-1894. He asserts with determination that the Bosnian church has always been and remained Greek Orthodox, and that the Roman curia merely slandered it since it did not make any distinction between the heretics and schismatics. In the arsenal of his proofs we find besides the Bosnian decrees (which have been quoted also by Petranovich and Atom) also the handwritten code of the Cristian Hval, with the sign of the cross. The monograph of Glushats made a deep impression in Serbian circles and received from the Serbian Academy of Science the grand prize of 6,000 dinars.

Ten years later the Croatian scholar, Dr. Yaroslav Shidak decided, under the influence of the work of Glushats, to examine the literature dealing with the issue of the Bosnian Church. The arguments of Glushats have convinced him that this church was not heretic, but true canonical and that the thesis of Rachki was in error. He admitted that there are only three scientific monographs on this subject: the works of Petranovich, Rachki and Glushats. Everything else, in his judgment, was "entirely fruitless" or was presented by writers who were not competent to deal with this problem. The result of his investigations is his uncompromising

rejection of Rachki's thesis as historically incorrect.

In this respect Shidak follows Glushats, but he cannot accept the latter's thesis about the orthodox nature of the Bosnian Church, since he knows that the Serbian Orthodox Church has stricken "The Bosnian and Herzegovinan Heretics with anathema." Therefore, he provides a rather nebulous assertion, that this was an independent canonical Church. "This church did not acept any connections with either the Roman Church for it did not recognize the primacy of the Pope, nor did it consider itself a part of the Eastern Church. This was an entirely independent Christian Church which ascribed to itself Apostolic origin."

In the same year the Franciscan Brother, Dr. Marko Vego, contributed a fairly similar, however, still bolder assertion. He considered that the Bosnian Christians were Catholics "who could not, nor would not because of their special culture, accept all the principles and norms (standards) of the Roman Church"; that this was a "Catholicism fitted to the spiritual needs of the population", with the Slavic services, a "purely national Catholic religion, which did not have its well perfected system."

The works of Yaroslav Shidak and Marko Vego had quite an echo in the collective work entitled: "Bosnia and Herzegovina Croatian Lands", which had been prepared before the war, but published only in 1942. Setting out from the political history of Bosnia, Marko Peroyevich speaks in this collection of "Patarenes"—in quotation marks—"of the alleged heretics" and explains the well known act of 1203 in the following manner: "The Bosnian clergy did not want to recede from the age old method of election of the Bosnian Bishop, and was opposed to either the Pope or King to impose upon them an alien Bishop. Perhaps this is the cause and the beginning of the later religious struggles in Bosnia". Then again, he still speaks of heretics, yet does not expound their teachings, but merely says: "*It appears that all the Bosnian heretics were against interference of the king's policy in the Bosnian political and church affairs.*" By the end he says: "*True enough, there were Patarenes in Bosnia and perhaps they were so strong that they were shaking the very foundations of government,* but with all that the Patarenes were not to blame for the fall of Bosnia. It has not been established by anything, that Radak had become a traitor to his country from some religious hatred and revengefulness. Therefore one cannot see that the religious strife had been the cause of the fall of Bosnia. *Neither can one assert that the Patarenes, immediately after the conquest of Bosnia were passing en masse to Islam. There is no proof of that."* Thus this is a very cautious but undecisive opinion.

However, in the same colective book the eminent scholar Chiro Truhelka, who wrote all his life about the Bogomils in Bosnia, changes his opinion entirely under the influence of Yaroslav Shidak.

He speaks of the entanglements in the issue of the Bosnian Church and says: "This issue has been brought in this truly hopeless situation by Francis Rachki.

Now Truhelka proves that the Patarenes were not Bogomils. In his estimation "The Bosnian Church, which during the stormy years of migrations and occupation had suffered much, and by its position was separated from Rome and the rest of the Catholic world living its own independent life, and developing into a special national church, as of old the Armenian, Coptic or Abyssinian churches which remained Catholic, but in course of time accepted some customs and rites by which they are differentiated from the rest of the Catholic churches." According to Truhelka the Bosnian Church disappeared in the Islam. "This tide of Islamic flood has gradually engulfed it and kept submerging it in its waves."

But the third writer, the Franciscan Yelenich in his article about the "Catholic Church in Bosnia" remains true to the view of Rachki asserting that the Bosnian Church was of the Patarene type, that it was heretic and that it conducted a decisive strugle against the Catholic Church. Thus we see three different opinions about the Bosnian Church in the same volume dedicated to the history of Bosnia and Herzegovina.

Against the thesis of Shidak only Dr. Miho Barada rose in Zagreb and produced potent arguments in favor of the opinion that the Bosnian church actually was heretic. However these arguments could not convince Dr. Shidak, who renewed his thesis in a condensed form. He states: The kernel of the problem is in the fact whether the native sources—those which origi-

nated in the circle of the Bosnian Church—confirm the accusation of the alleged dualistic heresies, or not. Only a conscientious analysis of the single data and expert comparison of the native and latin documents led me away, finally, from the thesis of Rachki to its complete negation. In this I became aware that "The Bosnian Church" did venerate the symbol of the cross and by this very fact it essentially differed from any dualistic sect. Furthermore, I have ascertained that in this church both Mother of God and the Saints were venerated, together with the relics of Saints and their pictures: that it accepts in their entirety the Holy Scriptures and that it recognizes the worth of alms and the prayers for the deceased; that it has its own monks and organized hierarchy including the cloisters and churches; that they do not reject the baptism and marriage, nor do they condemn the animal food. All this is in the head-long clash with the teachings and practice of dualistic sects both those in the west and east, and is entirely contrary to the accusations of the Latin documents.

In the meantime Dr. Vaso Glashats remained stoutly on his own position. In 1941 he began to publish an extensive book entitled "The Truth About the Bogomils". In its introduction he took note of the work of Shidak and also of the confidence which Shidak reposes in his work as "Scientific work with the most serious intentions". But Shidak's opinion that "Bosnian Church" was not Serbian Orthodox, he cannot accept. He figures that the attacks against the "Bosnian and Herzegovinan heretics do not issue from the official representative of the Eastern Church, nor are they taken from unimpeachable historical sources". Therefore they do not deserve to be taken into consideration. Vaso Glushats states stubbornly, that all the accusations from the Roman and the Orthodox sources against the Bosnian Church are false and slanted. He goes a step further to establish the truth about Bogomils and analyses "The Sermons of the Presbyter Kozma" claiming that the Bogomil sect as a heresy did not exist at all, but that this was a political movement in Bulgaria, unjustly slandered by its enemies. Then he engages in criticism of the sources which speak of Bogomils and Paulicians, namely Patriarch Fotius, Euthymius Zigabenus and Anna Komnena, and arrives at the conclusion that whatever they say of heresies is only a "monastic mystification". Hence the conclusion with the words of the author himself: "When all the Greek, Latin and Slavic writings on the basis of which Rachki created his Bogomils in our historiography are studied from all sides and with proper critical approach, we shall arrive at the unadulterated historical truth, that Bogomils have actually never existed in the Balkan peninsula. They are the monastic mystifications of the middle ages and historical error into which we have been pushed by Rachki. The historical sources claim that they did not exist in Bulgaria, in Serbia nor in Bosnia. Yet these three countries had their own independent states and in each state a special Greek Orthodox Church. At the same time the Roman Church was attacking the Orthodox churches, and conducted against them a violent propaganda, and was calling them all possible heretic names and ascribed to them all possible heretical doctrines.

"This is, definitely, the honest truth about the Bogomils".

From the foregoing we see that 80 years of study of the Bogomil issue in Bosnia, had gradually arrived to the following conclusions: (1) That the Bosnian Church was not Bogomil, but true canonical—whether Catholic or Greek Orthodox, according to the sympathies of the writers, and (2) that the Bogomil sect did not even exist in the Balkans.

It is time to solve this problem but not on the basis of the study of the literature, nor by unjustified rejection of the alien sources and the analysis only of single, native sources, but by a conscientious analysis of the ecclesiastic Bosnian manuscripts.

In order to become acquainted with the religious teachings of the Bosnian "Church" we should study the few literary monuments which survived it. Both Dr. Glushats and Dr. Shidak are analyzing only the Hval Code of 1404 and the Testament of the guest Radin from 1466, two monuments from the later period, but they ignore all the other spiritual books which could throw light on the religious concepts of the Bosnian "Christians."

There is quite a number of the Bosnian spiritual books, which had been published mostly by the experts in philology. These scholars have

been studying only the orthographic and dialectical features of the text and did not evaluate the contents of the texts published by them. However, they should be congratulated for establishing, with their analysis, the Bosnian origin of these manuscripts.

Among the monuments of the Bosnian-Herzegovinan literature of the middle ages we should class as originating from the 12th century: (1) the Gershkovich fragment of the Deeds of Apostles and Epistles, written in glagolitic script. (2) the Mihanovich fragment (only two sheets) also written in glagolitic. (3) Mirosav Gospel, written in Herzegovina in cyrillic script.

These three manuscripts are of no significance for our effort, for they are fully orthodoxal by their contents.

From the 13th century come only the Grigorovich-Hilferding fragments of the Gospel written in cyrillic script.

In the 14th century all the manuscripts are written in cyrillic, but traces of their transcript from glagolitic script are present. They are: fragments of the Mostar Gospel, which is preserved to this day in 32 sheets.

Further we should consider Hilferding's "Acts of the Apostles" in fragments.

To the 15th century belongs: The Code of Hval, by far the most complete of all the other manuscripts, containing all the books of the New Testament (353 sheets) and written in 1404 by the Christian "Hval, for the Duke of Split, Hervoye."

The Radosav Code written by "Christian Radosav for Christian Goysav" during the reign of King Stephen Thomas (after 1443) containing the Apocalypsis, Lord's Prayer and other prayers (containing 60 sheets).

There is quite a number of other fragments so poor and so damaged that they cannot be taken for a serious study of the contents.

However, after the first glance of this rather poor literary heritage, its simplicity cannot be missed. They are all only the Books of the New Testament and chiefly the Gospels, Apocalypsis and the deeds of Apostles, with Epistles: There is only one text of Psalterium.

That far we can follow Dr. Solovyev in his analytical effort. With all his labor he did not bring out much new evidence whether to identify the Bosnian sectarian canons with either Orthodox or Catholic Church, or differentiate them from either. He eventually reverts to the thesis of Francis Rachki, significantly by leaving out of consideration the archeological evidence of stechaks (tombstones) as Rachki did. Only Rachki could not come close to them because of physical obstacles, while Solovyev, who could inspect every one of them, ignored them altogether. So the age-old problem still hangs in the balance.

For conclusion we should mention the work of Dr. Leo Petrovich, O.F.M. Dr. Petrovich was a great historical scholar, and his capital work entitled: "The Christians of the Bosnian Church," was published in Sarajevo in 1953. Based on the works of Glushats, Shidak and Truhelka, he carries his investigation into the chanceries of the Roman Curia and the court of the medieval kings of Hungary. Among other amazing results of his investigation, he concludes that the clergy of the Bosnian Church represents the localized variety of the glagolitic Croatian Benedictine order, which resisted the pressure brought to bear on them both from Rome and Buda. The initial cleavage grew in time through ever increasing friction into a wide moat of antagonism and hostility.

The Military Might of Bosnia in the Service of Sultans

Only among the armies of the first four khalifs, we shall find an enthusiasm similar to the one with which the new Croatian Moslems of Bosnia had been inserted into the Ottoman war plan. From Bosnia, continuous attacks are made against the Croatian, German, Hungarian and Venetian territory, with a series of devastating and terrifying raids.

Only five years after the fall of Bosnia the natives are being trained and engaging in the practice of war so that even before the fall of Herzegovina, before the fall of the banates of Srebrenitsa and Yaytsa, immediately after the death of Skanderbeg in 1468, they break through, across Lika and Kerbava, to Senj (Segna) and in the Venetian Dalmatia. In the year 1469 the Bosnian Governor Isa Beg breaks in with 20,000 "Turks" into Croatia and Carniola and hauls away into Bosnia an army of 60,000 slaves. In the same year three new raids are recorded with the capture of additional 10,000 slaves. In 1470

again a new raid. In 1471 the breakthrough to Split, Zadar and Shibenik, is recorded; in the second raid of the same year Isa Beg breaks through to Lubyana, Kran and Tsel (Klagenfurt) and drives into Bosnia another 30,000 prisoners; in August of the same year there is a new raid to Goritza. In September they reach Goritza once again; in November they push to Zagreb.

In the year 1472 they break through to Ptuy (Petovio) and Maribor (Marburg); in September of the same year 12,000 Bosnian horsemen break into Furlandia up to Udine; in November they plunder in Istria and Goritza. In the year 1473 Isa Beg again appears in Carniola (Slovenija), Styria and Cartinthia. In 1474 again our former "Christians" are plundering throughout Turopolye, south of Zagreb, and the Drava region, and drive home 14,000 prisoners, while in the fall they return once more. In the year 1476 there are two more inroads; in July and October. In 1477, 30,000 Bosnians break into Croatia, Carniola and Styria, and for two months are ravaging the area, without any serious obstacles. In 1499 a new raid in Dalmatia; the second raid is in February; in the third raid of the same year they haul away 2,000 slaves. In 1500 they attack Zadar, Split and Trogir. In 1501, the same; in 1502, they laid siege to Yaytse; in 1511 they attack the Modrush district; in 1512 they attack Skradin, in 1513 Tsetin; and in 1514 they launch an attack against Knin; in the same year they capture and drive from Croatia 3,000 prisoners; the same year they stage another raid with "much slave capture." The Governor of Bosnia informs the Croatian prince Ivan Karlovich, that he will come every two weeks to "visit" him. The terror and misery are such that no one ever thinks of writing ballads about the fighting with the "Turks."

At the time the Ottoman empire does not conclude with the Christian states either peace or truce, as an equal with an equal.... As they establish a truce, then the sultan "merely permits the truce." But this "permission of truce" is of no value at the Croatian border, for the raids continue as ever. In the year 1555 the sultan "permitted the truce," yet the Bosnians raid the Croatian lands nevertheless; in 1568 the sultan again "permitted the truce," but new raids were coming from Bosnia. Hassan pasha Predoyevich hauls in 1592 from Croatia so many slaves that the price on the head of the slaves was heavily reduced; before a boy could be bought for 1 horse, but now "the Wallachians" offer 5 boys for 1 horse.

Occasionally, the Bosnians, too, suffered defeat. On one occasion King Mathias breaks through in 1480 up to Verhbosna (Upper Bosnia's Sarayevo) and sets it on fire; further he defeats Dawut pasha near Travnik where 10,000 "Turks" are killed. The Croats from Croatia proper intercepted in 1478 a Bosnian army at Sisak where a true "Croatian battle" was fought by Croats on both sides of the front. Those of Bosnia had been so badly defeated that the Turkish Chroniclers called that year "The year of disintegration." The sultan himself became worried to the point that he cancelled his truce and started his "imperial" or great war. After a series of battles the war was ended with a first treaty on the terms of equality, concluded in 1606 in Zsitvatorok (confluence of Zhitva river with Danube) in the present day Slovak territory. This time Turkey gets nothing, but starts slowly her descent from the zenith of her power. Only then originate also those popular ballads, in which the Christians find pride and glory in this prolonged and difficult wrangling.

Besides this Croatian war, the Croatian-Moslems from Bosnia join up with every sizable expedition of sultans; we find them also before Vienna, Güns (Köszeg), and before Sziget. And even in the 19th century they do not neglect their special Croatian war. Still in 1834 they launch their attacks at Tsetin and even Banus Yellachich had to defend himself from their raids. Even before the Austrian occupation the visiting writers report of guardhouses on watchtowers and, of "no man's land" at the border because of the hazards from the raids.

How can we explain these terrifying devastations and massacres which have reduced the number of Croats as a nation by at least 7,000,000 persons? From where stems this offensive enthusiasm of the Croatian-Moslems of Bosnia? Is it through the love or grandeur of Turkey as an empire; by their desire to loot? Was it the Bogomil revenge on Catholicism? Neither of these interpretations is quite sufficient even though each one of them separately and all of them together, have their own part. The love for Turkey was never so effectively developed. The desire

for loot was sporadic and too low for such a century old policy. The Bogomil revenge may have lasted for one or two generations and it would go, as it actually did go, into oblivion. Therefore something else was there which entered and remained permanently in the spirit of the Bosnians, something that could constantly evoke "a crusading" enthusiasm. And this alone was the religion. Therefore one has to take into consideration also the religious interpretation of this phenomenon.*

No matter what the immediate motives of those Bosnians have been while they took over the Islam, they soon became fond of it, they made it their own and were practicing it. But the tradition of Islam was inexorably offensive and military. While Mohammed carried on in Mecca as an unarmed prophet, he got but a few adherents, suffered many insults and persecutions and almost lost his life. But when he fled to Medina, equipped an army and started his guerilla raids, and battles, he finally conquered Mecca and all of Arabia, so that the armed prophet was much better listened to, respected and accepted. In his lifetime Mohammed was conducting some 50 battles and in 9 of these battles he personally took part. The Islamic army was a predecessor for the missionaries in Persia, Egypt and North Africa while guerilla troops often preceded the armies.

Before Tarik went to Spain the guerilla troops of the Moslem Berbers roamed through the country several times. The same guerillas which raided Italy to Rome and France to Lyons and Avignon as well as all the European shores up to Great Britain, according to the Moslem concepts, were by no means simple plunderers and brigands. This was the process of groping the terrain and weakening of the enemy which had been adhered to by tradition, so that the regular army which had to come found the ground prepared. This was the army which at no time has ever lost out of sight the Islamic domination of the world, and the eventual campaigns of conquest.

These ideals carried away also the Islamized Bosnians. Incidentally, of course, they found it profitable to get hold of booty and riches. But if somebody loses his life in a war so hallowed,

* See section V, Islam's laws of wars.

the fighter will not lose the salvation of his soul. No matter how bad the situation was, they were always prepared to fall into brotherly embrace with all those who would accept their ideals. Therefore they were amazed, with a mixture of contempt and anger why the Croats across the Sava and Velebit so doggedly resisted them when essentially they wished them good, the greatest good—either to become Moslems themselves or to come under the protection of Islam. And this is precisely what they wished most arduously to their closest brothers across the Dinaric Alps and Sava river; this is, in all appearance, why they attacked them so often.

Perhaps the most typical example is that of the Bosnian Yakub pasha, when he massacred in the battle of Udbine some 5,700 Croatian noblemen and dished up, after the battle, to the unfortunate Banus Derenchin the head of his son on a platter. With the booty he amassed, Yakub pasha set up the Vakufs (religious foundations). He himself was a pious dervish. On his own grave he had carved an inscription which he himself had set up. In it he refers to his fights from the religious point of view, and fervently recommends his soul to God.

One should stress the disproportion in the Turkish genius: The Turks were exceptionally dynamic. They were devoted to Islam, but for their great tasks they were not sufficiently original and not sufficiently intellectual. The Bosnian Moslems almost immediately felt their superiority over the Turks. Physically they were one of the fittest races in the Ottoman empire, by their courage they were among the first and by their intellectual talent, they were far above the Turks. For this reason in spite of their distant periphery, in spite of the difference in language and temperament, they succeeded in getting into the central government; they looked down upon the true Turk, and the Bosnians were leading the most brilliant century of the empire, the 16th century. Between the year 1544 and 1612 Bosnia provide the Empire with nine Grand Vezirs, and on the whole she gave Turkey 23 of them, in addition to a large number of Pashas, Sanjak Beys, Beglerbeys and other dignitaries. For a certain length of time the Croatian language is at the imperial court only second to Turkish and the Croatian is used by all the important men "of the military profession." When, after the failures in the 17th century Turkey was too weak to defend Bosnia, the Bosnian Moslems take over themselves both the defense of their country, with their old practice of inroads in the neighboring countries. When the sultan at the Congress of Berlin in 1878 ceded Bosnia to Austria, they rise, unaided by anyone else to the defense of their country, and furnish an exceptionally powerful resistance to Austria.

Not only did these Croatian Moslems from Bosnia make raids on the Croatian, Austrian, Venetian and Hungarian areas, not only did they participate in all the major wars of the sultans, but they were, like the cossacks of Russia, frequently settled along the menaced borders of the empire, as, for instance in Nubia, as in Serbia. They were settling the newly conquered territories not only of their expanded Bosnia, but also areas in Dalmatia, Lika, Croatia proper, Slavonia and Hungary.

Chronological Sequence of the Bosnian
Bani and Kings

1. Semi-mythical characters whose reign is placed between the 7th and 8th century:

Zhelimir, Kreshimir, Leget and Vukmir

Prince Styepan as vassal of King Bodin of Zeta 1082/83.

Borich (1150-1163)

Kulin (1180-1204)*

Stephen and his son Sebislav (1204-1232)

* Regardless of his fame and the success of his reign, the name Kulin (by others also Chulin) leaves us in the dark as to his racial and ethnic background. The name has no slavic etymology, but its root syllable shows clearly a Touranian or Turkish word *kul* (slave, servant). Similar is the case of the mythical Croatian leader Kluk, one of the five brothers: Horvat, Mohor, Kluk, Lovel, Kossinats. By their stymological indices Kluk seems to be a contraction of Turkish Kulluk (slavery, servitude); Lovel coming close to the Hungarian *lovas* (horsemen); Russian loshak (from Tartar) *mule;* Mohor with the change of the voiced guttural *g* to its spirant "h" (Greek X), as in the pre-Bulgarian "utrigur"; kutri-gur; bul-gur; the Hungarian: hunigar, hungarus and Magyar, in Haloti beszéd (funeral oration) *magar,* with the assumed meaning "seed; substance," etc.

Finally: *Kossinats* representing a variation present in Kazak, kozak, kazna (Russian loanwords from Tartar); and Hungarian gazda (a wealthy owner), gazdag, "rich," etc.

In contrast with this the names of the two sisters: "Tuga and Buga" seem to reflect Indo-European and more closely Germanic origin. So *Tuga* could be etymologically connected with N.H.G. "taugen; tauglish, jugend tüchtig," Lithuanian "daugas, daug" (large; much); Russian "djuzhiy" (brave, substantial) and Polish "duzhiy; duzho" (large, much).

Finally, "Buga" seems a cognate of N.H.G. "biegen, beugen, Bogen." Bucht "bend; bow, bright"; cf river name "Bug," lit. winding course of river, etc.

Mathew Ninoslav (1232-1250)**

Priyezda (1250-1254)

Duchess Agnes (1264-1268)

Adalbert (Béla) (1268-1272)

Stephen (1272-1279)

Queen Elizabeth (1280-1282)

Stephen Charles (Styepan Dragutin) (1282-1314)

Stephen Kotroman (condominium with his father-in-law St. Charles)

Paul Shubich (1298-1302)

Mladen Shubich (1302-1322)

Styepan Kotromanich (1322-1353)

Styepan Tvartko, first king of Bosnia (1353-1391)

Styepan Dabisha and his wife Yelena (Helen) Gruba (1391-1398)

Interregnum and struggle for the throne (1398-1421)

Styepan Ostoya (1398-1404) and (1408-1418)

Styepan Tvartko II Tvartkovich (1404-1408 and 1421-1443)

Styepan Ostoich (1418-1421)

Styepan Tomas Ostoich (1441-1461)

Styepan Tomashevich (1461-1463)

** The name Ninoslav reflects its Slavic origin, however leaving the first word of the compound in the dark, unless we restore it to the form "nynye-slav," as of the Latin "presentum inclitus," i.e. "famed right now"; Greek Peri-cles "famed all over"; Sophocles "famed for his wisdom," etc.

Section III

DALMATIA FROM 1380 UNTIL 1718

Sale of Dalmatia

THE death of Louis the Great of Hungary, who left behind two daughters, Mary and Hedwig, became the signal for great disturbances in both countries. Almost all of Hungary and Dalmatia recognized Mary, the older daughter of the late King Louis, as the legal king. However, she was under the guardianship of her mother Elizabeth, since Mary was only 12 years old at her accession to the throne.

At the same time a number of Croatian and Hungarian magnates who wanted to restore their ancient privileges and independence, conspired against the queen and expressed themselves in favor of Charles III of Durazzo (Drach, Duresh), cousin of the late King Louis, who had succeeded to the throne of Naples following the reign of Queen Johanna, in the face of the opposition of the latter who had adopted Louis, the son of John, King of France. A conspiracy in Zadar against the two queens had been drowned in blood. But Charles of Durazzo, proceeding with due haste, landed on the coast of Croatia, and when he arrived in Buda he was crowned King of Hungary, Dalmatia and Croatia.

His reign was short. On February 26, 1386, under the instigation of Queen Mother Elizabeth, he was assassinated, and in order to avenge his death the Croatian barons seized Elizabeth and Mary and confined them to the castle of Novigrad near Zadar.

Pursuing their policy of revenge, the conspirators, headed by the prior of Vrana (Aurana), John Palizhna and the powerful Horvath brothers assassinated the Queen Mother Elizabeth in Novigrad on January 16, 1387.

This murder was a true windfall for the Venetians, who were eager to ingratiate themselves with Sigismund, and whose good will they needed for their future plans. They were to use this stroke of fortune to keep out, at the same time, the forces of Margaret, mother of Ladislas and son of Charles of Durazzo, and a pretender to the crown of Hungary and Croatia. So they armed a fleet and, upon the request of Sigismund, laid siege to Novigrad, and liberated Queen Mary, the bride of Sigismund.

After the death of Louis the Great, the situation of the Dalmatian cities became evermore precarious, even critical. Ladislas of Naples, Sigismund, Venice and the Bosnian kings all reached out for this territory which constituted a base from which a conquest of the Orient could be started, as well as domination of the Mediterranean. Further, it became known that the Venetians were making preparations for a furious attack against Ragusa (Dubrovnik). The Republic of Saint Blaise became alarmed and made an effort to unite the Dalmatian cities in a defensive league, but conflicts of interests were so sharp that nothing came out of the league.

In connection with these circumstances a delegation of Croatian and Hungarian barons set sail to Naples and offered the throne of Croatia and Hungary to Ladislas, the son of Charles of Durazzo. Ladislas accepted. In 1390 he issued a proclamation whereby he announced to the people of Naples that he had decided to avenge the death of his father. The audacity of the Neapolitan party was matched only by the weakness or the apathy of Sigismund. Ladislas of Naples was accepted with misgivings by Venice since this Angevin was at the same time a potential ruler of the lands of southern Italy and those of Croatia and Hungary. This union forebode a great danger for even though Venice was deprived of Dalmatia, she assumed a dominant position in the Ionian Sea by acquisition of the Island of Corfu.

Venice became restless, and through her agents she set to work in Hungary to consolidate the anti-Neapolitan party. Indeed, she got the upper hand of the situation. The barons elected Sigismund as king of Croatia and Hungary.

Yet all these developments did not bring any succor to the Dalmatian cities which were being plagued and devastated by the partisans of Naples and the Bosnians simply because they could not get any aid from the king. And yet, ever since the 15th of April, that is two weeks after Sigismund's coronation, Venice, acting under a request of the latter, making virtue out of necessity, wrote to the Dalmatian communities reminding them of their oath of allegiance to the crown of Hungary which they had given to

Queen Mary. In their reply to doge Antonio Venier they accepted the terms of the ducal message and Spalato (Split) in particular assured the doge "that neither death nor the sword could turn it away from its loyalty to the king." At the same time Venice mobilized its fleet—twenty-four galleys—in order to join the king's army against the Neapolitan party. In July, 1387, Sigismund had achieved a double purpose; he had liberated his bride whom he wed in Zagreb, and reestablished a semblance of calm in Croatia.

King Tvartko of Bosnia was a man with a program and resolution to make his ideas a reality. But he was confronted with sharp opposition on the part of the king of Croatia and Hungary. However, Tvartko did not let this intimidate him. He signed a treaty of alliance with Ragusa (April 9, 1387). By use of clever propaganda accentuated by frequent raids, he alarmed the Dalmatian communities to such a degree that Spalato sent him a message in which—naturally without hurting the rights of the Hungarian crown—it placed the city under Tvartko's protection. The stronghold of Klis submitted to him, together with the strongholds of Ostrovitsa and Nona (Nin), all of which fell under Bosnian power. Sigismund was undecided as ever, while Dalmatia was hesitant and deeply distressed. Trogir (Trau) settled the question by submitting to the king of Bosnia.

The surrender of its eternal rival had an antagonistic effect on Split, which at this time stuck to Sigismund. An emissary who was sent to Buda (January 19, 1388) was given instructions to submit the plight of his faithful city to the king. The picture of Split's distress was greatly overdrawn but even that did not change the fact that the Bosnian sword was hanging over Dalmatian communities, and Sigismund did nothing but supply hollow rhetoric. Therefore, moved by despair, they concluded an alliance with the Croatian barons (6th of October, 1388) for the defense of their territory. The attempt was useless, for Hungary was weak and divided, Sigismund inactive and unreliable, while Tvartko was a man of action. Even Split, after some hesitation, submitted to Tvartko's sovereignty. Similar action was followed by Shibenik and Trogir as well as by the islands of the arcopelago. By 1390, Tvartko possessed all of Dalmatia and proclaimed himself king of Croatia.

After a life crowned with success and glory, Tvartko passed away on the 15th of February, 1391. His younger brother Stephen Dabisha succeeded to the throne and soon the work of the great king of Bosnia began to flounder.

In the meantime, Ladislas of Naples had himself crowned on the 11th of May, 1390. By this very fact he established his claim upon the sovereignty of Hungary and Croatia. A powerful Bosnian baron, Hervoye Vukchich Hervatinich, a very shrewd and energetic leader, was appointed banus of Dalmatia. This was the first step to a high scale of honors achieved by this man of peculiar talent, who all his life aspired to royal crown without ever reaching it.

Even though she was expelled from Dalmatia, Venice, relying on her powerful navy, still held control of the Adriatic. Nothing could take place between the two seacoasts without her intervention. Thus, Ladislas, thinking himself master of the situation, had to submit to their rejection of his request to cross the sea on a Venetian ship (February 8, 1392).

The Sovereign from Naples took revenge on Venice for its refusal to do him the required service, by offering his alliance to Sultan Bayezid Ilderim. But the only result of this move was to turn away the feudal Hungarian and Croatian nobility from a sovereign who did not sufficiently realize the Turkish threat to southeastern Europe. The prospect of such a distasteful alliance, was the more repugnant to all concerned for it came merely three years after the battle of Kossovo which destroyed Serbia in her attempt to avert the Turkish threat.

This was a painful and strange situation. Dabisha kept exercising the rights of his sovereignty in Dalmatia, and so did Sigismund. The Dalmatian cities hesitated to join either camp. The count of Veglia (Kerk), a lieutenant of Sigismund, demanded three galleys from Venice in order to strike at Zadar and to subject it to the sovereignty of Sigismund. The conflicting sovereignties cancelled each other. The situation was such, that speaking out the mind of Dalmatian city republics, Split (Spalato) declares "that since the death of King Tvartko let no one, except the city rectors and city judges, mention the name of another king, nor anything else." Indeed, the cities regained their freedom, but due to their internecine rivalries they were incapable of forming a political league and were helpless to ward off the inroads of the neighboring barons. At one time they encouraged democracy, at another time they stood for installation of an aristocratic regime as such. Dabisha died in 1395, after renouncing all his rights over the Dalmatian communities in favor of Sigismund. The King of Hungary and Dalmatia recovers the whole seacoast due to the support given him by the banus of Croatia and Dalmatia, Nicholas Goryanski, who invested supreme power in Split.

But all this takes place in the middle of a growing danger sweeping the country through the inroads of the Turks. The Turks had invaded Bulgaria and Serbia and now threatened Hungary. A new crusade becomes a pressing need. This time Sigismund does not hesitate. He pleads with the Venetians and the King of France, Charles VI. The flower of French nobility joins the flags of Hungary and Croatia. The Christian and Moslem armies engage in a spectacular battle at Nicopolis, on the banks of the Danube. The Christian army is annihilated on the 28th of September, 1396. The Christians of the Balkans are dumbfounded by this disaster. Sigismund, himself a fugitive, embarks on a Venetian galley, reaches Ragusa and lands in Split on the 30th of September.

Since rumors were spread that the king had perished in battle, the Neapolitan party gained new adherents. But after Sigismund returned safe and sound he promptly called a diet in Temeshvar and invited representatives of the Dalmatian communities. The delegates received strict and formal instructions not to accept anything that would be prejudicial to their age-old liberties. However, after extensive discussions they were withdrawn and the communities were not represented at all, and the situation became ever more dark and complex. The absence of the Dalmatian delegates was tantamount to an assertion of their new autonomy.

The natural son of Tvartko, Stephen Ostoya, ascended the throne of Bosnia in 1398. Elected by his barons, he submitted to their authority and they exercised the effective power of the state. All of them were hostile to Sigismund and favored the claims of Ladislas of Naples, who in the meantime, had appointed one of their number, the Duke Hervoye, his viceroy of Croatia. In retaliation Sigismund invaded Bosnian land,

but suffered a terrific defeat in this engagement.

All this strife and uncertainty along the Adriatic seacoast was the result of equally discouraging conditions in Hungary herself. The country became the stage of the party fights of oligarchs who were distrustful of Sigismund as an alien, and did not tolerate in their own home sovereignty of others than their own. In a surprise attack a party of rebels seized Sigismund and incarcerated him in the stronghold of Shiklosh. In this new situation Ladislas of Naples became the strongest contender, being a scion of a famous dynasty, a candidate of Croatia, Dalmatia and Bosnia, a protege of Pope Boniface IX, that of the King of Poland, and that of the Duke of Austria. Finally he was supported by a party of Hungarian barons who favored choosing from among their own number a person capable of bearing the crown of Saint Stephen, but who had no such candidate in their own ranks. In the meantime Sigismund's captivity was ended after four months of confinement. Precisely those who imprisoned him, let him go free.

In the meantime, during Sigismund's imprisonment, the Neapolitan party had gained great strength. It was intensified by the Estates of Bosnia, which had espoused the cause of Ladislas, while their powerful magnate, the Duke Hervoye, exerted extreme effort to win over the hesitating Dalmatian cities to the same cause. So he negotiated with the city of Zadar, which eventually joined his side. The city of Trogir (Trau) was partial to this combination, but wanted to make a final declaration after the decision of the other communities. However, Split was won over by the legitimist party and took up arms against Hervoye, captured Almissa (Omish), one of the powerful strongholds of the Bosnian duke, and finally expressed its readiness to submit to Venice. However, Venice declined the offer.

Ragusa (Dubrovnik) likewise rejected the Bosnian domination. Venice was noncommittal while waiting for more propitious developments, for she was caught between two fires, the power of Sigismund, and that of Neapolitan Ladislas. All the Dalmatian cities became divided, one favoring loyalty to Sigismund, and the other to Ladislas, the King of Naples. A sort of civil war broke out. Ragusa sent a fleet to Split in order to restore the aristocratic regime. The opposing factions destroyed each other. The cities of Zadar, Shibenik, Trogir were crowded with refugees. The 15th century rolled in with the fantastic adventure of Ladislas of Naples.

In this condition of strife and confusion Ladislas finally decided to act. On June 17, 1402 he sent the chief commander of the Neapolitan navy, Louis Aldemarisco de Maresci, to the Adriatic, with a fleet of five galleys. He gave him supreme power in Dalmatia, a power which included the widest authority and fullest jurisdiction in the matters of peace and war. Upon the news that Ladislas' fleet was approaching the Adriatic Sea, the Venetian admiral, Capitano in golfo, requested instructions from the Senate. The answer was neutrality. The Neapolitan fleet arrived in the port of Zadar without incident, in the month of August, 1402. Under the pressure of Ladislas' galleys, Zadar submitted to the Neapolitan sovereignty, but in order to avoid any complication in case of the contenders' defeat, it raised the flag of both kings on the main square. All of Dalmatia, except Ragusa submitted to the authority of Aldemarisco de Maresci in the name of his king, Ladislas of Naples.

Everything seemed to point to the expulsion of Sigismund and to the success of Ladislas. The Hungarian and Croatian barons, his adherents, armed themselves and invited the Neapolitan to have himself crowned the king of Hungary and Croatia. At the same time Venice refused to pay Sigismund the tribute imposed on her by the treaty of Torino (1381). She claimed that this was merely a temporary matter since the kingdom was in turmoil, and because the king was absent from the country. Boniface IX, Pope of Rome also sided with the opponents. He dismissed the archbishop of Split, Andrew Gualdo, who was a loyal partisan of Sigismund, and replaced him with Pellegrino di Aragona, an agent of Ladislas.

So everything was ready. Ladislas landed at Zadar on the 19th of July, 1403, where he was received by his partisan, the prince primate of the church of Hungary and the apostolic legate of Boniface IX, Cardinal Acciajoli. However, the insignia of the kingdom, which included the bible on which the oath is taken, was in Hungary. Therefore Ladislas was encouraged to go to Alba Regia (Gyula Fehérvár) in order to have himself crowned with the crown of Saint Stephen.

But Ladislas was afraid of Sigismund and had himself crowned in Zadar, biding his time for the other ceremony. On the 5th of August, 1403, the prince primate of the church of Hungary, Archbishop of Estergom (Ostrogon, Gran) anointed and crowned Ladislas with a substitute crown and proclaimed him king of Hungary. But this ceremony was decried by the partisans of Sigismund as an illegal act bordering on sacrilege.

Ladislas, master of the two coasts of Adriatic, had upset the plans of the Republic of Saint Mark. But what could Venice do at this moment? She was still weak on the sea. Her fleet had been neglected ever since the treaty of Zadar. The treasury was exhausted after the war of Chioggia. The ships' crews lacked confidence ever since the conspiracy of Doge Faliero.

As far as Ragusa (Dubrovnik) was concerned, its diplomatic intrigue expressed itself in all its flexibility. Even before the problematic arrival of Ladislas, Ragusa made contact with Hervoye. Its envoy had to declare to the viceroy of Ladislas, who was not yet crowned, that Ragusa would pay its dues only to a permanent king and ruler of Hungary. The Ragusans hoped that Ladislas would never cross the Adriatic. But at the news of his landing in Zadar, they sent a priest as ambassador to Zadar, who made contact with the Hungarian and Croatian barons, and declared that Ragusa was religiously keeping out of the controversy to whom the crown belonged. As far as Ladislas was concerned, the ambassador had to genuflect before him, and with flowery protestations of loyalty, he had recommended the Ragusan republic to him.

Further, he lost no time in complaining about the Neapolitan naval units which were attacking Ragusan merchant ships and accused the king of Bosnia of felony and brigandage. But the ambassador had to conceal the real sentiments of the Republic, and merely declared that Ragusa had no power to set on the throne or depose from such the king of Hungary, since this power belonged to the barons of the kingdom. In compliance with his instructions he declared solemnly that the Republic did not bear judgment on the king himself but on the crown (of Hungary) and she would not recognize anyone unless he possessed the crown of St. Stephen. And no one could more sharply and obviously insult the king of Naples, than Ragusa who considered the constitutional ceremonies performed in Zara as null and void. Ladislas immediately understood this and in the way of a reply, he sent the Neapolitan fleet to ravage the Ragusan territory, yet his galleys were forced to retreat.

However, thinking that he had won the game, Ladislas put up all efforts to ingratiate himself with the Dalmatian cities by giving them decrees confirming their communal franchises. At the same time Sigismund displayed before the people in his palace at Vishegrad the authentic crown of St. Stephen. Furthermore he sent his expression of thanks to Dubrovnik, and made preparations to meet the Hungarian rebels face to face. He also announced wide-spread amnesty in order to win the good will of the people.

On the other hand, Ladislas was confronted from the first day with recalcitrance of the communities. He wanted to fortify these cities against the inroads of Sigismund's partisans. However the city of Trogir, as the moral chief of the prospective league, was opposed to his orders, and declared that in case of necessity it would resort to force in order to enforce respect for its privileges. The success of Sigismund in the wake of the coronation ceremony had greatly impressed Ladislas. He promptly left Dalmatia, after appointing Voyevode (Duke Hervoya) his vicar general in Hungary, Dalmatia, and Croatia. At the same time he conferred on Hervoya, in defiance of the basic statute of Split, the title of Duke of Split.

Nothing else was needed to inspire this Croatian-Bosnian magnate with his ultimate ambition to seize royal power in Dalmatia. He certainly did not restrict himself to the limits of modesty. And yet, he could not become a king. He remained a vassal and never changed this status for better. However he acted as a sovereign, governed as a sovereign, oppressed, tyrannized, and resorted to extortions. With remarkable ingenuity he made Split and the rest of Dalmatia accept a will power conscious of its purpose, while complete confusion prevailed in all the other wills and plans. Ragusa was the only city which remained outside of this imbroglio. She became rich and powerful and thereby drew more and more the wrath of those who laid their claims on Dalmatia. The king of Bosnia, Thomas Stephen Ostoya, who represented the unstable equilibrium of the politics of the Balkans, was looking for a quarrel with this Republic. On the other hand Ragusa plotted his deposition, sought all over for allies and, by the example given by the king Ladislas, she stooped even to sue for the Sultan's aid, who was only too glad to interfere in the affairs of the Christian nations. She made every effort, at the same time, to prevent an agreement between Bosnia and Sigismund. Her diplomatic action, which came to the point of offering to Sigismund the partition of Bosnia, and the flatteries with which it showered the Duke of Split, had for their result the downfall of Ostoya.

After a war which was conducted halfheartedly, just haphazardly, Ragusa formulated her terms very much in line with typical adjustments following each war.

But they did not get anywhere with King Ostoya. True enough, he was deposed by the barons, and the son of the great Tvartko was proclaimed the King of Bosnia under the name of Tvartko I. But Ostoya still enjoyed the protection of Sigismund. So, for a moment there were two kings and three garrisons, the third one being the Hungarian garrison. The confusion was complete. Ragusa wrote to a great Bosnian baron with a calculated exaggeration that "ever since the great flood there was nothing so upset and more resembling a chaos than the present moment". Only that chaos was to her advantage. With the new king, it was the peace and restoration of territories which Ostoya took from Ragusa.

Sigismund insisted upon carrying on war in Bosnia, a war without positive results, which weakened the country and made it incapable to resist the Turkish invasion. Moreover, it set the stage for the enslavement of Hungary. Venice, happy over Hungary's absence in Dalmatia, made a treaty of alliance with Ladislas and disregarding the peace of Torino, it took Albania by force. The Neapolitan naval forces found their way back to the Adriatic under the leadership of Jean de Lusignan, duke of Bari. He took the title of count of Zadar, seized the island of Rab (Arbe) as well as the cities of Novigrad and Skradin, but Shibenik and Trogir repulsed him. The presence of the Neapolitan flag finally excited Hervoye's jealousy. In order to spite his sire, he abandoned Ladislas' cause and declared himself, somewhat belatedly for Sigismund. The future king of the Romans and their emperor once more invaded Bosnia, and Tvartko II fell victim. The Neapolitan party was wiped out. The Dalmatian communities again acclaimed Sigismund who sent them the trophies of his victories. But Ladislas stuck to the last vestiges of his royal mantle. Zadar, with the castle of the Templars, and the small city of Novigrad, and the island of Pag continued to stand by Ladislas. Venice knew how to use such a situation to her advantage.

Since 1400 Venice refused to pay the tribute imposed upon her by the peace of Torino. An inquiry of Sigismund's court in 1401 was confronted with a stubborn refusal to discuss the Dalmatian issue, which had been resolved for the king ever since the days of Torino. On the third of September, 1402, Zadar made an oath of loyalty to King Ladislas. Venice saw her hour come. While Sigismund became more insistent in demanding his tribute, Venice was pushed toward a decision. In 1403 Sigismund and his court got wind of the secret negotiations going on between Ladislas and the Venetian senate. He promptly dispatched his protest to the Serenissime; "The peace of Torino formally forbids you to get involved in Dalmatian affairs. Besides, you should know that King Ladislas is not a legitimate master of Dalmatia, but an adventurer. Dalmatia belongs legally to the crown of Hungary of which, by the grace of God, we are the legitimate owner". Venice therefore was fully advised. She kept quiet for the time being.

Ladislas, in his fantastic action and bent for adventure, was a person who was cut out just right for the skillful and the cynical merchants of the lagoon. As all the sovereigns of his time, but more so than they, he was in need of money. Lacking all scruples, he contracted marriages and dissolved them for the jingling gold coins, and was even planning to marry a daughter of Sultan Bayezid for a sizeable purse.

"I am a poor king, protector of peoples and a friend of the plunderers", he inscribed on his flags. All his expeditions were organized with the view to a profitable business affair, financial, commercial, and industrial. Not without courage, after he was through with his Hungarian adventure, he placed his stake on Rome against Avignon, occupied a good part of the Papal territory

and threatened the cities of Tuscany. He was through with Dalmatia. After a brief infatuation the Dalmatians turned away from him. Moreover, he became embroiled with Rome and dreaded the might of Sigismund. But the principal motive, typical and decisive, which controlled all his actions, was money. And behold, a splendid opportunity came to sight. Venice wanted to buy, Ladislas was eager to sell. At this moment he needed funds badly to continue his struggle with his personal enemy, Pope Gregory XII. Dalmatia itself, was at all times for him only a business affair, good or bad, according to the circumstances. His constitutional oath, his sworn decrees for the benefit of the cities, his attachment to the main city of Dalmatia, were merely pretexts for him to reap some financial gain.

Venice, on the other hand, was not so urged. She wanted to keep tolerable relations with the king of Hungary, and in order to satisfy her appetite by conserving her good relations with Sigismund, she resorted to all the tricks of her remarkable diplomatic genius. But Ladislas was pressed and speed was essential. He asked from Serenissime three hundred thousand ducats for Dalmatia. The Venetian senate found the sum grossly exaggerated. A shameful bargaining followed the offer. On the 30th of January Ladislas was ready to accept two hundred thousand ducats, on the fourth of February, one hundred and fifty thousand ducats, and finally he decided to settle for one hundred thousand ducats. But the Venetians' counter offer was sixty thousand, utmost seventy thousand, payable in three annuities. Hard pressed by the need of the moment, Ladislas sent a naval fleet to the Adriatic to impress Venice with his presence in Dalmatia and also to pretend to defend what his legal possession was there. Disturbed herself, Venice decided to sign. Michael Steno in his rank of doge, signed on the 9th of July, 1409, in the church of St. Silvester, an agreement by the terms of which she purchased for one hundred thousand ducats from Ladislas, the "King of Hungary, all his possessions in Dalmatia, notably the city and castle of Zadar with its territory, the cities of Novigrad, Vrana, and the island of Pag, with all his 'rights' over Dalmatia."

Obviously this was fraudulent and illegal, having all the earmarks of nullity. Ladislas had no rights over Dalmatia. He resided abroad. He had not properly been crowned. Sigismund could not recognize this transaction. Neither could Hungary or Croatia. Naturally, due to the absence of a legitimate ruler, and by the ever growing peril of Turkish invasions, the possession of Dalmatia should not and could not have been consecrated by shreds of parchments or illegal charts, but only by force of arms. This act of sale and cession was received with consternation in Ragusa and Split. In Zadar, profoundly humiliated and offended, incapable of any reaction whatsoever, the people resorted to insurrection against the Neapolitan government and hoisted the flag of St. Mark in order to avoid the ignominy of recognition of the sale of their city.

Four Venetian proveditors arrived in Zadar in order to take possession of the city. Upon leaving Zadar, the Neapolitan garrison sacked the city and set it on fire. The Venetians put out the fire, restored order and took possession of the city. In the cathedral of Saint Mark, a Te Deum mass was celebrated in the presence of the doge.

The Venetians set out immediately to fortify the city of Zadar. They built a new citadel, surrounded the city by a wide and deep moat and severed an isthmus which connected the city with the mainland. Zadar actually became an island. The vanquished Patricians, in their expectations to be subjected, sent a dozen deputies to Venice in order to make an oath of loyalty to the Doge. A Dalmatian historian who dedicated his work to prince Eugene, vice-roy of Italy wrote: "There is not one single senator who accepted in good faith the protestations of loyalty of the Zadar deputies, guided by necessity rather than by sentiment." On the 5th of September all the citizens of Zadar were recorded as Venetian citizens.

During negotiations with Ladislas, Venice assured Sigismund that she had no greater nor more faithful friend than the Serenissime of Venice.

Upon the news of the loyalty oath made by the people of Zadar to Venice, Sigismund made preparations for war. He cast his eyes to the Friulian area which was a well-known road for all invasions, it being the neuralgic point of the Republic.

In July, 1411 Sigismund became King of Germany and King of the Romans. Therefore in his desire to take revenge for the loss of his maritime cities, he demanded land which the Venetians, in acordance with the Germanic thesis, retained as a toe of the empire. The war that broke out in 1413 was preceded by substantial negotiations which did not prevent Venice from seizing new areas in Dalmatia and placing Sigismund before an accomplished fact. Rab and Pag had been occupied, but Trogir resisted occupation. The Venetians laid seige to Shibenik and offered twenty thousand ducats to anyone who would surrender the city. The common people rebelled against the nobility which leaned towards the Venetian side. Some of them surrendered the external towers, but the city itself continued its resistance. A Venetian fleet, under the command of Pietro Loredan, came to the rescue, but the common people repulsed the attack.

These events interrupted negotiations with Sigismund. Venice pleaded to occupy Zadar and other places in the interest of the king, since the possession of same had prevented Ladislas from proceeding to Hungary. As Sigismund kept insisting on his demands, Venice raised her voice and replied that she held Dalmatia as compensation for services rendered to the king. If he gave up his title of the King of Dalmatia, Venice would offer him compensation in the amount of fifty thousand ducats, and furthermore in acknowledgement of his sovereignty (dominium eminense) over the country, it would pay him an annual gift of a golden mantle and a white shawl. Sigismund rejected the whole proposition. But up to this point it was not the war itself. War broke out when Sigismund demanded permission from Venice to pass through her territory in order to make his trip to Rome. Ill advised, the Republic denied this request, and war broke out.

The Hungarians invaded Italy in September, 1411. But apart from several conquests of the second order, Sigismund could not achieve any further sucess. Treviso could maintain its resistance. A party of Hungarian troops under the Florentine condottiere, Lorenzo dei Scolari, returned to Hungary.

This failure made Sigismund decide to assume a personal command in Italy. But he was short of money. He hesitated. Under these circumstances, Pope John XXIII offered his mediation. Through this channel Sigismund sent to the

Venetian ambasasdors Marco Dandolo and Lorenzo Bragadin in Rome the following terms: First, compensation for the losses suffered at Shibenik; Two, war indemnity of five to six hundred thousand ducats; Three, the transfer of Zadar to Venice, in exchange for an annual gift of a scarlet tent or falcon as a sign of Hungarian sovereignty over the city; Four, free passage to Rome. However, the negotiators could not reach an agreement. The ambassadors interrupted the negotiations and left Rome. The war was renewed at its best. Sigismund demanded an eighty thousand florin loan from Poland, the payment of which was guaranteed by the cities of the Hungarian county of Zips.

Sigismund's fleet, under the orders of Genovese Admiral Hugolin Doria, was almost bottled up in Trogir, and revealed itself unable to undertake any action of grand style. After a few partial successes in the march on Treviso, Sigismund's armies were defeated at Livenza, August 24, 1412. In Dalmatia things went from bad to worse. The siege of Shibenik, which cost much in both blood and money, was prolonged indefinitely. Under the bulwarks of the city, bands of mercenaries whom no one could trust, were operating. In April, 1411, it was reported in Venice that the Hungarian mercenaries intended to join the service of the Republic. They were replaced by fresh Hungarian troops. They were ordered to reinstate the expelled aristocrats and to be severe on the chiefs of the popular movement.

These Draconian measures against Sigismund's partisans provoked a complete change of mind in Shibenik. An ambassador of the community came to Venice in July, 1412 and declared to the Signory that the city, cruelly offended and vilified by Sigismund, would like to place itself under the protection and sovereignty of Venice. Shibenik surrendered in October. It retained its statutes and the Republic reserved the right to send a patrician of her own to administer the city. Following the agreements in Shibenik, the same conditions were offered to the city of Trogir in case she wanted to submit to Venetian sovereignty. But Trogir refused the offer. In 1413 Venice declared war on the city. A part of the fleet which was cruising around the beleaguered city landed and the territory of Trogir was devastated. The Trogirans answered this outrage by devastating the Venetian lands which lay closest

to their own territory. Split and the island controlled by Hervoye were left undisturbed. The Republic recognized the sovereignty of the Bosnian banus appointed by Ladislas. In this year of 1413, the condition of the affairs in Dalmatia was as follows: Venice was in possession of Zadar and Shibenik; Hervoye controlled Split and the islands. Only the city of Trogir was independent. Thus Ladislas' infamous bargain had taken its course, but Sigismund did not recognize his rights. This implicated great difficulties in the organization of the communities and their relations with Venice.

It was necessary to give some satisfaction to the citizenry. The Zarans, the eternal rebels—could not compromise with the Venetian regime. Its patricians had lost everything. They were deprived of the offices and privileges which they enjoyed under the royal regime. They recriminated against Sigismund, but profited from his rule by getting pensions and gifts. Some of them took refuge in Hungary in order to conspire with those who remained in their ancestral homes. There was quite a large number of impoverished noblemen who could be purchased, but who could be equally bribed by the enemies of Venice. The most dangerous elements were those who had been expelled from the city and who had taken refuge with some relatives on the mainland. As far as the poor people were concerned, they had been dispersed. In spite of all her dispositions, Venice could not remain tranquil until she had made some arrangements with Sigismund.

After the bargain was struck with Ladislas, and up to the siege and capitulation of Shibenik, negotiations never ceased for a moment. Due to the insisting demands of Sigismund—especially in the case of Zadar, a Venetian mission was sent to Hungary. It declared to the king that this occupation, from his point of view, should be peaceful. The Republic desired only to purge the Adriatic sea from pirates, and besides, the neighborhood of Venice could have automatically prevented any expedition directed by Ladislas against his kingdom. The ambassadors also brought to the king's attention the services rendered by the Republic to his Majesty by freeing Queen Marie.

The mission returned home rather discomfited. Then Venice produced her financial arguments. She offered Sigismund seven to ten thousand ducats a year, and further raised it to fifty thousand for Zadar, Shibenik and Trogir. In 1412, this sum was further raised to one hundred thousand ducats. Venice would renounce to Split. Later the Republic declared herself ready to pay Sigismund three hundred thousand ducats for the rest of Dalmatia, while Ladislas had to satisfy himself with a mere one hundred thousand—and two hundred thousand for Shibenik and Trogir. Still there was no end of surprises. After the fall of Shibenik, Venice made the following proposition to the king. She would restore all of Dalmatia to the king if she recovered the price paid to Ladislas and all the expenses incurred in organizing the land. This was a new stratagem of Venetian diplomacy for she was well aware of the financial difficulties of the emperor and the legitist policy of his court. The Senate was sure that Sigismund could not accept this offer, for it would place a heavy financial burden on his depleted Treasury.

After this clever move of the Signory, doomed to failure by design, the Venetians sought everywhere for Allies against Sigismund. In 1411 they sent a mission to Poland, to King Ladislas II, the Yagiellonian, and husband of the younger daughter of Louis the Great of Hungary, who was willing to make an alliance against Sigismund in order to prevent him from coming to Italy and have himself crowned as an emperor. The Venetians did their utmost to lay to rest the apprehensions of the Yagiellonian. For them the coronation was not important, but it was necessary to create a military situation which would prevent Sigismund from conducting serious operations in Italy. Venice took it upon herself to persist in the struggle to the end, and to prevent Sigismund from proceeding on his march to Italy. Ladislas II of Poland himself was after the imperial crown, should the Signory give him support and free passage in Italy. But the King of Poland was not a reliable ally; Sigismund made peace with him in 1412.

Venice then turned to the eternal trouble maker, Ladislas of Naples. The latter took advantage of the Serenissime's request in order to propose an offensive alliance with her against their enemies. However, Venice decided it was a poor bargain for it would involve her in all the Italian disputes of this quarrelsome indi-

vidual. So she took pains not to come to terms with him because, even under the best conditions, she would have to unstring her purse. Therefore Venice simply offered Ladislas an alliance to help him get hold of the Hungarian-Croatian throne. By recognizing his title as King of Croatia and Hungary, Venice proposed to send troops to the eastern coast of the Adriatic which was without defense because Sigismund, with all his available forces, was already in Friulia. Venice would have placed her galleys at the disposition of the Neapolitan troops across the sea; she would even transport them to the Dalmatian territory and what counted most for Ladislas—she would set up the whole expedition at her own expense.

Ladislas accepted the Serenissime's offer, but the whole plan was dropped because in the meantime, Sigismund made a truce with Venice. Before this agreement Venice even went to the Turks to get support. The Turks certainly could not refuse to interfere in the complications of the European policy. Long before the fall of Constantinople, they could well sound the entire depth of the strife among the "infidels", and they prepared their plan of conquest.

Lashed by the blows of adversity and in spite of his pretension of power and warlike appearances, and aided by the thought that he could impose his will upon Venice and the north of Italy, Sigismund saw himself forced to sign a five years' truce on the 23rd of April, 1413, on the basis that each party retain those lands which it had in its possession (uti posidetis). In addition, the king was permitted, in case of necessity, to pass through Venetian territory. Venice scored a triumph all along the line and was still to have future successes.

Throughout the duration of the truce, Sigismund became involved in religious disputes which resulted in the convocation of the council of Constanza, and consequently he fully neglected Dalmatia. Venice, on the other hand, outwardly conforming to the terms of the truce, undertook every means to win over Dalmatian sympathies. Not all the communities in Dalmatia shared the same aversion toward the Republic of St. Mark. The truculent Balkan princelings and the dangers with which their raids in the coastal areas threatened the cities, as well as the furious struggle of the barons unchecked by any authority, and finally the disastrous invasion of the Turks who were approaching the western part, greatly served the purpose of Venetian propaganda over certain points of the coastland. Thus if Trogir and Split—Ragusa standing apart —were still nourishing some hope of Sigismund's armed aid, without listening to the voice of Venice, Cattaro (Kotor), in a critical condition sent an embassy to the Venetian Senate, pleading to be taken under the Signory's protection. Yet, Venice answered negatively to this exasperated request.

Immediately after the truce, Venice was fortunate to witness the end of Sigismund's opposition and she resumed negotiations. The Venetian Senate offered the king a sum of seven thousand ducats yearly if he would renounce Dalmatia for at least a period of thirty years. The emperor of Byzantium Manuel II, also took part in these negotiations, being led by the hope that Sigismund would compose his differences with Venice so that he could aid him in his struggle with the Turks. But no entreaties could prevail upon Sigismund, whose obstinacy had no equal, except the absolute lack of means to support his exaggerated wishfulness. However, an unexpected event came to the rescue of the Serenissime.

This was the crisis which Sigismund started in Split in his determination to cause the downfall of Hervoye. But Duke Hervoye refused to face his doom without resistance. In the ensuing struggle he unfurled the flag of insurrection against the king and sued for the support of Venice as a citizen of the city of St. Mark. In order to preserve the city of Split with Venetian aid, Hervoye tried hard to capture the city of Trogir. At the same time he offered to reduce the other Dalmatian cities as well. But Venice did not care to be obligated to a powerful baron at a time when an agreement with Sigismund, kept away from the coastlands and involved in European rivalries, appeared to the Venetian Senate a more welcome solution. However the fall of Hervoye merely speeded up the end. The little Dalmatian republics, after the fall of the Duke of Split, remained defenseless before Venice, a power in its full ascendancy under the wise rule of Thomas Mocenigo, a doge of peaceful inclination. Therefore the immediate objective of Venice was to weaken these proud communities to unconditional submission to the power of Venice.

In 1415 Turkish troops appeared in the vicinity of Split and Trogir, probably remnants of the bands which Hervoye engaged against Sigismund.

Taking advantage of this situation, Venice sent instructions to the counts of Zadar and Shibenik to leave the Turks unmolested, which caused the just anger of Sigismund. Not without semblance of cause, he accused the Serenissime of taking advantage of the Turkish troops for an attack on Croatian territory. At the expiration of the truce, the Venetian government, in order to complete occupation of the Dalmatian cities, resorted to all manner of shady means and before all to ruse and graft. Parties were formed in Split and Trogir which were in the pay of the Signory. The new king of Bosnia, Stephen Tvartko II, took part in the plot at a time when Sigismund was deeply involved in Bohemia and was seeking allies among the Byzantines and Serbs in order to ward off the Turkish danger. At that moment Venice thought she could drop the mask and proceed with the double expedition against Trogir and Split. Split, which detested its own duke, received the anathema issued by Sigismund against Hervoye, with a sigh of relief. Split celebrated its deliverance by decreeing on the 8th of July, 1413 the construction of a church dedicated to St. Guy (Guy), acknowledging its liberation "from pharaonic slavery". In the meantime Hervoye sent his letters to Sigismund, which were left unanswered, and likewise his appeals to Venice. Left in the lurch, Hervoye appealed to the Turks for aid. In the year 1415 the Bosnians defeated the imperial forces. Hervoye was at the peak of his career. His great enemy, the banus Paul Chupor of Moslavina, had been captured, sewed in the hide of a bull, and thrown in the Bosnia River. But Hervoye did not survive long his triumph for he died in April, 1416. He belonged to that class of barons which expedited the fall of the Bosnian monarchy, a special personal class, egotistic, contaminated with oriental heresies, and hardly Christian. A grandee with inclination to rule in the way of a tyrant and exact pressure on those under his thumb, Hervoye did not leave —except a tower in Split—any cultural trail of his rise to power.

Sigismund compensated Ragusa for her fidelity

by awarding her three great islands; Brazza (Brach), Lesina (Hvar), and Curzola (Korchula). But stirred up by the agents of Venice, they refused to accept the sovereignty of Ragusa. Ragusa complained to the king, and armed a fleet (1413) in order to seize the islands, the ownership to which had been claimed by two Bosnian barons. Sigismund did not understand this complication at all. He renewed in 1414 a message to the island communities not to oppose Ragusan authorities. Brazza (Brach) and Lesina (Hvar) submitted, but Curzola (Korchula) refused, being sure that sooner or later it would fall under the power of venice. Fearing that Ragusa could not control the three large islands, Sigismund turned them over to a knight of his court, but Venice definitely got hold of them in 1420. Ragusa had to become satisfied with the cession of the southern part of Konavli (Canali) by the Bosnian baron Sandalj Hranich, and of the ancient city of Epidaurus (Tsavtat), by another, Radoslav Pavlovich.

The events shaped worse and worse for Sigismund. Carried on without sufficient means, the war degenerated into a long series of disasters for the king. The province of Friuli fell in the hands of the Venetians. The patriarchate of Aquileia (Oglaj) was occupied and suppressed.

In Dalmatia success had equally favored the arms of Venice. In November, 1418 she would have been satisfied with the possession of Zadar and Shibenik, as well as abolition of the reparations established in Torino. But three months later, the captain of the Gulf (Capitano in Golfo) received the order to capture Split and Trogir. Sigismund had in vain issued orders to build galleys in the arsenal of Trogir, and charged the banus of Croatia with preparations for a long campaign. The dynamic actions of Venice promptly bested the king's lack of will power. Venice had rebuilt her naval power. She hastened to achieve a goal on which nearly 40 doges were working. She did not care to attack the powerful Ragusa, which was and would forever be at the outer limits of her empire, but she would, at least, take possession of Trogir and Split. Trogir resisted the fierce assaults of the Venetian troops under Pietro Loredan for only three days. At nightfall of the third day the exhausted Trogir surrendered (22nd June, 1420). A week later Loredan received a delegation from

Split which submitted to Venice. The Venetian fleet pased in view of Ragusa, without sufficient courage to attack it, but it entered the gulf of Cattaro (Kotor), and the city authorities surrendered to the Republic. Venice had to promise the citizens of Cattaro that she would never deliver the city to kings of Croatia and Hungary. In September and October, Curzola, Brazza, and Lesina (Korchula, Brach, and Hvar) were occupied. Sigismund was forced to make a two years' truce (1428).

Activities took on a new impetus under the terms of Francis Foscari, the Doge following the death of Mocenigo. On the other hand, Sigismund did nothing whatsoever to defend or recapture his possessions in Dalmatia. On the contrary, the complications that broke out in the Empire forced him to make another truce with Venice.

Due to the course of circumstances Sigismund sank so low that he asked Venice for a loan of ten thousand ducats for his trip to Rome and Basel so that he could exert his influence in the election of a citizen of Venice (Eugene IV) to the papal throne.

Even as emperor, crowned by Eugene IV on the 31st day of May, 1433, Sigismund was equally helpless in his contest with Venice, and after a new truce was signed in 1433, he finally decided to make peace with Venice on the 7th of April, 1437. He recognized all the Venetian territorial gains in the north of Italy, and their annexations. But Dalmatia was not even mentioned. Apparently Sigismund was reconciled to the unpleasant fact of Venetian occupation, but did not want to make any concession de jure, and his successors observed scrupulously the non-possumus clause to the very end of the Republic (1798). As far as Venice was concerned, she was satisfied with the possession of the land, and never insisted on the legal recognition of her conquest. That was a provisional arrangement which lasted three centuries.

On the 9th of December, 1437, Sigismund died in Znaim, a small town of Moravia.

Upon the death of Sigismund the King of Croatia and Hungary still possessed the Croatian coastland (ancient Liburnia), but in Dalmatia he retained chiefly a part of the back-country, including Scardona (Skradin), Bribir, Ostrovitsa, Knin, Verlika, Sinj and Klis. Even later when most of this territory was lost either to Venice or to the Turks, the kings proudly attached to their royal titles also that of the King of Dalmatia signifying thereby that they never had relinquished their claim to that country and to the eastern coast of the Adriatic.

From the point of view of security it was high time for Venice to get hold of the Dalmatian cities, for the Ottoman (Turkish) flood, through the conquest of the Albanian coast, was approaching the central and upper (northern) Adriatic coast.

After a long string of victories the Turks appear in 1468 at the very city limits of Skradin, Zadar and Split. They broke through the frontiers of Croatia and the province of Friuli was threatened. Venice seized two points of strategic importance—the stronghold of Ostrovitsa and Klis, and the defense against the Turkish invasion was ahead of all other considerations. In 1480 King Mathias Corvinus attempted once again to reconquer at least central Dalmatia including Split. He planned a military campaign and captured the port of Senj (Segna) as his base of operation. Finally in 1481 the Venetians got hold of the remaining Dalmatian territory when they occupied the northern island of Veglia (Kerk) which still carried on with a semblance of independence under the rule of the princes of Frankapani.

Thus Venice founded her Adriatic empire with energy and skill, a characteristic which was particularly her own. On the other hand the Dalmatian cities, with the exception of Ragusa (Dubrovnik), had to submit to their cruel fate after long agony and desperate resistance.

Betrayal of Dalmatia (League of Cambray)

The 16th and 17th Century was the saddest period in the history of Dalmatia. The country was fully in the power of the Venetian conquerors, the communal life was either destroyed or reduced to a low ebb, the city statutes were revised, an dchanged, and had merely an effect of striving to restore the age-old memories; this situation was still further aggravated by civil wars between the aristocracy and the denizens of the cities, and by the Turkish invasion. As a result of it all came the loss of population, with devastations throughout the country, while the fields providing food supplies were left unculti-

vated. In the midst of general distress, epidemics and famine were taking their toll. Here and there there were still flashes of heroism in the service of Christianity. Finally the very thought of liberation was abandoned and the country fell into a lethargy from which Dalmatia was to be aroused only by the thunders of the French revolution. Napoleon's victories finally smashed the dominant republic of Venice with a series of fatal blows.

However even before the coming of the great French general there was a serious attempt to return Dalmatia to her freedom. Unfortunately, this effort was half-hearted and therefore doomed. This last opportunity was given through the complicated course of events characterizing the League of Cambray, which was concluded on the 10th of December, 1508 between Pope Julius II, Emperor Maximilian of Hapsburg, and the King of France, Louis XII. It was gradually joined by the King of Aragon, King of England, Duke of Savoy, Duke of Ferrara and the Florentine Republic. This league was aiming its arrow against both the Turks and Venice which were treated as an ally of Turkey. However, the Turks served more as a pretext to destroy Venice than as a real enemy. In fact that was an alliance to dismember the Venetian empire.

The organizer of this league was the "elected" Emperor Maximilian of Austria, who was influenced by his energetic daughter Margaret. The governing chairman of the league was Pope Julius II of the family of Della Rovere, who was a sworn enemy of Venice to the point of excommunicating the Republic. But as the course of events complicated the issues, this Pontiff changed his mind and became the very savior of the Republic in a desperate situation.

This European coalition against the Republic of St. Mark was deeply rooted in the past. In fact it was formed during the rule of the Doge Francis Foscari, when Venice set out on a policy to conquer the mainland (terra firma), with huge reserve of manpower and lucrative income, which had attracted the Serenissime. Through her continental expansion, this city of the lagoons, had come into conflict with the ambitious aspirations of the most powerful north Italian state, the Duchy of Milano, that is with France which had conveniently established herself in that province; in regard to Ferrara, Venice came at loggerheads with the Papal State, while Florence was fighting all her schemes of conquest.

Through her schemes upon Goritsa and Trieste, upon Friuli and Trentino, Venice provoked the hatred of the emperor, stirred up all manner of plans against her, produced no amount of jealous fits and finally a moment came when the princes and statesmen of Italy saw in her expansion an imperialist plan to subject all of Italy to her suzerain power. Quite naturally the House of Austria was at the head of this alliance against the hated rival. Goritsa, Trieste, Fiume, Friuli and the cities of the north of Italy, which for a long time in the past were in direct contact with the Empire and on which Venice set her envious eyes, prompted the Emperor to organize an alliance for powerful action against Venice.

Each of the allied powers made accusations against Venice. So the king of France, Louis XII, made a vitriolic charge against the Serenissime for cutting his road to Italy, in spite of his request to return and restore the border towns, castles, fortifications and other seaports which the Venetians held without a valid title. Therefore he sent his peremptory demand to the Venetians to restore to the Holy See, to the Emperor as well as to the Catholic kings of Spain and to other princes and communities the areas they had seized in violation of the law. In case of their defiance and refusal to comply with his demand, they would be held liable for all the damages and harm caused to these Christian States. Maximilian's manifesto was no less violent and the Emperor flooded with his tract all the countries which he thought were ready to shake off the yoke of these greedy merchants of the lagoon.

The project of dismembering the Venetian state consisted of "disannexations" in the following order: The Pope would recover the cities of Romagna which had not as yet been restored by Venice, namely Faenza, Rimini, and Ravenna; Maximilian, in his capacity of the head of the Holy Roman Empire, would get Rovoretto, Verona, Vicenza, Padua, Treviso, Friuli, and the patriarchate of Aquileia; to the King of France as the Lord of Milano, the cities of Brescia, Cremona, Crema, Bergamo and Chiara d'Adda would be given; to the King of Aragon, who was at the same time King of Naples, the

six forts of Apulia would be returned. The island of Cyprus would go to the Duke of Savoy. All the areas would be returned to the Dukes of Ferrara and Mantua which had been occupied by the Venetians. Finally, the powers of the League turned to Ladislas II King of Croatia and Hungary, with an urgent invitation to recover Dalmatia, usurped by Venice and which, by the public law of Europe, belonged to the crown of St. Stephen. Thus nothing but the city of Venice itself would remain for the Republic except a part of distant colonies and the land possessions which would become precarious the moment she lost Dalmatia.

The loss of Dalmatia and her possessions on the mainland was certain death for Venice within a short period of time. But why should one keep Venice in existence? A hail of speeches, manifestoes, and pamphlets showered Venice, a circumstance entirely out of the ordinary in those times in Europe. This plainly shows how the merchants of Venice could accumulate so much hatred and jealousy against themselves by their immense wealth, by the force and stability of their government, and also by the sum total of the treasonable and perfidious tricks of their policy.

A typical example of this appraisal we find in the mission of the Ambassador of France, Louis Eliano (Hélien), a Piemontese from Verceil, who was sent in 1510 to Augsburg in order to arouse the emperor and the German princes for an unsparing campaign against the Republic of St. Mark. This orator called Venice "The most venomous and striking viper" (venenosissima ac resurgens vipera). His speech was a passionate accusation in which the Ambassador reviewed all the crimes of the Republic, some of which were true, while others were exaggerated. He said that the Venetian thirst for domination was above all imagination. He mentioned the sneaky annexation of Cyprus, the robbery of the patriarchate of Aquileia, the fraudulent occupation of Dalmatia. "The king of Croatia and Hungary is the witness from whom the Venetians have robbed three hundred islands, ten episcopal cities, two provinces, that of Dalmatia and Liburnia, a multitude of ports, and five hundred miles of seacoast . . . " "The Ragusans knew this very well. On the very threshold of Turkey they have a strong aristocracy which, by Venetian vexations and the oppression perpetrated by their fleet, have been pushed to such a depth of misery and despair that they had to seek the support of the Turks for which they are obligated to pay a tribute. Both the Italian and the Illyrian coast on the Adriatic Sea were so inextricably connected with each other that one could not live without the other. However, they were so widely separated by pestilent Venetian decrees and by piracy, that their people would sail in the Strait of Sicily in the most violent of storms rather than navigate in the Adriatic. The Italians who were born free and predestined to the life of the sea, were forced into a position to look at the sea rather than to make use of it. How many ships did these brigands stop, destroy, confiscate; how many merchants did they ruin by forcing them into bankruptcy through the loss of their goods? How many noble families and rich cities have been forced into misery by the same crowd? And what did they do in Alexandria? In Syria? In Asia? In Greece? In Africa? and in all the other seas where no one is permitted to sail except the Venetians themselves?"

By this speech we can assay the others.

The offensive started against the Venetians had decisive results from the first combat. On the 14th of May, 1509, the Venetian army was fully crushed by the French army near the village of Agnadello, between Oglio and Adda. The dreadful disaster was further aggravated by the incapacity of the Venetian commanders. The commander-in-chief, Bartolomeo Alviano, himself was taken prisoner. The entire Venetian artillery fell into the hands of the enemy.

This disaster precipitated a series of baneful events which pushed Venice to the very verge of abyss. In the meantime the powers of the League made every effort to get Hungary to join their league, for a victorious campaign in Dalmatia would have sealed the fate of Venice. In the same year the Venetians were defeated at Agnadello, their arsenal, one of the best arsenals in Europe, caught fire. This conflagration was attributed to the intrigues of Maximilian, for many workers in the arsenal were Dalmatians and Istrians who were loyal to the emperor. In the meantime Maximilian sent secret manifestos to the population of the mainland occupied by the Venetians.

These seditious proclamations could not avoid the attention of the Dalmatians, who in the meantime had formed a considerable part of the crews and personnel of the Venetian fleet. The number of "Slavs" (Dalmatians and Istrians) on board the naval vessels of Venice, in the arsenal and in general in the services of the government, was quite considerable. There could not be the slightest doubt that such imperial proclamations produced a deep impression upon the Dalmatians. The Venetians knew well the "free and violent nature of the Dalmatians", as it was stated in a report to the Doge. Besides, the Dalmatian plebians nourished a deep seated hatred against the nobility of their country, a sentiment which was in common with the masses of Padua and of other cities of the Venetian mainland. The rebellions throughout the duration of the War of Cambray in all the main cities of Dalmatia were not pleasant to the emperor, for they went counter to his plans and the diplomatic campaign which he, with his allies, undertook in Hungary and Croatia. They knew that the nobility sided with Croatia and Hungary and was friendly to the emperor. On the other hand the proveditor General Sebastiano Giustiniani was blamed in Venice for the severity with which he had put down the popular movement.

There was a delicate situation in that area. Venice could not permit the nobility to be entirely eliminated, but on the other hand she found it in her favor to watch benignly the popular uprisings directed against the patricians, since they were loyal to the king of Croatia and Hungary. At the same time the masses were in ebullition in Hungary herself, as a result of the Venetian agitations. The moment was one of extraordinary gravity. If Hungary had joined the League with sufficient forces, the Venetian defeat at Agnadello would have meant final disaster.

Therefore it was necessary to take immediate steps. Venice sent Pietro Pasqualigo to Hungary as her ambassador, a very talented gentleman, adroit and full of energy, which shines through his messages sent between 1509 to 1512, that is throughout the entire duration of the great crisis. They are immensely interesting. They give a picture of complete frustration prevailing in Hungary; of the weakness combined with the sinful apathy of the king, of the general condition of the country, which was not interested in the reconquest of Dalmatia. The country had no other need but that of money, since, after the brilliant exploits of Hunyadi and his son Corvinus, it had fallen back into chaos.

Venice had a short period of failures after her defeat, but rapidly, under the leadership of the Doge Leonardo Loredan, she recuperated her forces. She recaptured Padua on the 17th of July and forced the imperial forces on the 20th of October, to raise the siege of the city which the emperor wanted to recapture at all cost.

This was not yet the salvation, but a distant prospect. Venice had many anguishing hours yet to spend. In November, Pasqualigo visited Zagreb and had several contacts with the Croatian barons. They were always in a state of rebellion but Venice kept relations with them throughout this critical period. Venice made good use of their weakness and showered them with gold and favors of all kinds. But the greatest weakness of the Croatian hinterland was the imminent Turkish peril, which resulted after the crushing defeat of the Croatian forces in the battle of Udbina on the Corbavian fields (September 9, 1493).

In November, 1509, Pasqualigo made contacts in Zagreb with the Croatian magnates: Andrew Bot, banus of Croatia, the three Frankapani, Count John of Kerbava, Count Nicholas Zrinski, the Counts of Blagay and some others. They were in alliance with the Palatin of Hungary and with other Hungarian barons to raid Zadar and Nin, and to devastate their territory in case the Republic lost Padua. But the Venetians' success before Padua changed their mind about the project and now they were scared of the possible loss of Senj, a fief of the Frankapani. The banus apologized to Pasqualigo for furnishing aid to the enemies of the Republic. He assured Pasqualigo of his devotion to the Republic. Another Dalmatian-Croatian baron John Berislavich—whose family scored later glory in the fighting with the Turks—had informed his peers of his readiness to invade Dalmatia, but after being informed of the retreat of the emperor from Padua, he also changed his mind. When, on the 18th of November, the ambassador reported to his government, on the insistence of the King of France and the King of Romans (that is the

emperor) upon the necessity of undertaking a campaign in Dalmatia, the banus Andrew Bot offered to wage war, but demanded 1,000 soldiers from the king for this purpose.

Among these developments Pasqualigo found out that in Budavár a grand council of barons and high priests of the kingdom had decided to start a campaign in Dalmatia. They would send their six thousand horsemen with a large number of footsoldiers in order to complete this undertaking. But the whole thing was strenuously opposed by the archbishop of Ostrogon (Esztergom), the primate of the church of Hungary, Cardinal Thomas Bakach, who was by far the most influential person at the court. He had ambitions of his own, for he wanted the papal tiara himself. Capable and violent by his character, Thomas Bakach, a Croatian by origin, was not satisfied to command such position of influence in the government of his country. He was deeply interested in a crusade against the Turks in spite of the opposition of the nobility to arm the lower classes of the people. Bakach, however, managed to raise a whole army of the common people but could not carry out his project. Moreover, his precipitous activity became, in 1514, the signal for a rebellion of the peasants against the nobility, provoked in all appearance by the example of the Dalmatian masses and also perhaps by the underground activity of the Venetian government.

The Cardinal Archbishop of Ostrogon was the only support that Venice had during this troublesome period. He became an intimate friend of the Venetian ambassador to whom he revealed all the secrets of the State, without concealing his disdain and his animosity against the Hungarian magnates and against his weakling king. This prince of the church—perhaps in paid service of Venice, or in exchange for a promise to get her support at the next conclave —was indeed a prelate of the renaissance who did not recoil before coarse expressions. One day when the dismayed ambassador came to tell him that the Bishop of Pechuh—a prelate who had a considerable influence at the court—declared himself in favor of the expedition to Dalmatia, the cardinal could not control his anger and in the terms of his native tongue he discharged it with some obscene expressions. It caused quite a stir in the Senate when Pasqualigo brought the episode to the attention of the Signory.

The primate of Hungary made himself chief of the opposition to any adventure in Dalmatia, and the palatin sided with him. The King, a feeble character, could not overcome such opposition headed by two great dignitaries of the crown. Even if he could have done that, he would not have wanted it, but at the same time, when solicited by the Republic to renounce to his rights to Dalmatia, he refused it. Pasqualigo, in Zagreb, won the confidence of a member of the Frankapani clan. This Croatian baron assured the ambassador that he was sorry for the part taken by his brother in the emperor's campaign against Venice. He assured the Republic of his devotion. As far as Dalmatia is concerned—he said—everything depended upon the attitude of the Croatian magnates. Without their assistance the Hungarians could not undertake anything in Dalmatia. But it was necessary to sow money. Three thousand ducats would be sufficient for one year. That was a small sum, said Frankapan, if one figures that with such modest means one could assure the fate of Dalmatia, and one could save the peace with Hungary. Pasqualigo fully agreed with this plan.

On top of everything else the Turks assumed a threatening position, and the Croatian barons trembled at the news that the Pasha of Bosnia made preparations for an invasion by crossing the Sava river.

On the 29th of December, Pasqualigo informed his government that the banus of Croatia, Andrew Bot, rebelled and that his men were laying waste to Slavonia. But, he added, they have neither leaders nor money. They are not united, and are unable to undertake anything in Dalmatia. In addition, the majority of the Croatian magnates inclined toward Venice.

In January, 1510, the situation became rather serious for awhile. The king had finally made the decision, and since Dalmatia in all certainty —he thought—would be lost for Venice, it was much better to recover it for the crown of St. Stephen rather than to permit its occupation by others. Therefore he had given an order to the palatin to levy an army for the invasion of Dalmatia. The chiefs of this expedition would be the prior of Vrana and John Berislavich, who had been raised to the rank of the despot of

Serbia. But at the same time the palatin was opposed to this campaign, since he was—said Pasqualigo—as friendly to the Republic as was the cardinal primate. He demanded the convocation of a council of the crown. To Pasqualigo, who did not despair about the king, Berislavich stated briskly; "I am telling you and repeat to you, you will get nowhere if you do not cede Dalmatia." Venice would have been entirely powerless to defend that country. In order to cary on the war on the Italian mainland, she called to colors the entire male population of Dalmatia. In the country itself nothing remained but the clergy, old men, women and children.

Deprived of all defensive forces, Dalmatia was promptly invaded by the Turks. They attempted to capture Almissa (Omish) and Split, but the bulwarks offered strong resistance and the Turks retreated. In spite of the bad situation on the mainland, Venice took measures which had been dictated for the defense of the country. She sent money and workers to Dalmatia, built blockhouses (pillboxes) at the frontier, and built the castle of Suchurats near Split, and that of Nadin near Zadar. The Turkish raids became less frequent. The Ragusan chronicle writer, Tubero Cerva, asserts that this would have been the propitious moment to expel the Venetians from Dalmatia, since many Dalmatian citizens were ready to abandon Venice. But it was necessary that the king do something. Yet, he did not do a thing. A Hungarian history writer, Istvánffy, states that several members of the council of the crown had been bribed by Venice. The king—since he was as much in need of money as his predecessors were—probably too, was the beneficiary of the Venetian grant. Whatever it be, the game was not won, although the Allies tried their best to win it.

In April, 1510, Emperor Maximilian wrote a letter to King Ladislas in which he urged him in lively terms to join the League, and to assume the obligation not to conclude peace with Venice if she happened to restore Dalmatia to his kingdom. In Budavár and Táta, where the king resided, a desperate gamble was made. The diet of the kingdom was called. On the 25th of May, Pasqualigo reports to the Signory: "The archbishop of Ostrogon inclines in favor of Venice. But the Republic—the primate told me—should offer some little incentive to Hungary. And then the diet would turn to favoring the Republic." A few days later the cardinal primate had this word to say: "Our Hungarians are barbarians and passion moves them more than reason."

The allies promised them impressive advantages if they adhered to the League. To the suggestions of the bishop of Pécs (Fünfkirchen): "Give up Dalmatia!", Pasqualigo replied coarsely: "Hungary could never keep it, and even if she got it, the Turks would get hold of it as they did with Croatia; furthermore the enterprise would cost too much; Hungary would lose the thirty thousand ducats which she draws at present from Venice for the defense against the Turks, while from the side of the Adriatic the Kingdom is defended by the Republic." A dispatch from Pasqualigo of June 25, 1510, reports of a dramatic scene which took place in the presence of the king during an audience he gave to the ambassadors of the king of the Romans and the king of France, who were charged with the extreme effort to induce Hungary to join the League.

The League, however, began to lose its glow and vigor, for in February the Pope Julius II suddenly changed his mind and started to preach a crusade against "the barbarians" who invaded Italy—who for the moment were no one else but the French—and promptly made an alliance with Venice in order to expel the French from Italy. Venice had to go through the most humiliating terms in order to get absolution of the Pope. Julius II declared to the Venetian ambassador, Francesco Corner, that he could not admit the imposition by Venice of the duties on ships crossing the Adriatic. The Republic replied that she had held jurisdiction over the sea ever since time immemorial at tremendous cost and much blood sacrifice for the common benefit of Christianity and with the approval of the predecessors of the Holy Father and of other sovereigns; therefore why should she renounce those duties? Besides, the Turks would immediately profit by the abandon of an ancient right, and would enter the Adriatic. That is to say it was not exclusively the matter of the duty imposts, but also of the policing of the gulf, which was the only defense in the confusion prevailing in Europe. In order to satisfy the Pope, Venice renounced the collection of duties from papal ships, but a few months

later she invited the Turks to swoop down on Italy in order to save herself before the offensive of the imperial troops.

Thus the League had been given the death blow. Further, the patriotic attitude of the population of the mainland (terra ferma), whose shouts Marco! Marco! have drowned out the shouts of the nobility: Impero! Impero! (Empire!, Empire!).

Still Venice was not yet saved. Hope was still high in the camp of the allies. Maximilian especially did not want to renounce the hope that Hungary would leave her neutrality and make a decisive blow in Dalmatia, for all the chances of victory would have been placed in the camp of the League. At a royal audience in which the grand barons and chief prelates, as well as the ambassadors of the Pope and the King of Poland, Sigismund the First, participated; the ambassador of France made some exaggerated statements, a scathing attack against Venice. He declared that the king of the Romans, who occupied Vicenza, Treviso, and Legnano, together with France, would lay siege to Venice from the side of the sea after retaking Padua and that he "will return the Venetians to the stage of fishermen and weavers as they have been in the past." He exhorted the king to join the League, to undertake an expedition to his own Dalmatia, which the Venetians have usurped for such a length of time by cheat and fraud, and let him not blind himself by this Venetian subsidy of thirty thousand ducats, for he would draw an immensely greater advantage through the conquest of Dalmatia with its three thousand large and small islands, fourteen dioceses and two provinces, and to choose between his own sons and the Venetians. He cast the gravest accusations against the Venetians. By their fault—he cried out Constantinople was taken and Jerusalem lost. The Turks would have invaded Italy herself, had it not been for the defensive actions of her Christian princes.

"Christianity had in its womb two dragons, one inside and one outside (unum intus et alium foris), one your own Serenissime and the other the grand Turk; therefore it was necessary to extirpate and strangle both of them." He also added that the Venetians boasted that they have the king as their soldier, as if they were his superiors and "he added several discourteous words calling the Venetians the wild beast, human trash, etc." Among the general amazement, the master of the palace rose from his seat and shouted: "Modestius agatis, domine Orator" ("Be more moderate in your expressions, sir, speaker") —but the French ambassador was not disturbed by this interference. He finished his speech by declaring that if the king did not want to proceed in this path, the allies themselves would take care of the conquest of Dalmatia, but would keep it for themselves. Another assembly of the barons and prelates took place at Táta in a Franciscan cloister. The ambassador attacked again. He spoke for two hours "with so much insolence and truculence," reports Pasqualigo, "that he tired out everybody." He used the most violent expressions to describe the Venetians whom he called "tyrants, without faith or law, sordid merchants, sycophants, foxes," etc. On the subject of Dalmatia he tried to demonstrate before the barons that the Venetians have usurped its possession against all justice and have unleashed, in consequence, an incredible tyranny in that country, with great prejudice to the crown of St. Stephen. He once more exhorted everybody to get hold of Dalmatia. "The King of France," said he, "the Duke of Ferrara, the Holy Father himself and Spain would help them by the sea. The Duke of Ferrara would put at the disposition of the king 16 galleys, the Pope 6, France and Spain 6, and if that were not sufficient, there would be others. In case of need the sovereigns themselves would take part personally in this undertaking. Once conquered, they would keep Dalmatia with all its resources. Furthermore, the Ragusans, who were on the side of the king, would place at his disposition more than 60 well equipped ships. With this fleet they would defend the islands against everybody in the world."

The Venetian ambassador, called to answer "with moderation" the French accusations, took pains to prove that Venice's ruin would bring no advantage to Hungary, since the Spaniards and French had never been their neighbors nor ever had anything in common with them. Neither had the Germans since they had at all times been mortal enemies of Hungary. As far as Dalmatia was concerned it had never been more Hungarian than Venetian, and further, she had been supported for a long time at high cost,

more for the benefit of this kingdom than that of Venice. As far as the promise of ships made by the speaker of France, it was nothing but a pure hoax.

On the 4th of July a bomb burst in the court of Hungary. The apostolic Nuncio declared that the Pope did not want them to go to Dalmatia and that he wished for peace. The next day the comedy was repeated in the court. Yesterday— Pasqualigo writes on the 6th of July from Tata— the war was decided against Dalmatia but the cardinal and the other prelates have once more assured me that nothing would happen. The money for the venture was fully lacking and the Diet would not assign a single cent. A magnate told me: "I would rather be torn to pieces and my soul should be sent straight to hell, if you ever see these men crossing the mountains in order to invade Dalmatia."

On the 9th of July, Pasqualigo reports to the Signory that the Cardinal let him know that nothing would happen in Dalmatia and that the assembly, the Diet, had been sent home. Besides everything else it was feared lest Venice arouse the Turks against Hungary. On the 15th of July Pasqualigo was called to the Council. They requested him to demand that the Republic restore Dalmatia peacefully, otherwise they would take the matter under advisement. They gave him 30 days to give an answer. His friend the cardinal-primate assured him that "nothing should happen and nothing will happen" (nihil fiet et nihil erit). Furthermore, he added that this decision had been made by the prelate and the barons hostile to Venice, since they were all Germans and probably had already been bribed.

But the Dalmatian baron, Peter Berislavish, a native of Trogir, the ambassador of the King in Venice, urged the court to undertake war in Dalmatia. He stated that he had many relatives in Shibenik and Trogir, and was so much interested in the liberation of these cities that he would place himself at the head of the fighting troops for the benefit of his Majesty. Berislavich also made it known that the Pope would abandon all interest in Dalmatia in favor of the king. One day, as a matter of irony, the Republic demanded one thousand horses from the king in order to organize the defense of Friuli. A few days later, the 22nd of July, the court decided to send four thousand footsoldiers and two thousand cavalry lancers to Dalmatia, but the next day the Cardinal tranquilized Pasqualigo.

At the court, they were convinced that the Dalmatian cities would open their gates and deliver the keys to the first Hungarian forces to enter their land. The Cardinal urged Pasqualigo to write to Venice to keep close watch on Dalmatia, and eliminate all the suspicious or malcontent elements in Zadar, Trogir and Shibenik, and to send garrisons to these cities. There was a certain tendency at foot to consider this Hungarian primate as one who had actually replaced the patriarch of Venice, and further he was under suspicion of having been bribed by the government of the Republic. On the 25th of July the court ordered an individual known as Felice Raguseo, who was the ambassador of the King in Spain, to stop over in Ragusa and ask the Republic of Saint-Blaise for galleys to be used for the war in Dalmatia.

The partisans of Venice grew in numbers because of the disposition of Julius II toward the Republic, and in view of the negotiations conducted with the Turks by the Serenissime. For she had stubbornly decided to save Dalmatia, even at the price of an armed intervention by the terrible Selim I (Yavuz), in the affairs of Italy. The fear of the Turks at this time was the beginning of wisdom. At Komoran (Komárom), Pasqualigo received a message from one of the chief Croatian barons, the Count John of Kerbava, who assured him of his devotion to the Republic. He would remain faithful to the Republic. Further, he would not take command of an invasion army in Dalmatia, an undertaking that would never take place, since the king had not a farthing to his name, the barons were not in agreement, Croatia had no more forces and could not provide food for a group of a thousand soldiers for more than fifteen days.

So new theatrical change came to pass! Pasqualigo, summoned to the council of the crown, was informed (10th September) that the king did not intend to declare war on Venice, but what would Venice do for the benefit of Hungary. Pasqualigo replied vaguely that the Republic would always take care of the interests of Hungary. This was too little, it was even received by some as a poor joke. The ambassador reported to the Signory that this assurance was not sufficient and that the Republic should make better commitments. But all these things finally became useless. Time had played for the security of Venice. Besides time, also the weakness and exhaustion of the neighbors of Venice, played in her favor. The theatrical gesture of the Council was followed by calm and oblivion.

In October, Hungary no longer thought of Dalmatia. The Cardinal assured the ambassador of Venice that the Dalmatian affair had become "an adjudicated matter" (res judicata), that is, they wouldn't do a thing. However, Venice was urged to increase the subsidy to the kingdom in order to defend itself against the Turks; even that proposition was disregarded. There is a gap from September 10, 1510 and the 3rd of August, 1511 in Pasqualigo's correspondence at which time events took a slow course. In Italy things remained unchanged, and Maximilian, ever implacable in his hatred of Venice, could not boast of any important successes. He sent a delegation to the King of Hungary in order to plead the allies' cause which, as a matter of fact, became his own cause, and to request Ladislas to invade Dalmatia. The ambassadors of the emperor offered Hungary the alliance of Spain which would provide considerable subsidies to Hungary in case it should move to Dalmatia. The king was undecided more than ever. The strife between the barons was unrelenting, for all the magnates aspired to be at the head of the government, while the king was alive "because of his indolence and continuing ill health." He was absent all the time. The bishop of Pechuh would say to the Venetian ambassador: "By God, the king is enclosed in a vault and we do not know what reduced him to this condition, but it will be necessary to look after the interests of the State and you will see that we make the right decisions on short notice; he will be king and master of us all, but he will not rule." What an ideal king for Venice!

The answer was given to Maximilian's ambassadors that the whole expedition had been delayed until the next year and that the Cardinal primate could again repeat to Pasqualigo the refrain: "nihil fiet, nihil erit." The emperor was the exact opposite of the king, even though he was somewhat confused, inconsistent, devoured by his ambitions. But in his hatred against Venice he was consistent. Therefore he presented the following concrete proposition: One thousand footsoldiers for three months, two artillery pieces, 18 light galleys, six other large galleys, and in addition, he would not sign the peace with Venice without the consent of the King of Hungary. In case the Turks invaded the kingdom, he would rush to his aid. These obligations would be passed on to the Allies' successors, "until all of Dalmatia is regained." So it was necessary to give a less vague answer to these proposals.

Therefore, Hungary promised, on her part, that her army would be ready in April of the next year; that after the conquest of Dalmatia she would supply armed forces to the emperor against Venice; that she would get from Ragusa a number of ships; that she would not sign peace with Venice without the consent of the emperor, but if she were attacked by another party, namely Turkey, she would not be bound any longer by the treaty. In the meantime the Turks invaded Croatia, without meeting any opposition. Pasqualigo assured the Signory that the Croats, abandoned by the apostolic king, had planned to make themselves the tributaries of the Turks, the inroads of which became more and more frequent. Deprived of any will power and interest, the king thought only of his own personal security. Besides, the treasury was empty. The magnates would rather accumulate wealth in gold ducats than strive for glory; "everybody," reported Pasqualigo, "is placing his faith in God Almighty in order to find a remedy for this situation, however, without being forced to open the strings of their purse." On the 25th of February, the ambassador of Venice wrote with some exaggeration: "One can consider Croatia as lost. Count John of Kerbava made himself a tributary of the Turks and there are no more bani for the defense of that country."

The events rushed with precipitous speed and the campaign against Dalmatia petered out into a far distant mist. A radical reshuffling of alliances took place. Terrified by the victory of the French in Ravenna (11th of April, 1512) over the forces of the new league between the Pope, Venice and Spain, Maximilian hastened to sign a truce with Venice (on the third of June). But six months' later Julius II, disgusted with both the Venetian wiles and the Emperor, who took the decision more firmly than ever not to abandon the game, plotted against the Republic of St. Mark, and signed a treaty of alliance against Venice. In retaliation, the Serenissime hurled at the Pope the threat of an alliance with France and an invitation to the Turks to invade Italy. But the storm eventually died down with the death of Julius II (21st February 1513). Furthermore, with the election of Cardinal John of Medici (Leo X) the fearful league of Cambray ceased to exist. Nothing remained of it except a few temporary rumblings of thunder which became ever more distant. Once more Venice was saved and Dalmatia, definitely separated from Croatia and Hungary (soon by the watertight bulkhead of the Turkish conquest) became nailed to Venice forever, to the last day of Venetian authority.

Colonial Policy of Venice in Dalmatia

Upon consolidating her power in Dalmatia, Venice was naturally tempted to exploit this country without restraint, placing her commercial policy, that is the colonial rule, as the chief objective of her reign. The commercial monopoly was practiced there with the skill of a virtuoso.

Industry and commerce had been monopolized to the limit. No new industry could be established without authorization of the government, which was almost always denied. The salt-pans, the producers of the most important article in Dalmatia, had been simply declared property of the Republic. The municipalities had to deliver their entire salt supply to the Venetian agents at a price fixed by the Government. Occasionally the price was fixed in agreement with the sellers, but most frequently without it. The main principle towering above all other considerations was that the interest of the Republic, that is of the central power, must be safeguarded before and above everything else.

Whatever wine or other branches of Dalmatian commerce had been in the possession of the native producers, they were not entirely despoiled of every right, but Venice took care to close all foreign markets. The importation of alien wines was forbidden almost everywhere. This prohibition applied with equal stringency to the importation of wines from neighboring villages. One should be satisfied with the wine produced in the immediate vicinity, suburbs, of the city. Some municipal statutes prohibited the peasants to plant vineyards in an area under the penalty of yanking out the stock. But in this case the central power intervened in favor of the peasants. All the requests of the city residents to prohibit the planting of vineyards outside the city walls, had been rejected. In one of its answers, the government declared that every constraint exercised on the cultivators had been considered by the Republic as dishonorable. One would be tempted to believe that these answers had been inspired by the sentiment of justice toward the lowly and dispossessed ones. A good dose of official egotism was mixed in this display of interest in the welfare of the peasants, for, at the same time she raised the taxes of the class which she intended to protect. To the citizens of Antivari, to whom Venice replied that it was unjust to destroy the vineyards of the poor people, she found it necessary at the same time to assess these same peasants a tithe on the wine, exactly the same tax rate which was levied on the city residents.

Venice prohibited the producers of the Dalmatian wines to export same to the neighboring markets. The communities did not have any choice other than to export their wine to Venice. In fact, that was their duty. The city of St. Mark got its food supplies from the Dalmatian towns in the same way that the latter were provided by the villages. The moral considerations were in effect only when their application did not injure Venetian interests. The entire commercial legislation of Venice was marked by the excessive protectionist character.

The bread could not be sold except in Venice. The Venetian proveditors purchased their bread in certain communities at the expense of the city. They exercised no preemption rights over the local consumers, and only when their needs were satisfied could the local purchaser bid for left-over supplies. This was a merciless struggle of interests which frequently ended in complete sacrifice of the local consumers. Venetian vessels exported the entire bread supply from the communities while the people of the countryside were exposed to famine. Frequently, the officers of the Republic, who worried only about their appetites and pleasures, intervened in order to mitigate the Draconian regulations of the city of St. Mark.

The Count of Zadar, Albese Corner, the captains Andrea Querini and Antonio Cocco, the General of cavalry in Dalmatia, came one day to a joint agreement to protect the land from the gullible administrators. This case—indeed very rare—should be reported with the very words of Querini. "The famine of 1559 imposed upon us the measures which made it possible for us to live throughout the whole year. But we have received some terrible letters from the chief of the Council of Fen, enjoining us to send a large quantity of cereal to the capital. We have carried out these orders. But since we had no more than a two months' food supply, we wrote to the Council of Fen explaining the situation. On this account your Serenity, in agreement with the Senate, made the decision to release us of all obedience in this matter, even though we should receive orders from the Council of Fen. As a result of these wise instructions, we have taken a cargo of cereals to the merchants in order to satisfy the needs of these people who are exposed to death from starvation. Finally and in order to obey your Serenity, each of us have decided to pay two hundred and fifty ducats for a part of the surplus cereals which we had distributed among these very loyal people. We hope that your Serenity will refund us what we have spent in order to preserve the city folk and the inhabitants of the islands. For they were ready to leave the country and to move elsewhere thus ruining the entire structure of this city (Zadar) and causing huge losses to your Serenity in every respect."

This took place in 1559. But as a general rule the requests of the municipalities for authorization to purchase bread for local needs, and subsequent permission to export, remained without reply. The counts who dared to retain quantities of bread for these starving people were subject to a fine of five hundred ducats. So the famine became, together with the pest imported from Turkey, almost an endemic evil in Dalmatia.

In 1557, the Count of Split, Alvise Ferro, reported to the Senate that the famine had continued there for several years without interruption. It was necessary, therefore, to apply to the Turkish Sanjaks and their lieutenants to import cereals in sufficient quantities from Bosnia. In 1559, under the administration of Andrea Corini, there was a terrible drop in crops. The result was pauperism and emigration of "the residents of the border area next to the Turkish possessions, fearing that they might be massacred. The proveditor of the fleet writes in 1558 that the residents of the borderland area have taken refuge in Ancona, in the Abruzzi and Apulia, where they settled down because of personal security and better chance of getting food supplies. Those who did not leave the country, took refuge in Senj, in Bakar and Fiume and in the other areas ruled by the emperor, while others went to work on board the galleys and have been lost. These are the reasons responsible for pauperism in Dalmatia. The survivors preferred to do any kind of hard and extenuating work rather than to serve on board the galleys."

There was practically no community in Dalmatia which could live exclusively on the produce of its own territory. The exchange of the excess of certain products with the products of the first necessity was the prime objective of their economic activity. However, this exchange had to be done with regions in the back country. In the interior the exchange did not bring anything because the conditions there were about the same as in the rest of the country. As a result, the first need of the municipality was the freedom of their commercial relations by the selection of profitable markets. But, instead of this, Venice, which was deprived by a set of arrangements and regulations of everything which the Dalmatian communities had in excess, eliminated her rivals, and by excessive customs duties made it impossible to sell their goods on all markets.

Turkish Invasion of Dalmatia

Ever since the beginning of the 16th century Dalmatia experienced not only the nightmare of a merciless exploitation by Venice, but also the horrors of the Turkish conquest. The fall of Bosnia and the plots of the Turks to acquire the rich Croatian and Hungarian lands have turned away the attention of historians from a fact equally important, namely, the Turkish invasion of Dalmatia and the role played by Venice in regard to this Moslem undertaking. It is generally believed that Dalmatia was always in the possession of Venice. However, this is far from being true. During a century and a half there were, side by side, a Turkish Dalmatia and a Venetian Dalmatia.

Ever since the fall of the Kingdom of Bosnia, the natural road for Turkish invasions was Dalmatia, a case of tragic interdependence of these two countries. Only the cities along the seacoast escaped the terrifying ordeal. Their wonderful churches have never been polluted. But the mainland of Dalmatia and certain tracts along the seacoast have become the loot of the Moslem conquerors. The picture that this country offers following the Turkish invasion is sickening. "The Turkish territory," writes Giustinian, "extends to the bulwarks of our cities, sometimes to the very houses."

Out of 800 large villages, 500 have been occupied by the Turks. The territory of Zadar, which had a periphery of 70 to 90 miles, was reduced to 6 miles in circuit and in this area, so dreadfully reduced, it was practically impossible to raise any crops. The population would have succumbed to famine if not for the islands where one could live in safety with his livestock. It was generally thought that the population could not maintain itself under these conditions and in despair of its future it would surrender to the Turks. The Morlackians, who lived in the territory occupied by the Turks, forced their relatives, residing in the Venetian territory, to abandon their lands and pass under Turkish authority in order to save themselves from being exposed to endless robberies. For there was no doubt that the day would come when they would be forced to surrender to the Turks.

The flood was rising without anyone being able to tell when it would stop. In the district of Shibenik, when this city was taken over by the Venetians, there were about 300 villages. During the long conflict with the Turks a majority of them had been destroyed, and in the 16th century there were only 15 of them left, all strung along the seacoast. The entire rural economy was destroyed, including the production of olive oil since the Turks had uprooted all the olive groves. The same situation applied to Split and Trogir. "The territory of Split," writes Alvise Feror in 1557, "is reduced by Turkish occupation to insignificant proportions. It covers no more than 5 miles in length and 3 miles in width up to the town of Salona. This is a Turkish possession. It is located not further than 5 miles from Split. This territory is so badly reduced, that except for the protection of the stronghold of Salona, of Kamen (Sasso) and by the tower of the Papalich family, it could not be cultivated peacefully, for the Turkish raids continued without interruption."

From the bulwarks of Split one could hear the crowing of the Turkish rooster. In Trogir, the entire territory surrounding it was encircled by Turkish possessions. Count Alessandro Bolani (1569), ascertained that at no other place in Dalmatia have the Turks come so close to the bulwarks of a city as at Trogir. Regarding Zadar, Moro writes in 1520: "The peasants here are despondent. They plan to leave the country if they are not compensated for the terrible damage the Turks have caused them."

Cioran writes in 1525 as follows: "This poor city, the vicinity of which provided cereals for all of Dalmatia in the past, nowadays has nothing to its name. Its supply of wheat cannot last for more than 3 months. It cannot cultivate more than 6 miles of territory and that, with the greatest hazard for the cultivators to become captured by the Turks." Baglioni writes in 1524: "One must aid this poor population—both the nobility and the artisans—who have suffered tremendous damage in cattle, crops and human beings. They are despondent. Rather than keep suffering, they prefer to submit to the Turks." Vallaresso reports in 1527: "Ever since Obrovats fell into the hands of the Turks they come every day to the very gates of Zadar. One can no longer keep soldiers in the county of Zadar, since the Turks come and mix with them." Barbarigo wrote in 1528: "The whole territory is abandoned in dread of the Turks. Our poor subjects abandon their homes and possessions. They wish to move to some foreign country and even to Turkish territory in order to escape capture and slavery."

About Shibenik, the proveditor Moro writes to the Senate in 1520: "The very day of my arrival here, the Turks have plundered 3 villages, dragged into slavery 106 persons, driven away 2,000 head of cattle. This is terrible. I sailed aboard my galley toward several coastal villages in order to defend those poor people who, with their animals and their children carried in their arms, ran towards the sea. I managed to chase away these perfidious Turks. The people have deeply moved me because of their profound distress. In the meantime the Turks had finished their foray, for our cavalry detachment came too late. I took aboard my galley a few of these unfortunate people. They have complained of their misfortune and have been assuring me that this could last no longer, that they had had enough of it. I was consoling them. I told them that your Serenity had sent me specifically to attend to their needs and to guarantee their security. They have expressed their satisfaction over my effort to hasten with my galley to defend them. They hope that your Serenity will make friends with the new pasha of Bosnia."

Venier and Contarini write in 1525: "The entire territory of Shibenik is ruined and depopulated through the Turkish inroads." Andrea Diedo stressed: "The Turkish invasion resulted in Shibenik being deprived of all its territory. Everybody has fallen into misery." Due to the never ending raids, the whole eastern part of the Shibenik territory and even a part of its western possessions have been completely abandoned. A part of the peasantry have been dragged by the Turks into slavery and the others massacred. The survivors took refuge in the city or on the islands and the rest migrated to Abruzzi or in the March. Thus, all these villages became deserted.

After the Turks captured Scardona (Skradin), the residents of this town were sent to the abandoned land in order to cultivate it. But over protests of the Signory the High Porte agreed that Ottoman subjects should abandon the fields in favor of the inhabitants of Shibenik. As the result of the Porte's decision, the Morlacchi made an arrangement with the owners of the abandoned villages to keep using the pasture lands and their waters in exchange for one-fifth of their wheat crop and several heads of cattle. Venice demanded the restitution of 33 villages from the Porte, but could not obtain anything in spite of the repeated promises of the Sanjak of Klis.

According to further reports "the poor residents of Shibenik, former masters and owners of so many villages on the mainland, have been fully deprived of their lands." In a dispatch of December 23, 1560, Paolo Marcello, Count and Captain of Shibenik, reported to the Senate that the Sanjak of Klis had sent him letters in Slavic, in which he assured him that he would restore said villages, but that he would have to be compensated in the amount of 55,000 aspers, the true value of these 33 villages. But one of the worst scandals denounced by G. B. Giustinian.

was the permission given to the Turkish Emin, that is, customs supervisor, to establish his residence in Shibenik itself and to collect duty on the articles imported to that city by the Morlacchi. At the same time he presided over the distribution of the revenue between the sultan and the Republic of St. Mark, derived from the sale of salt, which came in part from the Turkish territory.

The landowners became beggars. Cultivation of the soil was discontinued. Cattle-raising was the only source of income for the population could drive its cattle to the areas relatively secure under the bulwarks of the city. But cattle raising alone could not extricate the population from their misery. Among the refugees there was a number of gardeners, farm hands, oil producers. This great number of men, condemned to unemployment, changed into bands of brigands who terrified not only the Turks, but also their own countrymen.

Not only the savage tribes with the instincts of plunderers were destroying the culture in Dalmatia, a heritage acquired in the course of centuries, nor causing a relapse into barbarism, but the very character of the nation changed and a class of individuals emerged which assumed the looting methods of their oppressors. This torrent of savagery rolled to the very bulwarks of the cities, but there it stopped.

Nevertheless the exchange of goods resisted this hurricane. The back country remained, in spite of all, the food source for the coast. The proveditors and syndics of the Republic reported to the Senate: "The commercial exchanges which the Dalmatians are carrying on with the Morlacchi and with other Turkish subjects are so important, useful, even indispensable, that, if they are interrupted or simply cut off, the Dalmatians would starve to death. As a matter of fact they received from them flour, cheese, meat, honey, wax, flax, hides, wool and blankets which they exchanged for salt, salted fish, oil, sugar, white wax and textiles." They purchased a great deal of salt. The turn-over was 5,000 ducats a year. The interdependence of the Dalmatian cities and the Morlacchian villages has been described by Giustinian as follows: "If trade between the Morlacchi and Shibenik were cut off, the town would perish, since the inhabitants of the city would have no means of support." And

the wise Giustinian declared without ambiguity that "the Morlacchi are the source of life and welfare of Dalmatia."

A rapid survey of the territorial losses suffered by Dalmatian communities plainly shows that Venice did not fulfill her first and supreme duty, namely, the defense of the territorial integrity of Dalmatia in its vital sectors.

This trade with the Dinaric back country was in vogue by a formal violation of the written laws of the Republic. It was merely tolerated. By outlawing external markets, and strict enforcement of same, the citizens would be deprived of the possibility of exchanging their goods for the raw materials which constituted the first vital necessities heretofore imported by the Morlacchi.

The depth of Dalmatia's misery can best be evaluated by the following report sent by the Rector of Split in 1574 to the Senate: "The territory is abandoned. It is badly taken care of. This cannot continue so any longer. If vital matters are still going on, it is a true miracle. Famine is everywhere. The people no longer think of tomorrow. They are not awake except in the hour of danger. But the flood rises higher and higher and they are drowning. Only then did they turn to the government. They sent them wheat and salt and other supplies but not in sufficient quantity."

The ravages of time, but especially war have totally ruined Dalmatia. Nobody lives there except the peasants. Nin (Nona) is in a lagoon. Its surroundings are very fertile, but the last war with the Turks had destroyed everything. Fortunately Nin had not fallen to the Turks. In 1553 Paolo Giustiniani reported to the Senate: "Nin is without defense structures. The enemy will be able to take it whenever he makes up his mind. And yet with very little money one could fortify it. It is an excellent natural port, but it needs to be properly equipped. In the absence of water a large army could not camp in the territory of Nin." Six years later the syndics Bon and Erizzo established the same facts: "Nin is an area created to become a powerful fortification. She is surrounded by a wall belt which is dilapidating. In the past it was a noble and populated city. At present she is abandoned. The air is polluted and, in addition, the war has destroyed everything."

And what about Zadar? The powerful and magnificent city which had resisted for several days a combined attack of the French-Venetian crusaders in 1202, which so often resisted Venice, which at a certain moment represented the will to live of the whole country? The bulwarks of Zadar by this time were entirely worthless. They were old, antiquated and decayed. A violent storm has demolished a part of it. It is necessary to rebuild the walls. In 1556 Girolamo Dolfin reports that the city is not even guarded at night and that the garrison is insufficient.

Taiapietra informs the Senate in 1526 of the condition of Shibenik which is called by Jacopo Baldu "a place of refuge for all of Dalmatia in case of danger." The walls are old and weak. If they are not renewed, the city will be exposed to the gravest danger. It is of utmost necessity to build a stronghold on the hill of St. John which overlooks the city and from where the enemy artillery could easily destroy or seriously injure the city.

Malatesta Baglioni, the captain general of the arms, visited the Dalmatian fortifications in August and November of 1524. It was he who urged the building of a fortification on the island of St. Nicholas, which controls the remarkable entrance to the port of Shibenik, a miracle of defensive points invented by the hand of nature, where a powerful fleet can anchor. The Turks in possession of Scardona (Skradin) where there is a large supply of timber, iron, tar and rigging for the construction and armament of the galleys and other ships, will naturally long for the port of Shibenik in order to accommodate their fleet. The fortification was actually built and completed in 1542, according to a report of the great military architect, Michel San Micheli, pupil of Bramante, builder of the Loggia de Lesina (Hvar) and numerous palaces and gates in Venice and Verona. But this "most beautiful" fortification of St. Nicholas did not have the food supplies needed for the garrison, nor the artillery pieces with which it should supplement the number of existing guns. "And since so much has been spent on the construction of so beautiful and powerful a stronghold, one should keep there a supply of biscuits, since the times are very uncertain, as your Serenity knows perfectly well."

In Trogir (1525), with the Turks at the very gates of the city, the stronghold is in bad shape without any ammunition and if there is some, it is of poor quality. One could fortify the city much better. Thirteen years later (1538) a bastion collapsed and it was necessary to build another one. Giustinian ascertained later that there was very little ammunition in the fort and that the stronghold had been totally neglected. Fortunately, the coast of Trogir was studded with fortified castles, all of which were built on the coast or even in the sea and connected with the mainland by a bridge.

There were seven such castles built in the 16th century with the funds of the Trogir patricians. These castles offered a valuable place of refuge in time of war. The walls of Split, according to a report of Bollani in 1534, were in very bad condition and needed urgent repair work. By the report of Alvise Ferro of 1557, Split was a very weak city. "In case of war her only hope would be God Almighty and your Serenity." The garrison of Split is practically non-existent (Giustinian). "In the city itself there are 15 footsoldiers, with two companies of cavalary which are cruising in the country in order to defend it from the Turks and Martolosian bandits. Therefore Split is continuously visited by the Turks who behave there with less respect than in their own country. It would be necessary, consequently, to increase the garrison for the security of the city and also for the prestige of your Serenity."

"At the entrance to the fort of Split" reports Antonio Diedo, "a castle tower is erected with two pieces of artillery and with no other ammunition as is the case in all the other cities of Dalmatia. The artillery pieces, which are the glory of all the princes, are in many places buried and visibly abandoned." In Kotor everything should be repaired, or, still better, rebuilt. The garrison is entirely inadequate.

This is the condition in which Dalmatia of the 16th century was carrying on her defense on the mainland. And what about her maritime defenses?

We have seen with what morbid jealousy Venice exercised her control of the Adriatic. That was her possession, her heritage, "her domain ever since the origin of the world," as they fancied it. Venice and the Adriatic Sea formed, in the opinion of the Serenissime, one indivisible whole. Therefore it is quite amazing that Venice did not keep a permanent naval force in the Adriatic before 1523. In that year on the 18th of January, the Senate made a decision, motivated by an ever increasing number of Turkish raids both on the mainland and at sea, to have a squadron of four light galleys stationed permanently in Dalmatian waters. The chief of the naval Adriatic forces would bear the title "Captain of the gulf for the safeguarding of Dalmatia" and would be subordinated to the general captain of the sea (Capitan da Mar), with the rank of chief admiral, and to the proveditor of the navy, a sort of Chief of Staff of the naval forces. Yet, the piracy in the Adriatic assumed ever more menacing proportions, and from their Albanian center in Durazzo, the Turkish pirates were emboldened to raid the Bay of Kotor. In view of this situation, the Senate decided to detach a galley to cruise permanently between the Ragusan cape of Molonta and the Albanian cape of Rodoni to protect the Venetian vessels sailing to Albania in search of wheat. This decision was made on the basis of a report by the naval authorities, corroborated by the rector of Kotor, Domenico Gritti. The stationing of galleys in the waters of Zadar during several months of the year became entirely useless. Moreover the rugged nature of the Dalmatian coast was equally fit for the defense and attack. Two natural ports, Shibenik and Kotor, were safe from attack: In his famous itinerary (travel description) G. B. Giustinian forcefully expressed his evaluation of the defensive characteristics of the Bay of Kotor. He found that fiord so important for the defense of the Dalmatian coast, that it could play a decisive role in a naval war in the Adriatic.

"The importance of this city (Kotor) and its sound," writes he, "issues from the fact that all the navies of the world could anchor in perfect security in the Bay of Kotor, without being exposed to the slightest danger. If the Turks, Almighty forbid, got hold of this city, they could maintain there a powerful navy, and with this fleet they could, within the blink of the eye, be at the coast of Apulia, Albania and elsewhere. To this, one could add two additional fortifications; one at the Trinity and the other at the entry to the Bay. Thus the Kotor bay could be instantly turned into the key of the whole sea. This was precisely the plan of the Sultan, revealed by an Emin (port and customs supervisor) to a Venetian official, who promptly relayed this information to the Senate. This intelligence produced a deep impression upon the Signory. Venice promptly took measures to fortify Kotor. She sent munitions, artillery and soldiers. For in the past the country was defended exclusively by local manpower. They realized that Kotor should be forfeited with impregnable bastions, for the freedom of the Adriatic depended upon Kotor."

In the meantime another problem raised its ugly head. Dalmatian sailors, an excellent fighting force, were being recruited for Venetian galleys. The recruiting of crews in the Archipelago of Zadar became more and more difficult. While the fleet was absent, the women were deprived entirely of their men. Also the Captain of Zadar, Paolo Giustinian, was of the opinion that the Dalmatian galleys should make their winter quarters in Dalmatia, without which the islands would be deprived of their population. In 1554, Antonio Civran reported to the Senate: "That the territory of Zadar is entirely depopulated because of the Turkish raids. Without this the Republic would not experience any difficulty in arming several galleys. However, this is not feasible at present because the male population is very scarce. If pressure were put on them to man the Signory's ships, they would go to Turkey for work." In this report of 1556 the Captain in Golph Guoro paints a moving picture. "The difficulties of recruiting the crews of the fleet, are enormous. The ordinary galleys are manned by Dalmatian sailors, in part Venetian and in part Turkish subjects. In the past they would swarm around the ships of their own port. The life was then more liberal and gratifying. Their salaries were sufficient to enable them a certain comfort and even to make savings. They bought and sold land and engaged in commerce which yielded money at the end of their trip. Nowadays everything is changed. The necessities of life became very expensive and salaries remained the same. Trade is no longer possible for the galleys do not pass any more by the Island of Zante and no longer visit the Greek Archipelago, where one could find goods at a low price. But nowadays the trips are so numerous, both in winter and summer, that the crews have not been disembarked for a three months' leave. They no longer have free time on the mainland, they cannot earn anything and, since they work a whole lot more than in the past, they deserve a better living and better sustenance. On the contrary they must content themselves with a bowl of soup and a small portion of bread, which is a poor meal for so much hard work. People will emigrate and the Republic will lose much population.

"The naval forces would be weakened, which would mean that both the arm and the nervous system of the state would weaken. They call all their crews 'Dalmatians' but they are made up of two parties, the Dalmatian Croats and a part of Greeks and a mixed section of Venetians and Istrians. Cristoforo da Canal, proveditor of the fleet in 1558, ascertains that there is a need for the Dalmatian crews, which have been depleted because of the last war and which has resulted in the escape of the population to Italy. These others, plagued by famine, took refuge in the territories of the (Austrian) Empire, in Senj, Bakar and in Riyeka (Fiume). Those who remained would prefer any other job to that of serving on the galleys of your Serenity. They have been informed by the spectacle revealed before their eyes by those who returned to their homes nearly naked and penniless. Their pay has been raised but they spent everything abroad and returned poor. I have set up a list of the whole population from Labin and Fian down to Ultsin. The area has 103,000 inhabitants from which one should deduct 12,000 exempted from military service and if one deducts 73,000 priests, members of religious orders, old men, women, girls and boys, there wouldn't be more than 18,000 men capable of bearing arms. From this number only one-fifth can serve in the fleet, since the other fifth is composed of nobility and citizens, another of partisans and another fifth of fishermen. Thus all in all only 3,600 of them are sailors of whom the government may dispose in order to man 22 galleys.

"At about the same time the commander of the light squadron Fabio da Canal, ascertained a high mortality in the Dalmatian crews (from 300 to 400 lost their lives in Dalmatia). This high rate of mortality, in his opinion, was due to the light-mindedness of the commanders who assign the Dalmatian sailors to crude services which they cannot endure. They did not care at all about that since they did not belong to them

and they left them to die in the streets. Furthermore, they used the bastinado. Therefore in the future one must strictly prohibit commanders of the galleys to take men from one galley to another, since in the absence of regular maneuvers, the sailors accustomed to another method of navigation, pass away. It is necessary to place the crews under the orders of Capitano in Golfo (Admiral), for the rear guard and allow them to row slowly."

Apart from the famous arsenal of Venice, there was in Lesina (Hvar) at the port entrance a well-equipped and expensive arsenal designed for servicing the entire fleet, and in Curzola (Korchula) there was a great shipyard which built all manner of ships.

The Venetian arsenal needed timber for construction. They got it in Albania and Dalmatia. One of the main complaints against Venice, is the complete eradication of the Dalmatian forests for the needs of the State. This includes not only shipbuilding, but also the lofty palaces which have been built with timber originating from Dalmatia.

The Venetians themselves covered Dalmatia with flowers of praise and in a memoir of 1577 one could read: "The nervous system of all the Signory's forces is located in Dalmatia, for on that country depends our maritime power, and on which the security of the state and the salvation of Italy is based. The Signory draws an immense benefit from Dalmatia, due to the sacrifices made by its fighters for the increase of naval power in the Adriatic."

This picture of Dalmatia, naturally incomplete under the Venetian regime, becomes ever more plastic in an anonymous journal found in the library of St. Mark. After the struggle between the Spaniards and Moors, nothing can present more graphically the life of a Christian people in a deadly struggle with the Mohammedans. But one special circumstance was aggravating the situation. There were many Slavic renegades among the Turks. The journal is prefaced with the following remarks:

Year of 1572.

The terrible year. In three years the territory was reduced by one-third. The Turkish scimitar reduced the population by one-half—the rest was done by famine and epidemics.

In 1570 Selim II (the Sot) demanded that

Venice should abandon the Island of Cyprus in his favor. Venice answered that he may come and take it. The battle of Lepanto had no effect. Besides Cyprus was already lost for good.

In the meantime the Morlacchi died as heroes for the defense of the fatherland and the altars. No one noticed that. The possession of Dalmatia became precarious for a great number of years from the time of Lepanto up to the discomfiture of the Turks, through the united efforts of the Christian League. In the meantime, hoping for liberation of the territory, every rupture between the two powers produced bloody repercussions, fraught with mortal perils and dangers, on the long Dalmatian frontier. The war continued, violent and murderous, from one end to the other up to the peace treaty of 1573.

The style of the journal is crude, but beautiful, it rivets the innocence of the truth. The Turks and Dalmatians are at each other's throat, they kill each other without mercy. The justice of God spread its wings over both the master country and the subjected country.

Trogir, the fourth of August 1571.

"The Turks made an inroad to the bulwarks of the city. Two young girls came as refugees. They related to Captain Orazio Ascoli all the phases of fighting between the Turks and the Christians. The women rushed to the rescue of their husbands. The Turks simply massacred all of them. The arrival of the Venetian troops forced the Turks to flee leaving behind the loot and the prisoners except two children, 13 years of age. In the course of the fighting they passed away.

"On the 21st of August, a troop of Morlacchi, sent under the command of Stanko Jurjovich by Colonel Chierigatto, to chase the Turks from the territory of Trogir, have come across four Turkish spies. Summoned to reveal the Turkish plans, the spies refused to betray their secrets and were hanged on the beach. Two others were taken in captivity."

Zadar the 3rd of September, 1571. "A Turkish felook came to sight. It had disembarked munitions and food supplies for Saint Philippe. The garrison of Zadar was alerted and two galleys sent in their pursuit. All over there is confusion, agitation. The peasants, pale and sallow, take refuge in the city with their herds and scant belongings. The women of Zadar are trembling

for their husbands, but at the same time they incite them to grasp their arquebuses and march against the invaders.

"A touching episode is unveiled. A poor woman, who ran with her companions to take refuge in the city, carried two children in her lap. Arriving at the borderline, she collapsed, removed the children from her lap and placed them on the ground. Then she stretched her arms as if she were asking some good Christian soul to receive them, and in the presence of a crowd that milled around her, she passed away.

"A Morlacchian, who had escaped the vigilance of the Turks, arrived in Zadar by swimming three miles at night and hiding under the water to avoid being discovered. By midnight they noticed the scattered fires set up by the Turks on the hills, and their approach to the city at a distance of the artillery fire range. They were sure that the gunners would not shoot so late at night, and besides they drove Christian prisoners in front of their line of advance.

"As they were advancing, they got hold of two parsons, Antonio Beglish and Francis Starich, who were members of the Order of St. Francis. Francis was in a good mood. He ate with them as if they had been friends. He told the legends of Saints to the Turks, who were stupefied. However, after a Turkish khodja (priest) declared that Messiah was the friend of Mohammed, and that Mohammed liked him, Father Francis replied to him that Mohammed was not a Saint, which provoked the Turk to hit him on the face."

Next morning the Turks demanded with amazing insolence that they surrender. The proveditor replied: "Let them come and take the city." The enemy opened fire with his guns. They made a breach and were crowding for assault. They had been repulsed at great losses. A renegade, Luke Lukovich, a giant who has killed his own sister and ran away from the gallows, took aim at a brave and honest citizen of Zadar, Zuane Katich, and said to him: "Scoundrel, your ancestors were working the land for my family. You will pay me now for your resistance." With this, discharging his gun, he wounded one of his sons who placed himself before his father to defend him. But he was captured and hanged on the bulwarks.

Split, 27th of September, 1571. The Turkish raids in the Split area were devastating. They laid waste the plain of Salona. The peasants are arming themselves in order to repulse the invader. But the appearance of the Turkish cavalry put them to flight. The commanders were begging them: "What is the matter, children? Do you want the Turks to grab our homes? What will the prince of Serenissime and the world say?"

A contingent of the Turkish cavalry at Nin (Nona) was defeated on the 3rd of October, 1571.

"Zadar, 6th of October, 1571.

"150 Turkish horsemen have been spotted by the city guards. 30 of our own cavalrymen left the city to meet them. The Turks and Christians engaged in negotiations. The Turks proposed a single man combat with lances. Our men accepted. A Turk, dressed in red with a large cap of the same color in the Turkish way, rushed at our captain George and killed his horse. The captain knocked down the Turk's cap with his lance, and when they again started to negotiate the captain complained that they killed his horse in violation of the rules of chivalry. The Turk promised to send him his own horse in four days; then they embraced each other and departed.

"23rd of October. The Turks challenged the Christians in front of Zadar to a combat on horseback. The cavalrymen embraced and then they rushed at each other.

"A Turk asked permission from Marquis Rongoni, the military commander of Zadar, to visit the churches and to attend a mass. They politely took him to church. The Turk was, so it appears, in love with the Marquis' daughter, whom he saw two years ago in Nin (Nona)."

According to the rector of Split, the winter of 1573 was unusually severe in Dalmatia. Storms at sea, famine and epidemics—they all broke down on this unhappy land. The people of the countryside were without shelter and exposed to want, which lasted for four years. In their ignorance the people attributed all these evils to magic. Fantastic stories were circulating in the country. Accordingly, witches were circulating at night between the plants turning the soil into pebbles and sand. Processions had been organized. Amulets and crosses have been suspended from the trees but the "witches" continued their mean trickery.

The rector further reports: "The provisions which are delivered from Venice, must be disembarked at full noon. Their delivery is inspired by the good will of the Government and not by some secret influences. Avoid the offenses perpetrated by the officials. One should try to understand people when they speak in Slavic. One single word can cause fire. One should stop it before it gets a good start because it could turn everything into ashes. With the noblemen (Patricians) one has to be gentle and friendly. One has to have patience. The young ones are sneaky, saturated with new ideas."

"The proveditor of Zadar has brought food supplies, tools and munitions. Biscuits, salt, heavy linen, gunpowder, hatchets, spikes, chains, etc. with twenty-eight plows. All this has been distributed in public."

"The distribution has been preceded by a mass in the cathedral. All the officials were present, together with the patricians and the common people. There were crowds everywhere. The windows and balconies have been decorated with bunting, with festoons, flowers, as if it had been some important holiday. The flags of the Serenissime have been hoisted all over. A signal was given from the galley. Three shots of cannon have been fired. Everything was hushed up in great silence and the rector made an inspiring speech. He said: 'Patricians, merchants and people of Split! Ever since you have placed yourself under the protection of the illustrious Signory of Venice, you have always received plain and sincere tokens of her benevolence and of justice. Your fathers and grandfathers have been living happy and united. Never have they repented for becoming the subjects of our protector St. Mark. Now, the Serenissime Republic has heard of your suffering. Promptly and generously she hastened to satisfy your needs. She promises you, in the same way as she has done in the past and as she does nowadays, she will bestow aid to the beloved people of Split in the future. Patricians and gentlemen in your presence we have brought aid so that everybody may see that you have been considered the beloved sons of Venice.' We gave the signal and the guns continued their salute, while the people shouted: 'Long live our honorable proveditor and that of Zadar; long live Venice'. The wives of the patricians waved their handkerchiefs and applauded, while flowers were strewn all over the place. People were crying and we were overjoyed. The articles of aid have been drawn by lot."

"A young widow, 28 years of age, a beggar woman, whose husband had been killed by the Turks, was going about with three children, a boy and two little girls, practically nude. She was selling raspberries at the market place which she picked in the fields. After selling them at a ridiculously low price, she begged with her children as the others did. At that assembly she drew lots and got salt and biscuits. Her joy could not be described. She prostrated herself and invoked the blessings of the Holy Virgin and St. Domnius, thanking them for this grace. The whole crowd surrounding her was deeply touched.

"An old, blind soldier, who spent his life fighting the Turks, drew biscuits by lot. He was led by his daughter, a beautiful youngster tall in stature, but completely confused. She was not over 16 years of age. The soldier took his biscuits, greeted everybody, and departed singing in Croatian a ballad about King Mark. The crowd joined him in chorus as if they had been prepared for a concert, for they all knew this ballad."

"We have done all in our power to bring into prominence the donations and the generosity of your Serenity; but I must say in full truth that the subsidy was rather poor when one thinks of the urgent needs of the people. But the people are satisfied and this replaces quite a number of pressing things."

Trogir, 23rd of April 1574.

A conspiracy of some common people was formed to take possession of the food store-houses. This conspiracy had been exposed by a servant. He confided in his master, since he did not want to stir any trouble in the office of the rector, and because he did not speak Italian. The rebellion that had been carefully prepared came to a swift end, due to the tactfulness of the rector of Trogir. But the rector reported to the Government that the situation in Trogir was absolutely desperate. One of the conspirators declared to the rector: "For quite a number of years there has been no business and we are at the edge of an abyss. Famine prevails every-where. This winter has carried away such a number of dead that we all wanted to abandon

Trogir. We refused to emigrate because of the affection that attaches us to our homes. Please help us."

"Another commoner told the rector that the city is simply crowded with poor and destitute. The beggars are crowding the gates of the city, weeping and begging for charity with the same refrain: May Almighty and Holy Mass be generous to you." "Dear lady, may Almighty give you and your children good health while to the dead members of your family may he give heavenly glory."

The rector reminds his Government that the expected subsidies to be distributed among the common people should calm the spirits and remove the evil moods.

"Twenty-eighth of April 1574.

"For several days past, the Turks have descended from the hills in order to sell their goods in the area. But since they refused to surrender their arms—as the others are doing, they have not been received. They sent their chief. They have empowered him to offer 25 sequins if they are allowed in with their arms. The authorities refused. The Turks threatened our messenger. They told him that they would force their entry but the authorities left them without reply. It appears this attitude of the Turks has been aroused due to an insult to a Turkish chief by a citizen of Trogir.

"We are quite watchful about everything that takes place in our midst but without getting involved in private disputes."

While western and southern Europe was in full vogue of the Renaissance producing miracles of art such as the Sistine Chapel and the loggia of Vatican, the whole of central and eastern Europe from Vienna to Kotor and from Friuli to Durazzo, was being devastated, brutalized and crushed by the terrible onslaughts of the new Asiatic invasion which came at the end of the Byzantine empire. The tragic end of the 15th century was merely a forebear of the great misery of the 16th century. The Adriatic area became one of the invaders' objectives. Dalmatia began her ascent to her Calvary.

In 1491 the Turks invaded the Dalmatian continent in force. Numerous and large detachments were pushing toward the well-guarded gates of Shibenik, but the Venetian galleys placed themselves in their path and prevented the Turkish advance toward Scradin. The Croatian barons, poorly supported by the weak and spineless King Vladislas, had to pay a tribute to the sultan. In 1497, the Turks invaded the territory of Trogir. In the next year they besieged Knin and invaded the coastland of Makarska. Finally Venice decided to equip 20 galleys with arms for the protection of Dalmatia.

In the midst of these events a war broke out between Venice and the Porte. Anthony Grimani was defeated near the Island of Sapienza, at the western coast of Greece, at the entrance of the Gulf of Coron (12th of August 1499). The galleys were manned by crews recruited in Lombardy. The entire fleet fled. Panic spread among the Dalmatian population. Alarms were sounded everywhere. Confused, poorly defended, the people began in their despair to emigrate, starting a movement which came to an end too late.

The territories of Zadar and Nin had been invaded. A new attempt against Shibenik was frustrated. The Croatian barons fraternized with Venice. Yet, the move was entirely useless. Nobody could do anything. Plunders and arsons were reported everywhere. Trogir and Shibenik and the proud strongholds of Klis trembled more than once. Finally peace was signed on the 20th of May, 1503 between Venice and Turkey. With the exception of Omish (Almissa) the whole area between the Tsetina and the Neretva River fell to the Turks. A great part of Dalmatia was delivered to the Asiatic master. But the peace itself was merely an official formula. For the Turks, it was a meaningless word, and it was fully understood that the invasions of other Dalmatian territories would not interfere with the peace "so happily" reestablished.

As far as the king of Hungary is concerned, who drew from Venice an annual subsidy of thirty thousand ducats to fight the infidels, he was, after the crisis of Cambray, still more weakened and even more involved than before. Dalmatia, robbed of the last means of defense, was abandoned to herself. Time made a step backward when the municipalities and bishops headed the armies. The archbishop of Split, Bernard Zane, placed himself at the head of a strong contingent of Dalmatian troops and resisted the Turks who had already besieged the city of Diocletian. A new attempt against

Split was repulsed. The stronghold of Karin, however, fell in the hands of the Turks.

At this time a church council was deliberating in Rome, at the Lateran, under the chairmanship of Pope Julius II and later renewed by Leo X. There was much talk at this council about the Turks. It centered around the never-ending projects of crusades which the popes preached with no more tangible results than exercises in rhetoric, which have been sarcastically commented upon by the contemporaries. At the sixth session of the council, on the 17th of April 1514, the Dalmatian bishop Simon Benya delivered a stirring speech in which he strove to explain to the fathers of the council that, Venice, Hungary and Poland were the true bulwark of Europe, upon which the salvation of the entire Christianity depended. He surveyed the Turkish invasions of recent months; in one diocese alone, the Turks have taken two strongholds and dragged into slavery two thousand persons; near Skradin four cities were taken and Skradin itself was beleaguered; it had resisted more by divine intercession than by foresight of men for a period of six months. Six strongholds in Illyricum have been taken and set on fire, together with their inhabitants. The fathers of the council shed tears but they could do nothing. The grave affair of Luther, the accession of Charles V, obscured the attention of Rome before a desperate situation in which eastern Europe was struggling.

Klis and Polyitsa were forced to pay tribute to the Turks for not being molested. The curious products of this spirit of autonomy, with which Dalmatia had prided herself for centuries, was the diminutive Croatian republic of Polyitsa. It was located on a peninsula bordered in its rear by the course of the Tsetina River. This tract of land formed a triangle between the river and the sea, and was overlooked by a hilly massive, the Mossor, consisting of several chains, the highest summit of which rose to over 4,000 feet. Among them small rivers flowed or cascaded on their way to the sea. This Dalmatian San Marino came into being in the 11th century. Polyitsa had, just like the republic of San Marino, a half aristocratic and half democratic type of government. A grand count was elected for one year, with autocratic powers and yet responsible for the acts of his administration after leaving his office. He was the grand judge in both civil and criminal affairs as he had at his side a voyevode (general) and was assisted by a council of four attorneys as well as a chancellor appointed for life, who was usually a priest.

The country was divided into twelve counties administered by vice-rectors. The elections were held every year on the 23rd of April, by an age-old custom. In this national assembly the Croatian and Bosnian nobles formed two electoral groups apart from each other. And then by a curious operation, the Bosnian nobles elected the great secretary from among the Croatian noblemen; the other secretaries were chosen by the rector and two secretaries; while the voyevode were elected by Croatian noblemen from among the Bosnian nobles. The election had taken place on a field next to a small bridge spanning a creek. The delegates from the counties spread out red dolmans (mantles) and threw small pebbles on these mantles.

The one who obtained the largest number of pebbles was elected as the head of the state. He put on the insignia of his rank; a tunic made of violet velvet decorated with golden embroidery, the dolman with silver buttons, a collar of black velvet and a large mantle made of red linen. A case containing the scrolls of laws, statutes, and privileges of the republic was placed in his hands, and the assembly was dissolved with the acclamation of the people who had been watching the procedure from the surrounding heights.

After the collapse of the Hungarian authority in Dalmatia, the little Republic was ruled for forty years (1443 to 1483) by a Venetian count. Without formally rupturing its ties with the republic of St. Mark, the rule of the count was terminated and the citizens of Polyitsa began to rule themselves. Split had exercised a certain influence over the chief families of the land. The times were inauspicious, and the Polyitsans did not find it to their advantage to sever ties with Venice. Moreover, the chief of the state offered Venice an echelon of troops against the allies of Cambray, and the Venetian Senate addressed itself to the chief of the diminutive states as an allied prince.

In 1537, Venice confirmed in a solemn manner the franchises of the small Republic, which

was soon to deliver a tribute to the Turks. The residents of Polyitsa lived over a century under the purely nominal authority of the Sanjak of Klis, but in 1647, they emancipated themselves and as a small belligerent power they took part in the liberation of Dalmatia. The republic of Polyitsa, with the other survivors of the Dalmatian municipal independence, was suppressed by Napoleon. The last great count took refuge in Russia, with its parchments and the seal of the diminutive but heroic state.

The years 1515-1526 passed in a distress without equal. In spite of the heroic acts of the armies of the banus of Croatia, the Dalmatian, Peter Berislavich, who became a true terror to the Ottomans, the Turks did not give Dalmatia either peace or respite. They advanced up to the stronghold of Trogir, but were repulsed by a Venetian fleet. Zadar, Klis, and Skradin were equally distressed. Skradin finally bowed before the Turks and resigned itself to pay them a tribute. Klis and Skradin applied for Venetian protectorate, but the Signory declined the offer in order to remain on good terms with the Turks. The population, all alone, was defending itself the best it could.

Not being able to resist the Turkish attacks by force of arms, the Signory came upon the idea of maintaining peace in the border areas by giving lavish gifts to the Turkish chiefs. However the costs for these gifts were laid upon the cities themselves, thus further aggravating their precarious plight. In order to acquire the good graces of the Turkish administrative officers and military commanders in the immediate vicinity, the cities had to give bounties without end.

The municipality alone paid to the Turkish administrative officers thirty thousand Venetian ducats within thirteen years which, by the way, brought profit to Venice as well. The Venetians sold their old clothes to the city hall of Trogir which they then gave to the Turks. Paolo Giustinian wrote from Zadar in 1553: "The Turks continuously raise incidents. They are nothing but poor alibis to extort money. The city treasurer spends much money (from five to six hundred ducats a year) in order to assuage them". —"What is left of the fiscal income, (reported Giacomo Pisani in 1566) is spent on gifts and banquets for the Turks who come to the city in order to negotiate the settlement of some border incident . . . The chief item of expense is the gift which is given every October to the Sanjak-bey when he comes to inspect the borderline and naturally this is net loss because one could not obtain anything from him. After getting three imperial decisions in the matter of the village of Bitchina, a very important locality for your Serenity since the village is located on the frontier itself, we have offered him our gift. The Sanjakbey received it with a pleasant expression of face but he declared that the imperial decisions are not final, because they are merely conditional: I am, therefore, of the opinion that the next time it is necessary to negotiate with the Sanjakbey we should obtain his decision first, and deliver the gift later . . . " Paolo Giustinian has still another suggestion. "I think we should introduce in Dalmatia what has already *been* resorted to in Kotor, that they offer the Turks a collective gift for the cities of Kotor, Budva, Dulcigno and Antivari. Thus Zadar as the principal city of Dalmatia, should also make the same arrangement with Shibenik, Trogir and Split. The three municipal treasuries should shoulder the whole burden together."

From time to time there was some revival of dignity.

Thus the Count of Trogir Bollani wrote to the Senate in 1569: "The general captain of the sea has wisely limited the expenses for the gifts to the Turks to one hundred ducats in all, for everybody. This measure brought more peace at the borderline and less incidents. In the past the Turks, greedy by nature, caused trouble by capturing children, etc. so that we should give them gifts. They knew well that the mayors of the city had full power in this matter and it was they who gave them magnificent gifts. It so happens that the Sanjakbey who did not come at first to inspect the frontier line, except for taking over their functions, has developed the habit of coming there every year which puts your Serenity under obligation to spend much money and thus increase the grief and distress of your subjects. As a matter of fact, at the departure of the Sanjakbeys, the Turks come to the very gates of Trogir, which they do not do in any other city of Dalmatia, robbing your subjects and subjecting them to all kinds of indignities.

"Of course sometimes it is necessary to make the sacrifices and pass on gifts to the big Turkish turbans in order to avoid conflicts, instead of complaining to the Porte and, consequently, having much trouble." About Trogir G. B. Giustinian writes: "It costs an enormous amount to live in peace with the Sanjakbey and other Turkish officials. But the rectors of Dalmatia are perhaps more generous with their gifts than is necessary. Under the pretext of acting as merchants, they sell their robes and clothing, in exchange for which they easily obtain permission from the Turks to procure the number of horses they need from their country. If anyone should refuse this service, the Turks would promptly retaliate with their customary arrogance and haughtiness."

Zuane Mocenigo reported to the Senate on the third of March 1567: "The conference which we have every year with the Sanjakbey of Klis, without any advantage to us and to the detriment of the public dignity, implies further, much annoyance and some grave inconvenience. For some time in the past, the Sanjakbey comes to inspect the frontier line every year in order to demand gifts, which the Dalmatian cities have usually given to him. When he arrives at the frontier of Zadar, he comes with many horses and a large crowd of attendants. And as if he were a superior, he sets up his tent and waits for the Proveditor to come to him and to deliver his usual gifts. In the past, two old denizens of the city were charged with this mission which, after the ceremonial delivery of the gift and some conversation, returned to the city without fanfare. But after a certain time they introduced the habit of having the proveditor meet the Sanjakbey in person, deliver the gifts to him and discuss the matters of good neighborliness. Well, since the proveditors are now accompanied by a whole cavalry division and the armed soldiers from the country, they are unfailingly exposed to some disrespect due to the bad faith and arrogance of the Turks.

"With an obvious lowering of the public dignity, they must actually dismount and walk up to the Sanjakbey, leaving the cavalry and the fusiliers at a certain distance. In the course of these interviews previously introduced, one does not discuss things and one cannot hear anything but expressions of sorrow and complaints made in the past and renewed by the subjects on both sides. The Sanjakbey forces his subjects to suppress the truth and to exhibit some new complication. On the other hand, the proveditor brings his own men who present their griefs and complaints against the damage and thefts of the Turkish frontier guards (Martolosians). But the Sanjakbey has never given them any satisfaction, although frequently one has pointed out the wrongdoers in his own suite. Being interested only in the gifts which he is to receive, as soon as they are delivered to him, he issues the order to move on, and he departs by saying a few words and leaving all manner of complaints unsettled and without any result. Moreover these conferences are dangerous. While the proveditor and the Sanjakbey have their conference, the two accompanying suites get together and throw recriminations at each other such as thefts, assassinations and plundering. Naturally, the passions mount and they separate inflamed with the sentiment of revenge. One day, something grave could happen here at these conferences. Therefore one should discontinue the proveditor's trips and return to the old usage of sending two elderly residents of the city to transact the business."

Domenico Gritti writes from Kotor in 1528: "The Signory has to sustain enormous expenses for the purchase of the gifts. Each rector during his administration must send gifts: first to the Sanjak of Montenegro; then to the Sanjak of Herzegovina when he comes to Herzeg Novi (Castel Nuovo); thirdly to the chairman, voyevode and subashi of Castel Nuovo, Risan and other places. This disgusting practice has been introduced recently, and if the rectors discontinue to follow this course, they cannot live in peace with the Turks. The Sanjakbey of Montenegro received gifts from four sides. He sends six ewes and one cow to our rector, all of which are not worth more than three florins, but to him and to his men, we have to give fifteen florins. Every year in the month of March he comes down in the low valley of Kotor and we have to send him refreshments, bread, wine, and other liquors, all of which represents an expenditure of twenty-five ducats each time."

"The residents of Kotor (observed Giustinian in his description of the trip) are carrying on friendly and neighborly relations with the Turks, which is the result of the skill and wisdom with which our rectors treat the high Turkish officials, by cuddling them and presenting them with gifts at an exorbitant price. The proveditors could acquire the benevolence of the Turks without so many gifts, by which the state is being degraded, and increasing the force of the enemy who wants to offend us."

To prevent the Turks from seizing the Dalmatian seacoast; from having them change, as they did with St. Sophia and many other Christian churches in Constantinople and Salonica as well as in Bosnia, the Dalmatian cathedrals into Mosques and to have a minaret towering in the shadow of the Mausoleum of the Emperor Diocletian and the persecutions of the martyrs of Salona, was the first duty of Venice towards herself and toward "The first-born state" as Dalmatia was called in Venice. Did Venice fulfill this great mission of hers? Yes, if one could judge by the simple fact that the Turks never got hold of the Dalmatian cities. Venice removed this disaster from the civilized world which would have had infinite repercussions in the Mediterranean and would have certainly exposed Italy to bloody and fatal trials for their entire future. But should we attribute to Venice alone the honor of having repulsed the Turks from the Dalmatian cities? Did she make them impregnable? Did she organize the continental and maritime defenses of Dalmatia, or did some other factors emerge to prevent this great disaster?

Jacopo Baldu reported in 1542 to the Senate: "In 1539 Barbarossa (Khair-ed-Din) could have gotten hold of Shibenik. He did not capture it, as the Uskoki assert, because this great corsair (sea pirate) had but mediocre intelligence. Had we lost the port of Shibenik, all our navigation would have collapsed. The danger is permanent. The Turks disposed of powerful means to build a great fleet and Apulia, the Marches, all of Istria and Venice herself would be within their striking range." Well then, why didn't they do it?

The losses suffered by the Venetians since the end of the 15th century, Scutari in 1479, the fortifications of Nadin and Vrana in 1540, Ultsin, Bar, and Budua in 1570-75 were significant (however recaptured by Venice in 1573 after the battle of Lepanto). Finally the conquest of the Dalmatian back country by the Turks to include the stronghold of Klis, at the very gates of Split, displayed eloquently what Dalmatia would have endured if the Turkish conquerors—distracted by the expeditions infinitely more important to them against Hungary, Vienna, Archipelago—had not given up an organized campaign against the Dalmatian cities. And also, one must admit, that the rise of the Venetian power at sea discouraged even the most pugnacious sultans from the costly adventure. It is beyond argument that the Venetian victories in the waters of the Mediterranean and especially the stupendous destruction of the Turkish-Barbaresc-Egyptian fleet at Lepanto—removed the bitter chalice from the Dalmatian seacoast. Except for several sporadic attacks by the minor forces of the Turkish naval power, which did not fit into any overall plan, the maritime Dalmatia was not disturbed.

And, yet, how dissolute were the conditions. How little Venice did to make Zadar and Kotor impregnable! Whatever defense was set up in Dalmatia, its evaluation was twofold and contradictory: one optimistic and one of pessimistic character. The optimism came from an official source and was expressed by the Venetian Ambassador in Constantinople, Marino Cavalli (1560). But the other one acquired much more weight, since it had been passed on to us by the governors which the Serenissime sent to Dalmatia. To neither of them could one dispute the experience or sense of loyalty or the acuity of observation.

Cavalli reported to the senate in 1560: "We have to live in fear of the Turks. They are inspired with specific intention since they are perfectly aware that the Republic can defend herself. About Dalmatia one can be absolutely sure. Kotor, Trogir, Shibenik and Zadar cannot be taken with a weak army. A considerably sized army could not exist in a mountainous country, deprived of water, without vegetation or food supplies. How could one feed a cavalry in large numbers? All this is impossible. In addition to that, there are good fortifications. If they are well defended they would resist as well as Naples or Romania. One should imitate the procedures of the Turks towards their slaves and persons of obscure origin. They in turn make excellent captains, sanjaks and beylerbeys, by giving them credit and reputation. Thus they are not afraid of desertions or of treason. Who could live after he deserted his master? You could do the same thing with the subjects of obscure origin who distinguish themselves in the time of war. You

could give them rich wives, grades, higher ranks in the army, and positions of authority. In many cities you would have colonels and even high ranking commanders who would serve you faithfully, without thought of desertion and treason. But let us get rid of the Morlacchi whether they be settlers or sharecroppers. Let the Dalmatian lands be neglected or deserted altogether rather than inhabited by the Turkish subjects. For, taking everything into consideration, we would lose these areas or, should we keep them, we would be confronted with so many parasites that we would have to pay them a whole lot, more than we expect to."

Against this thesis a chorus of formal testimony arises. At the head of this categoric declaration, the testimony of the Captain of the Arms, Malatesta Baglioni (November, 1524) should be invoked: "I am respectfully calling the attention of your Serenity," he wrote to the doge Andrea Gritti, "that Dalmatia is in a condition so grave that it is absolutely necessary to take immediate steps for her defense. In fact we have a neighbor so powerful that no city could resist it for more than 8 days if that neighbor made up his mind to besiege it." To these "immediate steps" suggested by Baglioni, the Senate was quite deaf. The syndic for Dalmatia, Antonio Diedo, a few years later, reminded the Senate "that the bulwarks of the cities are weak and insecure" and at the same time he praised the Dalmatian people, who are, under the authority of the Venetian patricians, of exceptional courage. Then he adds: "One can state that their chests are the shields and stronghold of this province which has, throughout its domain, nothing but a frontier."

The rector of Split reported to the Signory in 1574 as follows: "The Dalmatians are ready to strike. They are very brave. One should assign the defense of this province exclusively to men of the country, men without fear who charge in the depth of enemy ranks, especially when they defend the country in which they were born.

"For many serious engagements have been lost because of the cowardice of some Italian soldiers, as for instance when we lost the stronghold of Kamen (Sasso), the tower of Salona (Solin) and the stronghold of the Archbishop. The residents of Split were crying like little children and were in a mood to massacre the Italians. They certainly would have done that if not for the intervention of the Rector and the respect they have for your Serenity." The residents of Split said amid groans of pain: "But why didn't they let us guard the fortifications? We would not have run away. We would have died with our wives and children in order to furnish an example to the whole world."

The truth is that the most beautiful pages of Venetian military history ever since the 13th century would not be recorded without the bravery of soldiers and sailors of Dalmatia and Istria, and especially of the former, whose people were producing great sailors, incomparable merchandisers, ideal soldiers. They would have retarded by a century the unavoidable decadence of the Serenissime. These were the elements which gave Venice a tremedous ascendancy over the other Italian states in the 15th and 16th centuries, where the weakening of the military spirit exerted a marked influence on their political decadence." The nervous system of the Venetian power was in Dalmatia.

But, in addition to the stanch resistance of the manpower, should not one have protected himself against the violent temper of the atrocious enemy by a set of defensive structures? It is useless to say that human chests had been sufficient at any epoch for the defense of a country, no matter how heroic they were. Therefore the state of dissolution which the Republic had left Dalmatia, has often been denounced by the rectors of the Dalmatian cities.

In 1525 Bertuccio Civran submitted a number of measures in his proposals to put the strongholds of the area of Zadar, Nadin, Novigrad and the ruined city of Nin (Nona), in a condition of successful defense. So Novigrad, in the past a powerful fortification, with a Paleologue as its commander, was entirely abandoned. "One should destroy everything," writes Antonio Diedo, "or put up bastions and powerful bulwarks. The wind has blown away the lazaretes, while the soldiers' residences are open to the wind and rain. They cannot store their arms in a safe place. The bread baking oven cannot be used. The bell used to call the guard is broken to pieces. There is no gunpowder or ammunition. There is no water. One must repair everything and without delay. Novigrad is a military key of the first order. If it is lost, the whole country of Zadar is definitely lost for the Republic."

The fortification of Vrana, the famous stronghold of the templars, is not in a position to resist the Turks, and in spite of prodigies of valor of the Venetian commander who was a Croatian, became Turkish in 1533. Knin, Obrovats, Klishevats unable to defend themselves, fell in the hands of the Turks. As far as Knin is concerned, Giustinian gives (in 1553) a sickening picture. "Knin is in ruins. This is an old city inhabited only by peasants. But she has her bishop. There is a beautiful, fertile countryside surrounding it, but the land is not cultivated. Towards the north there are many forests and green pastures. The appearance of the residents resembles more that of the beasts than the humans, apes in hiding who would attack the travelers, disrobe them and kill them. They're boasting of their brigandage. Their food consists of milk and cheese. Their whole possessions consist of cattle. They are Serbians and heretics, Turkish subjects. They are filthy and live together with the animals." In a report of Antonio Diedo one can read: "Knin has a marvelous location. It should be fortified under all circumstances. In the past it had magnificent edifices, and a high nobility."

But on the 28th of May, 1522 the stronghold of Knin surrendered and the King of Hungary sent an ambassador to Venice in order to seek aid in favor of Hungary against Suleiman who was mustering a powerful army for its attack. Antonio Grimani was at that time 87 years of age and in the Doge's seat. The Hungarian envoy urged the necessity of making an alliance against the Turks. He stressed two decisive facts: If, during the attack by Mahomet II against Constantinople, Christianity had been listening to emperor Constantine's pleas, to his prayers, the Greek Empire would not have collapsed and the king of Mameluks would not have gone through the same fate: these two empires were actually the counter weights to the arrogance of the Turks; their safety would have been a guaranty against every danger the Hungarian kingdom and the entire Christianity would have to face.

Further, the existence of Hungary was needed for conservation of the Venetian State and its dependencies; if this kingdom is lost, which on many an occasion had repulsed the violence of the Turkish armies, and in general had retarded the course of their victories, what would remain in the world? What obstacle would there be then against the invasion of Austria and Germany as well as the Venetian states? The safety and common defense must be the fruit of a common effort. But the Duke of Crete, Marco Minio, formerly the Venetian Ambassador in Constantinople, wrote to the Senate that the Turks did not think much of the Hungarians after they had so poorly defended Belgrade. It is quite true that Minio defended them and explained their retreat when taken by a sudden attack of the Turks.

The Senate did not know what decision to make. Western affairs had entirely absorbed its attention. But the danger was serious. Ever since the 21st of September, 1520, a great sovereign occupied the Ottoman throne, Suleiman I, named the Magnificent. He had definitely decided and he had all the means at his disposal to continue the policy of his predecessor Selim I (the Fierce) and to snatch from Christianity the entire eastern Europe. In 1521, the Island of Rhodes had to surrender, in spite of the heroic defense of the Knights of Saint-John of Jerusalem, who from the Knights of Rhodes soon became Knights of Malta. In the same year the general proveditor Giovanini Moro sent to Venice a distressing report about Dalmatia. The mainland population has dropped from 60,000 to 5,500 inhabitants. He hopes that all the refugees who have fled to Italy will eventually come back to their native seats. He advocates the construction of three new fortifications. He set up the list of those places which were still keeping the Turks at bay; these were the Croatian strongholds of Obrovats, Ostrovitsa, Tsetin, Knin, Skradin, Senj; and the Venetian strongholds of Nin, Novigrad, Nadin, Vrana.

But the Turks had already occupied Knin and Skradin. The other conquests will follow. In the meantime, Hungary is made the target, since she blocked the way to Suleiman, and therefore must be smashed. In vain did Christopher Frankapan achieve prodies of heroism. Just one man cannot stop the fate. The Moslem tide rises with the force of a torrent which sweeps everything away. At the head of an army of 200,000 men, Suleiman crossed the Sava river and in the Hungarian plain of Mohach on the right bank of the Danube, he annihilated the Hungarian army (29th of August, 1526). King Louis fled and was drowned in a creek. The commander-in-chief of the Hungarian army was killed. Seven prelates, 22 magnates, 22,000 men were left on the battlefield that day in an engagement that did not last more than 90 minutes. Hungary practically did not exist any more as an independent nation. She became one of the major Turkish provinces, the vice-roy of which resided in the ruins of the once sumptuous court of Mathias Corvinus.

Resistance of Kruzhich

Hungary will remain a Turkish province up to the end of the 17th century. By smashing the kingdom of St. Stephen, the road was open for all the Turkish raids. Khair-ed-din Barbarossa penetrated for a moment the Adriatic, but was chased out by a Ragusan fleet. All the efforts of the enemy were concentrated around the stronghold of Klis, the strategic key of the maritime Dalmatia. Klis belonged to Ferdinand of Austria, elected in Pressburg in December, 1526 against his rival John of Zapolya—already elected and crowned a month before—the apostolic king of Hungary. But this Hungary was nothing but a shadow of her former self. On the first of January, 1527, Ferdinand, favored by good luck, was elected king of Croatia and Dalmatia by an Assembly of Estates in a Dalmatian Franciscan monastery at Tsetin.

Therefore the kingdom was divided, but Klis, neglected by Zapolya, was only under the authority of Ferdinand. He clung to this last remains of an obsolescent dominion, desired by Venice and Turkey, even though there was almost nothing of value to guard and defend in Klis. By a stroke of good luck Ferdinand obtained the services of an ingenious leader who had taken his assignment seriously and who believed stanchly in the good faith of the Hapsburgs. This was the commander of Senj, Peter Kruzhich, an obscure Croatian nobleman, of whose year of birth or birthplace nothing is known. This knight without blemish and without fear was fighting for a thankless court, a gallant fighter of old against the predatory colonial policy of Venice in Dalmatia. Nonetheless, he could not doubt the uselessness of his efforts since the city of Split, separated from Klis only by a distance of 13 kilometers, was already over a century under the Venetian authority. In 1531, Sultan Suleiman established his sovereignty over a good part of

Dalmatia. Disposing of the diminutive Republic of Polyitsa as of his own possession, the sultan appointed a Venetian renegade, Alvise Gritti, as the chief of the land. At the same time he gave the city of Senj and the stronghold of Klis to the same renegade although both of these places belonged to Ferdinand. But Peter Kruzhich did not take this arrangement at its face value. He openly resisted the Turks while Venice protected them in the hope of getting hold of this important spot. Furthermore the Signory strove to disestablish the authority of King Ferdinand, with the aid of the Turks. Never in Dalmatia had Venice played a more contemptible role. Although she did not approve of the surrender of Klis to Gritti, she prevented the delivery of food supplies to that stronghold. To an envoy of Kruzhich, who was pleading with the Republic for food supplies and ammunition, the doge answered: "Peter wants to embroil us with the Turks."

In the midst of these events the Turks got hold of Salona which by this time was nothing more than a village, the ruins of which still stood halfway demolished. There they set up a fortification to besiege Klis. In May, 1532, a comedy was enacted in this fortified town. Probably at the instigation of a Venetian emissary, the inhabitants of Klis yielded the city to Nicholas Querini, a representative of Gritti. But in a few weeks they chased him out and accepted Kruzhich in triumph. The Turkish garrison which was installed in the city had been put to the sword. Kruzhich got hold of the Turkish stronghold of Salona and set it on fire.

With no interest towards the plight of his subjects in the south, Ferdinand refused every aid to Kruzhich and his heroic friends, refugees from Bosnia, who later became famous under the formidable name of Uskoki.

On the 12th of January, 1533, a truce was signed between Ferdinand and Suleiman, but it did not prevent the Turks from besieging Klis. Thirty-seven attacks could not break the spirit of the stronghold's garrison. Finally on the 4th of July, 1534, the siege was raised. Ferdinand and his brother, Charles V, in the hope that a stable peace would be established with the Sultan, sent a mission to Constantinople. However, the mission came back empty handed.

This failure made Pope Paul III (Alessandro Farnese) declare a crusade against the Turks.

Bad news came to Rome from Dalmatia. An elegy of a piet of Split, Francis Natalis, compressed in a few words a desperate appeal to the Pope describing the horror of the situation: "Poor Dalmatia grieves and complains day and night; she no longer possesses her wealth or population; the cities have been destroyed, the women dishonored, the children torn from the embrace of their mothers and killed; old men and young women have been torn apart by the wolves' teeth. With hands tied we are chased from our native places. The Turks set our crops, our churches, our houses on fire. Their horses are prancing at our altars and we are being sold as slaves at the markets. Split has not yet sunk to that depth and probably never will, but its territory certainly is laid waste." Natalis begged the Pope not to abandon his loyal province, since Klis is close to the Bay of Salona, from which the Turks could reach Ancona in 12 hours. With the fall of this stronghold, Dalmatia, the Adriatic, and even Italy would be menaced. The worst thing was that Venice continued her policy of collusion with the Turks. She accused Kruzhich, in the face of Ferdinand, of wanting to provoke at all cost a war between the Republic and the Turks. On the other hand, the entourage of Ferdinand preferred the same accusation against Kruzhich. But the defender of Klis pleaded his own cause and that of the stronghold with so much convincing ardor in the presence of the king that Ferdinand had, in spite of his own will, to renew his old friendship (February 29, 1536) with Peter Kruzhich. However, he begged him not to create any conflict between the Venetians and the Turks, but to hold loyally to Klis to which he would promptly provide food. Kruzhich fully convinced of nothing but the hollow promise of the king, once more turned to Pope Paul III to provide the necessities for the defense of Klis. One must admit that Ferdinand was in an extremely delicate situation. The Turks had invaded Croatia, which almost entirely became their prey. The stronghold of Pozhega had to surrender (in August, 1536). On this occasion the Turks drove 60,000 persons into slavery.

Amid these events the sanjakbeg of Bosnia, Husrevbeg, after conquering and dividing Slavonia, hastened to the bulwarks of Klis (August 31). Kruzhich was no longer there. The Turks had cut off all communications with the stronghold, with Split and the sea. Ferdinand kept sending message after message, but nothing more than hollow promises. The residents of Klis convened to a council. What good purpose did it serve to keep fighting and just prolong their martyrdom. Christianity is deaf and dumb. Would it not be better to emigrate to other places? But where to? To Hungary? A country unknown. To Italy? They could not live there since they were not acquainted with the language of the country.

Capture of Klis by the Turks

Finally in March, 1537, King Ferdinand sent 3,000 German soldiers under the command of Count della Torre to deliver Klis. Kruzhich and della Torre left Senj together, while the Uskoki were cruising in the sea looking for Turkish vessels. In the night of 11th-12th of March, a small army, consisting of Croats, Italians and Germans, disembarked in Salona. At first the Christian troops reaped some advantages, but a sudden attack by an auxiliary Turkish echelon on the plain of Salona caused general panic. The Italians and Germans were first to flee. The Croats slowed down the flight. Kruzhich decided to resist the general flight, but in vain. Embarked on a disabled Italian ship, which could not shove off, the Turks captured the ship with Kruzhich on board. Kruzhich was killed and the aga of Janissaries got his head. The small garrison of Klis continued to fight. Then the aga of Janissaries came under the bulwark of the stronghold and paraded in front of the garrison with the head of Kruzhich. Without water, supplies and ammunitions, Klis surrendered on the 12th of March, 1537.

The Uskoki, who heroically defended the stronghold to the last minute of its resistance, retreated to Senj and deposited the keys of the fortification in the Cathedral. The head of Kruzhich, together with his body, was redeemed from the Turks by his sister Helen for 100 ducats, and was buried in the Church of Notredame of Tersat near Fiume. By a bloody irony of history, the conqueror of Klis, Husrevbeg, announcing the victory to the Sultan, proposed to remove the ruins of Salona and to settle it "with the heroes of Islam" in the environments which had been drenched with the blood of Christian martyrs and consecrated by the retreat of Diocletian, the great Emperor of ancient Rome.

The fall of Klis, which for Venice was more than a crime, had a painful echo in Rome. Paul III went to the Church of St. Mark on foot and to the Church of Holy Mary of Minerva, in order to issue an urgent appeal to all Christianity to forget all its dissensions and to arm itself for the defense of the Christian faith. The Pope's appeal did not fall on deaf ears. A league was concluded in Rome between Paul III, Charles V, Ferdinand and Venice (8th of February, 1538). The word of this first "Saint League" broke out immediately. The plan of the League was too comprehensive: it wanted to capture the whole Ottoman empire including Constantinople. It was an obvious miscalculation of the political conditions in Europe and of the power of Suleiman which was getting ever more formidable.

Ferdinand felt he could not risk a campaign in Hungary. His armies had been defeated the preceding year by the Turks and all of Slavonia fell in their power. Therefore, everything depended upon the Allies' success on sea. Vincenzo Capello took command of the Venetian naval forces. They had 200 galleys, forty of which under the orders of Girolamo Pesaro had to cruise in the waters of Corfou in order to maintain the loyalty of the population. On the other hand, 160 galleys had to cruise in the Adriatic under the command of Giovanni Vitturi since they had a good reason to believe that the Turkish naval forces under the effective command of Khair-ed-din Barbarossa had for their objective Dalmatia and Venice.

The Turks opened the campaign with 100,000 men and 400 vessels.

For the first time in history the neutrality of the Republic of Ragusa, a tributary of the Porte, came up for discussion. Instructions had been given to the Venetian captains general to seize in the ports of Ragusa and Gravosa all the ships which could be found there in order to place them at the disposition of the Serenissime Republic. This was an obvious violation of the sovereignty and neutrality of Ragusa, which was helpless in view of the combination: Venice-Turkey-Spain.

Venice insisted that Ragusa become a member of the League which would have exposed her to the reprisals of the Sultan and probably to her very doom. Clement Ranina was sent to the Pope in order to explain her situation. Finally he won the cause for Ragusa. The neutrality of Ragusa was proclaimed under the guarantee of the Pontiff. The Francophile policy of the Archbishop of Ragusa, the Milanese Philip Trivulce irritated the Allies, but everything calmed down. In spite of that the patriarch of Venice Grimani, who was in command of the papal naval forces, abused the weakness of Ragusa, or rather her non-armed neutrality, in order to ravage a part of her territory.

Summoned to pay her part of the tithe assessed by the Pope on the Confederates, Ragusa refused payment in view of her neutrality. She complained of the handicaps which Pesaro imposed on the navigation in the Adriatic, but the sly Venetian replied that this interdiction was advantageous to the city; it could serve Ragusa as an excellent pretext to refuse compliance with the Turks' demands. In the month of March, 1538 the Turks opened the campaign while Capello received the flag of St. Mark from the hands of doge Andrew Gritti. They immediately set out to Shibenik. But soon disorganization was at its peak. The Venetian troops demanded their pay and refused service in a defenseless and exhausted land. Camillo Orsini, appointed the general-in-chief of Dalmatia, openly lectured the Government. "If you cannot make war," wrote he, "make peace." Never in the past had the Republic received a similar message from a paid general. Convinced of Orsini's loyalty, the Senate took the lesson calmly. Orsini insisted. "The peoples' ruin is as much of a blasphemy as the one directed against God, for his Divine Majesty is gravely offended by humans."

Orsini insisted that a concentration of considerable forces be made in Dalmatia. The country cannot be defended by the dispatch of small "bundles." While Francesco Barbaro ravaged the area of Zadar, occupied by the Turks, these, with 20,000 men, concentrated their forces at Knin. The strongholds of Nadin and Vrana fell in the hands of the enemy as a result of treason and cowardice by the Venetian commanders. Sebastian Sagredo, who surrendered Nadin to the Turks, was beheaded on the 16th of July, while Vittore Soranzo, who cowardly abandoned Vrana, escaped capital punishment by his own death a few days later, haunted by disgrace and fear. The case of Stefano Trevisan, who had been elected proveditor general in Dalmatia and who refused to return to his post, had aggravated the situation. The doge Gritti declared that Venetian patriotism had vanished. "In the course of this war we have seen for the first time," he declared before the Senate, "that a patrician has refused to assume a public duty when the Republic herself was in danger." In the place of Trevisan, Alvise Badoer was sent to Dalmatia invested with full powers.

The truth is that the native population, the Dalmatian Croats, had been abandoned to themselves. They saved themselves and what additional things could be saved. The castle Venier near Trogir, deserted by the Italian soldiers, had been heroically defended by the local Croats and Trogir was saved. Orsini did not have more than 4,000 Croatian footsoldiers and 100 Croatian cavalrymen. However, he took Obrovats from the Turks. In regard to the suggestion of the Duke of Urbino, who offered to expel the Turks from the area of Zadar, the Senate could not make any decision. Furthermore, a strong group in the Senate, convinced of the uselessness of the grand campaign, were already inclining toward peace. The campaign in Dalmatia was open for discussion.

Senator Leonardo Emo pleaded for continuation of the war. He stressed the need that all the resources be placed at Dalmatia's disposal. The essential point for Venice was the abundance of construction timber for the Arsenal which would compensate the Republic for the impending loss of the archipelago. Alvise Gradenigo pleaded for peace. The treasury is empty. One has to pay the mercenary troops, without which they would plunder Dalmatia. The Emperor and his brother do not stir at all, Venice is isolated.

In addition to these developments, came the "flight from Prevesa" as was called the naval battle lost through the assumed fault of the Genovese admiral, Andrea Doria, commander of the Spanish fleet. He was accused of letting the Turkish fleet escape when it was already on its way to disaster. The Christian fleet left the coast of Epirus in haste and sailed to Corfu.

However, it was necessary to do something for this campaign, initiated with great fanfare, for in case of its failure, it would provoke the general laughter of Europe and especially that of Francis I, who loyally kept his word to the Infidel. At first the decision was made for a peculiar expedition, an eloquent testimony of the ineptitude of the allies to patch up their own differences. The new plan was to take from the Turks Herzeg Novi (Castelnuovo) in Dalmatia. It was a fortified city, founded by a Bosnian king, at the entrance of the gulf of Kotor, adjacent to the Ragusan territory. This picturesque stronghold, set up in a forest of pines and cypresses had been occupied by the Turks. The task was to chase out the Turks.

On the 24th of October, 1538, the combined Christian army, with their emotions somewhat quieted down relaxed for a month anchored at the roadstead of Corfu. They then made preparations to return in the Adriatic and promptly moved to the Bay of Cattaro (Kotor), which, with its deep fjord offered protection from the storms. The troops disembarked on the beach of Castelnuovo (Herzegnovi), without firing a shot. The light vessels entered the basin of Kotor; the ships and galleons assumed a position of vantage ready to repulse any attack from the outside. Gonzaga, on his part, protected the entrance of the Strait of the bay, by four companies of soldiers in case it was raided by horsemen from Herzegovina. The place to take was a fortified city, with its citadel. Five hundred Turks defended the city, while twelve hundred persons took refuge in the castle. The Italian and Spanish infantry deployed, under the orders of Gonzaga, around Castelnuovo, surrounding it, and began to attack the suburbs. In the night of the 26th to 27th of October, five large artillery pieces had been installed in the position of active batteries; at daybreak the galleys came near in order to participate in the attack. A violent firing kept up for several hours, but could not bring out any decision; the vessels finally decided to disembark their crews. Now the sailors and foot-soldiers assaulted the bulwarks from two different sides.

Musketry of the defender, in spite of serious losses inflicted on the besieging army, could not prevent these brave people from setting foot in the city. And even there it was necessary to fight from street to street. This bloody struggle cost the lives of many Christians. Captain Boccanegra, an officer who displayed great courage in the fight at Prevesa, among others, found his death here. The Ottoman garrison finally surrendered to Vicenzo Capello. It was stipulated

that the Turks would have the right to redeem themselves at the rate of forty golden ducats per head; their baggage would remain at the discretion of the victorious party. The next day, the 28th of October, 1538, the discouraged defenders of the castle sued for the terms of surrender. The booty captured at Castelnuovo was evaluated at more than 70,000 ducats.

Vicenzo Capello left the conquered town in care of two companies under the command of Captains Valerio Orsini and Augustino Spinola. Ferdinand de Gonzaga wanted to allocate a garrison of four thousand Spaniards in the citadel; he wanted more rights than the governor himself claimed. His selection was an excellent one from every point of view. He chanced to come across an officer of great determination, Francisco Sarmiento. The usurpation was no less flagrant. Castelnuovo belonged, by virtue of the treaty concluded under the auspices of Paul III, not to Spain, which had no interest in the Adriatic but for sure to the state of Venice, owner for several centuries of Corfu, of Kotor and almost of all the cities of Dalmatia. The Senate kept its resentment in concealment but Capello did not hide his. Ever since that day the rupture of the league was uppermost in the Senate's mind. Lorenzo Gritti set sail for Constantinople with the mission to negotiate a separate peace with the Sultan.

Castelnuovo was already in Christian hands when Barbarossa was informed that this place was threatened. He left the Bay of Arta in haste, hoping that he would arrive in time to avert the undertaking which would deprive him of his campaigning glory and restore to a certain degree his renown shaken up by the Christian armies. However, a violent storm, the famous Bora, overtook him on his course. The Ottoman fleet was dispersed and a number of its ships were lost. If not for the port of Valona, which fortunately offered him a place of refuge, Barbarossa had run the risk of losing his entire fleet. The Bay of Valona is not, as the Bay of Prevesa, protected by a narrow entrance. In Valona Bay one can deploy full sails. Capello and Ferdinand Gonzaga insisted that one should promptly take advantage of the unexpected chance, which placed for the third time the Sultan's fleet at striking range of the Christian fleet. This chance, in their opinion, called the vessels of the League to attack the assemblage of the storm-ridden vessels, half way destroyed, deprived of its installations, since it was learned by reliable report that a part of their oars was gone. The careful ways of the hesitant Doria saved once more Barbarossa's fleet.

The admiral of Charles V said in a formal declaration that the season of maritime operations had passed; attacking the Ottoman fleet in the open Bay of Valona one exposed himself to perish; for his part he would never associate himself with a project so foolhardy. Nothing could shake his determination.

Fighting for Castelnuovo

His decision was made, his orders were already given; as soon as the disembarked crews returned aboard, he would sail with all his fleet towards Sicily. At these words Capello could not restrain his indignation; anger was choking him and he forgot all proper bearing. He immediately returned to his galley in a state of despair. He blamed himself in loud words that he had been taking orders from an alien for such a length of time, from a natural enemy of Venice, and counseled his officers and crews never to take orders from anyone but a general of their nation. "Doria," he repeated with an increasing impetus, "is depriving us of a certain victory; thus it took a Genovese to tarnish the glory of the Venetian name."

Since Admiral Capello gave vent to his hatred in such violent terms, it really would be most unusual, had his subordinates abstained from outbursts of anger in their own name. "Don't you ever go for Doria," said Valerio Ursino; "Doria does nothing but faithfully follow the intentions of his master. What did Charles V want? He wanted to start a war between Venice and Turkey without endangering his own fleet. His purpose has been achieved. Others went even further. Accusations were made against the Emperor that he, with calculated moves, had pushed the Venetians to take up arms against the sultan in order to have them, after their own forces are exhausted, at his mercy. "Doria," grumbled they, "is managing his confrere Barbarossa. Is there anything surprising in that? Don't we know that the pirates are the same as the wolves; they never jump at each other's throat." Doria was not only a sailor; his entire

career was one of a politician. The abuse of the Venetians did not excite him for a moment. At the appointed day, he equipped and led the imperial fleet to Messina. Nothing else remained for Grimani and the Venetians, too weak for a continuation of the campaign by themselves, than to return to Venice; they went there to express their disappointment and griefs.

As far as Barbarossa is concerned, he continued his stay in the Adriatic to a point of gravely endangering the security of his vessels. As soon as the damaged ships had been repaired, he sailed back to the Bay of Lepanto. There he had divided his fleet into two parts: Dragut (or if we recite his Moslem name Torghud-Reis), was charged with 25 galleys and some brigantines to lay waste the Adriatic coast and the coast of the Tyrrhenian sea; the bulk of the navy commanded by Barbarossa himself, took course towards the Bosporus and reached Constantinople without damage.

The loss of Castelnuovo angered Suleiman. This anger was not diminished in his estimation even by the courage and tremendous service which Barbarossa had performed. The long ambition of the sultan had been achieved, the empire of the sea belonged from now on, without challenge, to the Ottoman fleet.

Perhaps it would have been wise to postpone hostilities along the Adriatic coast until the next spring. However, the impatience of the Grand Signor would not accept this delay. On the first of January 1539, three sanjakbegs guided by a Christian renegade, Morato of Shibenik, appeared with six guns, large cavalry forces and infantry troops before Castelnuovo. Morato pretended to have good information about the place; the garrison, asserted he, would surrender at the first call, especially if favorable conditions were offered to them. However, the reception was entirely different from the one the Turks expected. By a vigorous sally the Spaniards captured the Turkish artillery, and routed the Ottoman forces advancing to Split. The residents of the city rushed to arms: The Moslems fell in an ambush; they lost 70 men. The failure merely raised the pride and the anger of the sultan, eager to retake Castelnuovo. Barbarossa received orders to take to sea with 200 sails, 150 of them galleys and 50 fustae or galleots. For his part, the old bey of Bosnia, Khosrew Pasha, recently raised to the rank of Beylerbey of Roumelia, set his troops on march towards the coast of Dalmatia at the head of an army sixty thousand strong.

On the 13th of July, 1539, the vanguard of the Ottoman fleet consisting of 27 galleys and under order of Sinan-Reis sent his crews to fetch water at a fountain about a mile from the town. The Spanish garrison swooped down, in a surprise movement, at the landed Turks and forced them to flee in disorder back to their ship. In this engagement the Turks left 400 fighters on the ground. The Christians quite clearly indicated by their attitude that they did not intend to stay on the defensive. Unfortunately the enemy was in a position to oppose them with overwhelming forces.

On the 17th of July, Barbarossa led his entire fleet from Valona to the walls of Castelnuovo. There were some stiff encounters both on land and sea.

One could see the Ottoman army under the leadership of its best generals: Salih-Reis, Murad Aga, Murad-Reis, Dragut, the young Moor from Alexandria, and a short corsair known by the name of Zeffut. On the Christian side likewise excellent fighters were supporting the actions of the chief, Francisco Sarmiento, such as don Luis d'Argia, don Luis d'Aragon, don Juan de Biscaya, Sangio de Frias, Oliviero Selina, Lazzaro and the captain of the Albanian cavalry. The advantages were for a few days well balanced. However, on the 23rd day of July the victory tipped the balance in favor of the Ottomans. Barbarossa brought ashore 84 guns borrowed, for the most part, from the artillery of his galleys. Three well posted batteries were directing a thundering fire at the city and shelling it from three sides at the same time. Thirteen thousand shells had been fired at the city in less than 3 weeks. In this number there were shells weighing 100 lbs. which caused a terrific noise when dropped at the target and were fired from gun-carriages rolling on 8 wheels. Huge breaches were soon struck in the walls; the beleaguered garrison filled these breaches with fascines and retired toward the interior bulwarks.

Up to the 7th of August the Ottoman batteries did not stop firing for a single instant. Already several partial assaults had cost the Turks dearly. On the 7th of August, in a pouring rain, Khosrew-

Pasha and Barbarossa made a general assault on the city. The struggle was terrific; the number of assailants was growing without stopping; Sarmiento had to abandon the first circuit of forts; the Turks threw themselves in the breach. On the 10th of August the last attack took place. The most terrific of them all, it was also decisive. Sarmiento could not oppose more than 300 capable men to the masses which were pressing from all sides. As the last means of defense he was figuring on the mines which had been disposed within the walls. However, these mines had been drenched by the rain; they remained without effect. Sarmiento lost ground; finally he resigned himself to surrender. The janissaries shouted aloud that the prisoners should be delivered to them. Barbarossa did not permit this soldatesca to dishonor his victory. He imposed upon the janissaries all his energy and authority, and managed to save the remnants of the brave garrison of Castelnuovo from a terrific slaughter. The Turks had lost since the beginning of the siege more than 8,000 men, 500 of which were janissaries. On the side of the Christians, 3,000 dead bodies were counted. At no time can one say without exaggeration that a stronghold had been defended with more heroism. The Spaniards, under great indignation of the Venetians, had claimed this heroic resistance for themselves.

The proveditor Matteo Bembo was in command of Kotor. Disinterested entirely in the plight of Castelnuovo, the besieged city in distress, he provided the beleaguers with food supplies. "We do not need only the food supplies," reported Barbarossa, "but also the keys to the place of which you are the commander." At this haughty remark the Venetian pride came to full expression. "Kotor," Bembo replied, "belongs to the Republic. If you attack it, in disregard of the truce which exists between the Porte and the State of Venice, you will find promptly that our guns will reply to you." Barbarossa did not want to believe this boast. On the 15th of August, he disembarked his troops and pretended to start the siege. The death dealing fire which he experienced promptly made up his mind to call off this undertaking. After a gun duel more devastating to the Turks than to the Venetians, the two parties came to explain it to each other in this way: "Disembarking of janissaries, the gunshots, and the musket fire were merely a case of misunderstanding. Barbarossa made his soldiers return aboard the galleys and the proveditor promptly sent him in token of his friendly feelings, a sum of 500 scudi in gold and a silver vase."

The year 1540 and the years following it definitely confirmed the ascendancy of the Ottoman arms. The influence of Rustem-Pasha, a Bulgarian renegade and favorite son-in-law of Roxelana, Suleiman's wife, replaced the statesman-like policy of Ibrahim. Far from moderating the ambitious desires of his master, Rustem, on the contrary, kept whetting them. Why should limits be assigned to the grandeur of Islam, when the heaven itself made such visible moves in its favor? The land and the sea were obeying the sultan by this time. Venice, retiring in the shadow, after ceding Naples of Malvesia and Naples of Romania, was loyally paying the tribute of Cyprus; France looking wherever she could find enemies of the Emperor, made a secret offer to fight on the side of the Sublime Porte; the Ottoman flag was flying on the bastions of Buda.

Hungary at this time tended to become a fief of the Ottoman Empire. Suleiman left her, true enough, a nominal sovereign; but this sovereign, a child of not more than a year, brought into the camp of his Imperial protector by his nurse, had to send his ambassadors every year to deliver at the feet of the sultan 30,000 ducats in gold as a token of his absolute submission.

As it quite frequently happened in the course of her stormy history, Venice had negotiated with a powerful, barbarous Empire face to face, while deserted by all her Allies. For all the others, the war with the Turks had been merely an episode, but for the Venetian community it was a fateful drama, since all her life was concentrated on the waves and on the shores contested by the Asiatic Power. In an austere introduction to the history of this sterile war, the Senator, Francesco Longo, insisted on the necessity for the Republic to maintain peace with the Turks. "In order to plead this cause," wrote he, "is to perform the greatest service to the Republic. As long as I began to take part in the counsels of the Republic, ever since I could get a clear account of the weakness and poor administration of the state, different from that of our ancestors who by their justice and candor, by their great benevolence

and wisdom could conquer the love of the people and the State, I have been forcefully sustaining my opinion about the peace. The report on this war has for its main purpose to show that the only remedy to our evils is to keep peace with the Turks." Indeed nothing else was to be done.

Tommaso Contarini was sent to Constantinople in order to negotiate the peace. The Turks demanded all the territories between Kotor and the latest Venetian possessions in the eastern Mediterranean. Contarini accepted merely the surrender of Nauplia (Napoli di Romania) and Malvasia (Napoli di Malvasia). The negotiations had been broken off. On the 27th of December, Alvise Badoer, Proveditor General of Dalmatia, continued the negotiations. He had to accept the surrender of Nauplia and Malvasia on the eastern coast of Peloponnese, he had to accept a tribute of 300,000 ducats for reparations, but he demanded a counter service, the restitution of the Dalmatian fortifications of Nadin and Vrana. Yet on these points the Turks were adamant. Finally these two fortresses have been assigned to the Turks, but Badoer counseled the Senate to destroy them before surrendering them. In this way the Turks encircled Zadar. Nothing was saved except the cities and territories defended by the Croats. The peace was signed on the 2nd of October, 1540, which for 30 years had been officially respected, but merely officially, since it did not prevent the Turks from continuing their raids against the Dalmatian territory.

The mainland of Dalmatia became in a large part the Turkish sanjakate (military district) headed by the resident Sanjakbeg of Klis, and the muezzin was offering prayers to Allah only two hours' walk from the cathedral of Split. The population was despondent. The Franciscans of Bosnia came from time to time to bring it the solace of religion. They were celebrating the Holy Mysteries in the cemeteries and were secretly dispensing the sacraments. Dalmatia was reduced to that depth of misery under a regime incapable of defending it. Only the seacoast cities were the beneficiaries of the presence of the Venetian fleet, but also of the unceasing alertness by the local residents.

The year following the humiliating Turkish-Venetian peace, the Adriatic became a closed area where the Croats and Venetians were bordering on each other as in the 9th century when the doges took to sea in order to combat the formidable Narentans. The Turkish conquest had repulsed the new Croatian unities to the eastern coast of the Adriatic which, having nothing to do after the fall of Klis, took refuge in Senj, an ancient city carved in a hollow of the Croatian-Austrian coast, not far from Fiume (Riyeka). There they formed a State living on the waves of the Adriatic, under a collective and vague name of Uskoki of Senj (Senia, Segna, Zengg).

The Uskoki at first were chasing the Turks in order to revenge themselves for Klis. They were also a powerful defensive group in warding off the continental Turkish attacks in the face of the existing official peace treaties. Embarked on their small ships, imitating unconsciously the ancient Illyrian vessels which caused so much trouble to ancient Rome, with an audacity unmatched in the annals of the 16th century, they started an impetuous campaign against the Turkish ships, casting the lightnings of anger of the Sublime Porte at Venice.

Indeed, Venice was held liable by the Turks for everything that took place in the Adriatic. It was Venice who had to exercise the sea policing in the Adriatic, or otherwise in the Turkish eyes she was nothing whatsoever. Therefore Venice for the first time in her history, could do nothing, at least nothing decisive against this handful of Croats, who despised death. All she could do was to turn to King Ferdinand, since the localities inhabited by the Uskoki (Senj, Bakar, etc.) belonged to Austria. But disgusted with war, under the terrors of the Turkish power, Venice ordered the Captain in the Gulf to blockade the port of Senj. Ferdinand at first was impressed by the Venetian complaints. In turn he gave the order to destroy the Uskoki ships, but this order was never carried out. Furthermore, in his own courts they were delighted with the difficulties from which Venice could not extricate herself.

Some Turkish naval vessels penetrated the Adriatic, but chased by the Venetian fleet, they immediately left the sea. Only in 1566 did the Uskoki turn against the Venetians. Since the Venetians protected the Turks, they decided to fight the Venetians themselves. Without the slightest worry about the "rights" of the city of St. Mark on the Adriatic, which claimed the Adriatic sea as its internal dominion, the Uskoki were snapping contemptuously their fingers at the "Queen of the Adriatic." They insulted her, and exhausted her on board their primitive boats. At the same time Venice had a correspondence, replete with threats and misunderstanding, with the son of Ferdinand, the Archduke Charles who from Graz administered, in his capacity of vice-roy, a large portion of the hereditary States of the Hapsburg House, namely, Styria, Carniola, Istria and the Croatian seacoast. The Uskoki were formally under his jurisdiction. Charles played a two-faced role in the matter of the Uskoki, officially taking part of Venice, but underhandedly protecting the Croatian avengers, the naval exploits of which interrupted the Venetian control of the Adriatic.

As if the offensive of the Uskoki had not been enough, the Republic was confronted with a problem of vital interest to her; the problem of Cyprus.

To eliminate Venice from its Mediterranean Empire was one of the fundamental points in the program of three sultans, Selim I, Suleiman I, and Selim II. After Hungary, which had been reduced to a Turkish pashalyk, after the capture of Negropontus and Rhodes, after the acquisitions of the peace of 1540, Turkey cast her glances at the rich island of Cyprus which caused it too much inconvenience. Furthermore, Venice took it away from the last King of Lusignan by getting hold of the dowry of Catherine Cornaro, widow of Jacob II, King of Cyprus, and adopted by the senate "as the daughter of the Republic of St. Mark." The island was defended with true heroism. The epilogue of the defense of Cyprus took the proportions of a Christian epic by the martyrdom of its defender Marc Antonio Bragadin (2nd of August, 1570) whom the Turks, in violation of their faith, after the most terrible tortures skinned alive.

During these terrible events, the Uskoki had obtained full freedom to navigate in the Adriatic and to capture any Turkish vessels which they could find. Besides, the sanjakbeg of Klis attempted an offensive against Split which had been repulsed. The entire Venetian fleet, under the command of Jerome Zane, was concentrated in the waters of Zadar. But the fortification of Zemunik, 15 kilometers from the city, fell into the hands of the Turks. Novigrad resisted. Ragusa trembled and put on more solid fortifications.

The Turkish admiral Karahodja penetrated in the Adriatic, attacked by surprise Dulcigno (Ultsin), Antivari (Bar) and Budua (Budva), which were in part set on fire by the Turks. The Dalmatian population took up arms. Women were furnishing men examples of courage. Two memorable war episodes are credited to them. In Rogoznitsa, armed with nothing but oars, they assaulted the Turks and only one of them escaped. The next year (1571) the women of Curzola (Korchula) disguised as men seized weapons from the Venetian officers and soldiers, put in position several pieces of artillery, and repulsed the Turks who laid siege with 15 galleys on the city which the Republic entrusted to mercenaries.

A Turkish attack against the Lesina (Hvar) took place from the 17th to the 21st of August, 1571. The Turks destroyed and set on fire the main localities of the famous island. Their fleet consisted of 70 sails under the orders of Uluk Ali Karahodja. "We have lost all of our revenue— our goods and our supplies," wrote a patrician from Lesina to a friend. "I think that we shall have to look for another country if compassion of Christ does not come to our aid."

Solin (Solona) fell again into the hands of the Turks, along with the stronghold of Sasso (Kamen) which has been abandoned in a cowardly manner by its foreign garrison. Ettore Tron could not recapture Klis, but Almoro Tiepolo, a great soldier, recovered Skradin. Astore Visconti laid waste the Turkish vicinity of Shibenik. This city and Zadar resisted all Turkish attacks. Dalmatia was saved by a new crusade—the last one of those which could still be called actions of Christendom.

Unable to resist all by herself this formidable Turkish offensive, especially after the loss of Cyprus, Venice made a new alliance with the Pope (Pius V) and the King of Spain (Phillip II), which was joined by the Duke of Savoia and the Maltese Order. This was the second "Holy League."

It was more successful than the first one, but merely in its immediate manifestations. Don Juan of Austria, a young man of 24 years of age, and natural son of Charles V, was placed at the head of the most formidable fleet which the world had ever seen before. Venice equipped 114 galleys, under the command of Sebastian Venier, Spain armed 103, the Pope 12, the Duke of Savoia 4, the Maltese Order 3 galleys. Christian naval forces numbered 243 galleys. Marc-Antonio Colonna, commander of the papal fleet, was the next in high command and, with the Venetian Admiral Venier, these 3 men formed the supreme council which was to decide the operations.

Ragusa again obtained a solemn declaration of neutrality, in spite of the desperate opposition of Venice, which however, did not prevent it from sending underhandedly 30 "vessels" to the Christian League, mainly freight ships, which, in case of necessity could be transformed on short notice into fighting vessels. Dalmatia considered it an honor to contribute her own forces to this supreme struggle against the Infidel. The state of desolation in which this country lingered, did not prevent it from arming 7 galleys—Arbe (Rab), Cherso (Tsres), Veglia (Kerk), Lesina (Hvar), Trau (Trogir), Sebenico (Shibenik) and Cattaro (Kotor), which were distributed between the two flanks and the center. The Dalmatian galleys were under command of the local patricians: Colane Drascio (Tsres-San-Nicolo), Lodovico Cicuta (Kerk-Christo Risuscitato), Giovanni Balzi (Hvar-San-Girolamo), John de Dominis (Rab-San Giovanni), Louis Cippico (Trogir-La Donna), Jerome Bisante (Kotor-San Trifone), Christophoro Lucitch (Shibenik-San Giorgio).

The Turks had also a considerable fleet of two hundred and ten galleys with 63 fustae and galeots, under the high command of the admiral Ali-Pasha.

The two fleets sighted each other at dawn of the 7th of October, 1571 at the entrance to the Bay of Lepanto near the Curzolari islands. The battle continued from morning to night. The Turkish fleet was annihilated and if not for the refusal of Doria, nephew of the great admiral, to engage in battle, not a single Turkish ship would have escaped. By this idle move of Doria, who was in command of the right flank of the grand fleet, the squadron of the Algerian Uluj Ali managed to escape. For the first time in history the Croats, represented by the sailors and fighters of Dalmatia and Istria, took revenge on the Turks for the defeat at the Kerbava field, and incessant inroads of their Asiatic hordes in the Croatian lands. The prow and the lantern of the galley of Trogir, which up to this time can be viewed as relics of the great battle in the court of the palace of Cippico, are the mute witnesses of the world-wide conflict.

On the 14th of October, the anonymous journal which has already been referred to, has the following notation:

"At dawn the galley named 'Giustiniana' was sighted arriving speedily from the Levant under sails and oars with a damaged prow. Three men disembarked and announced that the Turkish fleet had been beaten. The galley continued immediately on its course to Venice, loaded with booty. An hour later the galleys of Giustiniano and Pasqualigo entered the port, firing all the guns they had aboard. The city responded with the ringing of all the bells and forty shots from their guns. They had confirmed the great victory and reported the course of the battle. About an hour later the entire artillery of Zadar and its fortification fired shots amid the general rejoicing of the residents of the city. In the churches the 'Te Deum laudamus' solemn Mass was celebrated and in the evening the city paraded with innumerable torches."

On the 16th of October at sunset twenty Turkish horsemen came to the pasture grounds of the city to inquire about the cause of rejoicing observed by them earlier in the day. But without learning anything, they retired. On the 17th of October, a solemn procession in Zadar was repeated for three days in commemoration of the Christian victory. Three squadrons of Turkish cavalrymen came close to the city. An alarm was raised. The infantry occupied the trenches and the whole cavalry force joined them. Ten Turkish horsemen came close to the trenches in order to find out what the celebration in Zadar meant.

"Since the proveditor was informed of the events, he passed on the message that one Turkish soldier may come in the city and they will tell it to him. The disdar (castellan) of Zemunik (Zemonico) came under the assurance of safe conduct, and the commander-in-chief of the city's Venetian forces imparted to him all the reports on the victory of Lepanto, after which he let him go.

"On the 18th of October still another solemn procession was arranged. The troops were mustered up on the Column square. The relics of the saints were carried enclosed in gold and silver sarcophagi, studded with precious stones. The troops followed them four in a row, the pikemen, the flag carriers, the musketeers. The procession ended very late at night, and the troops were disbanded. A solemn mass had been celebrated for the salvation of the souls of the Christians who gloriously died in this historic battle."

The battle of Lepanto was one great blow that weakened the Ottoman power, and, on that score it was worth more than its immediate results. The traditional animosity of the court of Spain against Venice, forced the latter into compromise with the Turks, so that one would think that at Lepanto, not the Christian, but the Turkish navy had scored a momentous victory.

After the defeat the grand Vezir (Mehmed Sokolli-Sokolovich) thus described the situation: "We have obtained Cyprus," he said to the Venetian ambassador (bailo), "but you have defeated us at sea. However, between our two defeats there is one difference. That is, by recovering from you a kingdom, we have cut off your arm. It will never grow again. But the beard of which you had shaved us, still keeps roots for further growth. We have forests in abundance. We also have iron and men and before all we have the certitude that our recent disasters are a small thing alongside the joys that we have experienced."

In part the Grand Vezir was right, but the beard shaved at sea never produced energy to grow, with the ancient vigor. Besides Turkey could profit only by discord and strife among the Christians. The shabby policy of Philip II, the death of Pius V, the immortal chief of the grand enterprise, the huge losses which Venice had suffered, deprived her of all the fruits of this victory which is almost unique in the annals of European history.

She had to cede Cyprus, in Dalmatia she lost Zemunik (Zemonico), Solin and the stronghold of Sasso (Kamen), abandoned by its Italian defenders. It is, indeed, a curious fact. Venice by triumphing on land or on sea had always to pay for her victories by losses. Lepanto, Dardanelles, Morea and a quarter of a century of the prodigious defenses of Candia meant for Venice nothing but loss after loss.

The treaty of March 7, 1573, concluded between Venice and Turkey, did not solve by any means the problem of the Uskoki, which on the contrary grew more and more complicated every day. The Uskoki carried their attacks by this time against all the coastlanders of the Adriatic. Before long it became intolerable, even for the Ragusans, who used the same Croatian language the Uskoki did. The capture of the Venetian vessels was beyond control. Since all their ships were loaded with Turkish merchandise, it became obvious that the flag of St. Mark was no longer capable of protecting the commercial interests of the other powers. Venice protested vainly to Graz. Archduke Charles was either helpless or pretended to be such. The Pope Gregory XIII also intervened, but without results.

In 1582 the Uskoki, together with the residents of Split and Polyitsa, engaged in a campaign to recapture Solin and Klis. Being afraid that she might be accused of breaking the peace treaty, Venice sent Giovanni Contarini to Split in order to investigate, and to punish the chiefs or the leaders assumed to be involved in this venture, and to place a price on the head of the most redoutable chief of the Uskoki, George Danichich, who had been given the rank of Grand Duke by the emperor himself. As Danichich had seized a Venetian ship loaded with Turkish merchandise, Venice addressed her protest directly to the Emperor Rudolph II, who resided most of the time in Prague. At the same time the captain of the sea received orders to blockade the gulfs of Fiume and Senj, the bases of the Uskoki operations.

A peculiar game devolved in consequence. The Austrian court already had its designs to control the Adriatic. It was not at all disgruntled to see that the Venetians were humiliated in their own waters in a costly fight with their Uskoki foes who were able to escape unpunished from the vain pursuits of Serenissime's superb galleys.

Venice vs. Uskoki

After the peace treaty of 1573, this Uskoki campaign was not meant to raise the prestige of Venice. The specter of the Hapsburg power had already disturbed the sleep of the doges. But

why should the Turks get involved in this struggle? Venice should be strong enough to take care of the situation. That is true, but the city government of Shibenik is secretly siding with the Uskoki. The Turks have been repulsed from Senj and the Croats have laid waste the regions of Obrovats and Neretva; they set on fire the very suburbs of Klis. The Venetians enclosed them in the Morlachian Strait. The Uskoki escaped under the cover of night. The Emperor made it appear that he had given orders of peaceful conduct to his commanders. But these orders were never carried out. All at once, an unforeseen event placed Venice in a dilemma; either to display utmost cruelty and so win the fight, or get involved in a new war with the Turks under deplorable conditions. The city government of Split can no longer stand the sanjakbeg of Klis. It issues a call to the Uskoki. Promptly an expedition is organized. A nobleman of Split, John Alberti, whose ancestors came from Florence, places himself at the head of a small army consisting not only of the Uskoki but also of the natives of Polyitsa. Emperor Rudolph sends them ammunition. The expedition takes on an Austrian aspect. The Emperor, residing in Prague, is well pleased with the situation. But the Venetians take the opposite view to the emperor's project. In their desire to prove to the Turks that they are not accomplices of the emperor, they sent ammunition and food supplies to the Turks only a few years after the Turks had skinned alive their commander Bragadin. But this, of course, will not prevent them from sending an ambassador to Prague, with congratulations to the Emperor over his successes and victories over the Turks. The expedition of Alberti was crowned with complete success. On the 8th of April, the city and the stronghold of Klis fell in the hands of the Christians, who, to the utmost disgust of the Venetians, raised the great imperial flag over the bulwarks of the captured city.

The armed victory of April 8, 1596 caused joyous applause throughout Christendom. But this very Christianity which set fires of joy for the slightest success against the Turks—providing that it should not be disturbed in its local ways—no longer had the fervor, though so moderate, of Philip II. The Catholic king died. The Emperor was submerged in his studies of alchemy and astrology.

In the meantime the Turks sent an army of 15 thousand men to recapture Klis. The Venetians took it upon themselves to prevent the passage of Christian reinforcements. The Venetian authority of Split would have suffered from the presence of the imperial troops at Klis. It was necessary to help the Turks to recapture the stronghold at all price and then let happen what may. The rejoicing of the Christians was short lived. In spite of the reinforcements which came with an imperial general, complete absence of discipline on the part of the Uskoki disrupted the operations. After the attack and counterattack, the Christians had many reverses. Alberti was fatally wounded, and the Bishop of Senj, Anthony de Dominis, with 3 canons, had been killed. The garrison surrendered and left the city with military honors. But the Turks took revenge on those of their subjects who had any sympathy with the imperial cause. The Venetians, in turn, were merciless in their chastisement of the citizens of Split who had manifested attachment to the emperor in his capacity of the king of Croatia.

In the meantime the Uskoki had taken oath to exact revenge on the perfidious ruler of the Adriatic. From now on there is nothing but a struggle of life and death between Venice and the Adriatic Croats.

The Uskoki plundered Rovinj (Rovigno) under the very eyes of the Venetian fleet. From this moment on the struggle became general. The Croats of the Adriatic, victims of the Venetian wars and Turkish massacres, of the arsons, joined up with the Uskoki. With a force of no more than 2,000 men they made the Venetians tremble for their trade and life.

In view of the heavy damage caused by the Uskoki fighters, the Venetians hurled the most abusive names at them, but always in relation to the Austrian court: "Rebels of St. Mark, Spaniards, traitors, brigands." Yet they forgot— as an anonymous writer of the 17th century say~—"That the Venetians owe it to the courage of these very Uskoki that the Turks had not become the absolute masters of the entire Croatian territory, of Senj, of the provinces of Lika and Kerbava (Corbavia), while in Dalmatia they could not resist the Turks who have become the masters of Nadin and Zemunik (Zemonico) at the very gates of Zadar, and of Skradin (Scar-

dona) at the very gates of Shibenik." Pope Gregory XIII found means to keep them more moderate. To the chiefs of the Uskoki he assigned (1580) two thousand scudi per year and to others four hundred scudi a year. During the lifetime of this Pope everything went fine. But as soon as Sixtus V ascended the papal throne, he discontinued their subsidy, and in retaliation the Uskoki returned to looting.

In Venice it had been rumored that the Archduke of Styria and all the magnates of the Archduke's court had been sharing in the loot. It had been whispered that in the possession of a certain archduchess a wreath of magnificent pearls had been seen, which belonged to a Jewish merchant who had been held up by the Uskoki. The gossip also had it that the caps and other headgear of the aristocratic ladies were adorned with precious ston.es But the Uskoki defended themselves; "Slanders"! In order to express their gratitude to the governors of Senj, they showered them with the objects retrieved in the course of their expeditions, such as an ornate sword, tapestry, sable fur coats for their wives. The Turks redeemed these frequently not only in cash but with racing horses, lynx furs, mantles adorned with silver buttons, etc.

On the contrary, the Emperor and the Archduke condemned the exploits of the seafarers and the Archduke himself issued orders to behead some Uskoki fighters found guilty of plunder and robbery. Reference was made to the capture of a vessel loaded with scarlet fabrics, satins and other precious textiles. The Archduke, upon being advised, issued severe orders to prevent the sale of these goods in his territory. The Uskoki disregarded this order and sold their loot at a low price. Their best customers were the Venetian magistrates throughout Dalmatia and Istria. The magistrates sent these very fabrics back to Venice selling them again to the Turks, or to the merchants of western cities.

The Emperor played a double game with Venice, that is, he acted the way the Venetians did. He did not want to break with the Republic, but on the other hand the Uskoki were his precious allies. Yet he did not want war with the Signory. Likewise he sent a mission to Senj ordering them to come to terms with the general proveditor of Dalmatia, Giovanni Bembo.

Interned for a spell in the interior of the country—so called the military district—the Uskoki came back in force. The Uskoki pushed their raids further over the Ragusan territory down to Herzegovina. The Ragusans did not take this lightly. They took most cruel measures against the Uskoki. They got hold, by mean trickery, of the voyevode (archduke) George Danichich and his associates and beheaded them.

At Lesina (Hvar) the Uskoki suffered another defeat. But in combat with a Venetian squadron between Split and Neretva they were victorious. Christopher Venier, the commander of the squadron, was taken prisoner, and beheaded.

Venice vs. Spain

Spain intervened, through the vice-roy of Naples, whose Adriatic coast was at the mercy of both the Uskoki and the Venetians at the same time. A Neapolitan squadron made its way into the Adriatic, negotiated with the Uskoki, and set Durazzo on fire. But soon the Venetians chased out the Neapolitans from the Adriatic.

In 1612, Rudolph II passed away and his brother Mathias was elected king of Germany. On the 14th of June he was crowned Emperor. He succeeded at the same time his brother in the kingdoms of Hungary and Bohemia. The chase against the Uskoki continued. In turn the latter were chasing their enemy. They attacked the Venetian possessions, they sacked them, seized their light vessels and shared the loot among themselves. A Venetian fleet consisting of 70 units had been disarmed by the small enemy, striking with lightning speed. The Archbishop of Zadar, Minuci, a Venetian-Dalmatian historian of the 17th century, compares them to a mosquito fighting a lion. The proveditor Marcello himself was made an Uskoki prisoner. They did not harm him. The Archduke Charles interposed his authority and Marcello was set free. Even the best organized expedition of the Signory did not have success. The proveditor blockaded the Croatian coastline, attacked Lovrana and Novi which were almost entirely destroyed, but in vain. From this paradoxical situation nothing but war could result.

This was a peculiar war. An expedition in the Adriatic had been promptly organized by the ambitious and undertaking vice-roy of Naples, the Duke of Ossuna, who in collusion with Marquis Bedmar, ambassador of the Catholic king,

in Venice, engineered a formidable conspiracy in order to blast the arsenal of Venice, together with the rest of the city.

In fact the whole expedition was engineered by Ragusa, the cunning and implacable enemy of Venice. However the immediate cause of the plot was the Venetian subsidy to Charles Emmanuel of Savoia in order to have him expel the Spaniards from Milan.

This war, in which no one was defeated or victorious, ended with the peace of Madrid made on September 6, 1617 through the mediation of Savoy and France.

The Venetian fleet could hardly get away from the Istrian coast, which was the very seat of war. Ossuna did the rest. He ruined the Venetian trade, and in triumph delivered in Naples the loot which his fleet had seized from the Venetians. Bedmar, who was making ready to strike the final blow at the city of Saint-Mark, insisted in his report "on the desolation in some of the provinces which had been caused by the war against the Uskoki." "There were no more than three officers in each garrison of Lombardy who actually drew a salary." It is quite certain that Bedmar and Ossuna could never have set up their project without the distress in which the Republic of Venice carried on under the administration of Giovanni Bembo as Doge, and his successors. Ossuna made his attempt in Venetian-Albania in order to detach it from the Republic. He attempted to get hold of Klis, but the Turks had put up a good defense. Girolamo Contarini had watched with his own fleet all the movements of the Ragusans and Spaniards. In spite of many harassing experiences, Venice remained safe. "Heaven did not want to abandon the work of 12 centuries and of so many wise heads in favor of a courtesan and a group of reckless individuals," reasons Saint-Real.

Twenty-seven years after said events, Candia replaced Cyprus. After the war of Cyprus the war of Candia followed. The first was stretched out over a part of the 16th century, the other exhausted the forces of Venice for over a quarter of the 17th century. It lasted 24 years, used the efforts of 7 doges and caused a considerable number of casualties and victims. It deprived Venice of the most beautiful diamond of her crown. Venice achieved wonders of heroism in the face of a Europe which was indifferent to her fate. In compliance with the program of its great sultans, especially that of Selim and Suleiman, Turkey could count upon the expert administration of the powerful Albanian family of Kőprűlű. The weak Mahomed IV, in spite of his other faults, had enough good sense to choose from this family two grand vizirs, statesmen of the first order, Mehmed and Ahmet Pasha. The latter, rivaling in tenacity the Venetian heroes, took in 1669 the last Venetian stronghold of the island which belonged to the republic ever since 1214. But if Venice could not keep the precious island, although poorly administered, she had won a decisive victory in Dalmatia. She recovered, with few exceptions, almost everything that she had lost in the war of Cyprus and could trace between herself and Turkey a more logical frontier which was secure from surprise attacks. In truth, it is in 1645—the first year of the war of Candia—that liberation of the Dalmatian soil begins with the combined activity of a great Venetian general and the brave Croatian troops of Dalmatia, whose remarkable exploits have been transmitted to this day in the form of heroic ballads of the Croatian people.

At the beginning of hostilities, in Dalmatia and northern Albania, a small army of 4,700 footsoldiers and 600 cavalrymen, had been assigned to defend the fortified places. The rest of the territory was, quite fortunately, defended by the armed Croatian population. The defense of Dalmatia was entrusted to the proveditor general, Leonardo Foscolo, a remarkable military leader of a firm character and strong will power, who knew how to channel the energies of the people to rise in rebellion and recapture its own native hearths.

Liberation of Dalmatia from the Turks

Foscolo had under his command some other brilliant generals, such as Marc Anthony Pesaro, chief of staff, and the German born Degenfeld as well as the Italian count Ferdinando Scoto. The troops, which consisted almost entirely of the local Croatian population, were impatient to combat their age-old enemy. It was the first time on the continent since the fall of their national state that the Croats came to blows, in an impressive force, with the Ottoman power. The plan of Foscolo provided for an offensive in open country. He figured that the defeat of the troops sent by the Pasha of Bosnia would result in the surrender of all the strongholds occupied by the Turks. But the Senate was opposed to this project and imposed on the commander-in-chief a purely defensive campaign. At the same time three state inquisitors sent the general a barrel containing arsenic "of the best quality" to make use of against the enemy. And Foscolo replied: "Pervaded by the sentiment of the need to defend this part of the state against the Pasha of Bosnia, who is, according to the information, on the point of attacking Novigrad at the head of an army which has already invaded the territory of Shibenik, I have given definite orders to poison the three wells where the enemy will most likely pitch camp."

The Turks attacked first. Bernardo Taiapietra, entrusted with the defense of Novigrad, abandoned the stronghold and retired to Zadar under the pretext of asking for aid. Foscolo put him in the dungeon. The Turks got hold of Novigrad. Its defender, Francesco Loredan, was released but the garrison was massacred. Foscolo counterattacked, chased out the Turks and organized a liberation of the other strongholds and towns of the Zadar territory. They fell one after another

Pisani at the head of eight hundred horsemen and fifteen hundred footsoldiers was supported by Foscolo and the rest of his army in the siege of Vrana. The Dalmatians got hold of the suburbs of the ancient residence of the templars. Vrana was surrounded by a lake, which was actually a swamp. Yet the beleaguers discovered a patch of solid ground and placed their single piece of artillery upon it. For eleven days they bombarded the stronghold. But the bulwarks ruined in daytime had been repaired by the Turks at night.

In the midst of these events, Nadin fell. The Turkish population was put to sword. A rich booty was recovered consisting of gold, silver and cattle. The castle of Karin was taken in turn, set on fire, and its garrison massacred. This news gave impetus to the troop beleaguering Vrana. Finally the garrison surrendered. The Turks demanded to leave the place with the honors of war but Foscolo had them massacred and Vrana was plundered for ten days. The native land of the great sculptor Francis Laurana and his cousin Lucian Laurana, architect of the palace of the Duke of Urbino, was completely destroyed.

At Vrana precious arms have been found which belonged to the Emperor Maximilian II and Sigismund Bátory, prince of Transylvania, as well as many other precious objects which enriched the Venetian palaces, in order to be dispersed later among all the museums of Europe.

The conquest of Dalmatian soil, initiated under these fortunate auspices, had been pursued tenaciously throughout the duration of the war of Candia. Everything was committed to plunder, to destruction; cultivated lands, mills, orchards, salt pans, chattel. For a long time the word liberation was synonymous to "impoverishment or destruction." Venice was in the hands of her fate. She must continue to fight. "Her struggle was that of an exhausted giant losing its lands, but not capable of stopping it. She must fight to the end. The night descends. Her destiny runs its course." Hence she must keep fighting.

Liberation of Dalmatian Cities from the Turks

The campaign in Dalmatia and the naval battles in the Archipelago, in the course of which Tommaso Morosini found his heroic death, while the captain general Grimani almost lost his fleet, moved the Serenissime to issue a pressing appeal to the Great Powers. With a certain dose of ingenuity, Venice, which had assisted the Turks during the entire period from the peace treaty of 1573 to the war of Candia, sought at this moment to set all Europe against the Turks. The ambassadors of the Republic made ingenious moves to prove at the foreign courts that the salvation of Christianity was at stake. Venice alone could go through the struggle in Candia, in Dalmatia, in the Friuli, and over a huge line of territory which skirted the Ottoman conquered lands. For this defense she exhausted the means of her arsenal, had emptied her public treasury, had sacrificed her citizens, had invited from all over subsidies in manpower and ships. The world of Christendom should be advised—the Venetian envoys stressed—that after Candia is taken, the enemy will become still more haughty and powerful, and will swoop on Italy, seat of the religion, after which the Turkish greed will have no limits. The princes of Europe must intervene in their own interests; they must compose their differences, so that they all, in common, may point their weapons towards an objective so noble. On the other hand, if the Republic is left in the lurch as in 1573, she will be forced to think only of her own salvation and make decisions dictated by the necessity of the moment and by her geographic situation.

All these beautiful words lacked convincing power, and were blown away with the wind. Venice was left alone and remained alone. Only the French sent a contingent to Candia, among which were a number of great names from the military history of France. But in the absence of true discipline, in spite of its prodigious courage, the small troop of French fighters perished almost to the last man. Venice will remain isolated until the day the Empire shall decide to humble the Ottoman power. In contrast with the Venetian affairs which had taken a bad turn in the Orient, in Dalmatia lady luck was smiling at the Republic. Step after step, blow after blow, Zemunik, Skradin, Ostrovitsa, Solin and the stronghold of Kamen (Sasso) fell into the hands of the Dalmatian Croats. Shibenik resisted a powerful army of the Pasha of Bosnia made up of twenty thousand Circassians. The capture of Zemunik was not the only one. The city so rich in the past, located in a plain in the greater vicinity of Zadar, had been surrounded by two rectangular bulwarks, and was housing a Turkish garrison. The fortifications had been powerful. A minaret was piercing the skies of Dalmatia. The force charged with the capture of the stronghold consisted of Croatian, German, French and Italian troops. The cavalry was for the most part, French. It was under the orders of Colonel Briton. In a sally from the city the garrison was repulsed and thrown back in disorder to the stronghold.

The Turks had attached much importance to Zemunik. The sanjakbeg of Lika, Ali-bey, had taken personal command of the city. An octogenarian, he enclosed himself in the citadel with his son Durak, who in the course of a night sally was captured and beheaded. The suburb had been taken, with rich booty. The artillery was destroying the fortification. The city population demanded surrender. After repeated assaults, and after the artillery destroyed the bulwarks, the Turks surrendered on the 19th of March. Pisani sent Marco Silla, a captain of the Croat troops, to negotiate the conditions of surrender. After being plundered, the stronghold was entirely demolished.

The capture of Zemunik was celebrated in the

churches of Zadar with a Te Deum mass. Upon a survey of the situation, it developed that 6,300 Turks perished during the siege while 200 of them had been made prisoners. After the capture of Vrana, Foscolo and Pisani organized an expedition to Skradin in order to completely relieve Shibenik.

Gabriel Emo and Nocolo Suriano could not take Skradin in 1652, in spite of the considerable forces they had at their disposal (six thousand infantry and two thousand cavalry). The Venetian vessels, 70 units strong, appeared on the 7th of May. The armed forces were made up almost exclusively of native Croats, with some Albanian and German detachments. In the midst of a headlong panic, the Turks evacuated the city which was captured after several small engagements. According to the reports of Bailo (Venetian ambassador) in Constantinople, the Sultan, deeply impressed by the disasters in Dalmatia, wanted to send there an army of 20,000 men, but a plague broke out in Constantinople which prevented this plan. A great leader of the troops, the true prototype of a Croatian hero, enduring, contemptuous of death, the priest Sorich, with the consent of the Government, placed himself at the head of a proven warrior troop and laid waste the whole area up to Knin, then took Knin and Verlika. In the meantime Foscolo in severe cold captured the important stronghold of Dernish.

But the greatest blow and the one which echoed throughout Europe was the liberation of Klis after a century of Moslem domination. Klis was, like Cyprus and Candia, a symbol of the Christian fighting spirit.

The beach of Solin was selected for this operation. The Venetian fleet consisted of seven large galleys, fifty other armed vessels, two fighting ships and a number of freighters on which the infantry forces were embarked under the orders of the proveditor Zorzi. Echelons of the free city of Polyitsa and from across the sea took part in the expedition.

An advance position called Greben (ridge) had been captured by Venetian and Dalmatian troops. Artillery pieces were disembarked and installed there. The stronghold itself was defended by a Turkish force of two thousand eight hundred men under the orders of sanjakbeg Mustafa bey. After a continous artillery fire, the Croatian, Albanian and Italian troops captured the front lines of defense. Shortly after the second line of defense had been taken, a hand to hand fight issued. The assailants were at first repulsed. But after an obstinate defense the Turks surrendered. They demanded the honors of war. The Venetians agreed that women and children should be set free, but the garrison should be taken prisoner. Later they would be exchanged for the Christians who were still in the power of the Turks. The latter insisted. They made a comparison between Canea and Klis, but the Venetians retorted that Klis, by the very mass of its ruins, proved that its military value had been greatly exaggerated.

The priest Sorich, the chief of the Morlachi; the governor of Polyitsa, Yanko Mariyanovich; the captain Gregory Detrico of Zadar; and Frederic Maroli of Split were heading the expeditionary forces participating in the recapture of Klis. Finally the garrison departed. They killed the aged Aga Barakovich, and carried a dozen dying Turks on a precious rug. Two hundred and forty-three Turks with five women had been put to the sword in violation of the given promise. Plunder and massacre continued for some time. In a frenzy of rage the Albanians, Croats, Italians and Germans mowed down the defenseless Moslem population regardless of the frantic pleading of the latter to spare their lives.

The news of the capture of Klis arrived in Venice on Palm Sunday and set off a general explosion of joy. The Doge himself came to the cathedral of Saint Mark, where the Te Deum mass was sung in the presence of the papal Nuncio. All the bells of Venice were rung, the guns were fired, the plaudits of the crowd and the felicitations of the diplomatic corps were attached to the joy of the Senate and to the congratulations addressed to Foscolo, who had been called "Benefactor of the Fatherland" (as per letter of the Doge of April 7, 1648).

A shower of decorations was distributed among the chiefs of the expedition whether Venetians or Croats, for Venice appreciated the effort of all those who had humiliated the Turks by seizing "their most secure haunt and one of the chief gates through which they were steadily making their inroads to the detriment of the Republic and Christianity."

Priest Sorich continued his campaign. Finally

he was captured and skinned alive. The entire year 1648 was marked with fighting, destruction, and incendiary activity. Venice took revenge for her losses of Cyprus and Negropont and for the siege of the Cretan cities. From that time on no quarters were given. Destruction was systematic. A proposition was made to destroy Klis, but it was rejected by the Senate. It was decided to rebuild and fortify the city, not only because of its dominant position, but also to express gratitude and acknowledgement to Foscolo. In 1649 Foscolo entered the Bay of Kotor. Due to the aid given him by the Croatian population of Perast and Pastrovich, he took hold of Rison, the ancient Illyrian capital. The Moslems launched a counter offensive. They threatened Zadar and Nin. Another Croatian chief of great talent, Iliya Smilyanich, defeated them at Karin and Zvonigrad. The population of Solin (Salona) repulsed them. All this action was effected in a secret agreement with the Franciscan friars of Bosnia who were from time to time their councilors, priests and soldiers. Furthermore, the Franciscan friars repopulated the deserted areas of Neretva and Nin (Narenta and Nona) with numerous families from Herzegovina.

The Croatian leaders did not take recess or respite. Everything was placed on their shoulders. The more Venice got embroiled in her long war in Candia, the more the native chiefs became involved in a war without mercy against the Turks, impatient to liberate their own country without any alien assistance. The historians could not pass up in silence the heroic exploits of priest Sorich, of a Smilyanich, of the aged voyevode Todor of Zadar, the chiefs of the troops Kralyevich and Shandich, as well as those of the "terrible warrior" Vuk Mandushich, of whose death an Italian contemporary of the capture of Klis, had written "that he had been bemoaned by all Dalmatia and that his actions will be recorded in all the history books."

Wars of Liberation

Smilyanich and Mitrovich of Possedaria, as leaders of the revolutionary liberation movement, declared war on the Turks in their own names and those of their co-fighters. This war was declared in 1651. The new proveditor, general Lorenzo Dolfin, reported to the Senate their victory record under the walls of Zadar. Smilyan-

ich chased the Turks to the banks of the Una river in Bosnia. In one of the many engagements, however, he was surrounded and killed. The year 1656 was probably one of the most terrible years in the history of Dalmatia with nothing but bloodshed, fighting, pestilence, famine, raids and invasions throughout the country. The country had been reduced to extreme poverty, while cities and strongholds evacuated their civilian population. No more trading, selling or buying—the country was in the throes of complete misery and yet the Dalmatians resisted all that without having any doubts that one day their country will be free from all strangers.

The Pasha of Bosnia renewed his expedition against Shibenik and also against Klis, but was thrown back to Bosnia. Nin, Skradin, and the area of Split knew more than once the distresses of invasion. The Turks even laid siege to Split. They were ready to capture the fortification Grippi, one of the external bastions of the city, when proveditor Antonio Bernardo, at the head of the Croatian troops recruited in the tract from Polyitsa to Trogir, forced the Pasha to raise the siege. The next year, Yanko Mitrovich and Iliya Milkovich chased the Turks to the gates of Sarayevo. Another Dalmatian whose name has never been known in the past, had been placed in command of the Venetian galleys in the waters of Cattaro (Kotor). The proveditor general, Andrew Corner, could therefore write to the Signory that "the chief support of Dalmatia were the Dalmatian peasants."

In August, 1664 an imperial army under the command of Count Montecuccoli crushed a powerful Turkish army at Saint-Gothard on the banks of the Raab river. However, this victory was followed by a shameful peace to which the emperor submitted, while five years later (in September, 1669) Admiral Francis Morosini, after a brilliant defense, surrendered and placed in the hands of Ahmed Kőprűli, the city of Candia. The island was lost to Venice for all times to come. She reserved for her own use three small forts, which were soon seized. From her conquests in Dalmatia she kept merely the coastline and the stronghold of Klis. The frontier was not precisely traced, so the Turks claimed Zemunik, Vrana, Ostrovitsa, Dernish, Knin, and Duare (Dvori). The delimitation of the frontier line had been carried out by two commissars who finished their work on the 30th of October, 1671. The Venetians gave the frontier line so established, the name of Linea Nani, borrowed from the name of a Commissar.

This line issuing from the Gulf of Novigrad continued northwest, then ran west and at the height of Nin, to the direction of the shoreline, except between Shibenik and Trogir. From this side, leaving to the Venetians the entire peninsula which runs southwest, the frontier line followed the last incline of the Tartar hills. The territory yielded by the Turks was stopped at the Tsetina river. The Venetians had to yield also the area of Makarska, but the Ottomans became satisfied with nothing more than a titular possession. The same happened to the County of Polyitsa which was left out of the Venetian frontier. However, the Turks never risked putting their foot there in order to exercise their suzerain rights. They called this line also Acquisto Vecchio (the old acquisition) in contrast with the more liberal Acquisto Nuovo, the fruit of the more recent conquests.

The great victories scored by the combined armies of the King of Poland and Duke of Baden, under the walls of Vienna (September 12, 1683) followed by a complete disaster of the Ottoman army and the execution of the Grand Vizir Kara Mustapha, finally persuaded Europe that it was time to finish with the Ottoman nightmare, which some 16th century writers called "Dragon of the East." Promptly a league was formed, the third "Saint League" (having for its slogan: Habeto nos foederatos et serviemus Tibi; "Take us (Oh Almighty) as allies and we shall serve you"— between the Pope, Emperor Leopold I, Venice and Poland. It was crowned with a complete success not only because of the multitude of forces, but also by the inexorable law of history, which set up a barrier against the Ottoman flood so that this flood could only recede. Hungary and Slavonia had been delivered of the Ottoman yoke within the confines of one single campaign.

As the news spread about the victory at Vienna, the Dalmatian population took up arms and organized itself into a regular army under the chief command of the proveditor-general Lorenzo Donati. But these national troops selected as their leaders some of their famous compatriots; the Count Yankovich of Possedaria, the serdar Smilyanich and the general Count Radosh. Ever since 1684 up to the peace treaty of Karlovtsi in 1699, the Dalmatians did not stop hostilities except at the moment of the epidemics of plague, and were fighting not only against the isolated bands, but also against the entire Turkish armies. In the next year, Girolamo Cornaro, supported by a Spanish troop under the command of Alessandro Farnese captured Sinj, a fortified place in the position of the continental Dalmatia, as well as Castelnuovo (Herzegnovi) at the entrance to the Bay of Kotor. Castelnuovo (Herzegnovi) with the adjacent shores, became one of the main naval stations of the Republic. Of all the Turkish-Venetian wars this is the one which can be said that it had been carried on exclusively by the people of Dalmatia.

While Francesco Morosini was carrying his blows against the Turks at sea and carried his attacks against Negropont, due to the onslaught of the Dalmatian troops a powerful fortification had to fall in the hands of Venetians. The operations in Dalmatia followed their course of bloody engagements between the army of the Pashas of Bosnia and Herzegovina, and the Dalmatian troops under the command of Count Augustin Tartaglia and the serdar Vuzhich. The Turks have been defeated on several occasions. Count Yankovich pushed with his own forces up into Bosnia and with Cornaro took again Sinj from the Turks, for the last time. With manpower of 50,000 men, Venetians and Dalmatians invaded Herzegovina and smashed a Turkish army near the River Trebinshchitsa.

In the midst of this development, taking advantage of the Dalmatian victories, Ragusa approached the Emperor, being afraid that Venice would encircle her. On the 20th of August, 1684, the Republic of Saint-Blaise signed in Vienna a treaty with the Emperor Leopold I, by the terms of which she placed herself under his protection, in his capacity of the King of Hungary, and Croatia, by renewing the pact signed in 1358 with Louis, King of Hungary and Croatia. This protectorate was restored under the auspices of Spain which saved the Republic of Ragusa at the time of the negotiations of Pozharevats. Due to the combined intervention, paradoxical as it may be, between the sultan and the emperor, Ragusa obtained her territorial isolation from the Venetian-Dalmatia. Surrounded by all sides with Turkish territories, the diminutive Republic could resist the imperialist designs of Venice and could preserve her independence up to the time of Napoleon.

In 1688, the capture of Knin and Verlika, freed by the Dalmatian troops and their recapture of Verhgorats completed the liberation of Dalmatia up to the frontier areas of the Ragusan Republic.

Peace Treaties of Karlovtsi and Pozharevats (1699 and 1717)

However, the struggle continued even after 1688. This time it does not take place on Dalmatian and Venetian territory, but on Turkish territory. The Turks had been smashed by the Imperial forces under the command of the Duke of Baden at Slankamen in Sirmium (Sriyem). As the momentum of the Imperial campaign intensified, the Dalmatian offensive became more definite. The stronghold of Chitluk was seized by the proveditor Dolfin. The Pasha of Bosnia hastened to its rescue with 16,000 men. He was repulsed but again renewed his offensive, yet he was finally defeated by the troops of the Count Fanfogna, Nonkovich and Vushkovich. Trebinye and Klobuk fell into the hands of the Dalmatian Croats.

In the next year Prince Eugene of Savoia smashed the Turks at Zenta on the banks of Tissa in southern Hungary. In their turn, the Venetians scored a brilliant naval victory at the Dardanelles, while the aged Doge, Francesco Morosini, captured a number of important places in Peloponese and later died at Nauplia (Napoli di Romania) in full triumph for which he was given the distinctive title: "The Peloponnesian." The Dalmatians renewed their offensive in Bosnia. But the grave problem of the succession to the throne of Spain cut off the victorious offensive of the Christian coalition, and in 1699 peace was signed on the Croatian territory in the town of Syrmian Karlovtsi. The Venetians keep their conquests in Peloponnese. In Dalmatia they were given all the territories conquered by the Dalmatian Croats for the last 14 years.

The act of boundary marking was signed on the 14th of July, 1700 by the proveditor Giovanni Grimani and thus the borderline was given the name "The Grimani Line." The frontier was set up by a very simple method; the points of Knin, Verlika, Sinj, Duare (Zadvorje), Verhgorats and Chitluk (Gabela) were united by straight lines

passing over mountains and through valleys. Around each of the six points, an area of about an hour's walk was left as the defense zone. The territory of the Bay of Kotor was left entirely to the Venetians with the exception of three villages north of Budua, occupied by the Montenegrins, and the county of Zhupa situated in the level plain separating Budua from Kotor. This Grimani borderline determined the frontier which the Venetians named "Nuovo Acquisto" (new acquisto).

In 1714 the war was renewed in consequence of the invasion of Morea (Peloponnese) by the Turks. Venice entirely neglected to provide for the military defense of Dalmatia, but in spite of this negligence—due to the initiative of the Dalmatian-Croatian troops—the Venetians were the beneficiaries of new successes. The Dalmatians took the offensive and the Pasha of Bosnia, who was marching on Senj and Knin, must have withdrawn in haste in spite of the army of 20,000 men which he had under his command. The Dalmatian offensive was supported by the victories of Prince Eugene of Savoia who at this time had in his hands the future of the countries of the southeastern Europe.

On the 13th of August, 1716, Eugene of Savoia, a new John of Austria, destroyed a Turkish army of 200,000 men under the command of the Grand Vezir Ali Pasha, at the stronghold of Petrovaradin on the banks of the Danube. The entire province of Banate had been delivered, while the Dalmatians, exhausted by famine, heroically resisted the repeated assaults of the Pasha of Bosnia, and saved Klis and Dernish. Count Nonkovich captured Metkovich—at the estuary of Neretva, and Utovo. Following up Nonkovich's success, proveditors Emo and Mocenigo broke into Bosnia and Herzegovina, and took Mostar (capital of Herzegovina) by assault in 1717. On this occasion 1,000 Christian families were taken to Dalmatia in order to repopulate certain districts of the land.

The Turks raised the siege of Corfu, defended by Marshal Schulenburg, and rushed in force to Dalmatia in order to check the Dalmatian offensive. But on the 15th of August, Prince Eugene of Savoia struck a crushing blow at the Turkish forces under Belgrade, the stronghold which had stood so many attacks in the course of centuries, and occupied it. On the other hand, the Dalmatian troops made still another advance to Livno in Bosnia, under the command of the new proveditor Alvise Mocenigo.

In the course of these developments, the Emperor called a Congress in Serbia, in the town of Pozharevats, and initiated negotiations with the Turks. The other members of the Alliance could merely submit, and especially Venice which had been exhausted to the point of collapse. Truly, one cannot view, but with a feeling of depression and regret, the sudden halt of Prince Eugene's brilliant campaign—a campaign of encirclement practiced of old by the Roman legions. It was stopped dead by the most foolish of conjunctures, provoked by a Spanish Minister.

One cannot disregard a realization so keen that the stopping of the campaign against the Turks, due to the policy of Philippe V, marked a decisive turning point in the history of Europe. For the victorious march of the Imperial troops— the army of which consisted of numerous ethnic elements—this march to the very heart of the Balkans under the inspiring command of the victor of Zenta, Petrovaradin, Belgrade and Sarayevo would have achieved the deliverance of the Balkan Christians from the Ottoman yoke. Furthermore Eugene of Savoia would have solved the painful Balkan problems two centuries ago, raising this peninsula to a high level of European civilization. Unfortunately the policy of the Cardinal Alberoni, powerfully supported by Elizabeth of Parma, the wife of Philip V, destroyed in several weeks this magnificent perspective. The encroachments of Spain in Italy, the violation of the treaty of Utrecht and Rastatt—the decadent Spanish monarchy which aspired to return to the times of Philip II and deprived the Empire of its Italian possessions—precipitated a set of events which made Charles VI decide to make peace with Turkey. To a certain point even this treaty was good, since the Empire obtained all of the Banate, the little Wallachia up to the confluence of the Aluta river with the Danube, and a certain part of Serbia, with Belgrade. Yet, its weak point was that it placed the Ottoman Empire again in its former position as the dominant power in the Balkans, which it preserved until the end of the 19th century (1878 and 1913).

Venice gained nothing by the peace of Pozharevats (21st of July, 1718). The Serenissime even lost Morea, and as far as Dalmatia was concerned, the regulation of the frontiers was made on the basis of "uti possidetis" (actual possession at a certain date), so adverse to the Republic that rumors of treason had cropped up.

The Mocenigo line, which is called Il Nuovissimo acquisto (the latest acquisition), was traced in the period from 1729 to 1733 by the commissioners Sebastian Mocenigo, for Venice, and Mehmet-effendi-Lialy for the Sultan. This frontier line divided the area between Turkey and Austria up to 1878. Setting out from Triplex confinium, a point where royal Croatia and the Turkish Croatia meet, it included the high valley of Plavno and moved to Stermitsa in the area of Prolog by running along a series of straight lines which left Dalmatia all the villages of the Kerka plateau, and all those situated on the left bank of the Tsetina river.

The town of Unishte, due to its commercial importance, had been partitioned into two halves so that one-half remained Turkish and the other half became Venetian. The tower of Prolog with its circular area of gunshot range remained Turkish. Then the straight line ran uninterrupted to Imotski by cutting in two halves the town of Arzano. From Imotski to Verhgorats there was a new straight line, interrupted by two zones of gunshot range, left in favor of the Venetians. Gabela (Chitluk), evacuated by the Turks in 1715, was never restored to them. Thus the Mocenigo borderline passed behind the Grimani line, including Metkovich, and from there extended to the sea at the valley of Klek. The Venetian conquests around Ragusa were restored to the Turks, but in the Bay of Kotor the enclaves of the district of Zhupa and Pobori, together with Mani and Braitsa, were reunited within the district of Kotor, as well as the area of Krivoshia. Furthermore, the entire Imotski district was ceded to Venice.

Conditions in Dalmatia in the 16th Century

When the Turks conquered the Croatian lands south of Velebit, they found them deserted for the most part. Multitudes of people were fleeing from the Turks wherever they could, especially to the Venetian coastland and the neighboring islands. Those who remained in their native land became serfs of the Turkish nobility, that is, of the Turkish officers and soldiers to whom the

Turks gave the land taken away from their previous owners. The entire Croatian territory conquered by the Turks was now called Bosnia, and was subject either to the sanjakbeg of Klis in the south, or to the sanjak of Lika in the north.

Throughout the entire 16th century, up to the peace of 1573, all of Dalmatia was steadily exposed to the threatening Turkish danger. For not even then, when peace was officially established between Venice and Turkey, was there actually peace in the borderland. The Dalmatian coastal cities under the authority of Venice were at the very Turkish border, since it passed only a few miles away from Zadar, Shibenik, Trogir and Split, and the frontier quarrels frequently degenerated into plunder and massacres.

Dalmatia—Population

When war broke out, the territory surrounding these cities and the cities themselves were mercilessly attacked and plundered, the population was decimated while defending their own possessions and that of their cities. In addition, starvation set in, poverty, plunders. Then also the islands with their towns and cities were set on fire and plundered by the Turks.

But in spite of all the Turkish dangers and disasters, the Dalmatian cities and towns, made rich in the middle ages, and especially on the islands where the Turkish incursions were relatively rare, kept living comfortably as cultural centers.

All these cities, in their overwhelming majority and some of them entirely, by their language and population have been Croatian. The old Romanic element changed into Croatian. The Roman language disappeared and in the place of Latin the official language was Italian, imported to Dalmatia by the Venetian rectors and their chanceries. In 1484 Felix Faber arrived in Zadar. He was not able to converse with the sailor who gave him transportation for he, as the rest of the population in Zadar in general, spoke only Croatian (lingua sclavonica). Giovanni Battista Giustiniani, as supervising Venetian syndic, made a tour of Dalmatia in 1553 and in his official report to the Venetian government he writes that in Zadar due to the large number of aliens (Venetian officials) the patricians live, speak and dress in the Italian way, "while all the lower population lives by its Croatian cus-

toms." For Shibenik, the same Giustiniani says: "the dress of the inhabitants, their speech and their communication is Croatian. All women are dressing the Croatian way and almost none of them speak Italian." And in Trogir: "the residents of this city live by the Croatian customs. It is true that some of them are dressing the Italian way, but these are rare. They can all speak Italian, but in their own homes they speak Croatian, especially the women for hardly any of them understand Italian. But even if some do understand it they will not speak any other than her native language." About Split the same syndic stresses: "all the Split customs are Croatian; their native language is so polished and musical that in Dalmatia the language of Split has its primacy." In regard to the women of Split he says: "They do not speak any other language except Croatian." In 1574 the Rector of Split reports to his government in Venice regarding the distribution of the presents sent to Split. He further writes how some soldier sang a ballad about Prince Marko upon which "the whole crowd was singing the hymn as if by collusion, for they all know this ballad."

The fact that the patricians of Zadar speak Italian and that in the Island of Hvar they knew also Italian, the Venetian Giustiniani ascribes to the intensive contacts with the Venetian officials, captains and sailors. In the Dalmatian women monasteries, in which only patrician or noblemen's daughters from the Dalmatian cities are received, few nuns could speak any language except Croatian. In 1611 none could speak Italian in the women's monastery in Shibenik. The population of Dalmatia, and especially that of individual cities was Croatian. Only in a purely Croatian medium could the oldest Croatian poetry originate. At that time in Split the member of the age-old patrician family Marko Marulich (born 1450, died 1525) writes his drama "Judith" in Croatian. And also another Croatian poet of that time, Matulich, resides in Split. On the Island of Hvar resides Hannibal Lucich (1485-1553), Peter Hektorovich (from 1487-1572), Jerome and Hortensius Bertuchevich and Miksha Pelegrinovich while Vinko Priboevich lectures in Hvar in Croatian on the "Origin and history of Slavs," emphasizing his own Croatian origin and that of his fellow islanders.

Residents of Zadar are: Zoranich (1508-1569),

the poet of the mountains (Planine) and Bara-kovich (1548-1628), the poet "of the Slovinka fairy" (Vila Slovinka), both deeply inspired with Croatian national feelings, which they stress in their poetical expressions.

The Ragusan poetry in Croatian started out with a pleiade of literary stars. Ivan Guchetich died in 1502. Shishko Menchetich (1457-1527), George Derzhich (1461-1501), Andriya Chubra-novich (1480-1530), Mavro Vetranich (1482-1576), Marino Derzhich (1520-1567), Dinko Ranina (1536-1607), Dinko Zlatarich (1558-1609), and so many others set out to display their poetical talents and develop poetry to en-viable heights in their native Croatian.

The entire seacoast, both under the control of Venice and that of the Ragusan Republic, ex-pressed through the art of their poets, who are in personal contact with each other, its frame of mind and attachment to the Croatian language.

At first religious plays are presented in the cities, and then also ballads and dramas, in the national language which echoes in the churches where the sermons are held in Croatian, the messages and gospels are read in the same native language. In the courts the interpreters explain to the Venetian judges the statements and testi-mony of those who do not speak Italian.

The Social Conditions in Dalmatia in the 15th and 16th Centuries

When Venice took over the Dalmatian cities and their surrounding territory, she found every-where two sharply divided social classes: the patricians and commoners. The clergy itself forms a distinct Estate, but as such it had no effect whatsoever on the municipal, that is, on the general communal administration. A certain priest could exert his influence only as a member of the individual patrician family, but the clergy as such did not have access into any patrician council, nor into the assemblies of the plebeians.

Venice, upon sending a rector to the Dalma-tian municipality, took away from these the most important symbol of their complete autonomy, but everywhere the "patrician council" kept going. But this council strove to keep in its hands as large an autonomy as possible in the internal affairs of their community. This council selected the judges and the entire municipal officialdom. It made various decisions for their territory which

later on were subject to confirmation by the Venetian government. In spite of all the limita-tions of the autonomy, the patricians were those who, in addition to, and on the side of the rector, had been carrying on administration in the com-munity and were controlling it to the benefit of their own interests. On one hand, because of the conflict of interests, and on the other, because of the depressed feeling of social inferiority, the conflict between the patricians and plebeians took place in almost all the Dalmatian cities. The plebeians strove to become equal to the patri-cians, while the latter never agreed to that. These quarrels, for the most part, in the presence of the government in Venice, and frequently incited by the representatives of Venice herself, resulted several times in noisy and bloody con-flicts in some cities. The patricians assembled in the "patrician council" or "grand council," strove at least, in the face of the plebeians, to retain in their hands the municipal legislation and munici-pal offices.

On the other hand the plebeians, which since the 15th century had their own assemblies called "congregations" strove to have their own de-cisions assume an official characteristic and to get for themselves certain municipal offices, at any rate the supervision of the decisions of the patrician councils. This became conducive to struggle and to sharp and bloody conflicts. Such events took place in Split, Trogir, Hvar and Shibenik.

The second cause of conflict between the patricians and plebeians was in some cities the haughtiness of certain patricians. So the ple-beians of Shibenik, indignant over the acts of sexual violence by the patrician young men on their maidens, killed several patricians. This started a hatred between the one and the other party which has never been stopped, and which is reported in 1553 by the syndic Guistiniano.

The third cause for this conflict was the in-sistence of some plebeians to be received in the grand council and thus to become equal to the patricians.

The municipal statutes applied equally to the patricians and plebeians for they were free men, on one side and the other. There were no serfs in Venetian Dalmatia, and the landowners had their fields cultivated by sharecroppers, who received a certain portion of the yearly income.

This "colonate" relation was set forth in the colonate agreements, made in proper legal form in the presence of a notary, attaching only the land but not the person who was cultivating it. The land remained the possession of its owner, but he could no longer dispose of his possession while the agreement was in force. The contract was usually in force throughout the lifetime of the grapevine or, in the case of other produce, for a certain determined period. Throughout this period the cultivator was an entirely free man. He was not attached personally to the landowner himself, but was under obligation to give the landowner a certain portion of the produce.

The patricians were always the owners. The farmers, artisans, merchants, fishermen, sailors and others were the "common people." However, in the 16th century in some cities also a third Estate began to emerge, one between the plebeians and patricians, called "citizens." Their purpose was to become separated from the common people and to create a special closed corporation. In some places this arrangement was quite successful (as in Split) while in other cities they had to content themselves only with the title. The "citizens" were rich merchants and owners who were opposed to being treated as common people. In the first place they strove to be exempted from the taxes and contributions which the commoners had to pay, and from doing some distasteful services such as to keep watch on the rampart, to ply the oars on the municipal galleys whenever it was needed, to perform manual duties during the forced work time (kulluk), and the like. And thus from the 17th century in the Dalmatian cities, three estates are formed: the patricians, citizens and plebeians.

In the long struggle which lasted for over several centuries, the plebeians succeeded in their aspirations and in many respects they became equal to the patricians. Yet this equality was not enforced everywhere, since the struggle was conducted in each town independently and there was never any common action among them.

Some municipalities in Dalmatia remained throughout the Venetian period closed corporations with their own special municipal life, with their own special statute entirely different from that of other cities. This autonomy of theirs was impinged by the State whenever it felt like it by subjecting them to some legal provision. However, the State always saw to it that their statute was kept in force so that the residents might live in accordance with the provisions of their statutes—naturally in such a way that it did not conflict with the interests of the Republic.

Each Dalmatian municipality had its own internal struggle, the struggle of the plebeians with the patricians, the struggle of the "citizens" with the patricians on one hand and with the plebeians on the other. These struggles became under circumstances, now more vehement and then again less impulsive, but it also happened that they flamed into a large movement not only for small concessions but also for the entire upheaval in the social life of the city, as it took place on the Islands of Hvar and Vis.

The nobility of Hvar (Lissa) trampled, without the slightest regard to the common people, the rights of the plebeians and manifested on every single occasion its haughtiness and superiority as well as contempt for the plebeians. This haughtiness reached its climax when some of the estate holders raped some plebeian women. The plebeians of Hvar, humiliated and insulted, formed in 1510 a conspiracy and under the leadership of the Canon Mathew Lukanich and Thomas Bevilakva they decided to kill several patricians in order to get rid of those who oppressed and despised them mercilessly. However, a "miracle" in the house of Bevilakva frustrated their plans. On February 6, 1510, the crucifix in Bevilakva's house began to bleed, and this phenomenon caused such a panic both in Hvar and on the whole island that Lukanich himself, the leader of the planned rebellion, desisted from it, became insane and died.

But the people soon came back to their senses and a well organized rebellion broke out in May of the same year under the leadership of Mathew Ivanich from Verbanya, called "duke John." The whole island was now in flames. The rebels attacked several patricians in Starigrad, and wounded them. With a thousand rebels Ivanich set out for the city of Hvar where he was joined by the plebeians of Hvar, and at the head of 2,000 people he went to the rector's house where he set down the demands of the common people of the Island of Hvar and Vis. Their chief demand was that the members of the grand council had to be both plebeians and patricians, and that the patricians will carry the same burdens that the commoners do. The common people, that is, the plebeians, sought equal rights with the patricians.

As they submitted their demands to the rector, the plebeians attacked the houses of the patricians, plundered them and destroyed everything that they found. Some houses were set on fire and others were destroyed, while the captured patricians were either killed or thrown in the sea or maimed, while the others were thrown into prison. Those patricians who did not lose their head in the turmoil, fled to Brach, Korchula, and wherever else they could. Upon this the plebeians took over the reins of government and summoned the patricians to return to their homes unless they wished to be exiled forever.

Rebellion in Hvar

At this turn the plebeians armed 30 ships, under the command of Mathias Ivanich, and blocked the island to keep watch so that no patricians could leave for Venice in order to make their complaint. In the meantime some patricians of Hvar, who fled to the island of Brach, set sail to Venice, upon which the Government ordered the proveditor of the Navy, Jerome Contarino, to set sail for Hvar.

The great-Hvar rebellion left a deep impression throughout Dalmatia, while the Dalmatian patricians did everything to check the spreading of these rumors.

In the meantime the plebeians and patricians came to terms. However, this agreement was not confirmed by the Venetian government which was influenced by the patrician refugees. But, in order to make some arrangements, the government sent the proveditor Zuano Navaiero to Hvar. In May, 1511, after a full year of struggle, the plebeians of Hvar became tranquilized and the quarrel between the plebeians and patricians came to an end. In order to have the excited elements fully pacified, the Venetian government sent the proveditor Sebastian Giustignano to Dalmatia, who with his brutal ways spoiled everything. Giustignano came upon the idea to punish the plebeians of Hvar for the damage caused the patricians. For this reason he issued a manifesto in 1512, in which he condemned 65 participants of the Hvar rebellion; 14 to death, the others to maiming, prison or exile. The mani-

festo caused a new uprising far more dangerous and more intensive than the first one. And again the whole island was in rebellion. Under the leadership of the chiefs condemned by the new governor, the plebeians set out for Hvar to see Giustignano himself who did not manage to tranquilize them. "Here are such conditions, Giustignano reported from Hvar to Venice, that one can really say the Venetian government no longer rules, but 3 or 4 plebeian chiefs." Failing to bring about a settlement, Giustignano attacked the village of Verbovsko which his troops plundered first and later set on fire. After this Giustignano came to terms with Starigrad. But the main part of the rebels, under the leadership of Ivanich, did not even want to hear about settlement and defeated Giustignano when he landed with his troops at Yelsa. Ivanich's fleet kept cruising around the island.

When the patricians realized that the government was supporting their side they became still more antagonistic and again started to humiliate the plebeians, in the face of which the plebeian leaders raised a new and far greater rebellion on the whole island in 1514. Six thousand plebeians laid siege in a violent storm, they broke through the gate, climbed on the walls and cut 24 patricians to pieces. They broke also into the rector's palace in which the patricians took refuge, and putting to sword all those who had been there, they threw out their bodies through the window on the square. Then they hunted down the other patricians and put to sword all the patrician males who happened to be in the city. However, with the conciliatory intercession of the rector Vincenzo Donato, the plebeians became tranquilized and invited the patrician refugees to return.

In the meantime the success of the plebeians of Hvar also had an effect upon the other plebeians throughout the country, and there was great danger that all of Dalmatia might rise in equally violent rebellion.

Signs were appearing that similar rebellions would break out in other places, especially in Split and Trogir. Fearing this outbreak, the government sent the proveditor Vicenzo Capello to Hvar with a strong fleet of 14 galleys and 3 light ships. In the presence of such a force on the sea the plebeians were really helpless. After Capello had sunk all the plebeian ships they did the same thing at the island of Vis in Starigrad, Yelsa and Verbovska. After this he wanted to punish the plebeian leaders, but they retired in the central mountains of the island. Surrounding the island with a strong navy, he attacked the plebeians with 1500 well-armed soldiers, and after he caught 20 of their leaders he returned to Hvar. On the 10th of October, 1514, in the presence of his troops and the patricians of Hvar, he had them hanged on the lateen masts of his galleys. Thus the greatest popular revolution of the Croatian people at Hvar was ended. Venice had eradicated it.

The plebeian rebellion was beaten down but the Venetian government knew well that it would break out again if some satisfaction were not given to the plebeians. For this purpose in the same year (1514) the government complied with one of their chief demands—control over the spending of the municipal incomes; from that time on the city of Hvar got two treasurers (Camerlengo): one selected by the patricians and the other by the common people, while both had equal rights. The plebeians accepted this, but under the leadership of the "people's attorneys" which they had elected themselves, they continued their struggle until they achieved full equality of rights. Even though they had never achieved this equality, namely the patrician council and the popular assembly made on the 9th of July, 1611, a lasting and mutual peace with which both parties were satisfied. Then Venice recognized also the third estate for the city of Hvar, that is, the citizens who were permanently residing in the city.

The struggle of the plebeians of Split, Trogir and Zadar for equal rights with the patricians was never so bloody as on the island of Hvar, but it was steady for centuries and was never relaxed. Also in these and other places, the plebeians who followed in many ways those of Hvar and under the leadership of the citizens, achieved much which made them equal to patricians. As a result of this change in the 17th century there was no municipal affair of some importance in which the plebeians had not taken part. Throughout this period many plebeian families who became rich and prominent, were received in the class of the patricians.

Commercial and Economic Conditions

Venice, which had taken away much from the Dalmatian city government when it took them over, left them, even though limited, sufficiently important internal autonomy. It started immediately to follow its commercial policy of favoring the capital city, thus destroying the life of the Dalmatian seacoast communities. Already in 1422 the Venetians issued the order that, should the Dalmatians export some goods to other lands, and not to Venice, they must pay the same custom rates for these goods which they would have paid if they had imported them to Venice. When the Dalmatian cities rose as one man against this regulation, Venice withdrew it but soon after, others similar to the first one, were issued so that all the food articles such as olive oil, cheese and the like, if shipped north, had to be shipped only to Venice (1425).

This was followed by high customs rates for goods imported from abroad, the prohibition for trading with iron and iron goods by the Dalmatians, and the limitation, respectively prohibition of trading between individual cities, without permission of the rector. The heaviest blow felt by the Dalmatian cities was when the Venetian government ordered on the 15th of January, 1452 that all the commercial goods in general which should be exported from the Dalmatian cities had to be shipped to Venice and to no other place. This order meant not only a complete stagnation of the commerce of the Dalmatian cities, but even life was made impossible, since they had to import wheat for their own consumption from Pola and the Marches. Inversely, they had to sell them their own manufactured goods and those shipped from the Turkish areas. When the Dalmatian cities again rose against this order, the Venetian government made it slightly milder. Moreover, the Signory admitted itself that "this prohibition destroys Dalmatia, and in the meantime increases the income of Ragusa, strengthening this city, enriching its citizens and increasing the number of its commercial ships and naval vessels."

The Venetian government prohibited the Dalmatians to buy alien ships, to sail on board the ships and to ship their goods on board alien ships. This was soon loosened up and again tightened. Due to these machinations the Dalmatian cities' trade dropped to the lowest point, and concurrently their former wealth was also reduced to misery. The cities have been made so poor that, for instance, Split around 1540 could not pay a municipal physician. The richest Split families had no more than 200 ducats yearly income, while the greatest part of the population was poor, as the syndic Gianbattista Giustiniano reported to his government in 1553. Only the islands were better off economically.

In 1577 Venice began to set up a commercial port for trade with Turkey, in an effort to enliven her own trade, which because of the discovery of America was taking a different course. After much effort and work, struggle and antagonism Split warehouses have been set up and opened in 1592. A great volume of trade began to pour into Split both from the mainland and from the sea. The warehouse itself was one of the largest and best in the world, and it was provided with a sanitary installation of its time. The Turks were coming from the Ottoman empire, even merchants from India and Persia, creating—by the words of a contemporary writer—a golden chain between the East and Venice. The port and warehouse of Split rapidly prospered from year to year, because numerous caravanseries were coming and going, and likewise commercial galleys.

Moreover in 1592 a bank was established in Split. However, the merchants who had benefitted from all this were in the first place Venetian citizens, then the Turks and Jews, while the citizens of Split were on the side, contenting themselves with that small trade which was going on between their city and its vicinity. In order to engage in a large-style trade they had neither knowledge nor funds. They were contented with a small income which the inns and the hostelries provided. Soon the new hospital (lazarett) was too small and a new one was built. Trade grew in proportion, yet it brought no progress to Split, only ruin. In 1608 the plague appeared in Split which destroyed two-thirds of its population, and from 4,223 inhabitants only 1,405 of them remained alive. The same visitation appeared also later in 1731, 1732, 1763, 1764 and 1784.

The rest of Dalmatia carried on in her misery. The only exceptions were the islands. The closed Turkish borders and the incessant conflicts interfered with the peaceful development of both agriculture and other economic pursuits. The overseas trade was limited to commerce with Venice, which at all times moved within narrow limits.

Migration of People Inside Dalmatia, and Settling of "The New Residents"

In 1423 the clan of Pashtrovichi, which inhabited the area between Spich and Budva, decided to recognize the sovereignty of Venice if the Signory would confirm some of their demands. Among these was the franchise to select their own rector every year, who would be confirmed by the Doge. Further, they will not have to pay any import duty for the produce of their own territory whether in Venice or in any other place of the Venetian republic. The Venetian government confirmed all of this on the 17th of May, 1424. These privileges were extended in consequence by the Pashtrovichi clan.

By accepting the demand of the residents of Krayina and the Seacoast, and upon taking them under his authority, the Doge Francis Molino gave to the residents of the Seacoast and Krayina "the Pashtrovichi privileges" on February 8, 1647, and ordered the general proveditor of Dalmatia Foscolo to make it possible for them to move their families to the neighboring islands, as protection from the Turkish attacks. Thus, the migration of the residents of the seacoast was initiated by shipping them to the islands of central Dalmatia, a movement which on different occasions, continued up to 1714. At this time the general proveditor of Dalmatia, Emo, decided that in the future no new families can be accepted among "the new residents of the islands." These seacoast dwellers, whom Venice transferred to the islands, were divided into groups whose continuous obligation it was to guard the islands from the attack of the Turkish population and the Turkish troops from the neighboring Turkish seacoast. In compensation for these services these new dwellers obtained land on the Islands of Brach, Hvar, Vis and Korchula. They were exempt from paying taxes, were not compelled to perform compulsory public works, did not have to serve aboard the galleys, and enjoyed the "Pashtrovich privileges" in regard to import duties.

These "new residents" on the islands counted already in 1669, 230 families and in 1699, 282 families, which were settled on the Islands of

Brach, Vis and Korchula. These newly settled inhabitants enjoyed their privileges even when Turkey was forced out from the sea, and there was no longer any need to guard the islands from Turkish attacks. And when Venice left in 1797 and Austria took over Dalmatia, they retained the privileges which had been taken from them by the French.

In the 16th century we find Greek orthodox people in Zadar and Shibenik which had been imported from the Venetian possessions in Greece. When the Turks conquered Croatia south of Velebit, a large number of people fled to the seacoast and on the islands. At that time many Serbian families were settled in these areas. During the war of Candia some Serbian families left their native country and settled down in Shibenik and Zadar.

Conditions in Dalmatia After the War of Candia

Twenty-five years of continuous and embittered warfare in Dalmatia destroyed every vestige of its welfare. The acquisition of Klis meant good security for the Venetian possessions around Split and Trogir and the free passage way in the Turkish regions, while everything else was exposed to continuous Turkish attacks and plundering.

Since it had been determined, at the tracing of the borderline, that in Dalmatia each party will retain ("uti possidetis") that area which is in its possession, the Venetians had hoped that they would considerably expand their territory, but when it came to determining the borderline, by the terms of the agreement of October 13, 1672, they had to return almost everything except Klis to the Turks.

Truly poor was the appearance of everything that remained in Venetian hands. All in all there were 78,288 inhabitants at that time in Venetian-Dalmatia and Albania. The well-inhabited cities of the past, in spite of the influx from open places within their bulwarks, had very few residents. Thus, Zadar which in 1527 had 7,051 residents, and in 1559, 8,100, had only 3,597 inhabitants in 1682, 12 years after the peace treaty. Split and other cities had at this time only 3,315 inhabitants. Especially tragic was the fate of Shibenik. In 1553 it had 8,200 inhabitants and now in 1682 it had only 4,172 inhabitants. Kotor had all in all 1,086 inhabitants; Tsres, 2,050;

Osor, 129; Rab, 2,353; Kerk, 1,585; Pag, 1,365; Trogir, 1,032; Hvar, 1,159; Korchula, 1,231; Perast, 1,488; Budva, 578. During this war the proveditor general, Antonio Bernardo, reported in 1656 to his government that Dalmatia "had fallen to such depth that the few inhabitants which survived the plagues and the present-day war, had no means of taking care of their food supplies—had no trade whatsoever." Bernardo urged the Venetian government to help people in such a distress "which cannot be any greater." From year to year during the war which lasted for nearly 25 years all this misery became ever more oppressive.

For this reason the Dalmatians were glad to hear that the peace of 1669 had been concluded. Yet it brought no immediate advantage to them. They had hoped that normal conditions would be restored and the land, so dreadfully devastated would be reconstructed. But this peace was not of long duration. The war which broke out in 1683, between Emperor Leopold and Turkey involved also Venice which, on the 5th of March, 1684, joined the Holy League.

The Venetian-Turkish War of 1684 to 1699
The War of Morea

The smashing defeat of the Turks under Vienna on the 11th and 12th of September, 1683, stirred up the populations all along the Dalmatian-Turkish border. The faith of the coming defeat of the Turks had become contagious. Numerous refugees were inciting the people which otherwise were angry at the Turks because of their continuous attacks, depredations and plundering.

And while Venice was still keeping peace with the Turks, the Dalmatian Croats, together with the rebels from Lika, attacked the Turks in October, 1683, and captured from them Obrovats, Plavno, Ostrovitsa, Benkovats, Dernish, and Skradin. At the beginning of 1684, at the time when Venice formally kept the peace with the Turks, the Turks kept in their possession only Knin and Sinj.

But when war was declared the Turks promptly lost Duare (Zadvorye). At this turn also the official Venetian army, being powerfully assisted by native fighters, began to attack the Turks.

The proveditor general Valier took Norin on the banks of Neretva river in November, 1684, and built a tower on Opus island. In the next year, 1685, he attempted to capture Sinj, but was defeated by the Turks and turned to flight. When the Turkish attack against Duare (Zadvorye) was repulsed, the native volunteer groups attempted to break into the Turkish territory, destroy some Turkish towers, and plunder the area. Among the leaders of these native troops who especially distinguished himself was "Cavalier" John who spread terror among the Turks in the vicinity.

Meanwhile decisive events took place on the great battlefields of the Danubian area. After defensive actions for over two centuries, the Empire and its allies carried on a successful offensive against the Turks. In rapid succession they took Vishegrad, Vats, Pest, Virovititsa (1684), Novi Zamki (1685), Buda (1686), Segedin, and broke into Transylvania. In Croatia itself, successful engagements were fought with the Turks, while Venice had succeeded, too. In 1686 Morosini took Navarin, Modon, Argos, and Naples in Morea, and after several successes in Dalmatia the proveditor general Jerome Cornaro, captured the fortified city of Sinj on the 25th of September. In the next year Morosini took Patras, Lepanto, Athens and Corinth. In Dalmatia the struggle was carried on around Sinj and Herzegnogi (Castelnuoso) which Venice captured with the assistance of the Papal and Maltese navy and their troops, on the 30th of September, 1686.

In the meantime the imperial army in Hungary, after its victory at Mohach in 1687, chased the Turks and cleared the whole country. Moreover the Turks retired even from Slavonia. On the 6th of September, 1688, even Belgrade fell into the hands of the emperor. Now the Balkan was quite open to the imperial and allied armies. When, on the 11th of September, 1688, Cornaro captured Knin and Verlika, the Turks did not have a single city any more in Dalmatia-Croatia. In 1689 the allies were joined also by the emperor of Russia, while the imperial troops penetrated deeply south into Serbia, Bosnia and Wallachia. Turkey was in a very bad condition.

Unable to capture Dubrovnik by feat of arms, the Venetians decided to make its prosperity impossible by taking the area in its background. They started this action immediately and on the 22nd of November they took Tsarina, the key

point for Dubrovnik, through which almost the entire Ragusan trade with Turkey was passing. At this turn the Venetians were also striving to capture the district of Trebinye. They were successful by taking it in 1689. In the same year they took Klek and Vergorats. The Venetian advance in Herzegovina, powerfully assisted by the outlaws (hajduci), extended up to Mostar. In 1694 the proveditor general Dolfino captured Chitluk on Neretva river, while the Turks evacuated Gabela.

With the armed forces, the core of which consisted of Dalmatian Croats, the Venetians conquered the same year Zazhablye, Popovo, Klobuk, and the district of Trebinye.

After the Turkish defeat at Zenta on the 11th of September, 1697, peace negotiations were started in June, 1698, between the emperor and sultan which were completed in the Sriemski Karlovtsi. In these negotiations Venice participated, too.

Conditions in Dalmatia After the War of Morea

Even though it lasted for 15 years, the war of Morea caused Dalmatia much less distress than that of Candia. In the first years of war the mainland of Venetian Dalmatia was exposed to suffering, but soon the struggle was carried on almost exclusively on Turkish territory. Consequently, only that part of Dalmatia-Croatia had to suffer which was still controlled by the Turks. The islands throughout the duration of this war were untouched since the Turkish navy was engaged in Greek waters and was not in a position to get into the Adriatic Sea. In such conditions the troubles and distress of the war of Candia in the maritime cities and on the islands were not renewed. The interior mainland of Dalmatia (Dalmatinska Zagora) was going through a heroic period and was repaying the Turks for their former depredations. In addition to the regular Venetian army, numerous troops appeared which were made up of native fighters who fought in their own way. Venice not only failed to obstruct their actions but from time to time was even praising them, especially those troops which succeeded in getting up a strong organization.

The most famous leader of such troops was the already mentioned "Cavalier" Yanko Mitrovich. Besides these irregular troops there were also such formations as had been made up of pure Dalmatian Croats. These troops were received in the regular army, but as special territorial units under native commanders, among which the most famous were the Split patricians Yakovlyevichi, called Tartaglia, and Ivan Markovich in Central Dalmatia, the knight Mitrovich, serdar Smilyanich and prince Posedarski in northern Dalmatia. The Dalmatian Croats took the war with the Turks as their own. They were not fighting for Venice, but for the freedom of their native soil. And since the concept of delivery from the Turks was combined with the concept of coming under the authority of the nearest Christian sovereign, they were also fighting as Christians against the infidel. Besides this, frequently there were such elements in the irregular troops who were not fighting for any ideal, but were chiefly interested in plunder and adventure. Such was for instance "the indomitable" Iliya Mitrovich, the brother of John. His forces caused terror among the Turks and Christians alike; there were also the brothers Tsernitsa, who had been captured by the Venetians and thrown into Shibenik prison where they died.

"Terrible are the Morlacchian troops," according to the report of the general proveditor Daniel Dolfin in 1697, "which in the upper Dalmatian areas are called outlaws (hayduks). There is no doubt that they constitute the greatest attacking and defensive force in the conditions prevailing there. There are around 30,000 men capable of bearing arms. They are of a tall and powerful bodily build, they are men of firm resolution, they are standing the worst effort, they go sleepless and stand the worst weather, they are used to the farmers' simple life, and need no luxury whether in garments or in residence. They do not know certain established rules in the struggle, but they are expert both in gun and sword fight, they are as good footsoldiers as cavalrymen, they are courageous and fast, they skillfully pursue the enemy during its flight, and they also know how to retire skillfully when they suffer defeat. From my own experience I know that they are also ready to follow discipline." The same proveditor has not enough words to praise the heroism, ability and courage of the Dalmatian troops who by thousands joined the regular Venetian army against the Turks, and recommends his government to be very careful in respecting their

customs, to regulate their temperament, and to carry out every commitment given to them, that is, that each of them get as much land as is necessary for the support of his family, under the provision that he should keep a horse, with which, in case of need, he will rush to the defense of the land.

In the meantime, not waiting for the approval of the government, the proveditor General Dolfin distributed provisionally, land possessions to all those who had already participated in the struggle and, in addition, he gave them 18 lire of pay for each soldier and "a supply of biscuits." From his land each new owner paid the government only one tithe.

The Venetian-Turkish War of 1714-1718

On the 8th of December, 1714 Turkey declared war on Venice. Dalmatia again became the theater of war. Already in January the whole borderline was stirring. And again the Dalmatian troops were the best Venetian army in this area. At the beginning of 1715 they occupied Tril, Zazvina, Prolog, Plavno, Stermitsa, Clavash. In the meantime the Bosnian Turks broke with a great army (allegedly 40,000 men) into Dalmatia and laid siege to Sinj, but after desperate fighting they were forced to retreat. At the same time the Turks were fighting successfully in Morea.

In 1716 the alliance between Venice and the Hapsburg Empire against the Turks was renewed and Eugene of Savoia started his offensive. On the 5th of August, 1716 he defeated the Turks near Petrovaradin and soon he freed Banate. Venice could not do anything in Dalmatia for she needed armed forces in other parts, but individual native troops broke into Bosnia, harassing the Turks. Knight Nonkovich captured Metkovich and Utovo and penetrated up to Mostar.

Also in this war as in the last one and again in 1716 as the Emperor's ally, Venice tried to conquer the territory in the Ragusan background and to connect her possessions in northern Dalmatia with the ones in the Bay of Kotor. For this purpose she again started to capture the Turkish territory in this area and the general proveditor Emo, conquered Tsarina and Popovo and the whole Ragusan background, thus cutting off all trade between Dubrovnik and Turkey

(1716). In 1717 the Venetians conquered Herzegovina up to Mostar, which they had set on fire. Ragusa again was in the same difficult position as during the last war.

When Eugene of Savoia defeated the Turks under Belgrade on the 15th of August, 1717 and two days later captured Belgrade itself, the condition of the Turks in this area was very bad. The general proveditor Alvise Mocenigo captured Imotski, but did not advance any further.

Forced by events in the west, Charles VI, made peace with the Turks on the 21st of July, 1718 in Pozharevats, which was accepted also by Venice. Besides the loss of Morea, Venice had to return to the Turks all that it captured in the background of Ragusa. The Venetian territory from Klek north had been expanded and of the larger places she got the town of Imotski. The new borderline (linea Mocenigo) was accurately marked out on the terrain itself by the Turkish plenipotentiary Mehmed effendi Sialy and the Venetian Alvise Mocenigo in 1721-1723. It ran from Klek to Zhabska hill, over Metkovich, Imotski, Sinj, Verlika and Knin so that in regard to Bosnia and Herzegovina it was the same which persisted up to 1878. The area which Venice acquired at this time was called its latest acquisition (acquisto novissimo). In order to have the republic of Ragusa separated from the Venetian territory, Turkey got two narrow strips from her own Herzegovina to the sea, which ended at Neum-Klek, in the north, south of the estuary of Neretva, and Sutorina in the south right at the entrance in the Bay of Kotor.

Plate 6.
A. Konits, typical of the towns of both Bosnia and Herze-
govina in their lofty setting and studded with minarets of
Moslem houses of worship.
B. A Moslem priest standing at the entrance of his mosque.
(Engraving by courtesy of A. L. Zivich.)

Plate 7.
PHYSICAL BACKGROUND: Winter landscape in Bosnia,
typical of Bosnian mountains in spite of their southern loca-
tion. Above are seen the Yahorina hills in southeastern
Bosnia.
(Engraving by courtesy of Dr. John F. Ruzich.)

Plate 8.
Contrast in vegetation. Above, produce of rich Bosnian conif-
erous forest. Below, a huge platan tree of southern Dalmatia.
(Engraving by courtesy of Mr. and Mrs. Andrew Livovich.)

Plate 9.
Wild-life in the Bosnian highlands.
Above, a herd of agile chamois.
Below, flocks of water-fowl at their best.

Plate 10.
The Bosnian karst-lands are frequently used for roads and
overland traffic.

Plate 11. The highlands of Bosnia and Herzegovina as they appear by deep gorges and river canyons, while their tops are frequently dotted with medieval castles. The lofty mountains are usually skirted throughout the land.

Plate 12.
Tombstones or stechaks scattered all over Herzegovina and
Bosnia throughout Middle Ages by the followers of an
heretic sect.

Plate 13.

MISCELLANEOUS GROUPS. On top, the family castle of the famous Corvini (Hunyadi) clan, with its illustrious scions: John, the governor of Hungary and intrepid fighter against the Turks at the climax of their crusading zeal, and his son, Mathias, king of Hungary and Croatia, a brilliant general, patron of arts and promoter of Renaissance scholarship in his royal domain. Below, the family crypt of Corvini, with the tomb of John in the center, his son Ladislaus, beheaded in a feud with a coterie of opponents, and John's wife at his left.

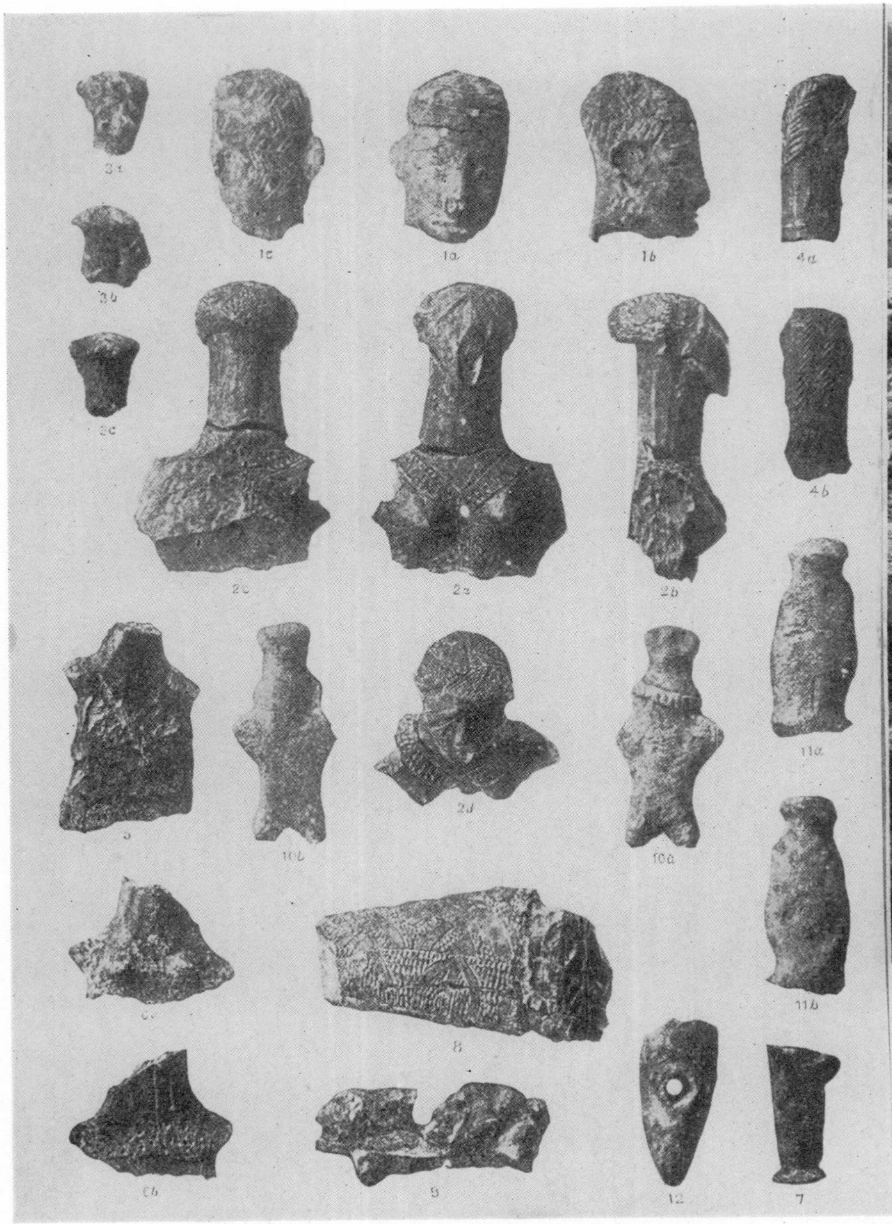

Plate 14.

B. Wheel tracks left by the Roman vehicles on Roman highways leading through Herzegovina and Bosnia to lower
Danube regions.

A. Clay figurines unearthed at the neolithic station at Butmir.

Plate 15.
Top. Moslem faithful at prayer in a mosque.
Below. Typical citizens of Sarayevo of Moslem faith.

Plate 16.
Top. Moslem betrothal ceremony.
Bottom. Elders engaged in a chat and parlor game of younger
set at a social gathering.

Plate 17.

Garments of Moslem ladies for wear at home and in public.

(Engraving by courtesy of Mrs. Augusta Mertz)

Plate 18.

Types and Costumes from Bosnia and Herzegovina, both Christian and Moslem.

A. On the left, a lady from Herzegovina listens, together with a Bosnian, to the ballads of glory and heroism recited by an aged bard to the accompaniment of the gusle, a string instrument of hoary past.

B. A typical Moslem date (ashik) at the side gate of future bride's home (kapijik) where they plan their future.

(Engraving by courtesy of Mr. Matthew Mertz)

Plate 19.
Customs of the Christian peasants of Bosnia and Herzegovina.

A. In spite of centuries of Turkish oppression and unceasing martyrdom, the good-natured Croatians kept up their love for song and dance.

B. In a solemn, tragic mood, middle-aged ladies listen to bard's chant of the lost freedom of their land and a hopeless future. Submerged in painful thoughts, one of the ladies probably thinks of her teen-aged son dragged away to be forced into the Janissery troops for the oppression of their own Christian kinfolk. The other may think over the lot of her marriageable daughter dragged away as merchandise for a white-slave market.

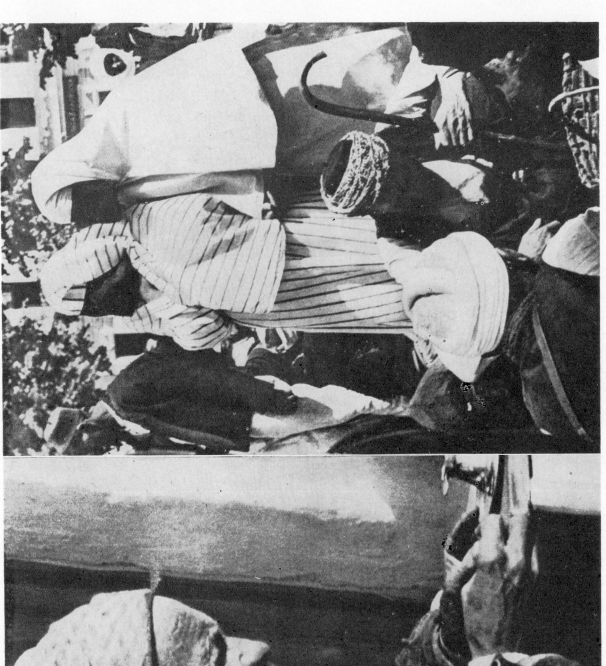

Plate 20.
MOSLEM TYPES:

A. A Moslem priest studies the sacred text.

B. A Bosnian bazar with veiled Moslem buyers.

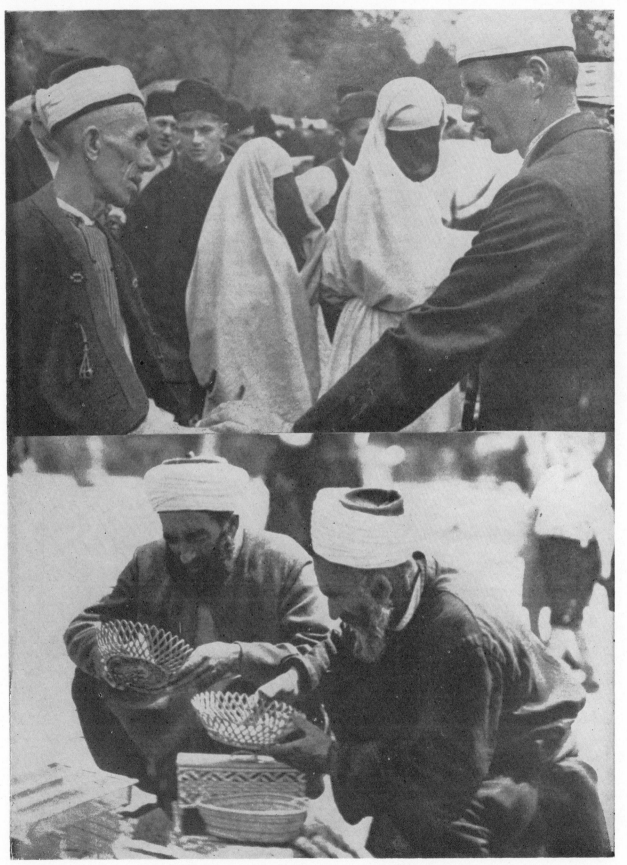

Plate 21.
Top. A Bosnian market visited by Moslems and Christians
alike. Moslem women still veil their faces in public.

Bottom. Two Moslem priests look over domestic ware.

Plate 22.

Two Croatian women from Herzegovina in their native dress.

A. The fibula adorning the waist of the maiden was widely distributed over the Adriatic area including Albania and Greece.
B. The matron wears a head-gear which was common in Herzegovina.

Plate 23.
Typical Croatian peasants of Bosnia in their daily dress.
(Engraving by courtesy of Croatian Catholic Union.)

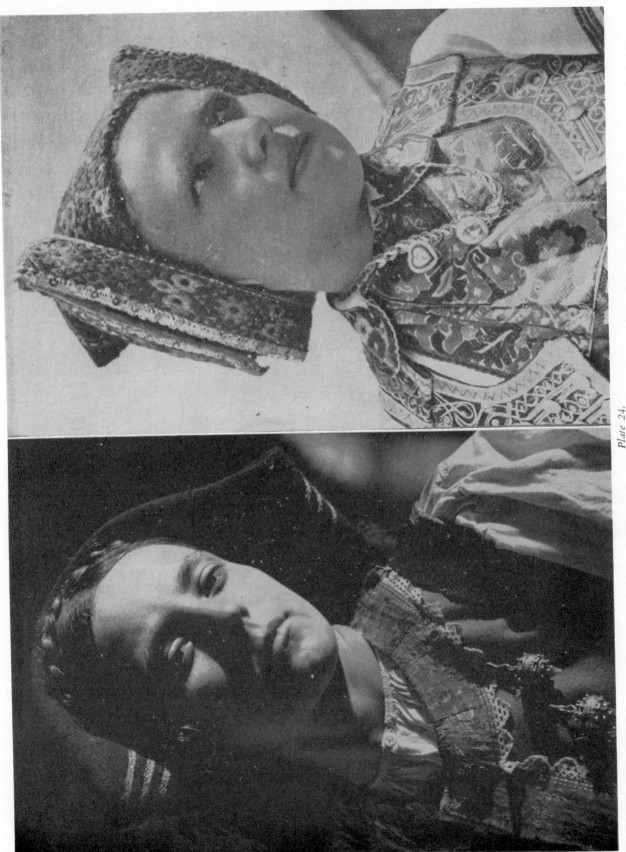

Plate 24.

COMPARISON OF CROATIAN TYPES AND COSTUMES

A. The maiden on the left is a Bosnian peasant.

B. The matron on the right is a peasant woman from the Zagreb area.

(Engraving by courtesy of Croatian Catholic Union.)

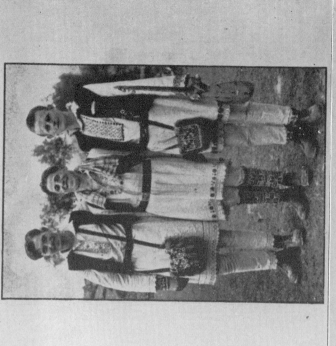

Plate 25.

On both banks of Sava River

A. Young man from Slavonia, in richly decorated silk raiments.

B. Bosnian youth in his jovial mood displays a variety of oriental costumes and racial features.

(Engraving by courtesy of Mr. Dagmar Kriegseis)

Plate 26.
Contrasts in dress between Bosnian and Croatian peasant women.

The lady on the left is a Bosnian, while the one on the right is a native of Croatia.

E. Chapple & C. Coon. Principles of Anthropology, 1942 (Chap. 5 & 10).

E. Perrier. The Earth Before History; Man's Origin, and Origin of Life, 1925

E. Baily & J. Weir. Introduction to Geology. 1939

Dalmatia, London, 1920

Bosna i Hercegovina, 1922. Engineers' Memorial Book.

L. Dudley Stamp. A Regional Geography, Europe & Mediterranean, 1940.

Lóczy Lajos. A Magyar szent Korona országainak földrajzi stb. leirása. (Geographical Description of the Countries under Sovereignty of the Holy Hungarian Crown).

    I. A Társországok: Horvát és Szlavonország, Dalmátország (Companion countries: Croatia, Slavonia and Dalmatia).

    I. Bosnia és Herczegovina, (Bosnia and Herzegovina).

Cambridge Ancient History. Vol. I.

Stjepan Ratković, Zemljopisni pregled Banovine Hrvatske. Zagreb, 1941. (A Geographical Survey of the Croatian Banate).

Nikola Žic. Istra. Dio I. Zemlja (Istria, Part I. Country) Zagreb, 1936.

E. W. Berry. Paleontology; 1929

E. A. Hooton, Up from the Ape, 1931

J. de Morgan, Prehistoric Man (A General outline of prehistory); 1924.

W. J. Perry, The Growth of Civilization; 1924

V. G. Childe, The Dawn of European Civilization; 1925

Christopher Dawson; The Age of Gods; 1928; Chaps. VI. VII, VIII, XIII, XV.

Sir Arthur Evans, New Archeological Lights on the Origins of Civilization; 1917

Sir Arthur Evans, The Palace of Minos. 4 Vol. 1921-35.

Sir Arthur Evans, Through Bosnia & Herzegovina on Foot; 1876.

Sir Arthur Evans, The Earlier Religion of Greece in the Light of Cretan Discoveries; 1931.

The Cambridge Ancient History, 1925. Vol. III, Chap. VII and XXV.

L. Wilby, A Companian to Greek Studies, 7th ed. 1931.

A. Holm, History of Greece, 1894. Vol. 1, chap. XXI.

G. W. Botsford, Hellenic History; 1922.

W. Smith, Dictionary of Greek & Roman Antiquities, 2 vols. 1891.

O. Seyffert, A Dictionary of Classical Antiquities; 1895.

W. G. East, An Historical Geography of Europe. Chap. XVIII "The Danube Route-way," 374 ff., 1935.

M. Rostovzeff, A History of the Ancient World, 2 vols., 1940.

M. Rostovzeff, Social and Economic History of the Roman Empire 1926.

Theodore Mommsen, The History of Rome. (5 vols.) Translated by: W. P. Dickson, 1903. Vol. III, 264, 290 f; 426 f. Vol. V. 103, 284 f.

Theodore Mommsen, Provinces of the Roman Empire, 2 vols. Translated by W. P. Dickson, 1887. Vol. 1, Chap. VI "The Danubian Lands."

R. Munro, Rambles and Studies in Bosnia-Herzegovina and Dalmatia. Chaps. VI, VII, VIII 2nd ed.; 1900.

A. E. R. Boak, A History of Rome; New York, 1943.

M. Rostovzeff, A History of the Ancient World-II-Rome. Oxford, 1927.

Dio Cassius, History of Rome, 6 Vols. Translated by: H. B. Foster, 1905. Vol. IV, pp. 196-221.

C. Suetonius Tranquillus, The Lives of the Caesars. Translated by J. C. Rolfe, 1914.

J. Hindmarsh, The New History of Count Zosimus, Sometimes Advocate of the Treasury of the Roman Empire. London, 1684.

J. B. Bury, The History of the Later Roman Empire (395-565). 2 Vols., 1923.

J. B. Bury, The Invasion of Europe by the Barbarians, 1928.

Ch. W. Ch Oman, The Dark Ages, (476-918). 1901.

P. Villari, The Barbarian Invasions of Italy. 1902.

Tho. Hodgkins, Italy and Her Invaders. 8 Vols. 1885-99.

W. G. Holmes, The Age of Justinian and Theodora. 2 Vols. 1905-07.

A. Carr, The Church and the Roman Empire. 1902.

E. Hatch, Organization of the Early Christian Churches. 1881.

James T. Shotwell & Louise R. Loomis, The See of Peter, New York, 1927.

Kidd, Beresford, The Roman Primacy to A.D. 461.

Chr. B. Coleman, Constantine the Great and the Christian Church, New York, 1914.

N. H. Baynes, Constantine the Great and the Christian Church, London 1931.

J. B. Bury, A History of the Later Roman Empire from the Death of Theodosius I to the Death of Justinian (395-565) I-II London, 1923.

W. Holmes, The Age of Justinian and Theodora I-II., 2nd ed. London, 1912.

Sir Arthur Evans. Les Slaves de l'Adriatique et la Route Continentale de Constantinople. London, 1916.

F. Preveden, The Vocabulary of Navigation in the Balto-Slavic Languages. 1927. University of Chicago dissertation.

J. Bary, The Chronological Cycle of the Bulgarians, Byzantinische Zeitschrift 19. (1910)

A. Vasiliev, History of the Byzantine Empire. 2 vols. 1928-29.

Ch. Oman, Story of the Byzantine Empire. 1892.

Ch. Diehl, History of the Byzantine Empire. 1925.

I. Goldziher, Mohammed and Islam. 1917.

Sir W. Muir, "The Caliphate," its rise, decline and fall. 1915.

C. H. Becker, Christianity & Islam. 1903.

N. W. Pickthall, The Meaning of the Glorious Koran. (Arabic Text and explanatory translation). 2 Vols. 1938.

C. Stephenson, Mediaeval History. 1935-43-44.

J. B. Bury, The early history of the Slavonic Settlements in Dalmatia, Croatia and Serbia.

J. B. Bury, A History of the Later Roman Empire from Arcadius to Irene (395-800), 2 Vols., London, 1923.

Franjo Rački, Scriptores rerum chroaticarum ante 1200 a.d. 1880.

Hodgson, F. C. The early history of Venice. 1901.

J. B. Bury, A history of the Eastern Roman Empire from the fall of Irene to the accession of Basil I (802-867). London, 1912.

I. Jirlček, Geschichte der Serben. Gotha, 1911.

G. Zenoff, Die Geschichte der Bulgaren.

John Farrow, Pageant of the Popes, London, 1943.

Attwater, Donald. A dictionary of the Popes, from Peter to Pius VII-1940.

G. Balashchev, Clement, the Slavic bishop, Sophia, 1898.

J. B. Bury, Life of Thomas the Slavonian. Byzant. Zeitschrift (1892).

Pastor, Ludwig, The History of the Popes (32 Vols.). 1891-1940.

Bower, Archibald, The History of the Popes (5 Vols.). 1749-1766.

Soranzo, Girolamo, Bibliografia veneziana. 1885.

S. Runciman, The Emperor Romanus Lecapenus and his reign. Cambridge, 1929.

August Theiner, Vetera monumenta Slavorum meridionalium, maxima parte nondum edita, etc. Vol. I-II. Zagreb, 1836-1875.

J. B. Bury, Roman Emperors from Basil II to Isaac Komnenos. Cambridge, 1930.

C. Neuman, Die Weltstellug des byzantinischen Reiches vor den Kreuzzügen. Leipzig, 1894.

J. B. Bury, Roman Emperors from Basil II to Isaac Komnenos. The English Historical Review 4 (1889).

Živko Jakić, Poviest Srba, Hrvata i Slovenaca. Zagreb, 1929.

Deér, Jószef, A magyar törszövetség es patrimoniális királyság Külpolitikája.

Jalland, Trevor G. The Church and the Papacy. 1942.

Milman, Henry Hart, History of Latin Christianity. 18 volumes. 1903.

Vj. Klaic. Poviest Hrvata (5 Vols)

A. Dizdarević, Bosansko-hercegovački muslimani Hrvati, Zagreb, 1936.

M. Mehmed Handžić, Islamizacija Bosne i Hercegovine i porijeklo bosansko-hercegovačkih muslimana, Zagreb, 1940.

J. Jelinić, Kultura i bosanski franjevci, II. sv., Sarajevo, 1915.

K. Draganović, Katolička Crkva u Bosni i Hercegovini nekad i danas, Croatia Sacra, Zagreb, 1934.

Hrvatska Enciklopedija, Bosna i Hercegovina, svezak III, Zagreb, 1942.

Rev. Charles Kamber, Islam u Hrvatskim Zemljama, Winnipeg, Canada, 1957.

Rački F., Bogomili i Patareni, Beograd, 1932 (2.izd.).

Vj. Klaić, Povijest Bosne do propasti kraljevstva, Zagreb, 1882.

Arthur Evans, Through Bosnia and Herzegovina on foot, London, 1877.

Prelog M., Povjest Bosne u doba osmanliske vlade, Sarajevo, 1942.

Note. The above represents only a part of the sources used in this work.

EXPLANATORY NOTE

Professor Dr. Francis F. Preveden, author of *A History of the Croatian People*, died suddenly August 31, 1959. At the time of his death Volume II was in work and required the final review of the author, the selection of illustrations, and final completion of corrections.

It is very difficult to take over such a task when someone as highly intelligent as Professor Preveden had done the work with special ends in mind. Mr. Stanley Boric, the editor of Our Hope, Croatian Weekly, and secretary of the Committee of the Croatian History in English, took upon himself all obligations for completing this volume and making publication of it possible.

VALENT SUSA, *President*
The Committee of the Croatian
History in English